The
Pastoral in Charles Griffes's Music

Musical Meaning and Interpretation
Robert S. Hatten, *editor*

T A Y L O R   A .   G R E E R

The

PASTORAL IN CHARLES GRIFFES'S MUSIC

Aesthetic of Ambivalence

INDIANA UNIVERSITY PRESS

This book is a publication of

Indiana University Press
Office of Scholarly Publishing
Herman B Wells Library 350
1320 East 10th Street
Bloomington, Indiana 47405 USA

iupress.org

Manufactured in the United States of America

First printing 2024

Cataloging is available from the Library of Congress

ISBN 978-0-253-069283 (hardback)
ISBN 978-0-253-069290 (paperback)
ISBN 978-0-253-069306 (e-book)

CONTENTS

PREFACE

This book presents a new way of hearing and understanding the music of Charles Tomlinson Griffes (1884–1920), a neglected American composer at the turn of the twentieth century. The breadth of his sources of inspiration is breathtaking including the British Aesthetic Movement, the sensuality of fin-de-siècle French harmony, and non-Western folk music drawn from China, Java, and the Arab Peninsula, as well as a wide range of poets including Oscar Wilde, William Sharp, Walt Whitman, and Samuel Taylor Coleridge. Yet Griffes's music has fallen into a stylistic oblivion, and many historians treat him and other American composers of his generation as marginal—lost among the dying embers of Romanticism just as the torches of Modernism were being lit. Since his death in 1920, his works have usually been described as eclectic, as if his musical aesthetic were flawed, a fragmented vision without a center.

In this book, I argue that the eclectic character of Griffes's musical style is inseparable from his revival of and reaction against the pastoral tradition. In the pages that follow, I propose a new interpretive framework for understanding Griffes's artistic achievement called the *ambivalent pastoral*, which confers a new unity on the highly diverse works of his mature period. My aim is to calibrate his stylistic eclecticism by identifying the musical techniques that he revived from the eighteenth- and nineteenth-century pastoral tradition as well as his own expressive features that he developed. One of his achievements was to expand the emotional spectrum of the pastoral from the bright colors of serenity and romance to the darker hues of grief and spiritual longing. Griffes's transformation of the pastoral was part of a new chapter in American music that was cut short by his untimely death.

My argument also has consequences for music semiotics in that I offer a new way of defining a musical topic—in this case, the pastoral. Considering that the pastoral has a long and distinguished history, one may wonder why the tradition needs to be reevaluated. The answer lies in the wide range of experimental pastorals that Griffes composed as well as in the shortcomings of topic theory as a whole. While there are works in his oeuvre that evoke traditional bucolic associations such as simplicity and serenity, there are others that might be called "outliers"—works that stretch the limits of what it means to be a pastoral. These include pastorals that blend with laments, bacchanals, and expressions of musical irony, thereby introducing other emotional associations such as grief, ambiguity, anxiety, and even aggression. To do justice to this heterogeneous collection as well as to Griffes's revival and transformation of the pastoral, a new definition of a group is needed.

One of my overall aims is to reconsider the process of empirical classification itself. Instead of merely reenacting the traditional procedure of topical analysis—matching an individual passage or movement with a preexisting type—I approach the concept of a unifying group from a philosophical perspective. After raising questions about the usual assumptions of what constitutes a group, I propose an alternative definition of group membership that lays a foundation for accommodating the extreme variety found among Griffes's various pastoral experiments. The philosophical foundation for this new definition relies on the writings of two twentieth-century thinkers: Ludwig Wittgenstein for his insight about family resemblance and Morris Weitz for his concept of openness in relation to group membership. By expanding the concept of a group, it is possible to consider a broader empirical field of works that still have some properties in common. The ultimate goal is to develop a theoretical model that, while still relying on logic and empirical confirmation, relaxes the criteria of necessary and sufficient conditions. In my conception of the pastoral, these logical constraints will sometimes be stretched but never completely abandoned. By integrating the processes of description, classification, and interpretation, I hope to expand our understanding of the pastoral tradition.

After establishing my initial assumptions and interpretive approach, I will then embark on a close exegesis of Griffes's pastoral sensibility as displayed in twelve works, both instrumental and vocal. My interpretive method will be eclectic, combining topical and philosophical investigation with more traditional motivic, harmonic, and formal analysis as well as, occasionally, Schenkerian reductive techniques. This study is interdisciplinary in character and integrates many disciplines including music theory, music history, literature, art history, semiotics, and aesthetics; it embraces speculative theory as well as hermeneutical interpretation. Likewise, my intended audience is broad, ranging from performers, music theorists, musicologists, semioticians, and philosophers as well as anyone interested in early twentieth-century American culture.

The book consists of ten chapters that are divided into two parts: Part I (chaps. 1–3) presents a biographical as well as a theoretical introduction to the project, and Part II (chaps. 4–10) offers detailed analyses of twelve works including solo piano pieces (most of which were orchestrated) and accompanied songs (three of which were also arranged for voice and orchestral or chamber ensemble). Each chapter is summarized below.

Chapter 1 can be divided into two parts: a biographical portrait that is crucial for understanding the significance of the ambivalent pastoral in Griffes's creative life and a detailed study of the multiple stages in his evolving musical style that display a polythetic pattern. In addition, I explore the various ways in which the writings of Oscar Wilde and William Sharp, as well as a handful of non-Western musical traditions, helped inspire his eclectic musical style.

The theoretical heart and soul of the project resides in chapter 2, where I present a panoramic overview of the following: a brief history of semiotic theory and the theory of musical topics; a primer of the literary and the musical pastoral; a synopsis of the concept of musical exoticism and its significance for understanding Griffes's unusual style; and, finally, a detailed summary of the philosophical foundation for a new definition of group membership based on the ideas of Wittgenstein and Weitz.

Chapter 3 grows directly out of the preceding chapter and offers an encyclopedic summary of thirteen musical cues: eleven from the pastoral tradition and two from the lament tradition. It can be read either from start to finish or in piecemeal, based on the cue in question. The chapter ends with some reflections on cohesion and fragmentation in Griffes's overall style.

Chapter 4 consists of my analysis of two works by Griffes: an early song entitled "Der träumende See," and "The White Peacock," a rich, ambivalent pastoral whose dual nature grows directly out of the sensual abundance of William Sharp's poem. While the initial section expresses languor through the use of multiple dance topics and non-Western scales, the eventual climax is a wondrous evocation of spiritual ecstasy by the expansion of registral space in the outer voices. This work is like a miniature genealogy of artistic culture at the turn of the century, spanning nearly thirty years and encompassing four different media: music, poetry, art, and drama. All told, a French playwright inspired a French artist (see fig. 4.1) who sparked a Scottish poet who, in turn, gave wings to an American composer.

Chapter 5 explores *The Pleasure-Dome of Kubla Khan*, Griffes's composition based on Samuel Taylor Coleridge's drug-inspired poem. The work is a showcase of the deep conflicts found in Griffes's ambivalent vision of the pastoral, combining the conventional emotions of the literary tradition—serenity amid the contemplation of nature—with other emotions such as the expression of grief, aggression, and bacchanalian frenzy.

My analysis of the *Three Poems of Fiona Macleod* in chapter 6 reveals that the pastoral and lament traditions are not only deeply intertwined in these songs but, in some cases, are incompatible. In each musical setting, the emotional balance between the two traditions constantly shifts, creating a distinct portrait of ambivalence. Overall, the aesthetic sensibilities of Macleod and Griffes intersect in their common love of sensual pleasure, bordering on the erotic, and a mutual yearning for spiritual deliverance.

Chapter 7 explores several dimensions of Griffes's passion for exoticism. In "Tears," his setting of a sixth-century Chinese lament, he blends elements from East Asian and Western musical traditions in a new pastoral synthesis, combining pentatonic tranquility with a brief outburst of chromaticism. By contrast, his setting of Oscar Wilde's poem "Symphony in Yellow" reveals his deep affinity for the Aesthetic movement by virtue of the piano's slow-moving kaleidoscope of harmonic colors and the implied irony in its final cadence. When the poem's reference to Whistler is taken into consideration, Griffes's setting becomes an intermedia festival where music, literature, and the visual arts all intersect.

My survey of Griffes's ambivalent pastorals continues in chapter 8 with a detailed overview of three works for solo piano drawn from the early 1910s: "The Lake at Evening," "The Vale of Dreams," and Scherzo/Bacchanale. Each one displays its own peculiar mix of pastoral and lament cues.

As the last work Griffes completed before his untimely death, Prelude #3 for solo piano is less a pastoral per se than a musical commentary on Griffes's fascination with the pastoral tradition. In chapter 9, I explain how this work is a musical-philosophical challenge that raises questions about traditional assumptions of interval quality, tonality, and formal closure.

The final chapter offers a brief summary of "Salut au Monde," Griffes's final artistic extravaganza, which combines music, drama, chorus, narration, and dance pantomime in a setting of a Walt Whitman poem drawn from *Leaves of Grass*. Although Griffes's music for the initial section was left unfinished at his death, the remaining sketches reveal his interest in experimental choral textures as well as his penchant for eclecticism.

One question I have been asked countless times during the incubation of this project is, Why Charles Griffes? There are several answers to this question that involve conscious as well as unconscious motivations. Above all, it is the music itself. I have always been moved by the sensuous pleasure in Griffes's piano, vocal, and orchestral music. Even though his compositions were widely praised in the final months of his life and immediately afterward, in recent years his music has fallen into neglect. His contribution to American music in the genres of piano and vocal repertoire is beyond dispute. By writing this book, I hope to inspire performers, listeners, and readers to discover (or rediscover) the joys it contains.

I am also drawn to Griffes's insatiable appetite for literature. Previous publications have neglected the rich correspondences that exist between the text—whether poetry, program, or title—and music in his songs as well as his instrumental works. My book will address this lacuna along with the absence of detailed commentaries and close analyses of his mature pastorals. Retracing Griffes's artistic path and tracing my own interpretive steps has uncovered a wonderous group of figures and events, including Theocritus, Virgil, Kubla Khan, Samuel Taylor Coleridge, Edgar Allan Poe, William Sharp, Fiona Macleod, W. B. Yeats, Heinrich Heine, Jens Peter Jacobsen, Octave Mirbeau, Walt Whitman, James McNeill Whistler, Théodore Roussel, Walter Pater, Ludwig Wittgenstein, Morris Weitz, Lydia Goehr, Eleanor Rosch, and Charles Sanders Peirce, as well as the Order of the Golden Dawn, Celtic faeries, symphonies in white and yellow, and two celebrated trials in late-Victorian London (*Whistler v. Ruskin* and *The Crown v. Wilde*). One of my goals has been to re-create Griffes's artistic sensibility by bringing this motley cast of characters to life.

Another motivation, perhaps less conscious, grows out of an artistic tension in my own life. As a professor for many years, I have had the privilege of simultaneously inhabiting two very different artistic worlds. One is in the classroom, where I have regularly taught Analysis of Twentieth Century Music, including composers such as Debussy, Bartók, Stravinsky, Schoenberg, Messiaen, Bill Evans, Pete Seeger, and even Deadmau5. The other artistic world I inhabit is the piano, orchestral, chamber, and operatic music of Western Europe during the late eighteenth and nineteenth centuries. As a late-bloomer pianist, I still hold this music close to my heart and, by performing excerpts informally in various tonal theory classes, I try to move my students' hearts. Based on what I have discovered about Griffes, I believe that he also struck a similar balance, but for him the pendulum swung between older music he admired and performed and new music he was trying to create.

During the years I have devoted to this project, it has gone through so many transformations that at times it felt as though I were staring at some ancient Greek mythological creature, like Proteus, who could change its shape before my very eyes. But eventually, I realized, to paraphrase Gilles de Van, that what I thought was a window into someone else's journey was often a mirror of my own.

Acknowledgments

I wish to thank the College of Arts and Architecture at Penn State for generously funding a travel grant in 2000 for me to visit archives in Washington, DC and Elmira, New York. My thanks also go to the Institute for the Arts and Humanities at Penn State University for providing a semester residency in 2012 to pursue the initial stages of this project. I wish to thank two librarians at the Music Division, New York Public Library: Jonathan Hiam, former Curator, for his generosity in giving me access to the Donna K. Anderson research files before they had been fully catalogued as well as Bob Kosovsky for his painstaking perusal of the Edward Maisel research files. I am also grateful for the Semiotic Society of America where, at their annual meetings over the years, I have shared my ideas about Griffes within a sympathetic and supportive community. I owe an enormous debt to Thomas Cody and Phillip Torbert for their technological wizardry in fashioning the musical examples and figures for this book and for never losing patience with my many second thoughts and changes of heart. In addition, I am grateful for the generous support of the Maureen Carr Endowment for Music Theory and Musicology Research to help defray the cost of creating all of the book's graphics. Finally, I must thank the entire Indiana University Press team for their consummate skill in shepherding this book through various stages of production including Allison Chaplin, Sophia Hebert, and Nancy Lightfoot, as well as Pete Feely at Amnet.

I also owe debts of gratitude to a number of people who have supported me along the way. First, I must acknowledge the generous support of Donna Anderson, who shared with me her vast knowledge of Griffes's life and music as well as her personal copies of his diaries and library inventory, and who graciously hosted me in her home in Cortland, New York. Although she died in 2018, the shadow of her artistic passion and scholarly commitment has loomed large throughout this project.

As the founding editor of the IUP book series Musical Meaning and Interpretation, Robert Hatten has been a pillar of support and a steady guide through the semiotic wilderness, offering a seemingly endless supply of encouragement and constructive criticism. I must also express my appreciation for the two anonymous external referees who offered numerous suggestions for revision of my manuscript that I took to heart. Many others have read various drafts and saved me from countless errors of fact and of judgment including Jason Charnesky, Michael Klein, Eric McKee, Charles Youmans, and Lawrence Zbikowski.

My heartfelt thanks go to my parents, John Taylor Greer and Martha Elizabeth Aitken Greer, who built an emotional foundation of trust and love that freed me to follow my curiosity wherever it led. Likewise, my sister, Helen (Penny) Greer, has provided her unflagging emotional support and a perceptive pair of editorial eyes along the way.

This book is dedicated to my three children: François William, Emile Philippe, and Juliette Dunoyer Greer.

The
Pastoral in Charles Griffes's Music

PART I
PRELIMINARIES

1

Biography and Style

Griffes's central contribution to American music was a new conception of the pastoral, which transformed the dance-based tradition he had inherited into a new and vibrant means of expression. Before we can appreciate the overall significance of the pastoral tradition for Griffes, it is worth exploring in greater depth what I mean by a musical style that is based on an *aesthetic of ambivalence*. Griffes's artistic achievement is ambivalent in four respects: biographical, literary, topical, and historical. Let me briefly consider each one.

In some ways Griffes's musical aesthetic mirrored the geographical shifts in his personal life in that, during his final thirteen years, he constantly rotated between a major urban center (New York City) and a small town (Tarrytown), secluded in the country, where he worked at a boys' boarding school. Although he eventually grew weary of this bucolic setting and longed to move to the city full time, he nevertheless drew inspiration from both locations. There are two other sources of tension in Griffes's personal life that may have helped shape his musical style: his sexual orientation, since he was a gay man living in a predominantly heterosexual world, and his interest in spirituality. Although he was adamantly opposed to organized religion, he felt drawn to literature with spiritual themes and occasionally set highly spiritual poems to music.

The second way in which Griffes's artistic approach can be considered ambivalent reflects two contemporary literary movements that previous

Griffes scholars have neglected, though they were continuing sources of inspiration for him: British Aestheticism, as represented by the writings of Oscar Wilde and Walter Pater, and the Celtic Renaissance, especially the spiritual poetry of William Sharp and his female persona, Fiona Macleod. Although Griffes never set foot in Great Britain, his compositional voice was shaped by some of the leading figures in Irish and Scottish literature.

The pastoral tradition itself, both as a literary tradition and as a musical topic, can also be characterized as ambivalent. It is defined by a series of oppositions: rural versus urban; utopian ideal versus daily life; nature versus society; nature versus art; and retreat from politics versus immersion in political life. My oppositional understanding of the literary pastoral relies on the recent theories of Harold Toliver and Annabel Patterson, both of which will be summarized in chapter 2.

Finally, the oppositions in Griffes's musical aesthetic also reflect the underlying tensions present in the styles of many other European composers and writers during the fin-de-siècle period, which can be described as *ambivalent modernism*. This conception of ambivalence is inspired by Walter Frisch's use of the term in his compelling study of a collection of German composers and writers from 1880 to 1920 entitled *German Modernism: Music and the Arts*. In his book, Frisch questions the traditional dichotomy between Romanticism and Modernism and instead develops an alternative he calls *ambivalent modernism* that is based on the conflict between composers' loyalty to the past and their fascination with the new.[1] The difference between Frisch's and my use of the term is that while he focuses on the tensions among a generation of German artists arising from their national identity, I am interested in the tensions within the artistic identity of a single American composer.[2] In the biographical portrait below and the pastoral primer in chapter 2, I will explore the connotations of ambivalence in greater depth.

The ancient Roman god of paradox, Janus, serves as an overarching metaphor for Griffes's ambiguous artistic attitude, looking backward and forward at the same time. His deep Romantic sensibility and respect for past artistic traditions was counterbalanced by his fascination with new aesthetic resources. On first impression, there is much about Griffes that suggests a Romantic artist par excellence. In some works he was content to speak the *lingua chromatica* of the late nineteenth century—the intense chromaticism and lyricism associated with such composers as Wagner and Strauss. But there is far more to Griffes's sensibility than sheer Romantic nostalgia. In some works, he was clearly an incipient Modernist, inspired by contemporary French, German, and British muses. In short, there is a fundamental ambivalence in Griffes's style: a sympathy for Modernism coexisting with an underlying Romantic sensibility.

Ultimately, Griffes's artistic outlook was as experimental as it was traditional, and the concept of the ambivalent pastoral provides a new framework in which to balance this conflict between opposites. In order to appreciate this balance, it is appropriate to provide a brief biographical portrait followed by a detailed study of the many elements that helped shape his musical style. As will become clear below, the source of ambivalence in his life serves as a lens through which we can view and interpret the landscape of his pastoral imagination.

Biographical Portrait

Anyone who undertakes a summary of the life and works of Charles Tomlinson Griffes is blessed with two comprehensive biographies by Edward Maisel and Donna K. Anderson.[3] Yet these chronicles could not be more different in style and method. Maisel's approach is highly personal and, at times, rhapsodic, merging biography and cultural history with a detailed analysis of a single mature work, the Piano Sonata.[4] By contrast, Anderson's style is measured and precise, balancing an exhaustive study of archival sources with insightful analytical observations about a host of works. Considered as a pair, these authors possess nearly opposite temperaments: one is Dionysian, poetic, and indulgent, the other Apollonian, judicious, and evenhanded. In this biographical portrait, my goal is to create a synthesis, blending the best of each author's approach, supplemented by new empirical evidence gleaned from primary sources.

Born in 1884, Charles was the third of five children. He grew up in Elmira, a small town in upstate New York, in an extremely close-knit family, which originally came from Wales and England and whose ancestors spelled their name differently.[5] Though his older sister introduced him to the piano at the age of ten, he began studying the instrument seriously only when he turned fifteen. One of the greatest fortunes of his life was his first piano teacher, Mary Selena Broughton, a native of New Zealand who grew up in England, emigrated to America, and eventually accepted a position at Elmira College, where she taught piano, music theory, music history, and later Spanish. A teacher of strong personality and eccentric taste, Broughton not only provided Charles with a solid technical foundation at the piano, she also encouraged him to explore other forms of artistic expression. It is no exaggeration to say that Griffes's artistic gifts were protean, for throughout his life he continued pursuing his mutual passions for composition, literature, and photography.

At an early age, Griffes already possessed an acute sensibility for color. Although apparently his favorite was orange, he developed strong emotional reactions toward a wide range of colors and their associations with musical keys.[6] These correspondences fall under the broad category of synaesthesia, though it is difficult to determine exactly to what degree Griffes experienced this phenomenon. His acute response to color shows his innate sensitivity to the sensual dimension of art and nature—an attribute that will become important when we consider the multiple sources of inspiration and influence that shaped his musical style.

When Griffes turned eighteen, Broughton insisted that he continue his musical study in Germany, where she had briefly studied piano herself. Armed with her advice and financial backing, he moved to Berlin in the fall of 1903 and, for the next three years, studied at the Stern'sches Konservatorium.[7] His coursework included the following: private piano lessons with Ernst Jedliczka, a student of Nicholas Rubenstein and, after he died, Gottfried Galston; counterpoint with Max Loewengard, who, in turn, had studied with the German composer Joachim Raff; and, most important, composition with Philippe Rüfer.[8] One indication of Griffes's integrity is that once he began earning a steady income following his return to America, he repaid every penny of the money Broughton had loaned him to live and study in Germany.[9]

Eventually, Griffes began to realize that he was not destined for a career as a solo pianist and that his gifts lay more in composing than in performing. However, it should be emphasized that throughout his life he was a highly capable soloist and accompanist of his own works.[10] When he graduated from the Stern Conservatory, he stayed in Berlin for an extra year in order to study composition with Engelbert Humperdinck and pursue a freelance career as a teacher and performer. During this period, he composed mostly songs based on texts by German poets.

A central figure during Griffes's four years in Berlin was Emil Joël, a student in civil engineering at the Technische Hochschule whom Griffes met soon after his arrival. Although Joël lived with his mother, he and Griffes became inseparable, attending concerts, operas, exhibitions, circuses, zoos, and gardens, and even vacationing together. He served as a combination of musical and cultural mentor, older brother, and possible lover.[11] In any case, Joël's influence could be felt in practically every aspect of Charles's life. For instance, he was pivotal in Charles's decision to concentrate on composition instead of performance and, later, to lengthen his stay in Berlin for a fourth year, which Joël helped finance. Eventually, the time came for Griffes to leave Berlin behind and make his fortune back in his home country. Anderson captures well this juncture in his life:[12] "Charles Tomlinson Griffes left Elmira in 1903 a rather immature, naïve, and self-centered boy of not quite nineteen. He returned to American in 1907 a far more sophisticated (if not worldly) and musically mature man of not quite twenty-three."

Upon returning to America, he immediately accepted a position at a private boarding school for boys called the Hackley School, located in Tarrytown, New York, thirty miles north of New York City, and worked there for the next thirteen years. The school was small and exclusive, the unstated goal being to prepare each student for entrance into an Ivy League college.[13] Though the administration regarded music as a purely extracurricular activity, qualified students were expected to participate. Hence, Griffes's duties were considerable. As the resident music director, he was expected to conduct the choir, play the piano for daily morning chapel and the organ for Sunday afternoon service, teach private lessons, perform in formal and informal weekly concerts, and attend most evening meals; he had only one day off per week. It is fair to say that his job was both a blessing and a curse. The advantages included a modest but steady salary, free room and board, and ample time to compose in a cloistered and supportive environment. However, as the years wore on, the scarcity of any genuine musical community among the students and faculty became more and more stifling. According to Maisel, "to the end his duties remained the purely menial chores of a musical drudge."[14]

In some respects, Griffes's life is a case study of the contrast between rural and urban life and the mixed emotions he felt toward both. Beginning with his early years in Elmira, he took great pleasure in spending time outdoors, especially in gardens, collecting flowers and bird-watching. His extensive collection of photographs taken at the Hackley School and in the Hudson Valley region shows a marked preference for scenes of nature such as lakes, trees, streams, landscapes, and various farm animals as well as athletic events, self-portraits, and portraits of students. A friend and fellow composer, Burnet Tuthill, observed that "Griffes was a great lover of nature and the outdoors, and told me of walks he made to the countryside about Tarrytown and how he loved to lie in the grass."[15] Griffes confided in his diary entry from May 31, 1915 "This evening a while after coffee we went out and sat on the bench by the chapel. . . . At such times one appreciates what a beautiful place this is up here."[16]

But he not only savored the country, he also constantly tried to escape it.[17] Griffes's true home was a studio apartment in New York City where he sought refuge during summers and school vacations. Only an hour away from Tarrytown by train, the metropolis offered concerts, plays, exhibits, and opportunities for professional advancement as well as companionship. He immersed himself in performing at private concerts as well as in trying to get his works published, usually at G. Schirmer Inc., which became his primary publisher during his lifetime. In a diary entry on May 6, 1912, Griffes confided, "I wish I could get one or two real big successes for Schirmer and then they would take my other things which they don't want to risk now."[18] He also consulted various colleagues for their aesthetic advice. The routine was always the same: first he would perform his latest compositions on the piano, and then he would report the listener's judgment in his diary, whether positive (Ferruccio Busoni, Arthur Farwell) or negative (Daniel Gregory Mason).[19]

Considering Griffes's passion for New York City, one may wonder why he never ended up quitting his job and moving to the city. The reason is financial. Tuthill describes his conservative approach toward managing his finances: "Griffes' mutual friends often tried to persuade him to leave the Hackley School and set up a studio in New York where he would receive pupils. This of course involved financial risk in the time it would take to develop a class of pupils. He was always unwilling to take this risk, for fear that it might interrupt his regular monthly contribution to the expenses of his mother and sisters."[20]

During his final thirteen years, he spent an enormous amount of time in transit to and from the city. By his own admission, he composed the opening phrase of "The White Peacock" on the train (for detailed discussions of this piece, see chap. 4).[21] In a deep sense, Griffes was perpetually in motion between two extremes: the urban parade of the city and the rural retreat of the country. It is safe to say that he developed a love/hate relationship with life in a small town, a paradox that partly defined his life. When asked by a colleague if he liked living in the country, he responded, "I long to be in the city. The country does not inspire me especially; perhaps I take it too much for granted. I get much more inspiration from reading Oriental folk tales than I do from looking at a tree."[22] Although composers' reports about their sources of inspiration are often less than reliable, in this case Griffes's comment must be viewed as part of a broader ambivalence toward rural life. While at times he loathed living in the country, he repeatedly found artistic inspiration in visions of the pastoral, some more Arcadian than others.

Living in flux between small town and big city, Griffes also had ample time to indulge in literature. A voracious reader, he also was a meticulous record keeper of his literary adventures, a fact that makes it easy to eavesdrop on his expansive literary tastes. Maisel observes, "Concerning Griffes's tastes in reading it is almost impossible to frame any valid or approximate generalization, so diverse and almost crazily unrelated were they in scope. One fairly programmatic year, however, included Baudelaire, Poe, Verlaine, Goethe, Hawthorne . . . Hearn (especially the letters), Gordon Craig, Mirbeau, de Amicis, and d'Annunzio, outside of his reading on music."[23] Table 1.1 provides a comprehensive record of his reading between 1912 and 1916, based on his diary entries. The breadth of his literary taste will be crucial when we consider the eclectic character of his musical style.

Another key to understanding Griffes's life and art is his sexual orientation. Anderson summarizes well the broader social context: "In the atmosphere of sexual repression in America at the time, Griffes had no one with

Table 1.1. List of Griffes's readings based on his diaries, 1912–16.

1912–13

de Amicis: *Novello, Nel Regus de Cervisso*; Morocco; Constantinople; La Spana; Furio

d'Annuncio, Gabriele, *Il Fuoco* (*The Flame of Life*); *Il Piacera* (*Child of Pleasure*)

1001 Arabian Nights

Baudelaire, Charles, *Oeuvres posthumous*

Beckford, *Vathek*

Brontë, *The Tenant of Wildfell Hall*

Bulow, *Briefe*

Cervantes, *Don Quixote*

Coulevain, Pierre de, *Sur la branche*

Craig, Gordon, *Art of Theater*

Dostoevsky, Fyodor, *The House of the Dead*

Evelyn, John, *The Diary*

Flaubert, Gustave, *Education Sentimentale*; *The Temptation of St. Anthony*

Fogazzaro, *Fidele*

Gadow, Hans, *In Northern Spain* (1897)

Hawthorne, Nathaniel, *Legends of Province House*

Hearn, Lafcadio, trans., *Japanese Fairy Tales*

Hearn, Lafcadio, trans., *Chinese Ghost Stories* and *In Ghostly Japan* (Selon Anderson)

Howells, William D., *Essay on Valladolid*

Keats

Loti, Pierre, *Fleurs d'ennui*

Lowell, Percival, *The Soul of the Far East* (Selon Donna Anderson)

Mallarmé, Stephane, "L'après-midi d'un faune"

Mantagazza, *Amori delgi nomini*

Marlowe, Christopher

Mignet, Antonio P., *Philippe II*

Mirbeau, Octave, *Le Jardin des supplices*; *Le Professeur*; *Le Journal d'une fleur de chambre*

Moore, George, *Celibates*

Petrarca

Piranesi

Poe, Edgar Allan, *The Masque of the Red Death*

Shaw, George B., *Man and Superman*

Sherard, Robert, *The Life of Oscar Wilde*

Soulié, Charles George, *Essai sur la literature chinoise* (Selon Donna Anderson)

Strindberg, August, *Lebensgeschichte (Autobiography)*

Synge, John Millington, *The Playboy of the Western World*

Teasdale, Sara, *Helen of Troy and Other Poems*
Vasi, *Rome*
Verga, *Eros; Vito dei campi; Tigre reale*
Verlaine, Paul, *Oeuvres*
Lepelletiers, *Paul Verlaine, Sa Vie, Son Oeuvre*
Whitman, Walt, *Leaves of Grass*

1914
d'Annuncio, Gabriele, "Francesco da Rimini"
Balzac, "Sarrasine"; "Girl with the Golden Eyes"
Chinese Stories from Lodge of Leisure, trans. Soulie
Dostoevsky, *Notes from Underground*
Flaubert, Gustave, *The Temptation of St. Anthony*
Gautier, Théophile, "Une Nuit de Cléopâtre"
Hoffmann, E. T. A. "Fermate"
Schaffner, Powers, "Er ist Irlander"
Wilde, Oscar, *Lady Windermere's Fan*

1915
Baudelaire, Charles, *Collected Works*
Dostoevsky, "The Gambler"
Farrère, Claude, "Les Civilisés"
Flaubert, Gustave, "Légende de St. Julien"; "Hériodias"
Gautier, Théophile, *Espagne*
Loti, Pierre, *Fantôme d'orient*
De Maupassant, "Une vie"

1916
Baudelaire, Charles, *L'Art Romantique*
Galsworthy, "The Silver Box"; "Man of Property"
Loti, Pierre, *Le Roman d'un enfant; Un Pélérin d'angkoi*

whom he could feel at ease discussing his homosexuality, without generating at least shock and embarrassment, if not censure." She adds, "Griffes felt no shame about his homosexuality; rather he expressed frustration that homosexuals could not meet openly."[24] It is significant that he never married nor found a permanent companion. While he seldom became close to the younger male students at Hackley, New York City offered ample opportunities for physical and/or romantic encounters, which he fully exploited. Griffes not only frequented homosexual bathhouses such as Lafayette Place Baths and Produce Exchange Baths, he also developed a long-term close relationship with a city policeman named John Meyer who was married and had a family.[25]

One telling clue about this aspect of his life can be found in the intimacy of his diaries. Amid the painstaking records of his daily activities, he always wrote in German whenever he penned the details of his romantic encounters with other men. While one can speculate about his motivation for using a different language—security, fantasy, or even nostalgia—the systematic shift into German adds a layer of linguistic complexity in his sexual identity.[26]

An additional source of paradox in Griffes's life was his attitude toward spirituality. On the one hand, by the time he arrived at Hackley he was deeply opposed to institutional religion. Two books with which he strongly identified were Jens Peter Jacobsen's *Niels Lyhne* and August Strindberg's autobiographical novel, *Tjänstekvinnans son* (*Son of a Servant*).[27] The narrators in both books passionately renounce religious authority amid their search for a personal identity. On the other hand, most would agree that Griffes had a highly poetic sensibility that occasionally led him to set texts involving mysticism and spirituality. Maisel argues that, as early as his childhood years, he possessed "a strongly religious, nostalgic, poetic temperament seeking to ground the elements of religion in life itself."[28]

Considering this profound ambivalence toward spiritual experience, it is not surprising that the poems, programs, and dramatic scenarios of some of his mature works show a marked sympathy toward some form of spirituality, whether it be mystical contemplation, an evocation of epiphany, or a longing for transcendence.[29] This facet of his personality will take on more importance in my close exegesis of two late works: his tone poem "The White Peacock," which is suffused by the spirit of a magical bird in a luxuriant garden (see chap. 4); and his vocal settings of Fiona Macleod's poetry, which expand the pastoral tradition by merging the serenity of nature with elements of lament, physical desire, and spiritual longing (see chap. 6).

During his many years at the Hackley School, Griffes continued to submit compositions to G. Schirmer with some success. However, for most of his career he never achieved the recognition that would have led to more publications and greater financial independence. When success finally came, it swelled like a tsunami. In a four-week marathon at the end of 1919, six of his orchestral works received premieres along with a song cycle and a string quartet earlier that year (table 1.2). Of these various works, I will provide close readings of four: *Bacchanale* (orchestral version of Scherzo, Op. 6, no 4); *The Pleasure-Dome of Kubla Khan*, Op. 8; "The White Peacock," Roman Sketches, Op. 7, no. 1; and *Three Poems of Fiona MacLeod*, op. 11. Even though several orchestral works were transcriptions of previously composed piano pieces, all six required scores and parts to be copied.[30] Unfortunately, Griffes had neither the funds to pay professional copyists nor the confidence that their work would be reliable. So, after enlisting help from his family, he ended up doing most of the copying himself.[31] Performances of these works took place in Boston, Philadelphia, and New York by three of the leading orchestras and conductors in the country: the Boston Symphony Orchestra (BSO), Pierre Monteux; the Philadelphia Orchestra, Leopold Stokowski; and the New York Symphony Orchestra, Walter Damrosch. Most important, after performing in Boston, the BSO repeated the same program at Carnegie Hall in New York.

Table 1.2. List of Griffes's works premiered in 1919

Orchestral

1. Bacchanale, conductor, Leopold Stokowski, Philadelphia Orchestra, Philadelphia, December 19, 1919 [version of Scherzo, piano piece, 1913].

2. "Clouds," *Roman Sketches*, op. 7, no. 4, conductor, Leopold Stokowski, Philadelphia Orchestra, Philadelphia, December 19, 1919 [version of piano piece, 1916].

3. Notturno für Orchester, 1908, conductor, Leopold Stokowski, Philadelphia Orchestra, Philadelphia, December 19, 1919.

4. *The Pleasure-Dome of Kubla Khan*, op. 8, conductor, Pierre Monteux, Boston Symphony Orchestra, Boston, November 28, 1919; Carnegie Hall, New York, December 4, 1919 [revised version of piano piece, 1912–15].

5. Poem for Flute and Orchestra, soloist, Georges Barrère, conductor, Walter Damrosch, New York Symphony Orchestra, New York, November 16, 1919.

6. "The White Peacock," *Roman Sketches*, Op. 7, no. 1, conductor, Leopold Stokowski, Philadelphia Orchestra, Philadelphia, December 19, 1919 [version of piano piece, 1915].

Table 1.2. *(continued)*

Stage

7. "The White Peacock," conductor, Erno Rapee, solo dancer, Marget Leeraas, Rivoli Orchestra, Philadelphia, December 19, 1919 [revised version of piano piece, 1915].

Chamber

8. Two Sketches for String Quartet Based on Indian Themes, Flonzaley Quartet, MacDowell Gallery, New York, A 2pril, 1919.

Vocal

9. *Three Poems of Fiona MacLeod*, op. 11, Vera Janacopulos, Charles Griffes, voice and piano, New York, March 22, 1919.

Afterward, the music critics sang his praises. One wrote, "[Mr. Griffes] is that rare bird [*sic*] an American composer with imagination, the gift of expression, pronounced originality." Another critic concluded that he was "unquestionably one of the most gifted composers this country has produced."[32] Indeed, it was the break of his life. But the effort of copying all the parts for these concerts, mostly at night, had left him physically broken. Following the first two premieres in Boston and New York, he was bedridden, too ill to attend any of the other concerts. Tragically, on April 8, 1920 he died of empyema resulting from influenza in a New York hospital at the age of thirty-five.[33]

Griffes's Musical Styles

For many, Griffes's musical style has proven to be something of a puzzle. Historians, performers, and listeners alike often treat early twentieth-century American composers like Griffes as marginal, occupying a stylistic oblivion that is neither fully Romantic nor fully Modern. There are three principal reasons for this historical judgment: the so-called "Emerson" problem—that is, the tendency of American composers to imitate European traditions; the upsurge of musical Modernism during the 1920s that overshadowed all that had come before; and the eclectic character of the music itself. Each one is worth examining.

Griffes grew to maturity at a time when American musical life was dominated by the aesthetic ideals of Europe, in particular of Germany. One of the biggest reasons for this was the absence of a vibrant tradition at home. Denise Von Glahn observes that American composers "were few in number, those consciously seeking to develop a representative, national voice even fewer, and their champions nearly nonexistent. . . . There was no single goal motivating all composers to develop an American high-art music, no overarching philosophy or point of view to unite their efforts."[34] No conservatories existed in America, and once you left the East Coast orchestras and opera companies were few and far between. Virtually all of the leading American composers between 1890 and 1920 not only studied in Germany or France, but when they came home, they heard their music performed by conductors who were either European or educated in Europe. More important, many critics felt their music had little to say. In his award-winning book *The Rest is Noise*, Alex Ross argues that composers of this generation "failed to find a language that was singularly American or singularly their own." He quips, "What classical music in America lacked was American classical music."[35] When Ralph Waldo Emerson bemoaned in his 1837 essay "The American Scholar" that "too long have we listened to the courtly muses of Europe," little did he know that nearly two centuries later at least one critic would still be making the same complaint.[36]

Another reason Griffes's music has been neglected is the radical shift in American musical taste immediately after he died. It is little exaggeration to say that during the so-called Roaring Twenties, especially in New York, Modernist music began to roar. In her comprehensive monograph, Carol Oja argues that Modernism "stood for one basic principle: iconoclastic, irreverent innovation."[37] Whatever its merits, Griffes's music paled in comparison to the soaring sirens of Edgar Varèse, the bizarre wailing of the theremin, or the well-armed tone clusters of Henry Cowell. In short, Griffes fell into the cracks of history because he reached maturity during a period of transition when late-Romantic styles were in decline and the Modernist revolution was on the rise.

But to treat Griffes's music as lost in a stylistic crevasse does it a serious injustice. Instead, we should focus on the reasons why his music often eludes conventional historical categories. One reason is that he was a musical pluralist. Within a mere thirteen years, 1907–20, Griffes's compositional approach and sources of inspiration underwent enormous changes. Yet amid this stylistic evolution, his fascination with reviving and reinventing the pastoral served as an overarching framework and source of unity. To appreciate exactly how the pastoral created this framework, it is important to consider the meaning of the terms *musical style* and *genre*.

According to the *Grove Dictionary*, an artwork's style can be defined in the broadest context as a "manner of discourse, mode of expression or presentation."[38] In common parlance, the term *style* is used to describe musical phenomena in a wide range of contexts: the music of a historical period, a country, an ethnic group, a group of artists, or a single artist. Leonard Meyer argues that musical style must be understood as a theoretical hierarchy consisting of three levels: universal laws (physical or physiological limits), rules (intracultural constraints), and the strategies of individual composers.[39] Using his terminology, my project falls at the margin where rules and strategies overlap. The question takes on special importance in the case of Griffes because his works exhibit so many different "manners of discourse" that it can be challenging to account for them as expressing a single style.

The concept of musical genre has recently been given new life by the analogy with literary theories. For example, Heather Dubrow proposes that "genre establishes a relationship between author and reader [that] might fruitfully be labelled a generic contract."[40] Poets, she argues, create a contract with their readers in the title, meter, and familiar patterns or conventions with which their works begin; in other words, readers give their tacit consent to an ongoing literary tradition. According to Jeffrey Kallberg, the same contractual relationship arises in music: "The choice of genre by a composer and its identification by the listener establish the framework for the communication of meaning. The genre institutes . . . a frame that consequently affects the decisions made by the composer in writing the work and the listener in hearing the work."[41]

My project focuses on the two most common genres in Griffes's oeuvre: tone poems, either written for solo piano or transcribed for orchestra; and accompanied songs. While I will not do justice to the full range of the "generic contract" surrounding Griffes's historical reception, nevertheless I will explore the questions of style and, to a lesser extent, genre in

Griffes's music, ultimately focusing more on how the concept of musical topic intersects and, to some degree, integrates them both.

Amid the rich diversity in Griffes's works, it is useful to identify four predominant styles: German, French, Non-Western, and Abstract/Russian. Of the four, three were at least partly inspired by late nineteenth- and/or early twentieth-century European traditions with which he was familiar.[42] As will become clear below, there is a certain degree of overlap among all four.

The first style emerged during his years in Berlin and continued after he had moved back to New York. It is represented by twenty-six songs, all of which employ German texts, and three unpublished works (two for orchestra and one movement of a piano sonata). It comes as no surprise that these vocal works bear the stamp of late nineteenth-century German composers such as Richard Strauss, Hugo Wolf, and Johannes Brahms. These early songs are characterized by lyrical vocal lines, regular phrasing, and coloristic piano textures. Although Griffes later dismissed them as student works, nevertheless many are significant contributions to twentieth-century vocal literature.[43] One of these songs, "Der Träumende See," will be briefly explored in chapter 4.

The second style can be traced to the experimental artistic traditions in painting and music that emerged in France during the last quarter of the nineteenth century, commonly called Impressionism. Following Griffes's death, historians and critics began using the epithet *American Impressionist* to describe his musical style, and since then the label has persisted.[44] To be sure, several of Griffes's works composed between 1911 and 1916 exhibit compositional techniques that are traditionally associated with experimental French composers at the turn of the century such as non-Western scales (e.g., whole tone), parallel textures, and ostinato rhythmic figures. In addition, his reliance on rich harmonic color and instrumental nuance in some of his mature works bears an unmistakable French fragrance. It is evident that Griffes was immersed in contemporary French music, for he frequently programmed works by Claude Debussy in his piano recitals at Hackley.[45] In fact, Griffes was so fascinated by Debussy's orchestral work *Ibéria* that he prepared a piano transcription of the middle movement, "Les Parfums de la nuit" ("The Perfumes of the Night") and tried unsuccessfully to get it published.[46]

That said, while some of Griffe's works certainly possess an impressionistic character, the term does not do justice to the broad spectrum of styles he explored within his entire career. Perhaps a more apt epithet for his emerging compositional voice might be "the impressionable American."

The Non-Western style reflects Griffes's prodigious appetite for the foreign musical traditions that he encountered in New York City. These include folk music from the following traditions: China and Japan (*Five Poems of Ancient China and Japan*, Op. 10 for voice and piano, and *Sho-jo*, pantomime for orchestra and solo dancer, unpublished); Java (*Three Javanese Songs*); and Native America (*Two Sketches Based on Indian Themes*).[47] Although one of the most common cues of these traditions is the use of alternate scales such as the pentatonic, Griffes was also sensitive to the treatment of rhythm, phrasing, and instrumentation. In chapter 7, I explore the fourth song in the Op. 10 song cycle, entitled "Tears," which is a stirring lament suffused by static harmony and an unrelenting rhythmic ostinato.

The final style represents the most dramatic shift of all, for it consists of a highly dissonant idiom that often employs alternative scales. These works tend to portray extremely contrasting emotions ranging from quiet introspection to explosive aggression. Two works that demonstrate this new idiom are themselves studies in contrast: the Piano Sonata, an extended canvas in three continuous movements; and the Three Preludes, exercises in brevity and, in one case, irony (see chap. 9). These pieces bear the traces of other experimental works from the early twentieth century such as Scriabin's Five Preludes, Op. 74, and Schoenberg's *Sechs kleine Klavierstücke*, Op. 19, both of which Griffes owned and performed.[48]

The relationships among these four styles pose the first of several interpretive and philosophical challenges that emerge in my study of Griffes's musical aesthetic. The following questions arise:

- Is each style an independent musical idiom with its own musical integrity that does not participate in a linear pattern?
- Are these four united by an ongoing pattern of organic growth, each new style being integrated into the previous one and ultimately culminating in an apex of stylistic maturity?
- Or are they related in some other way, balancing between independent and integrated?

I would argue that the third observation is true. In order to appreciate the nuances of my argument, it will be useful to represent each stylistic period as a letter: A = German, B = French, C = Non-Western, and D = Abstract/Russian. There are two ways of interpreting the shifts between the different stylistic periods: continuous change and modified polythetic organization. Let us consider each one.

The first interpretation is a succession of four letters with no repetition.

A B C D

This arrangement focuses more on the individual integrity of each period and de-emphasizes the elements of similarity and overlap that do exist. The only unifying theme would be a lack of unity—pure eclecticism, or continuous change for its own sake. In his monograph *Mainstream Music of Early Twentieth Century America*, Nicholas Tawa provides a useful historical backdrop for this interpretive approach.[49] He recounts the lineage of multiple generations of American composers between 1840 and 1930, linking Griffes with a second generation such as Edward Burlingame Hill, Daniel Gregory Mason, Henry Gilbert, Arthur Farwell, Charles Cadman, and Deems Taylor. There are two artistic features that unify this motley group: their early works had some kind of Germanic basis; and, more important, their music was characterized by eclecticism.

Despite its virtues, there are two problems with this perspective. To begin with, it overlooks the cross relations that exist among different stylistic approaches. Griffes did not completely reinvent himself and his compositional aesthetic in each stylistic period. In addition, it ignores the unifying power that the pastoral tradition exercised on his musical imagination.

The second arrangement emphasizes the degree of overlap among the four styles; it can be described as a modified "polythetic" pattern (this method of classification will be discussed in greater detail in chapter 2). Each horizontal line below represents either a single style or an amalgam of multiple styles in chronological order as they emerged in his career.

A			
A	B		
A	B	C	
	B	C	
		C	
A			D

To further clarify the above diagram, table 1.3 identifies representative works for each style and, more important, each stylistic blend, that Griffes developed in his music.

Table 1.3. List of representative examples of Griffes's styles and stylistic blends

Style/Style Blend	Musical Examples
German (A)	"Der Träumende See"
Blend of German and French (AB)	"The Lake at Evening" "The Vale of Dreams" Scherzo
Blend of German, French, and Non-Western (ABC)	"The White Peacock" *The Pleasure-Dome of Kubla Khan* *Three Poems of Fiona Macleod* Poem for Flute and Orchestra
Non-Western (C)	Five Poems of Ancient China and Japan Sho-Jo Three Javanese Songs
Blend of French and Non-Western Styles (BC)	"Symphony in Yellow" Two Sketches Based on Indian Themes "Waikiki"
Blend of German and Abstract/Russian (AD)	"Clouds" Piano Sonata Three Preludes

After having explored the full spectrum of stylistic diversity in Griffes's music, we are in a position draw some initial conclusions. The first thing to be noted about this arrangement is that while individual letters of the original four recur in various subsets, no single stylistic period is present in every subset. Thus, while there is no common ground, no overarching principle, that unifies all of the subsets, there is a considerable amount of repetition among them. The best way of describing this arrangement is *polythetic classification*, which can be defined as "involving or sharing a number of common characteristics of a group or class, none of them essential for membership of the group or class in question."[50] This type of classification is used in such diverse fields as anthropology, psychology, and religious studies.[51] As will become clear in chapter 2, this concept plays an important role in helping define the relationship between topical cues in Griffes's pastoral works.

Another striking feature of table 1.3 is that only two styles appear in isolation: German (A) and Non-Western (C). That the German style would appear by itself comes as no surprise since it represents his creative adolescence while living in Berlin, studying at a German conservatory, and composing mostly vocal settings of German poetry. By contrast, two types appear in combination with one or two others in a stylistic blend or fusion (e.g., AB or ABC). To be specific, the German, French, and Non-Western styles all participate in at least three blends.

The frequency of these stylistic blends raises questions about their exact character: Are all features of both styles preserved as if they were a union of both sets? Or are some features eliminated when two or more styles blend together and, if so, which ones? Finally, are new features created by these stylistic fusions? The answer is that there is no single formula that explains the dynamics of Griffes's stylistic blending because each example creates its own unique balance.

The best way to illustrate this balance is to consider one blend in closer detail: the French/German fusion (AB). One piece that illustrates this stylistic blend is "The White Peacock," originally written for solo piano and later transcribed for orchestra. The opening section of this work is a quintessential example of the composer's sympathy for a French sensibility in his use of non-Western scales, a colorful harmonic palette, and frequent shifts between contrasting themes and textures. However, later in the work Griffes reveals his Germanic temperament, for he creates an enormous climax, combining a peak in dynamics with a dramatic expansion in the outer voices' register that coincides with the return of the opening sonority. Hence, this work blends features from three different styles: non-Western scales, colorful French harmonies, and a climax of Germanic intensity. In addition, the extreme contrast between two rhetorical characters—the exaggerated as well as the understated portrayal of emotion—ends up being complementary, for the two approaches coexist in different sections of the same work. This work will be discussed in greater depth in chapter 4.

The polythetic arrangement displayed above also reinforces one goal of this study: to raise questions about using a framework that is based entirely on the principles of logic and empirical science to interpret a work of art. Rather than completely rejecting the scientific methods of classification by groups and subgroups based on criteria of resemblance, I wish to borrow theories of knowledge that have been proposed in the fields of aesthetics and cognition during the past few decades and then adapt them to a new purpose. In this respect, I hope to revive to some degree the skeptical spirit of Ludwig Wittgenstein's late work without completely abandoning the logical assumptions of sufficient and necessary conditions.

Finally, it is useful to locate Griffes's protean musical temperament in the context of two recent debates about the cultural climate of the early twentieth century: post-Victorianism and cosmopolitanism. In some ways Griffes's cultural outlook was a product of Victorian culture combined with a reaction against it. The foundation of Victorian culture depended on a strict dichotomy between, on the one hand, the civilized values of education, refinement, morals, religion, art, and family and, on the other, the so-called "animal" instincts such as sexual desire. It goes without saying that in his sexual identity and his rejection of organized religion, Griffes was anything but Victorian. However, his fascination with foreign cultures reveals the strong influence of late-Victorian taste and, especially, Aestheticism. The vogue for exotic culture was pervasive in late nineteenth-century England among the middle class as well as the aristocracy. During the second half of the 1800s, non-Western commodities became affordable, and as a result Great Britain became the largest importer of Chinese goods in the West.[52] However, instead of collecting objects of foreign culture, Griffes studied the musical traditions themselves, often setting non-Western melodies or using them as sources of inspiration for new artworks.

The Americanist T. J. Jackson Lears argues that many artists in early twentieth-century America experienced a general crisis of cultural authority, which he dubs "anti-modernist." This paradoxical category, which the historian Daniel Singal later renamed "post-Victorian," is suspended between two world views, Victorian and Modernist, without belonging to either.[53] If we characterize Griffes as anti-modernist (or post-Victorian), he would be considered an outsider, and his music would constitute an aesthetic vacuum. However, I prefer to conceive of his aesthetic posture in a more positive light rather than as a pure negation of both categories. While Jackson Lears identifies an important transitional period in American culture, I prefer to focus on an artistic tradition that Griffes cultivated and made his own—namely, the pastoral.[54]

The other experimental movement is cosmopolitanism. Although this ideal is an old venerable tradition originating in ancient Greece, during the late nineteenth century it underwent yet another transformation as a framework for understanding the explosion of experimentation in literature, music, and the visual arts of Western Europe. Recently, musicologists have revived the concept of cosmopolitanism as a means of revisiting the nationalist traditions of the nineteenth century and how they impacted the production and consumption of music. Sarah Collins and Dana Gooley propose that "there is now a burgeoning stream of scholarship that explicitly aims at undermining nation-oriented categories by focusing on transnational exchanges, border-crossing encounters, and expressions of the so-called cosmopolitan in music culture."[55] In many respects, the collection of Griffes's pastorals stands as a testament to the challenges of developing a cosmopolitan creative identity while living in New York City at the turn of the century.

At this juncture, let us take stock of this close exegesis of Griffes's compositional approach. Amid the evolution among the four contrasting styles outlined above, a source of unity slowly emerged: his ongoing fascination with the musical pastoral. Although he was by no means content to compose only pastorals during his career, it was a tradition he returned to again and again. In this study, I propose to use the pastoral topic as a unifying framework to *calibrate* his eclecticism and to reassess what may initially appear to be a larger pattern of constant change among the various stylistic periods.

Griffes renewed as well as redefined the pastoral musical tradition. He renewed his ties to the past by employing the same characteristics (or cues) that appeared in pastorals written in the eighteenth and nineteenth centuries. These cues are vital for determining a given piece's pastoral identity, especially when it lacks any specific reference to that tradition in its title, text, or program. By the same token, Griffes redefined the tradition in that virtually every one of his pastorals possesses a different combination of characteristic features. If one imagines each of these features as a separate musical color, then its presence in a work helps confirm its pastoral identity. Yet the presence of multiple features in different combinations creates a different blend of colors in each work—in short, a pastoral design. The goal of my project is to reveal the full abundance of Griffes's pastoral designs.

Non-Western Influences

Griffes's reliance on non-Western musical traditions as a source of inspiration must be placed within the context of his eclectic artistic sensibility. As shown above, during the final thirteen years of his life, his musical style underwent enormous changes. One impetus for these shifts in style was his fascination with the various traces of non-Western (or exotic) culture that he encountered, whether through fiction, travelogues, theater, books about music, performances, and/or transcriptions of folk music (for a detailed discussion of my understanding of the interaction between Western and non-Western musical traditions, see chap. 2).

Griffes developed his initial taste for foreign artistic cultures by living and studying in Germany for four years. But when he later returned to America, his interest in non-Western cultures expanded exponentially due to his voracious appetite for reading and to the cosmopolitan musical culture in New York City. Griffes never had the luxury of attending a World's Fair, whether in Paris (Exposition Universelle of 1889) or Chicago (Columbian Exposition of 1893). But he hardly needed them, for during most of his adult life he harbored a deep fascination with foreign cultures and, by extension, foreign musical traditions. His diaries from 1912–17 provide a virtual road map of his exposure to East Asian and North African culture. His reading list not only encompassed Chinese and Japanese stories in translation such as Lafcadio Hearn's *Some Chinese Ghosts* and *Japanese Fairy Tales, Chinese Stories from the Lodge of Leisure,* and Georges

Soulie de Morant's *Voyage en Chine, La littérature Chinoise,* and *Musique en Chine*; it also included travelogues and fantastic novels by various Western authors including Théophile Gauthier, Pierre Loti, Octave Mirbeau, Edmondo de Amicis, Gabriele d'Annunzio, and Robert Louis Stevenson. In short, for him to compose music inspired by non-Western sources was partly due to his catholic literary sensibility.[56]

Recently, there has been a resurgence of interest in the role that travel literature—that is, guidebooks, poetry, novels, and essays—played in nineteenth-century contemporary life. In a recent essay, Michael Allis observes that these publications contributed to "the intellectual culture of the nineteenth century . . . whether in terms of knowledge exchange, geography, ethnography, cultural identity, philosophy, aesthetics, or historical and political commentary"[57] In essence, the primary function of travel writing during the nineteenth century was to "[acclaim] the foreign as gratifyingly dissimilar from the familiar."[58]

By contrast, Griffes's exposure to non-Western musical traditions themselves was through treatises and manuals as well as transcriptions. For example, the inventory of his library includes a book on Chinese music by J. A. Van Aalst as well as a collection of essays by Francisco Salvador-Daniel that surveys Arab instruments, Arab music, and the relationship between Arab and Greek musical traditions.[59] Salvador-Daniel was a nineteenth-century Spanish composer, raised in France, who lived and taught in Algeria during the 1850s and who later prepared a collection of four hundred Arab folk songs, including French translations and piano accompaniments. As a composer, he wrote music that was highly influenced by his ethnomusicological studies, including *Danses Arabes* for orchestra, Arab fantasies for piano, and a *Messe africaine*.[60] While there is no evidence that Salvador-Daniel's book directly influenced Griffes's compositional process—in particular, his decision to use an Arabic melody in *The Pleasure-Dome of Kubla Khan*—it clearly demonstrates that his interest in Arabic music was far beyond that of a dilettante.

In New York City, he occasionally witnessed performances of non-Western music. For example, in a diary entry from 1917 he describes a private concert in Chinatown where he heard a Chinese folk song, which he took down in dictation, accompanied by "the Chinese harp or harpsichord. The tone was about the same as the clavichord. It is played with bamboo hammers."[61] That same year, Charles Griffes met the singer Eva Gauthier, who shared with him a handful of non-Western melodies from Japan and Java that she had collected in her travels in East Asia. According to Anderson, these melodies formed the basis for the following works by Griffes: *Sho-Jo: The Spirit of Wine—A Symbol of Happiness* (unpublished, 1917); and *Three Javanese Songs* (1917).[62] In his biography, Maisel describes Griffes's obsession with all things exotic: "For his part Griffes was fascinated by the fresh musical material that the singer disclosed to him and filled several little notebooks and scraps of paper with it . . . as well as the with the fruits of his own intensive studies in the field. Lullabies, war songs, lance ceremonies, a Malay song from Sumatra, a Malay song from Java, Javanese and Indian and Japanese and Chinese melodies, carefully detailed notes on Eastern structure. . . . He collected and mined them all."[63] In a fascinating article devoted to Griffes's setting of three Javanese melodies, Henry Spiller argues that his goal was less to reproduce authentic sounds of East Asian music than it was to express how he imagined they would sound.[64]

Griffes's treatment of these non-Western sources was often quite subtle. Though he used Western instruments in his settings, he often tried to re-create the textures and sounds of specific non-Western instruments. Regarding the pantomime, *Sho-Jo*, Griffes explained the details of his compositional approach in an interview in 1917:

> There is a striving for harmonies which suggest the quarter-tones of Oriental music, and the frequent employ of the characteristic augmented second; as well as the organ point common to both systems. . . . My harmonization is all in octaves, fifths, fourths, and seconds—consonant major thirds and sixths are omitted. The orchestration is as Japanese as possible: thin and delicate, and the muted string *points d'orgue* serve as a neutral-tinted background, like the empty spaces in a Japanese print. The whole thematic material is given to the flute, clarinet, and oboe—akin to the Japanese reed instruments; the harp suggests the koto.[65]

This quotation is unusual in two respects: Griffes is quite candid about his compositional method in that he confesses his artistic goal is to suggest the specific timbres of Japanese instruments as well as an alternative tuning system. In the detailed analysis in chapter 7, I will explore how

Griffes's organization of melody, harmony, and texture in *Five Ancient Poems of China and Japan* follows some of the same strict compositional regimen he describes in his setting of *Sho-Jo*.[66] Perhaps the most telling insight about Griffes's adaptation of non-Western musical traditions is found in his admiration for Michio Ito, the lead dancer and collaborator in the pantomime *Sho-Jo*: "Japanese music should not be too largely infused with Western ideas and procedures; yet Michio Ito himself, who understands the music of his native land *au fond*, believes that it will gain in breadth of expression, that its beauties will be more widely understood if brought into a modified contact with Western art influences."[67] Griffes's description of "modified contact" provides a profound insight about his artistic motivation and about the stylistic synthesis he tried to achieve.

When one contemplates the stunning diversity of traditions that inspired Griffes—Chinese, Japanese, Javanese, Celtic, and Native American—no single pattern unifies all the ways in which non-Western culture shaped his musical oeuvre. Instead, at different junctures in his life, various musical, literary, and even theatrical sources became individual threads that helped color the rich tapestry of his musical style. It is no exaggeration to say that his fascination for musical exoticism is inseparable from his overall eclecticism.

Aestheticism

At this juncture, it is appropriate to consider two sources of influence that are crucial for understanding Griffes's artistic sensibility. The early years of the twentieth century witnessed the cultural aftershock of two experimental literary movements: British Aestheticism and the Celtic Revival; notably, two of his favorite authors, Oscar Wilde and William Sharp, were deeply involved in each one. In order to understand Griffes's affinities with these two artists and the degree to which they influenced his music, it is necessary to provide a detailed summary of both movements.

For many, the term *Art for Art's Sake* (or *l'art pour l'art*) is so obvious that it ends up being opaque. How could such a simple, trivial statement—the art lover's equivalent of common sense—serve as a general aesthetic principle? The first order of business is to provide some clear definitions and then to briefly summarize the historical origins of this artistic approach.[68]

This origin of the Aesthetic movement can be traced to a group of English writers and artists, led by Dante Gabriel Rossetti, who formed the Pre-Raphaelite Brotherhood in 1848 to revive the artistic ideals of the Medieval and early Renaissance periods and to celebrate themes of nature. Later, after the initial group dissolved, another diverse group of experimental artists and intellectuals emerged, and it acquired a family of labels including *Art for Art's Sake*, *Aestheticism*, and the *Aesthetic movement*. According to *Grove Art Online*, Aestheticism was characterized by a common belief in the autonomy of art as well as a "cult of the beautiful and an emphasis on the sheer pleasure to be derived from it."[69] This loose-knit group included writers (Algernon Swinburne, Wilde, and Walter Pater), painters (James Whistler and Edward Burne-Jones), and decorative artists (E. W. Godwin and William Morris). While the late-Victorian dramatis personae of the Aesthetic movement changed at various points, depending on the source, the only name that appears on every list is Oscar Wilde.

Strictly speaking, the infamous Aestheticist motto *Art for Art's Sake* is a tautology. In mathematical terms, it could be described as the identify function: $X = X$. The art historian Elizabeth Prettejohn considers such redundancy a "non-theory or anti-theory."[70] When defined in this way, it is difficult to understand how such a verbal redundancy could have inspired anyone.

But there is another way of interpreting the Aestheticist motto that is more fruitful. The key to understanding the basis of the motto is to treat it as a form of philosophical relativism. According to Walter Pater, one of Oscar Wilde's professors at Oxford, the basis for assigning beauty is self-explanatory; hence, each artistic experience that is deemed beautiful provides its own contextual basis for inferring what the criterion of aesthetic value should be. In his volume of essays on the Renaissance, Pater concludes, "To define beauty, not in the most abstract but in the most concrete terms possible, to find, not its universal formula, but the formula which expresses most adequately this or that special manifestation of it is the aim of the true student of aesthetics."[71] This comment explains why in his writings Pater provides inventories of sample objects or experiences that he finds beautiful; "the lists enumerate the various objects of sensuous pleasure in lieu of authorizing a rule for taste."[72] Consequently, the group of works that are deemed to have aesthetic value resists any generalization: "a set of art practices that are linked by . . . a common agreement that no theory can ever be devised to link them."[73] In short, the Aestheticist motto could be restated as "Eclecticism for its own sake" or "The sum of the parts is greater than the whole."

To fully understand the basis of the Aestheticist manifesto, one must consider all of the historical threads that converged in the late nineteenth century. In a recent monograph, Gene Bell-Villata offers a scintillating overview of the concept of Art for Art's Sake that traverses three countries—Germany, France, and Great Britain—and spans over two centuries, beginning with the philosophical theories of Immanuel Kant in the late eighteenth century, continuing through the French Romantic authors in the 1830s, and finally culminating with the British Aesthetic movement.[74] His sweeping overview stresses that the idea of Art for Art's Sake associated with late-Victorian England initially came to light in the context of Immanuel Kant's critical philosophy, which synthesized human understanding, morality, and beauty. Bell-Villata summarizes the idea's point of origin: "Beauty can serve as transition to morality, but morality can also serve as foundation for taste. Hence, Kant's advocacy of what, in retrospect, resembles *l'art pour l'art* actually had as its broader premises our growth as social and moral beings, the human process of becoming more civilized—of which the love of beauty . . . was only one part."[75] For Kant, the contemplation of beauty could not be separated from a broader synthesis of human understanding and morality.

The crucial turning point in the history of the concept of Art for Art's Sake was during the 1830s in France, where early Romantics like Théophile Gautier and Victor Cousin adapted for their own ends a concept that had originally germinated in the German Enlightenment. Their goal was to refute the view that art should serve a higher moral purpose or should imitate nature. "Kant's mature ideas were . . . reduced to a number of set phrases and slogans. His grand synthesis was lost and his global totality ignored."[76] The infamous phrase *l'art pour l'art*, which Cousin himself penned, might be interpreted as "Metaphysics without the Morals" or

"Kant-lite": "Il faut de la religion pour la religion de la morale pour la morale, comme de l'art pour art." ("It is necessary that religion is for religion, morality for morality just as art for art.")[77] This attempt to purge from art any expression of religion or morality as well as any attempt to mimic nature eventually became the rallying cry for Pater and Wilde at the end of the nineteenth century. For Wilde, "aesthetics supersede ethics . . . [and] beauty matters more than morals."[78] The British revival of the French Romantics had another layer of justification, for it was a reaction against the prevailing philosophical and aesthetic climate in Victorian England, in particular John Ruskin's view that art should have a practical value and should serve as a means of moral instruction. For artists like Wilde, art should "not exist for the sake of preaching a moral lesson, of supporting a political cause, of making a fortune."[79]

In sum, we have seen that the historical evolution of the Art for Art's Sake movement is truly international in scope, weaving together ideas of German, French, and British vintage. Also, if one considers the fundamental artistic vision of British Aestheticism as negative, one source of that negation can be traced to the deformation of Kant's original philosophical vision that combined cognition, aesthetics, and morality. Yet this same vision also became a positive source of inspiration for some of Griffes's most inspiring music.

Application to Griffes

Let us turn to the relationship between Aestheticism or the Art for Art's Sake movement and Griffes's musical style. There are three principal factors that suggest the experimental art movement in late-Victorian England had an impact on his artistic approach: (1) Griffes's reliance on Aestheticist poems and programs in his music; (2) his fascination with non-Western artistic traditions that had a hedonist or sensual character and the resulting eclectic character of his musical style; and (3) his occasional use of musical irony. While these factors do not constitute proof of a direct influence, on balance it is reasonable to conclude that Griffes had a strong affinity for the Aestheticist movement.

The first reason is biographical in nature and reflects his working methods as a composer. Griffes was deeply inspired by the texts of writers who were self-avowed Aestheticists, such as Wilde, or writers who had strong sympathies with the Aestheticist outlook, such as William Sharp / Fiona MacLeod. Griffes either set their poems as vocal music or used excerpts from their poems as programs for his instrumental music. There is ample evidence that Wilde's life and work exercised a considerable influence on Charles Griffes. He set seven different poems by Wilde for voice and piano and two separate settings of "La Mer," making a grand total of eight collaborations.[80]

Furthermore, Griffes and Wilde shared a fascination with one of the two most common motifs of the Aesthetic movement: peacocks, especially white ones.[81] In one of Wilde's best-known essays, entitled "The Decay of Lying," for instance, he introduces the image of a white peacock as the epilogue to his argument that nature should imitate art rather than vice versa. [82] In addition, the same image of a white peafowl—now multiplied a hundred times—appears at a pivotal moment in his controversial play *Salome*. At a pivotal moment King Herod offers his stepdaughter a gift of one hundred white peacocks if she would withdraw her request for John the Baptist's head, an offer she refuses. Although no proof exists that Griffes read this particular essay, he was clearly enamored of the play, having attended it once and having heard Richard Strauss's opera based on it four times while living in Berlin.[83] As we will see in chapter 4, Wilde's and Griffes's mutual obsession with white peacocks was also shared by William Sharp.

The second justification for linking Griffes with Aestheticist artists is their common fascination with exoticism, which played a prominent role in a wide range of literature, painting as well as arts and crafts (Griffes's curiosity about and sympathy with various non-Western musical traditions was discussed in depth in the previous section). The Aestheticist interest in non-Western culture overlaps with a broader tradition called Japonisme, a French term that refers to a "broad range of European borrowings from Japanese art. . . . encompassing decorative objects with Japanese designs . . . paintings of scenes set in Japan, and Western paintings, prints and decorative arts influenced by Japanese aesthetics."[84] When one contemplates the stunning diversity of national traditions that inspired Griffes—French, Chinese, Japanese, Javanese, Celtic, and Native American, to name a few—it is reasonable to conclude that he was drawn to the traces of foreign artistic culture that he encountered in New York.

A corollary to Griffes's fascination with non-Western music is a desire to cultivate hedonism and sensuous beauty for its own sake, a feature that also lies at the heart of Pater's and Wilde's conceptions of art. As described above, this focus on hedonism was significant because the Aestheticists were all reacting against what they considered to be a highly repressive conception of art. Taken together, the preoccupation with non-Western artistic traditions and sensuous beauty confirms that artists in the Aesthetic movement were committed to eclecticism for its own sake—a belief they shared with Griffes.

A third reason for associating Griffes with the Aestheticist program is a common interest in irony. There are three factors that support this observation, beginning with his personality. According to the music critic Lawrence Gilman, Griffes "had a delicate perception of mortal ironies, both humorous and tragical. He was a poet with a sense of comedy." Maisel agrees: "The philosophy from which that comic awareness arose, the viewpoint that informed its irony, was something that Griffes retained all his life."[85]

Another factor is his fascination with Oscar Wilde. A detailed inventory of Griffes's personal library includes the complete works of Oscar Wilde, one of the leading voices of the Aesthetic movement.[86] Griffes specifically mentioned in a 1914 diary entry that he had just read Wilde's *Lady Windermere's Fan*. But the most telling indication is the following reflection about Wilde's relationship to the Aesthetic movement: "Read interesting things about Oscar Wilde, including 2 good essays by Carl Dietz from the Preuss Fahrbücher and Sherand's Biography. Dietz says that Wilde was a combination of Walton, Dorian and Basil in 'Dorian Gray,' an explanation which I like. He thinks the man will be remembered for his search for beauty and connection with the esthetic movement long after his works are forgotten."[87] Although no proof exists that Griffes modeled his works after any particular poem, play, or essay by Wilde, it is more than likely that he fell under the sway of the Irishman's ironic sensibility.

The final justification of Griffes's taste for irony is the direct evidence in the music itself: the paradoxical structure found in his final work, Prelude #3 and, to a lesser extent, "Vale of Dreams" (see chaps. 8 and 9). For example, Griffe's use of irony in the Prelude #3 has a critical character in that he questions the underlying theoretical assumptions about scale-degree identity and, as a consequence, the traditional concepts of consonance and dissonance. In addition, this work also exhibits and comments upon the model of binary form and the principles of balance and closure upon which that model is based. The presence of paradox in both works confirms Griffes's ongoing preoccupation with musical forms of ambiguity and irony.

Overall, it is accurate to say that the principles of Aestheticism—whether in Pater's elegant essays or Wilde's pithy aphorisms—reinforced Griffes's own artistic propensities. His underlying sympathy with the Aesthetic movement in literature and painting broadened the landscape of his artistic vision and his cultural aspirations.

Sharp/MacLeod

William Sharp (1855–1905) was one of the more enigmatic British authors at the turn of the century. Born in Scotland, he traveled widely during his youth but eventually settled in London and began writing biographies of major nineteenth-century English authors (e.g., Rosetti, Shelley, and Browning). Soon he became fascinated with assuming fictional identities and changing gender. For instance, in mid-August 1892 Sharp issued *The Pagan Review*, the first and last volume of a new periodical for which he was the editor and sole contributor, furnishing all seven essays/poems under various pseudonyms. Also, in 1891 Sharp completed a joint epistolary novel with a female author, Blanche Willis Howard, imagining a conversation between a husband and wife. It is significant that Sharp wrote all the wife's letters and Howard wrote the husband's.[88]

However, a sojourn to Italy in the early 1890s served as the turning point in his literary career when, beginning then until his death, Sharp assumed a dual identity—one male, the other female. To christen this new female persona, he invented the name Fiona MacLeod. With the help of his wife and his sister, Mary, he concealed MacLeod's true identity and continued writing under this alias as well as his own name for the final fourteen years of his life. By adopting this new persona, he discovered a new calling—to help resurrect the lost culture and traditions of the ancient Celts. Sharp, along with such figures as W. B. Yeats and George William Russell, helped inaugurate the Celtic Renaissance movement, or the Celtic Twilight, in late nineteenth-century England.[89] While immersed in the folk tales and myths of the ancient Celts, Sharp focused primarily on their deeper spiritual character: "So far as I understand the 'Celtic Movement,' it is a natural outcome, the natural expression of a freshly inspired spiritual and artistic energy. . . . There is no racial road to beauty, nor to any excellence. Genius, which leads thither, beckons neither to tribe nor clan, neither to school nor movement, but only to one soul here and to another there."[90] Using his pseudonym, Sharp fashioned an artistic credo that could be encapsulated in a single phrase: "To live in beauty—which is to put into four words all the dream and spiritual effort of the soul of man."[91]

While visiting Rome during the winter of 1891, Sharp wrote a collection of poetry entitled *Sospiri di Roma* (*Sighs of Rome*) that coincided with his discovery of his new female persona. William Halloran argues that three factors shaped the genesis of these poems: (a) recent professional impasses he had suffered in London; (b) his discovery of the female side of his personality; and (c) his romantic passion for a woman he encountered in Italy, Edith Wingate Rinder.[92] Sharp's biographer summarizes Rinder's impact: "Because of her beauty, her strong sense of life and the joy of life; because of her keen intuitions and mental alertness, her personality stood for him as a symbol of the heroic women of Greek and Celtic days, a symbol that, as he expressed it, unlocked new doors in his mind and put him 'in touch with ancestral memories' of his race."[93] Though he still signed his own name under these poems, Sharp felt transformed:

> That moment began, he declared, my spiritual regeneration. I was a New Man, a mystic, where before I had been only a mechanic-in-art. Carried away by my passion, my pen wrote as if dipped in fire, and when I sat down to write prose, a spirit-hand would seize my pen and guide into inspired verse.[94]

Central themes in the *Sospiri* poems include a fascination with nature, intense romantic passion, and hints of spirituality—themes that must have struck a chord in Griffes.

William Sharp / Fiona MacLeod played a pivotal role in the instrumental and vocal music that Griffes composed in his later years. Griffes was clearly a devotee of both dimensions of the author's literary sensibility, for he owned books of poetry by Sharp and Macleod.[95] In 1915–16, Griffes composed four works for solo piano that were inspired by poems drawn from Sharp's collection *Sospiri di Roma*, which he called *Roman Sketches*, Op. 7.[96] Preceding all four scores, he included excerpts from the poems as epigraphs. Then, in 1918, Griffes set a trio of Macleod's poems as a set entitled *Three Poems of Fiona Macleod*, Op. 11, which he later transcribed for voice and orchestra. In addition, he composed an isolated setting of Macleod's poem "The War Song of the Vikings."

There are several ways in which the lives and aesthetic values of Sharp and Griffes resemble one another. The first is a common duality about their identity and sexuality. For over a decade, Sharp flourished as a male writing with a female perspective. By contrast, although Griffes never developed an artistic alter ego, he also had two completely separate identities, one for his public life as a heterosexual—composer, performer, and teacher—and the other for his private life as a gay man. The dichotomy between public and private was all the more dramatized by his regular geographic rotation between Tarrytown, a small town on the Hudson, and New York City, where he sought refuge during summers and vacations.

The second aesthetic correspondence between Sharp and Griffes was an assumption that underpins the revival of Celtic folk traditions. By retelling or setting to music stories of Celtic magic and mysticism, both artists helped renew a tradition of rural beliefs and superstitions that rejected the modern urban world—whether the daily life of late-Victorian London or early twentieth-century New York. Viewed as a whole, the work of the Celtic Revival authors such as James MacPherson, W. B. Yeats, and Sharp served as a highly embellished protest against modernity, which had as a corollary a highly idealized view of the natural world. While Fiona Macleod devoted great attention to the physical settings of her poems and dramas, these settings were always based on an ideal of nature—often in an imaginary Celtic landscape. Neutral or scientific description of the outdoors had no place in her art. Thus, while Griffes never overtly showed a distaste for the urban life of New York City, his artistic taste, like hers, reveals a sympathy for an idyllic, Virgilian conception of nature and the pastoral.

Third, the two artists shared a common fascination with mysticism. While Macleod was consumed by it, Griffes's attitude toward spirituality is difficult to determine. Clearly, he was no full-fledged mystic; by the time he settled in New York in 1907 he was, according to his first biographer, "outspokenly opposed to institutional religion." Apparently, Griffes possessed "a strongly religious, nostalgic, poetic temperament" and sought "to ground the elements of religion in life itself."[97] Furthermore, the two books that most closely expressed Griffes's attitude toward religion were August Strindberg's autobiography, *The Son of a Servant*, and Jens Peter Jacobsen's controversial novel *Niels Lyhne*, published in 1880, which recounts the suffering of an avowed atheist. Judging from his late songs, piano works, and dramatic works, Griffes's literary taste reveals his affinity for some kind of spiritual experience. For example, the narrator in one of the three Macleod poems in Op. 11 longs to be touched by a faery's kiss. Also, his chamber setting of *The Kairn of Koridwen* portrays a druid priestess who must choose between her fidelity to religion and her love for a Gallic warrior. Based on these observations, it is reasonable to characterize Griffes's attitude toward spirituality as, at the very least, ambivalent, and, in some cases, sympathetic. Chapter 6 will be devoted to three of Griffes's settings of MacLeod's poetry that display their mutual love of sensuous pleasure and longing for spiritual fulfillment.

Conclusion

This chapter has had three aims: to provide a rich biographical sketch of Griffes's life; to uncover the spectrum of styles that informed his eclectic musical style; and to shed new light on the broader historical context that gave birth to his compositions. Griffes flourished at an unusual juncture in American music. His geographical location in a major urban center coupled with his own creative temperament enabled him to nurture a cosmopolitan sensibility. In addition, two sources of influence can be found in contemporary authors who helped inspire his music: the writings of Oscar Wilde, who championed the ideals of Aestheticism, as well as the poetry of William Sharp and his female persona, Fiona Macleod, who contributed to the Celtic Renaissance.

Within a thirteen-year span, Griffes developed an inimitable stylistic blend that balanced European inspiration with an American sensibility, German bombast with French sensuality, an Aestheticist love of non-Western culture with Celtic spiritual longing, and deep, heartfelt emotion with detached ironic commentary. At the end of her work, Donna Anderson comments that "Griffes ... spent his life in an incessant search for a musical language that could express his own artistic personality. ... He was neither decisively shaped nor permanently influenced by any one person or by any one prevailing musical style."[98] The concept of the ambivalent pastoral provides a way of tracing his search for a new "musical language." And that is the subject of the next chapter.

NOTES

1. Frisch acknowledges that he is borrowing the concept of ambivalent modernism from Marion Deshmukh. See *German Modernism: Music and the Arts* (Berkeley and Los Angeles: University of California Press, 2005), 8.

2. These artists include Richard Wagner, Arnold Schoenberg, Max Reger, Ferruccio Busoni, Richard Strauss, Hans Pfitzner, Hugo von Hofmannsthal, and Thomas Mann.

3. Edward Maisel, *Charles T. Griffes: The Life of an American Composer* (New York: Knopf, 1943; revised edition, 1984); and Donna K. Anderson, *Charles T. Griffes: A Life in Music* (Washington and London: Smithsonian Institution Press, 1993).

4. While Maisel frequently relies on primary source material, he often uses quotation marks without citing a specific source. To his credit, he also includes a meticulous formal and motivic analysis of the late "Piano Sonata," a work he felt had been unduly neglected.

5. Charles's Welsh ancestors on his father's side spelled the name *Griffith*. Family lore credits the name change to his great-great-grandfather, who spoke with a lisp and who was too embarrassed to correct the county clerk when the name was officially recorded as *Griffes*. See Anderson, *Charles T. Griffes*, 15.

6. For Griffes, "the key of E-flat, for example, was yellow or golden. C major was an incandescent white light, the most brilliant key in the tonality." Maisel, *Charles T. Griffes*, 11.

7. Broughton had studied piano with Karl Klindworth, a pupil of Franz Liszt. The school began as the Berliner Musikschule in 1850 but six years later was renamed in honor of the Stern family, Stern'sches Konservatorium. Throughout her book, Anderson uses the abbreviation "Stern Conservatory."

8. See Anderson, *Charles T. Griffes*, 52; and Maisel, *Charles T. Griffes*, 38, 64.

9. The total debt was $1,800, which Griffes paid as a bank note in March 1915—a sum that exceeded his annual salary! See Anderson, *Charles T. Griffes*, 114.

10. An undated piano roll recording of Griffes's own performance of "The White Peacock" exists at the Gannett-Tripp Library, Elmira College, Elmira, New York.

11. Maisel is convinced that the two had a physical relationship, while Anderson has her doubts. An additional anecdote is that when Griffes returned to Germany to attend Joël's wedding, he described Joël's fiancée as "an agreeable disappointment." Letter to Clara Griffes, July 8, 1908; referenced in Anderson, *Charles T. Griffes*, 60.

12. Anderson, *Charles T. Griffes*, 95.

13. In 1907, the year Griffes arrived, the total enrollment was 92; ten years later it had risen to 113. See Anderson, *Charles T. Griffes*, 102.

14. Maisel, *Charles T. Griffes*, 92.

15. For a series of 286 photographs that Griffes took of the Hackley School and Hudson Valley region in 1907–20 as well as drawings, etchings, and watercolors from his years in Germany, see JPB 97-68, Archives and Manuscripts, New York Public Library for the Performing Arts, Dorothy and Lewis B. Cullman Center. A smaller collection of photographs is on deposit at the Gannett-Tripp Library, Elmira College, Elmira, New York. Letter from Burnett Corwin Tuthill to Edward Maisel, June 4, 1938, Burnet Corwin Tuthill Papers, Music Division, Library of Congress, Washington, DC.

16. Griffes Personal Diary, May 31, 1915, Box 47, Folder 5-6, Series III, Donna K. Anderson Research Files on Charles Griffes, Music Division, New York Public Library for the Performing Arts.

17. In a diary entry for January 5, 1915, Griffes wrote, "It is very dull and stupid to be back [in Tarrytown]." Box 47, Folder 5-6, Series III, Donna K. Anderson Research Files on Charles Griffes, Music Division, New York Public Library for the Performing Arts.

18. Box 47, Folder 5-6, Series III, Donna K. Anderson Research Files on Charles Griffes, Music Division, New York Public Library for the Performing Arts. For a comprehensive list of Griffes's works as well as a list of the publishers for most of his works, see Anderson, *Charles T. Griffes*, 223–34. Anderson also completed a bibliographic resource for locating all of the extant sketches and manuscripts of his works: *The Works of Charles T. Griffes: A Descriptive Catalogue* (Ann Arbor, MI: UMI Research Press, 1983).

19. Anderson, *The Works of Charles T. Griffes*, 232–33, 436–37.

20. Letter from Burnet Tuthill to Edward Maisel June 4, 1938. Burnet Corwin Tuthill Papers, Music Division, Library of Congress, Washington, DC.

21. Maisel, *Charles T. Griffes*, 154.

22. Marion Bauer, "Charles Griffes as I Remember Him," *The Musical Quarterly* 29 (1943): 356.

23. Maisel, *Charles T. Griffes*, 108.

24. Anderson, *Charles T. Griffes*, 37, 40.

25. Ibid., 39–44.

26. Anderson provides English translations of nine relevant diary entries in 1914–15. She concludes that "his sexual perambulations, preferences, and strategies are revealed with fascinating clarity." See Anderson, *Charles T. Griffes*, 40–41.

27. Maisel, *Charles T. Griffes*, 99.

28. Ibid., 105.

29. A provisional list of Griffes's works with spiritual or supernatural themes would include *The Pleasure-Dome of Kubla Khan*, "The White Peacock," *The Kairn of Koridwen* (Edouard Shuré), "In a Myrtle Shade," "Phantoms," "Thy Dark Eyes to Mine," and "The Rose of the Night."

30. Although the titles of the two versions of his Macleod cycle differ slightly ("by" instead of "of"), I will refer to both as *Three Poems of Fiona Macleod*. Also, the orchestral version of *The Pleasure-Dome of Kubla Khan* should be considered as an independent work by the same name.

31. Burnett Tuthill explains, "In the year or two before his final illness, the demand for Griffes' work and the contract which he had entered into with the Misses Lewissohn . . . crowded him . . . to such an extent that he had to work long late hours not only finished the score of the pageant, *Salut au Monde*, but also in copying orchestral parts for *The Pleasure-Dome* for its premiere in Boston, under Monteux. It is this overwork and late hours that undermined his strength which was never too robust and laid him open to his fatal illness." Letter from Burnett Corwin Tuthill to Edward Maisel, June 4, 1938, Burnet Corwin Tuthill Papers, Music Division, Library of Congress, Washington, DC.

32. *New York Herald Tribune*, December 5, 1919, 11; *Globe and Commercial Advertiser*, December 5, 1919, 13; Referenced in Anderson, *Charles T. Griffes*, 162.

33. Anderson, *Charles T. Griffes*, 169. Considering that the Spanish flu pandemic was raging throughout the East Coast in 1918–19, it is reasonable to speculate whether that disease contributed to his condition. The autopsy, however, makes no mention of it—see Maisel, *Charles T. Griffes*, 325.

34. Denise Von Glahn, *The Sounds of Place: Music and the American Cultural Landscape* (Urbana: University of Illinois Press, 2021), 4–5.

35. Alex Ross, *The Rest is Noise: Listening to the Twentieth Century* (New York: Picador, 2008), 28.

36. Ralph Waldo Emerson, "The American Scholar," in *Complete Writings of Ralph W. Emerson* (New York: W. H. Wise, 1929), vol. 1, 25–36.

37. Carol J. Oja, *Making Music Modern: New York in the 1920s* (Oxford, UK: Oxford University Press, 2000), 4.

38. Robert Pascal, "Style," *Grove Music Online*, accessed February 22, 2021, https://www.oxfordmusiconline.com/grovemusic/view/10.1093/gmo/9781561592630.001.0001/omo-9781561592630-e-0000027041.

39. Leonard Meyer, *Style and Music: Theory, History, and Ideology* (Philadelphia: University of Pennsylvania Press, 1989), 13–23.

40. Heather Dubrow, *Genre* (London: Methuen, 1982), 31.

41. In Jeffrey Kallberg's study of Chopin's nocturnes, his aim is to uncover the social context of this "generic contract," connecting the musical structure of individual works with broader questions of gender and social class. See Jeffrey Kallberg, *Chopin at the Boundaries: Sex, History, and Musical Genre* (Cambridge, MA: Harvard University Press, 1996), 5.

42. In the final chapter of her biography, Donna Anderson provides a preliminary template of four "stylistic periods" in Griffes's output, which she calls Romantic, Impressionist, Oriental, and Abstract. However, she emphasizes that these terms are not exhaustive since there are pieces that either span multiple periods or do not belong to any of them. See Anderson, *Charles T. Griffes*, 195. Although in her book she identifies only four, in her

extensive program notes for a CD of Griffes's music in 1976 (New World Recording, 273-2), she includes two more: "Celtic" as well as "Native American."

43. In an article published after his death, Griffes was quoted as saying that the songs were "more the result of composition study than his own musical expression." See A. Walter Kramer, "Charles T. Griffes: Cut Down in His Prime, a Victim of our Barbarous Neglect of Genius," *Musical America* 32, no. 4 (22 May 1920): 39.

44. See Marion Bauer, "Impressionists in America," *Modern Music* 4, no. 2 (1936): 19–20; Beth J. Eggers, "Charles Tomlinson Griffes, Portrait of an American Impressionist," *American Music Teacher* 32, no. 1 (1982): 28–29. Anderson argues that this label is misrepresentative—Anderson, *Charles T. Griffes, A Life in Music*, 185.

45. For a representative list of Debussy works that Griffes either studied or performed in his recitals, see Taylor A. Greer, "The Unfolding Tale of Charles Griffes's 'White Peacock,'" *Gamut, the Journal of the Music Theory Society of the Mid-Atlantic* 3, no. 1 (2010), Festschrift issue, "A Music-Theoretical Matrix: Essays in Honor of Allen Forte," Article 7.

46. This movement is a triptych within a triptych. "Les Parfums de la nuit" is the middle movement of *Ibéria*, which, as a whole, constitutes the second section of the orchestral work *Images pour orchestra*. Griffes's piano transcription was premiered by Solungaa Liu, Coolidge Auditorium, Library of Congress, November 4, 2017.

47. In 1917 Griffes also composed arrangements for Adolf Bolm's *Ballet-Intime* of two Non-Western sources: *A Trip to Syria (Assyrian Dance)*, Alexander Maloof; and *Sakura-sakura*, a traditional Japanese Cherry Dance.

48. Anderson, *Charles T. Griffes*, 193.

49. Nicholas E. Tawa, *Mainstream Music of Early Twentieth Century America: The Composers, Their Times, and Their Works* (Westport, CT: Greenwood Press, 1992), 12; quoting from Rupert Hughes, *Contemporary American Composers* (Boston: Page, 1900), 13, 22–24.

50. Oxford English Dictionary Online. Oxford, UK: Oxford University Press, accessed August 20, 2023. https://www.oed.com/search/dictionary/?scope=Entries&q=polythetic&tl=true.

51. Rodney Needham, "Polythetic Classification: Convergence and Consequences," *Man, New Series* 10, no. 3 (September 1975): 349–69; J. A. Silk, "What, If Anything, Is Mahayana Buddhism? Problems of Definitions and Classifications," *Numen-International Review for the History of Religions* 49, no. 5 (2002): 355–405; Josef Parnas, "Differential Diagnosis and Current Polythetic Classification," *World Psychiatry* 14, no. 3 (2015): 284–87.

52. Qi Chen, "Aristocracy for the Common People: Chinese Commodities in Oscar Wilde's Aestheticism," *Victorian Network* 1, no. 1 (Summer 2009): 40.

53. According to T. J. Jackson Lears, examples of "post-Victorians," which he calls "anti-modernists," include Henry Adams, William James, Henry Wadsworth Longfellow, Charles Eliot Norton, and Edith Wharton; see *No Place for Grace: Anti-Modernism and the Transformation of American Culture, 1880–1920* (Chicago: Chicago University Press, 1981), 314–23; cited in Daniel Singal, "Toward a Definition of American Modernism," *American Quarterly* 39, no. 1 (Spring 1987): 10.

54. Griffes's propensity for opposition was also shared by later "post-Victorian" artists in the 1920s and 1930s such as Max Beerbohm, Baron Corvo, and Vernon Lee. According to Kristin Mahoney, these artists revived what she calls "late-Victorian Decadence" found in the highly diverse writings and drawings of Aubrey Beardsley, Oscar Wilde, and W. B. Yeats. These later writers had two motivations: to renew the spirit of skepticism and

critical detachment shared by the Decadent artists of 1890s and as a means "for subtly communicating distaste for the methods and values of the present"—that is, the extremes of modernism. See Kristin Mahoney, *Literature and the Post-Victorian Decadence* (Cambridge, UK: Cambridge University Press, 2015), 3.

55. Sarah Collins and Dana Gooley, "Music and the New Cosmopolitanism: Problems and Possibilities," *The Musical Quarterly* 99, no. 2 (Summer 2016): 139–65.

56. Griffes was particularly fascinated by color and ambiance in literary works. For example, in a diary entry during June 1912, he confided, after reading Pierre Loti's *Fleurs d'Ennui*, that Loti has "a peculiar faculty of transporting the reader at once into a strange and exotic atmosphere." In addition, later that summer he noted in his diary that the prose fragment "The Wanderings of Cain" by Samuel Taylor Coleridge "would be a good thing for a melodrama with piano.... The language is very dramatic and picturesque." Although he never set this particular work to music, he ended up basing one of his most ambitious orchestral works on another, more celebrated Coleridge poem, "Kubla Khan." Diary Entries, June 29, 1912, and August 9, 1912, Box 47, Folder 5-6, Series III, Donna K. Anderson Research Files on Charles Griffes, Music Division, New York Public Library for the Performing Arts.

57. Paul Watt, Sarah Collins, and Michael Allis, ed. *The Oxford Handbook of Music and Intellectual Culture in the Nineteenth Century* (New York: Oxford University Press, 2020), 103.

58. Chloe Chard, *Pleasure and Guilt on the Grand Tour: Travel Writing and Imaginative Geography, 1600–1830* (Manchester, UK: Manchester University Press, 1999), 4; quoted in Ibid., 106.

59. Francisco Salvador-Daniel, *The Music and the Musical Instruments of the Arab*, Eng. Trans. Henry George Farmer (London: William Reeves, 1914); reprint (Monee, IL: Forgotten Books, 2022).

60. Salvador-Daniel briefly served as the director of the Conservatoire Nationale Supérieur de Musique but was executed by the royalists in May 1871 during the *Semaine sanglante* (*Bloody Week*) of the Paris Commune. See the biographical summary https://www.amar-foundation.org/francisco-salvator-daniel.

61. Diary entry April 18, 1917, Box 47, Folder 5-6, Series III, Donna K. Anderson Research Files on Charles Griffes, Music Division, New York Public Library for the Performing Arts.

62. Anderson, *Charles T. Griffes*, 192.

63. Maisel, *Charles T. Griffes*, 204.

64. Henry Spiller, "Tunes That Bind: Paul J. Seelig, Eva Gauthier, Charles T. Griffes, and the Javanese Other," *Journal of the Society for American Music* 3, no. 2 (2009): 142.

65. Frederick Martens, "Folk-Music in the 'Ballet Intime,'" *The New Music and Church Music Review* 16 (October 1917): 764–65.

66. Other Griffes arrangements include "A Trip to Syria" (or "Assyrian Dance"), based on a piano solo by Alexander Maloof, and a Japanese folk song, "Sakura, Sakura." See Anderson, *Charles T. Griffes*, 450.

67. Ibid., 765.

68. Aestheticism can be defined in four different ways: (1) an artistic manifesto that reacted against the prevailing Victorian assumptions about art, but which had philosophical roots in the eighteenth century; (2) a highly disparate group of works in literature and

painting during the late nineteenth century that were loosely inspired by this manifesto; (3) an experimental movement in the decorative arts, interior design, and fashion; and (4) an individual artist, Oscar Wilde, whose sensational and self-parodying advocacy personified the manifesto. For the purposes of this study, I will focus primarily on the first definition.

69. "Aesthetic Movement," *Grove Art Online* (Oxford, UK: Oxford University Press), accessed August 20, 2023, https://doi.org/10.1093/gao/9781884446054.article.T000566.

70. Elizabeth Prettejohn, *Art for Art's Sake: Aestheticism: in Victorian Painting* (New Haven, CT: Yale University Press, 2007), 3.

71. Walter Pater, *The Renaissance: Studies in Art and Poetry*, ed. D. L. Hill (Berkeley and London: University of California Press, 1980), 19.

72. Prettejohn, *After the Pre-Raphaelites*, 12. A typical example of Pater's lists appears in the preface to his collection of essays: "the picture, the landscape, the engaging personality in life or in a book, *La Gioconda*, the hills of Carrara, Pico of Mirandola." See Pater, *The Renaissance*, xx.

73. Ibid.

74. Gene H. Bell-Villada, *Art for Art's Sake and Literary Life: How Politics and Markets Helped Shape the Ideology and Culture of Aestheticism, 1790–1990* (Lincoln: University of Nebraska Press, 1996).

75. Ibid., 24.

76. Ibid., 36.

77. Victor Cousin, *Du Vrai, du beau et du bien* (Paris: Didier, 1836).

78. Bell-Villada, *Art for Art's Sake*, 91.

79. Elizabeth Prettejohn, *Art for Art's Sake*, 2.

80. The only author whose poetry he set to music more often was Heinrich Heine.

81. The other preferred motif was the sunflower. See "Aesthetic Movement," *Grove Art Online*.

82. In the final paragraph of Wilde's essay "The Decay of Lying," the narrator says, "The final revelation is that Lying, the telling of beautiful untrue things, is the proper aim of Art. . . . And now let us go out on the terrace, where 'droops the milk-white peacock like a ghost,' while the evening star 'washes the dusk with silver.'" *Works of Oscar Wilde*, ed. G. F. Maine (London: Collins, 1948), 931.

83. Maisel, *Charles T. Griffes*, 86–87. Wilde had already introduced his unique brand of showmanship to American audiences during a twelve-month long lecture tour in 1882, but this would have had little influence on Griffes since it occurred three years before he was born. For a detailed account of this tour, see Richard Ellmann, *Oscar Wilde* (New York: Alfred A. Knopf, 1988), 157–91.

84. Phylis Floyd, "Japonisme," *Grove Art Online*, accessed August 20, 2023, https://doi .org/10.1093/gao/9781884446054.article.T044421.

85. Quoted in Maisel, *Charles T. Griffes*, 98.

86. "Appraisal of the Charles Tomlinson Griffes Library," Harold Ernest Wands, undated. According to Donna Anderson, the appraisal was completed sometime shortly after Griffes's death in 1920 (private communication).

87. Diary Entry, March 9, 1912, Box 47, Folder 5-6, Series III, Donna K. Anderson Research Files on Charles Griffes, Music Division, New York Public Library for the Performing Arts.

88. Written in a lighthearted spirit, *The Pagan Review* was dedicated to the new spirit of sexual liberation and literary cosmopolitanism. For more details on the epistolary novel, see Institute of English Studies, University of London, The William Sharp 'Fiona Macleod' Online Archive.

89. The title of W. B. Yeats's *Celtic Twilight: Faery and Folklore* (London: A H. Bullen: 1893) served as an emblem of the movement that helped inspire Fiona Macleod.

90. Fiona MacLeod, "Celtic," *Contemporary Review* 77 (1900): 672.

91. Elizabeth A. Sharp, *William Sharp (Fiona Macleod): A Memoir* (New York: Duffield, 1910), 428.

92. William F. Halloran, "W. B. Yeats, William Sharp, and Fiona Macleod: A Celtic Drama: 1887 to 1897," *Yeats Annual* 13, ed. Warwick Gould (London: Macmillan, 1998), 67–70. For a general introduction to Sharp's life and work, see Flavia Alaya, *William Sharp—"Fiona Macleod," 1855–1905* (Cambridge, MA: Harvard University Press, 1970).

93. Sharp, *William Sharp*, 222.

94. Ernest Rhys, *Everyman Remembers* (London and Toronto: J. M. Dent and Sons Limited, 1931), 79–80; quoted in Halloran, "W. B. Yeats, William Sharp, and Fiona Macleod," 68–69. In a letter dating from 1895, Sharp explained his new persona in detail: "I can write out of my heart in a way I could not do as William Sharp, and indeed that I could not do if I were the woman whom Fiona Macleod is supposed to be, unless veiled in scrupulous anonymity. . . . My truest self, the self who is below all other selves, and my most intimate life and joys and sufferings, thoughts, emotions and dreams, must find expression, yet I cannot, save in this hidden way." Catherine Janvier, "Fiona Macleod and her Creator William Sharp," *North American Review* 184, no. 612 (April 1907): 721.

95. According to his list of book purchases, in 1914 Griffes bought Macleod, *Poems and Dramas* and Sharp, *Poems*—see Anderson, *Charles T. Griffes*, 509. Although these titles differ from those of the original publications by Sharp and Macleod (e.g., Sharp, *From the Hills of Dream: Mountain Songs and Island Runes*), it is reasonable to infer that the volumes listed in Griffes's log were the source for his various settings.

96. The four works in *Roman Sketches*, Op. 7 include "The White Peacock," "Nightfall: Al far della note," "The Fountain of the Acqua Paola," and "Clouds."

97. Maisel, *Charles T. Griffes*, 105.

98. Anderson, *Charles T. Griffes*, 222.

2

Philosophical Prelude and Interpretive Method

One of Charles Griffes's greatest achievements was his ability to revive as well as reinvent the pastoral tradition. Although Griffes certainly composed other works during his final thirteen years that do not display a pastoral character, over and over again he kept returning to the pastoral as a source of inspiration.[1] The challenge that any interpreter of his music faces is how to account for the degree of his experimentation and how to classify it. For example, some of his experimental works contain characteristics that are not traditionally considered pastoral such as dissonant pedal chords and temporal ambiguity. Likewise, some of his pastorals not only portray feelings that are commonly associated with the tradition such as serenity and romance but also evoke more intense emotions such as aggression, grief, and spiritual longing. Also, some of his vocal settings blend his fascination with Chinese folk song with his personal pastoral sensibility. Finally, some works exhibit not only conventional pastoral characteristics but also elements of a different musical tradition, the lament. Instead of classifying these works as a hybrid of two musical categories, such as half pastoral, half lament, we need a more nuanced and more precise way of explaining their categorical blend.

In this chapter, I unveil a new approach to understanding what I call the ambivalent pastoral, which integrates insights from many disciplines including music theory, semiotics, philosophy, and cognitive psychology and relies on the work of a wide range of thinkers including Leonard Ratner, Robert Hatten, Ludwig Wittgenstein, Morris Weitz, Lydia Goehr, and Lawrence Barselou. The philosophical terrain that I will traverse includes epistemology, aesthetics, and, to some extent, ontology.[2] Most of my attention will focus on the nature of knowledge—that is, how we know things and how we classify them into groups. In particular, I will apply the philosophical insights of Wittgenstein about family resemblance and of Weitz about "open concepts" to the question of group membership in a musical topic.

My aim is not to invent a new theory of musical topics altogether but rather to synthesize existing theories and thereby provide a new philosophical foundation for the notion of a topic. At the outset, I will question as well as clarify the semiotic status quo—that is, the prevailing assumptions of topic theory in its original formulation and in its later adaptations. My ultimate purpose, however, is far more than a critique. Instead, I will offer an alternative approach to defining membership within a group that allows for greater variety among the works, including outliers, that belong to the pastoral topic. When viewed as a whole, Griffes's diverse pastorals do not all belong to a single logical category or, to put it another way, a group defined by a set of necessary and jointly sufficient characteristics that all members share. Instead, they constitute a looser category in which individual members possess different combinations of characteristics, some of which overlap and some of which do not. Most important, no single characteristic is common to all members. In short, my project is an attempt to develop a more nuanced method of classification that allows for a highly varied collection of works within a single category.

This chapter consists of six parts: (1) a brief history of semiotic theory, focusing on the thought of Charles Peirce; (2) a synopsis of topic theory as proposed by Leonard Ratner and developed by Janice Dickensheets, V. Kofi Agawu, and Hatten; (3) a pastoral primer, including various literary precedents as well as a limited panorama of the musical pastoral in different historical periods; (4) a brief overview of the concepts of musical exoticism and Orientalism and how they are relevant to Griffes's pastorals; (5) a philosophical foundation for my concept of musical topic, drawing on the ideas of Wittgenstein, Weitz, and Goehr; and finally (6) a polythetic model that describes a representative collection of Griffes's pastorals.

Semiotics

The pastoral constitutes a tradition that is deeply embedded in Western civilization. To better understand the nature of this tradition and how it shapes our musical experience, it is necessary to explore its philosophical ancestry in semiotics, or the theory of signs. The first stage in this history dates back to ancient Greece and the term Σημεῖον, which can be translated as a "semeion" or "sign"; a familiar type of sign is a phenomenon in nature such as smoke that signals a fire.[3] The litany of luminaries who contributed to the study of signs is vast, including Plato, Aristotle, St. Augustine, and John Poinsot. But the modern rebirth of the theory of signs can be traced to two monumental thinkers at the fin de siècle who independently developed their own formulations: Ferdinand de Saussure, a Swiss professor of linguistics, and Charles Sanders Peirce, an American philosopher and logician. Let us briefly consider the contributions of each one.

Saussure's posthumous publication, *Cours de linguistique générale*, helped inaugurate the field of structural linguistics, or what he called semiology.[4] One of his central proposals is that all human speech—and, by extension, any sign system—has two dimensions: the "signifier" (or the sound of a given word) and the "signified" (or that to which the word refers). Another of his key insights was the distinction between *langue* and *parole*. In his mind, language was not a collection of names each referring to a separate object but rather a social system created by a community of speakers and then assimilated passively by each individual. His term for this abstract system is *langue*—the aggregate of all words and the rules that govern them. By contrast, *parole* encompasses the individual speech acts that put *langue* into practice.[5]

The significance of Saussure's theories for my study of Griffes is in the difference between a general principle and a group of particular examples that test the limits of that principle. I am less interested in focusing on the highest level of generality, the system of musical topics shared by a generation of composers, than the collective features of a group of musical *paroles* or works at a particular period in music history that together embody the unique character of Griffes's pastoral temperament.

In sharp contrast to Saussure, Charles Peirce was more of a generalist who contributed not only to linguistics but also to the fields of logic, astronomy, and philosophy. He is considered the founder of the philosophical approach called pragmatism, although he objected strongly to the views of other pragmatist thinkers—namely, William James and John Dewey.[6] Peirce's central claim is that "all thought is in signs." In its simplest form, his concept of a sign can be summarized as "something which stands to somebody for something, in some respect or capacity."[7] His definition differs from Saussure's in that his model of knowledge is understood as a philosophical triad instead of a dyad: the sign itself (or representamen), the object to which it refers, and the means by which the sign is interpreted, which he calls the interpretant.[8] For him, human knowledge is more like a process that can also be divided into three broad stages: "firstness," in which the sign is referred to as an icon; "secondness," in which it is referred to as an index; and thirdness, in which the sign is referred to as a symbol.[9] It should be emphasized that, unlike Saussure, Peirce focused on *"parole*, not *langue*. Because his approach is abstract and general, it is not always obvious that he is reasoning about concrete sign occasions, but . . . it is this very orientation that requires abstraction."[10]

A question arises: in what way is a theory of musical signs different from a general theory of signs? To address this question, I take inspiration from two authors: Naomi Cumming and Vincent Colapietro. In her book *The Sonic Self*, Cumming combines a detailed exegesis of Charles Peirce's work with an investigation into subjectivity and musical intuition. On first impression, Peirce's theory of human cognition and his strict categories may seem like a fixed semiotic process—a perceptual symphony in three movements. Once the various trichotomies are defined and displayed within an overall scheme, it may seem as if they are addressed to philosophical interpreters obsessed with classification—fixed types of experience that never interact. But it is a mistake to treat each stage in this process as autonomous, isolated from the other two. In her book, Cumming emphasizes that for Peirce the purpose of erecting such a scheme is less "to provide fixed categories of signs" than it is "to separate out the kinds of questions that might be asked of them or the directions that answers could take."[11] Also, in a recent series of articles Vincent Colapietro proposes to soften the strict boundaries between Peircean categories and to blend them with ideas drawn from other American philosophers such as James and Dewey.[12] For both Cumming and Colapietro, the various stages in the cognition of signs are less like hermetically sealed concepts and more like semi-permeable membranes.

Two other features of Peirce's writings, though often overlooked, are central to his theory of signs and to my study. First, Peirce rejects the belief that knowledge is absolute or established with apodictic certainty. In that respect, he reacts strongly against the idealism of René Descartes, who proposed that any philosophical claim must satisfy an ideal standard of absolute certainty.[13] Peirce utterly rejects this search for a perfect philosophical foundation and instead embraces a realist approach, insisting that philosophers and, by extension, music analysts must begin their project wherever they find themselves and with whatever critical tools they have available. Although the term *realism* has various meanings and justifications in the philosophy of language, ethics, and aesthetics, it nevertheless places Peirce within a tradition that reacted against those who believed in universal and objective truth.[14]

Second, Peirce also embraces the principle of fallibilism, which is a corollary to his realist views. Fallibilism is the view that no argument can ever be proven conclusively or with absolute certainty; there is always the possibility that a new unforeseen explanation will appear or that new data will emerge that overturns the prevailing theory. Peirce believed that human knowledge was always evolving, and therefore any scientific model or philosophical system must have an open-ended character. The "imprint of Peirce's understanding of practical science on his semiotics is decisive. The dominant pictures of signs in his imagination are images of *developing* knowledge, of knowledge in progress rather than knowledge as a fixed block of information."[15] The Lithuanian semiotician Algernon J. Greimas describes the tension between openness and closure as follows: "When a semiotic theory is formulated as a trajectory (i.e. as an encompassing and encompassed hierarchical organization of models), it is necessary to examine this trajectory continually, and consider it as a construct. . . . Under these conditions, a theory claiming to have a scientific status is constantly on the lookout for its own deficiencies and weaknesses, which it tries to overcome and rectify."[16] The metaphor of a "trajectory," balancing scientific rigor with evolutionary change, strongly resembles the notion of "openness," which will be a central feature of the philosophical foundation of Griffes's musical pastoral to be explored below.

One of Peirce's greatest contributions as a logician was his notion of abduction. He proposed that there were three types of logical inference: deduction, induction, and abduction. In deductive inferences, the conclusion follows necessarily from the premise. By contrast, inductive inferences are reached by extrapolating from a group of individual cases and therefore are merely probable. Finally, the third type of inference is abduction, which Peirce defines as "the process of forming explanatory hypotheses. It is the only logical operation that introduces new ideas, thereby fusing logical reasoning with imagination."[17] The significance of the concept of abduction for this project is that since Griffes experimented with different approaches to the pastoral over the course of his career, we need to hypothesize a new type of pastoral topic that can explain the full range of his innovations.

Another distinctive feature of Peirce's theory is that while he aspired to establish a comprehensive framework for knowledge, this framework was essentially heuristic—that is, intended for each person to discover for himself or herself through trial and error. Colapietro observes that Peirce's framework "is deliberately designed to guide and goad inquiry. Its purpose is not to offer transcendental grounds for our historical practices; rather it presupposes that . . . evolving practices alone provide the grounds for all of our theoretical endeavors."[18] For Peirce, in some situations practice could help guide theory. In other words, thoughtful analyses can serve as abductions that lead to new theoretical clarity. As will become clear below, I have taken this heuristic approach to heart in my reconsideration of how Griffes's treatment of the pastoral reinforces and yet also departs from the assumptions of eighteenth-century topic theory.

Patrick McCreless offers a useful hierarchy to address the situation faced by anyone who pursues semiotic analysis. In his article "Semiotics and Music: An End-of-Century Overview," he describes an ongoing ambiguity about the very definition of semiotics and its philosophical aspirations. He concludes that "practitioners of semiotics do not even agree whether it is a *science*, as imagined by Saussure . . . and as founded by Peirce and Charles Morris, a *discipline*, a *method*, or merely a *point of view*."[19] While this comment may initially seem pessimistic, it nevertheless provides a hierarchical framework for understanding the history of semiotic analysis, proceeding from the most general to the most specific. It is as though we were looking through four different telescopes, each with a different level of magnification, ranging from the smallest to the largest depth of field.

Like McCreless, I believe that the fourth definition is the most fruitful: "What ties semiological studies together is less a consistent theoretical foundation and programme than a point of view and a praxis: the foregrounding of sign and signification, a faith in the notion of semiosis as an interdisciplinary and even universal path to insight and knowledge, and the appropriation of some theory or methodology of the central figures of semiotics."[20] In this remark, McCreless not only affirms the enormous variety of approaches that go by the name of music semiotics, but he also emphasizes that although there is no single theoretical principle that ties them together, they all rely in some fashion on a common semiotic concept or orientation. McCreless's emphasis of the importance of "praxis" suggests that despite the absence of a strict scientific method within the semiotic tradition, a given semiotic analysis can be vindicated by the quality of interpretive insights it affords. Methodological purity is less important than interpretive fertility. In other words, practice overrides theoretical consistency.

Given the complexity of many of Peirce's theories and, more important, his tendency to shift if not refute an early idea in one of his later formulations, I will not attempt to justify or reconcile the tensions in his various formulations. Several scholars such as David Savan and James Liszka have painstakingly explicated his ideas and the process by which they evolved over the course of his life.[21] My reason for offering this short summary of Peirce's thought and the ensuing semiotic tradition is to justify my assumption that the musical pastoral and, by extension, most musical topics are types of signs that have an ambivalent status or loose boundaries. In addition, his rejection of absolute certainty and his belief in fallibilism (or openness) are central to my understanding of Griffes's pastorals and to the philosophical foundation for my method of classifying them. Rather than adding yet another layer to the rich geological history of Peircean scholarship, I will adopt a different approach. By combining Wittgenstein's alternative concept of a logical category with a polythetic approach to classification, I provide a new way of conceiving of a group and new criteria for group membership.

Topic Theory

It is appropriate to begin our study of Griffes's pastorals by focusing on the founding father of topic theory; the twentieth-century musicologist and composer Leonard Ratner. While many acknowledge that Ratner inaugurated a new approach to musical interpretation, the written statements he left behind do not constitute a clear theoretical system, for they are fragmentary—like musical sketches without a final score. Were he alive today, he would hardly recognize the rich intellectual legacy that his writings set into motion. To appreciate my new conception of the pastoral, it is worth briefly summarizing the evolution of topic theory within the writings of Ratner himself and his followers.

The earliest version of Ratner's concept of musical topic appeared in his introductory textbook, *Music: The Listener's Art*, in which he distinguished between "types" and "styles."[22] Ratner's ultimate achievement in *Classic Music: Expression, Form and Style*, his magnum opus published in 1980, consists of the fusion of two different projects: a panoramic study of eighteenth-century musical style, integrating harmony, melody, rhythm, and form; and an encyclopedic method of identifying different types of dance patterns, textures, and gestures—what he called "topics"—in a musical texture.[23] Topics are by no means his primary focus in this work, but instead are located in the context of his comprehensive study of a wide range of musical features. One of the virtues of this work is the breadth of his historical vision and the sheer depth of his insights about individual works.[24]

It is worth emphasizing that while Ratner provided hints of his theoretical assumptions at various stages in the evolution of his ideas, he never unveiled a full-fledged systematic theory. Instead, it is something closer to a theoretical work in progress. In short, Ratner never conceived of the study of musical topics as a scientific theory, for he proposed neither a clear philosophical foundation for them nor a consistent analytical method for identifying them in eighteenth-century music.[25]

Let us consider the specific definitions Ratner presents in *Classic Music*. He identifies three kinds of musical *topos*, or topics: "types," "styles," and the general phenomenon of "pictorialism," which includes the concept of text painting. In his mind, a "type" refers to a "fully worked out" dance such as a gavotte or gigue. By contrast, a "style" is a section or passage that displays a distinctive musical character. Examples include a hunting signal, the French overture, and what he calls the "musette, pastorale." The latter refers to a pair of dances that share the same bagpipe-like drone texture. Although he explores the pastoral character in many excerpts in the compendium, his initial definition is rather meagre. In his mind, the study of topics becomes a "subject of musical discourse" that can be organized in what he calls a "thesaurus of characteristic figures."[26]

Ratner's conception of musical topic deserves a few comments. By presenting three distinct definitions of the concept, he displays a diffused approach: two are general categories (dances and styles), and one is a correspondence between two different art forms: literature and music. Instead of offering a single all-inclusive umbrella that unites all of the examples he has collected, he is content to let the diverse evidence speak for itself. His definition betrays an encyclopedic temperament, a painstaking empirical spirit that resists theoretical rigor in favor of precise yet piecemeal description. His conception of a topic does not rely on the principle of group identity—that is, on clearly defined properties that determine membership in a general category. The various topics he enumerates in this volume constitute a miniature catalogue of types, each of which is either loosely or tightly defined, but which all lack an overarching theoretical framework. In short, Ratner favors multiplicity over unity, and, as a result, the concept of a musical topic has been in flux since the day *Classic Music* was published.

The assumption of a one-to-one correspondence between a distinctive musical figure and a fixed cultural association has had both positive and negative consequences for musical interpretation. On the positive side, Ratner's fascination with dance types and expressive styles has awakened a newfound interest in deciphering musical references and associations that previously had been sorely neglected. As a result of his interest in musical rhetoric, our understanding of the intersection of eighteenth-century dance and instrumental music is richer and more multidimensional.

However, amid the scholarly enthusiasm for topics, there have been some excesses. At times, Ratner's encyclopedic approach has encouraged scholars to try to discover new kinds of topics—in some cases, to the point of diminishing returns. Whereas he originally introduced roughly thirty-five different types of dances and styles, Agawu expanded the catalogue considerably (which he dubbed the "Universe of Topics"), eventually positing sixty-one separate entries.[27] The underlying reason for the steady growth of these topical lexicons is not that new dances or styles had suddenly been unearthed in some secret musicological excavation, but rather that Ratner's original concept was so loosely defined. In a later article devoted to Mozart's keyboard sonatas, Ratner broadened the concept to include "a figure, a process or a plan of action." Ratner himself reached the point of furthest topical extreme when he claimed that "appoggiaturas, tiratas, arpeggios, suspensions, turns, repeated notes" could acquire the role of a topic.[28]

There have been many attempts to clarify Ratner's original vision, to anchor it within a systematic theory, and to develop a reliable method for applying it in analysis and interpretation. For example, Danuta Mirka proposes a more limited conception of topic theory, which defines a musical topic as a dance or style that is taken out of its original functional context.[29] Though her definition is provocative, I will not follow it strictly in this study. Since Monelle, McKay, and Agawu have all written detailed surveys of the history of music semiotics, I do not need to reenact them here in detail.[30]

In some respects, it is difficult to imagine how the concept of musical topic could ever become a systematic and verifiable analytical method—that is, it is impossible to put the topical genie back into a scientific bottle.

Topical analysis is clearly not an exact empirical science, and there will always be some flexibility in what constitutes a given topic and how it is realized in a musical work.[31] Nevertheless, if we acknowledge the spirit of Greimas's semiotic "trajectory" mentioned above, then hermeneutic interpretation using the lens of musical topics consists of balancing a set of predetermined historical associations and their application in a work of art.

Topics in the Nineteenth Century

Considering that topic theory originally emerged as a way of explaining music in the eighteenth century, it is reasonable to ask how it evolved in later historical periods. Several questions arise: To what extent did Romantic composers revive and/or adapt old topics in their music? Did new musical topics appear in their compositions? Finally, how did the tradition of eighteenth-century musical topics and its adaptation in the nineteenth century influence Griffes's music in the early twentieth century? The answers to these questions are not only complex but crucial for my project.

The story of the development of musical topics in the nineteenth century combines two conflicting principles: preservation and expansion. It comes as no surprise that Ratner himself was the first commentator to explore the frontier of nineteenth-century music through the lens of musical topics in his book *Romantic Music: Sound and Syntax*. Although he investigates how the topical language of eighteenth-century dances and styles reappears in many instrumental works, he never offers a comprehensive list.[32]

By contrast, Janice Dickensheets recently took the first steps at assembling a provisional lexicon for nineteenth-century musical topics. While she insists that her project is not intended to be exhaustive, in two essays she enumerates twenty-three distinct topics that encompass a wide range of dances, styles, and cultural rituals.[33] To begin with, she identifies seven older topics that continued the musical language of the eighteenth century and illustrates each one with a handful of excerpts drawn from nineteenth-century repertoire.

Dances

- minuet
- gigue/siciliano
- march

Styles

- pastoral style
- military style
- hunt music
- fantasia style

It goes without saying that Romantic composers also introduced new topics altogether. Dickensheets uncovers numerous examples of dance types, including the waltz (in both low and high versions), polonaise, mazurka, bolero, and funeral march, as well as broader stylistic types that include lied style, aria style, nocturne style, virtuosic style, declamatory style, *stile appassionato*, tempest style, heroic style, demonic style, *Biedermeier* style, and fairy music. Finally, in addition to Ratner's two categories of dances and styles, she introduces a third category called a "dialect," which consists of a collection of gestures as well as styles that can sustain an entire movement. Examples include chivalric style, bardic style, and the exotic dialect.

As insightful as Dickensheets's copious examples may be, the project of compiling a topical lexicon is a "rear guard action" that will never be complete. She proposes various patterns in melody, texture, rhythm, and harmony that recur in different composers' works as if they were universal—that is, understood by composers and audiences as a common language—like the dances and styles that appear in eighteenth-century music. Yet in the next breath, she also claims that some of these gestures were highly idiosyncratic musical signatures of individual composers. If that were the case, then her nineteenth-century topical lexicon would be infinite, for it would amount to an endless portrait gallery of individual styles, not a mural of the stylistic networks that bind them together.[34] My own topical aspirations are more humble—to codify and illustrate one composer's treatment of the pastoral as a window into American musical sensibility in the early twentieth century.

In recent years, other musicologists have explored the concept of topic in individual nineteenth-century composers. Márta Grabócz and Eero Tarasti have uncovered new topics in the music of Liszt and Wagner that assume a shared musical competency with their audiences.[35] More recently, Keith Jones explores a wide range of musical topics and structural principles in Liszt's symphonic poems.[36]

Yet other scholars have raised doubts about the viability of using topics to interpret nineteenth-century music. For example, Julian Horton casts doubt on the entire enterprise of topical analysis of post-eighteenth-century music. After praising the explanatory power of topics to explain the sensibility of the Classical period, he later decries the same model for its inability to account for the ways in which a topic's set of associations evolved during the nineteenth century. He claims that there are so many new layers of cultural associations that it is impossible to separate and make sense of them—a virtual topical Tower of Babel.[37]

While I do not share the degree of Horton's pessimism, I acknowledge the difficulty of doing justice to the many historical dimensions a given topic may acquire over time. As we will see, the modified polythetic model provides an interpretive framework for accommodating the ways in which one early twentieth-century composer reenacted and yet also transformed musical traditions of the eighteenth century.

In a recent essay Lawrence Zbikowski adopts a different point of view by portraying a shift in the social perception of dance and, as a result, dance topics in instrumental music. He describes a rising tension among social classes that resulted from the gradual democratization of dances like the waltz: "the cultural context that shaped the reception of musical representations of the dance had changed: The body that one imagined on hearing a strain of a waltz might be that of a social equal, but it might also be of someone of no distinction whatever."[38] He concludes, "As dance came to serve as an index of a cultural practice that was broadly shared across social strata, dance topics lost their value as part of a common vocabulary of musical figures through which musical discourse was shaped."[39] While no one can dispute that the older hierarchies of social class began to erode during the nineteenth century, it is not entirely clear how that gradual shift led to the loss of a shared musical "vocabulary."

The most ambitious study of the evolution of musical topics during the nineteenth century is Kofi Agawu's *Music as Discourse: Semiotic Adventures in Romantic Music*. His book is panoramic rather than systematic. Instead of proposing a single all-encompassing method, he offers a marketplace of different semiotic-based approaches using six different analytical criteria to interpret a wide range of works. In short, his critical aspirations could be characterized as heterophonic rather than monothematic, favoring multiple interpretive strategies rather than a single vision.

Most important, he argues that during this period a structural change occurred in the concept of a musical topic. Rather than new layers of associations simply piling on top of old ones, instead there was a fundamental shift in what a musical topic could signify. For him, in the nineteenth century there was a "dislocation of the signifier from the signified." He adds that "while the morphology of various topics is retained by Romantic composers, their conventional association is displaced. Thus, one way of describing the Classic-Romantic relationship is in term of a morphological continuity and a referential discontinuity."[40] Agawu also emphasizes the private nature of composers' expressive languages. "On one hand, the largely public-oriented and conventional topics of the eighteenth century often exhibit a similar orientation in the nineteenth century. . . . On the other hand, the ascendancy in the nineteenth century of figures born of a private realm, figures that bear the marks of individual composerly idiolects, speaks to a new context for topic."[41]

In the end, as insightful as Agawu's philosophical meditations on the status of a topic are, they go only so far. His remarks suggest a broad spectrum, stretching between the extremes of the "composerly idiolect" at one extreme and the "conventional" topic shared by a musical community at the other. Based on his comment about "idiolects," it might be tempting to christen a new set of topics for every composer or, by extension, for every piece. However, this would undermine Ratner's fundamental premise that composers and their audiences share a set of common psychological/cultural associations. In that case, the concept of topic would merge with autobiography. At the other extreme, amid the "morphological continuity," one wonders what common musical elements recur among the community of nineteenth-century composers that contemporary audiences would have recognized and understood.

In this study, I explore a region of Agawu's topical spectrum that is closer to the "composerly"—the ambivalent pastoral of Charles Griffes—than to the topical language shared by a broader community. My focus is to isolate traces of the eighteenth-century pastoral tradition that one early twentieth-century composer revived and to explore how they interact with other musical dimensions. By focusing on Griffes's topical language, I hope not only to provide a cross section of the innovations that he introduced within the pastoral tradition itself, but also to shed light on the American musical sensibility at the turn of the century.

Tropes

One of the central aims of this study is to explain a process by which features of multiple topics interact with one another in the same musical passage or movement. This sort of interaction needs to be placed in historical context, beginning with the writings of Robert Hatten. In his first book, *Musical Meaning in Beethoven: Markedness, Correlation and Interpretation*, Hatten reveals an expansive critical vision that fuses structuralist and hermeneutic aims.[42] The former is demonstrated in a general theory of musical meaning based on correlation and markedness, the latter in a collection of close readings of instrumental works by Beethoven. The ultimate aim of these two complementary processes is the "reconstruction of a stylistic competency."[43] Hatten's study of the pastoral tradition embodied in Beethoven's works was a turning point for the discipline of music semiotics, and I hope to emulate his mix of philosophy, theory, and analysis but now applied to music of the early twentieth century. One underlying characteristic in all of his rich theoretical and analytical contributions is a reliance on the concepts of *topic* and *trope*, both of which can be a source of terminological confusion.

To begin with, the term *trope* is laden with a rich rhetorical heritage, for it originally derives from the Greek verb τρέπειν (*trepein*), "to turn."[44] In ancient Greek manuals of rhetoric, a trope was a figurative or metaphorical use of language. For nearly thirty years, the theory of musical tropes in Hatten's writings has functioned like an ongoing theoretical leitmotif or, more precisely, an exercise in "developing variation" à la Schoenberg. To summarize of all of the various nuances in his proposals about tropes would be a considerable undertaking, more appropriate for a history of music semiotics than a theoretical introduction for a monograph. Nevertheless, it is necessary to provide a brief synopsis of his contributions to provide a road map of where his meditations have led and what remains to be explored.

In his initial formulation, Hatten defined a musical trope as the interaction of two or more distinct musical topics; such interactions could be characterized as different degrees of conflict or of harmonious blend. For him, musical tropes could occur at different levels: within a single passage, over an entire movement, or spanning a multi-movement work.[45] In his second book, *Interpreting Musical Gestures, Topics, and Tropes: Mozart, Beethoven, Schubert*, he considerably expanded his focus, exploring various ways in which meaning emerges from the synthesis of topic, trope, and the musical counterpart to human gesture.[46] In a more recent article entitled "The Troping of Topics in Mozart's Instrumental Works," Hatten's theoretical aspirations turned in yet another direction, investigating the general phenomenon of topics, whether as an imported style or a quotation.[47] Here he unveils a mini-catalogue of four possible troping axes—compatibility, dominance, creativity, and productivity—each of which describes the relation between a topic and its broader musical environment within a work.

Let us take stock of this brief tropological tour. Amid all of Hatten's prodigious theories and interpretive discoveries, there is one common assumption that they all share. He always relies on some version of Ratner's original formulation of the concept of topic that links together highly dissimilar objects into a loose assemblage—indeed, a catchall more than a clearly defined category.[48] The following question arises: How can you explain the relation between a topic and its new musical milieu or the process by which two different topics interact unless you have clearly defined the limits of a single topic? Since I am introducing a new, more open definition of the concept, the blending of two or more different topics must be reconceived. Thus, I prefer an approach that initially relies on a looser concept of type that, in turn, allows for a new way of conceiving the process by which aspects of multiple types interact.

In short, my study in no way refutes either Hatten's theoretical proposals or the rich panoply of musical examples he explores. Instead, we are both pursuing different approaches within the same terrain. While he is a musical cartographer, mapping out the different types of terrain and proposing a systematic theory to account for them, I am more interested in retracing the paths of musical topography and the process by which one type of terrain gradually changes into another.

My reason for elaborating on the potential ambiguities of Ratner's notion of topic and, by extension, Hatten's concept of trope is not to decry their logical flaws or to try and undermine their overall critical achievements. Quite the contrary. By clarifying Ratner's assumptions and then extrapolating from them, I am in a better position to discover how one composer at the turn of the twentieth century not only revived old musical topics but also combined them together in new ways, creating new forms of expression.

Pastoral Primer

Before establishing the philosophical foundation of my approach to Griffes's pastoral experiments, I need to briefly consider the history of the pastoral tradition on which it depends. The pastoral is one of the oldest of all Western literary and cultural traditions, with origins that can be traced to ancient Greece and Rome and that continue up to the present. In the ancient world, it occupied an idealized location—in such places as Sicily or Arcadia. Centuries later, the pastoral acquired a spiritual dimension when the New Testament scriptures recorded that shepherds were the first to witness the Nativity and, ever since, it has been directly or indirectly associated with Christmas. Beginning in the Renaissance, however, the associations became more secular as the themes of erotic love and worship of nature became more pronounced. As Monelle says, for many it is "the most profoundly mythical of all topics."[49]

Considering the complexity of the pastoral tradition, it makes sense to divide it into two dimensions: the literary and the musical. Within the literary dimension, four subtypes can be identified: the Theocritian pastoral; the Virgilian pastoral; the realistic pastoral; and a more controversial category called the "post-pastoral."[50] Of the four, the first two have the greatest resonance in Griffes's musical pastorals.

The original conception of the pastoral tradition initially arose in the didactic poem *Works and Days* by Hesiod (c. 700 BCE) and was perfected in the *Idylls* of the Greek poet Theocritus (316–260 BCE), who most likely worked at Ptolemy's court in ancient Alexandria. Although his fictional characters included "shepherds, farmers, serfs, goatherds, fishermen, neatherds and housewives," the tradition eventually crystalized around the ideal life of the shepherd.[51] The overarching theme in these works is the cycle of departure and return, usually from an urban to a rural setting. In these poems, shepherds balance the charms of country life in Sicily—singing contests and debates—with elements of realism such as complaining about the hazards of herding or lamenting about death. Theocritus not only celebrates the joy of romantic love, but he occasionally mocks it, saying that lovestruck shepherds "can't cut a swathe straight."[52] As we will see below, Griffes's ambivalent vision of the pastoral ideal resonates strongly with that of Theocritus.

The second subtype emerged several centuries later in the *Eclogues* of the Roman poet Virgil (70–19 BCE), who transplanted his shepherds from Sicily to Arcadia. Although Arcadia was an actual region in the Peloponnese mountains, Virgil transformed it into an imaginary landscape where it was always springtime and where mortals communed freely with gods and demigods such as Pan. Ultimately, the shepherds' simple life is something one can never possess, for Virgil filtered out most of the realistic aspects of Theocritus's original vision, instead focusing on idyllic themes of nostalgia and romantic love. For Virgil, the Arcadian paradise is a golden age, a "state of simplicity [that] has been lost and can never be recovered."[53]

The final two subtypes can be described as reactions to and revivals of the two ancient models. Poems belonging to the third subtype, the realistic pastoral, portray life in nature as rewarding but full of hard work and self-sacrifice. The emotions evoked include a loss of faith in Nature, sadness, and general melancholy.[54] Finally, the fourth type, the post-pastoral, is a recent rebellion against the idealistic pastoral visions of the past. In this tradition the traditional assumptions of the pastoral ideal have been turned upside down and replaced with the imperatives of so-called eco-criticism.[55] It should be noted that the latter two conceptions of the pastoral played no role in shaping Griffes's imagination.

My reason for recounting these various literary species in such detail is that one of Griffes's artistic innovations is that he revived the ancient Theocritian approach, evoking a wide range of emotions including anxiety and aggression as well as tranquility, and, in the process, developed a balanced vision of the pastoral. In order to appreciate my way of understanding Griffes's contribution, it will also be useful to summarize several of the leading critical theories of the pastoral during the twentieth century. One of the most influential studies is William Empson's *Some Aspects of the Pastoral*, published in 1935. After proposing a new broader definition—a "process of putting the complex into the simple"—he devotes most of his book to the classification of numerous subcategories.[56] In short, the plural noun in the title is significant, for, in his mind, the pastoral is a multitude, not a unity. Sixty years later, the literary critic Paul Alpers echoes this pluralistic approach in his article "What Is Pastoral?" which served as the basis for a book-length study by the same name. The foundation of his thesis is the same as Empson's: many, not one.[57]

For my purposes, the literary critic Harold Toliver proposes a more fruitful conception of this literary genre. In the opening chapter of his book *Pastoral Forms and Attitudes*, Toliver argues that the basis of the pastoral is not a single idea but rather a pair of opposing ideas. In his view, the history of the pastoral is a litany of dialectical opposition: "we begin with some of the broadest implications of the idyllic elements of pastoral . . . which habitually calls forth an opposite."[58] The nature of the pastoral opposition varies enormously depending on the historical period and the contrasting idea against which the idyllic element is juxtaposed. Toliver believes that all worthwhile pastorals possess a dialectical tension between the "golden age and the normative world." One central task of a theory of pastoral is to explain in what ways this tension is manifested in a work of art.[59]

Annabel Patterson expands upon Toliver's insight, providing extensive historical and philosophical evidence from a wide range of artistic traditions. In her book *Pastoral and Ideology: Virgil to Valéry*, she proposes a model for interpreting virtually any pastoral poem, painting, or illustration in the Western tradition in terms of the dynamic framework outlined in the opening lines in Virgil's collection of eclogues.[60] She argues that the dialogue between the pair of shepherds in Virgil's initial eclogue establishes the foundation for a recurring dichotomy in the history of the pastoral: Tityrus, who is content to play his pipe, aloof from the daily life of Roman politics, and Meliboeus, who berates his bucolic companion for his political and moral aloofness. For Patterson, this scene presents two different visions of the underlying ideological assumptions of the pastoral: one denies them; the other recognizes and tries to contextualize them. In her view, these two points of view together create a critical framework for a cultural history of the pastoral in literature and the visual arts, a kind of philosophical theme and variations, traversing sixteen centuries and tracing which of these two views is more dominant.[61]

Patterson's proposal deserves two comments. First of all, her theory shows that Griffes's literary taste for idealized pastoral texts reveals a fascination for Tityrus more than Meliboeus—that is, for an aloofness from moral and/or political questions. Her framework also provides a glimpse of the ideological foundation of British Aestheticism in its preference for sensual beauty and exoticism rather than a social and moral critique of late-Victorian England.

Second, her dialogical conception of the literary tradition serves as a loose interpretive framework that individual works realize in different ways and to different degrees. The oppositional nature of this interpretive approach allows for a new flexibility in understanding pastorals that blend contrasting elements into a new whole. This understanding of the literary tradition will be indispensable when we consider the wide range of Griffes's musical works with pastoral characteristics.

Equipped with this dialogical understanding of the literary pastoral, we are now prepared to consider the ways in which the tradition was manifested in music. In his panoramic monograph, Monelle adopts a useful distinction between the pastoral signifiers themselves—that is, the instruments used in pastoral music and the pastoral signified, or the emotions and associations that these instruments signify.[62]

The natural point of departure is the family of wind instruments played by shepherds in ancient Greece, which included the double-reeded aulos—whether made from bone, wood, metal, or ivory—the syrinx, and the panpipes, a wind instrument named after the chief satyr, Pan (later composers used the flute and recorder to achieve the same associations). The other instrumental family that evokes the pastoral is defined by a characteristic drone sound such as the bagpipe, musette, zampogna, and hurdy-gurdy (or vielle). Finally, other instruments with pastoral associations include the chalumeau (precursor to the clarinet) and the alphorn.

As it turns out, Griffes relied on characteristics and/or instruments from both families to evoke pastoral associations. By far the most important feature is his use of a bass drone as a single pitch, interval, or chord. This characteristic sound appears in such works as "The Lake at Evening," "The Vale of Dreams," and the middle section of Scherzo/Bacchanale as well as in numerous song settings. His use of pastoral wind instruments includes melodic lines for solo oboe and clarinet in the orchestral versions of *The Pleasure-Dome of Kubla Khan* and "The White Peacock," respectively. Griffes wrote only one work for flute and orchestra, *Poem*, which is replete with pastoral associations. Regarding the so-called "signified" dimension, the emotions evoked by the musical pastoral generally have traditionally mirrored the literary tradition over the course of its history including serenity, joy, spiritual fulfillment, and, to a lesser extent, grief and remorse.

To do justice to the vast history of the musical pastoral would in itself require a book-length study. Nevertheless, it is important to provide a brief sketch of significant pastoral milestones, especially in the nineteenth century, as a prelude to the polythetic model that is crucial to our understanding of Griffes's pastoral works.[63]

Since, according to scripture, shepherds witnessed the birth of Jesus, the tradition arose of including pastoral themes as well as instruments in Christmas music. The tradition of associating the musical pastoral with the ritual of Christmas dates back as early as the fourteenth century in Italy and Germany. Besides the overtly Christian associations of this music, the musical characteristics also overlapped with those of a more secular genre, the Renaissance madrigal, in Italy and England. For example, the text of a pastoral drama by Guarini, *Il Pastor Fido*, inspired over five hundred madrigal settings. During the early Baroque, the pastoral tradition renewed its birthright with the rise of opera in the Florentine Camerata. The Greek myth of Orpheus served as a recurring subject for operas by Italian composers such as Peri, Caccini, and Monteverdi.

During the late Baroque, J. S. Bach, in his Christmas Oratorio, borrowed and expanded upon earlier pastoral models that Corelli had developed in his concertos. Likewise, in Handel's early operas, such as *Aci, Galatea e Polifemo*, and *Acis and Galatea*, the pastoral language was highly refined—as much of a commentary as an application of the usual musical conventions.[64]

In the early Romantic period, both German and French composers revived the pastoral style. One piece that cast a shadow over the entire century is Beethoven's Symphony No. 6 in F major, Op. 68, a work that Monelle considers "the central pastoral work of our whole tradition."[65] In the second movement (*Szene am Bach*), the combination of a 12/8 meter, moderate tempo (Andante molto mosso), continuous rhythm texture, and simple melody create the quintessential example of the pastoral style. Other significant examples of the period include the *Scène aux champs* movement from Berlioz's *Symphonie Fantastique*, in which an English horn and offstage oboe engage in an improvisatory yet plaintive duet. As will be shown below, some of these same characteristics, along with other less common ones, combine to form Griffes's unique pastoral style.

At this juncture, it is useful to explore in closer detail an example of a pastoral work during the late Romantic period: Brahms, Symphony No. 2 in F major, Op. 73. The reason is that this particular work exemplifies an unusual musical and psychological fusion. In a fascinating book, *Late Idyll: The Second Symphony of Johannes Brahms*, Reinhold Brinkmann explores the concept of a twisted ideal, an idyllic vision that has been interrupted, compromised, and, in short, broken.[66] Brinkmann also attributes a sense of melancholy to this broken vision, creating a contradictory pair of emotions: part serene, part woeful. He describes it as follows: "At the onset of the modern age the compensatory dream of the idyll is seen through as such; the idyllic and utopian plan, on the one hand, and the thought of its unreality, on the other, will together generate that 'melancholy enthusiasm' which blends idyll and elegy."[67] In addition, Brinkmann argues that the character of this particular work is representative of an entire generation of composers: "Thus etched on the Brahmsian idyll, with its reflective intensity, is the consciousness of a late period."[68]

The importance of the concept of a broken idyll is twofold. First, it shows a precedent in the nineteenth century for pastorals that are conflicted and that fall outside the norm. While there is no evidence that Griffes was directly influenced by Brahms's symphony per se—in fact, he never wrote any multi-movement orchestral work—it still provides a larger context into which his pastoral experiments can be located. Second, Brinkmann's interdisciplinary portrait of late-Romantic *Weltschmerz* serves as a telling prelude to the panoply of cultural influences that were at work in the American musical landscape during the early twentieth century.

It is also appropriate to consider a recent article by Joanna Frymoyer devoted to musical topics in Arnold Schoenberg's instrumental music. She develops a method of classification for determining whether and to what degree a work displays adaptations of traditional dances, such as the minuet and waltz; in a previous unpublished paper, she proposed the same approach for the pastoral.[69] Her model is based on three types of features: "essential" (present in every case), "occasional" (appearing less often), and "idiomatic" (piece-specific), which can be abbreviated as all, some, and one. While Frymoyer's three-tiered approach to classification clearly has merits, it also has some drawbacks. Although her "occasional" category isolates a composer's characteristic features, she neglects the ways in which these cues combine to form specific pastoral works or blends. Her "idiomatic" category is the least useful since each case is sui generis. In short, while her project is to assemble a catalogue of pastoral anatomy, by contrast, my goal is to study pastoral physiology and to reveal how the disparate parts blend together within a work.

One of the most provocative recent monographs about the musical pastoral is by Eric Saylor, who explores a specific geographical area and historical period: England during the early twentieth century.[70] He relies on a nuanced literary foundation of two subtypes of pastoral, Arcadian and Utopian (based on a distinction by W. H. Auden), and then traces the evolution between these two in a whirlwind tour of works by English composers such as Elgar, Ireland, Vaughan Williams, Bliss, and Britten. The various English pastorals that Saylor explores have unmistakable analogies with those of Griffes, especially in the degree to which they incorporate experimental procedures. The difference, however, is that Saylor focuses on a national style displayed by an entire generation of composers rather than the interpretation of a personal style of a single composer. I am less interested in the question of whether and to what degree Griffes represented a twentieth-century American tradition; indeed, one of the hallmarks of his musical style is his propensity to blend together elements from different national styles such as French, German, and Russian, and transform them with his own artistic stamp. Finally, while Saylor explicitly avoids the detailed interpretation of individual works, a central goal of my study is to combine close exegesis of twelve pastorals within a broader historical and philosophical context.

Musical Exoticism

At this juncture, it is important to consider the broader cultural context of Griffes's relationship to non-Western music with respect to the twelve pastorals to be considered in this volume. Exoticism in Western music is far more than a single musical topic, style, or cue; rather, it can arise in a number of different ways, some clear and one-dimensional, others more paradoxical.

First, several terms need to be defined, beginning with *exotic*. In musical contexts, the concept of being exotic is based on difference. To be exotic, a given musical feature must be perceived as abnormal or unorthodox in relation to a predominant style. Two other terms arose during the nineteenth and early twentieth centuries: *Oriental* and *Orientalism*. The *Orient* not only referred to eastern Asia but "often designated a portion of the globe much closer to Europe: North Africa and the Arabian Peninsula, with the possible addition of Persia and India."[71] Since the term's connotation embraced such an enormous swath of territory, stretching from Morocco to China and Japan, it also encompassed a breathtaking variety of cultures, languages, and artistic traditions. It is a logical next step to treat the nineteenth-century understanding of *oriental* culture as a manifestation of the Other.

Recent scholarship on musical exoticism draws its inspiration from Edward Said's landmark critique published in 1978 entitled *Orientalism*.[72] Said revealed a host of political assumptions in the Western academic discipline devoted to the Middle East, including the many ways in which "the study of the languages, literatures, and cultures of the eastern world could amount to the appropriation, control, and ultimately marginalization and trivialization of those cultures and peoples."[73] However, according to Jonathan Bellman, Said's critique was also full of critical nuance in that "he consistently acknowledges the complexities of the multifaceted West-East equation, the tendencies of the West to 'read' the East not as itself but rather as an idealized object of desire, focus of evil, focus of good, bastion of purity, bastion of decay, or any of myriad other interpretations. ... The Orientalist discourse is only one of many present in the East-West encounter. There is, in short, a bewildering number of simultaneous conversations intrinsic to this cultural and geographic exchange."[74]

In recent years, there has been a virtual explosion of scholarly interest in the political implications of musical exoticism, which can be loosely arranged in a broad critical spectrum.[75] Toward one end would be musicologists such as Susan McClary, who describes *Orientalism* in the same breath as other cultural biases such as antisemitism and misogyny.[76] In his provocative article "Musicology on Safari," Matthew Head observes that "art's fictitious and imaginative elements" do not render it "ideologically neutral." On the contrary, "by resisting politics and thus according naturalness and neutrality to orientalism, scholars maximise orientalism's ideological force."[77] In a recent review, Andrew Chung goes even further by raising questions about the "politics of naming" as well as the universality of music theory's philosophical foundation—what he calls the "self-evident epistemological privilege for the music-theoretical concepts and values trained on particular Western notated traditions."[78]

Bellman occupies a central position in this exotic spectrum, acknowledging the colonialist implications of musical Orientalism while also investing in the detailed study of its morphology. He offers a useful distinction between three types of music criticism: orientalist, postcolonial, and transcultural. Of the three, my approach most closely resembles the latter, which he defines as the study of "music that references more than one culture, of any time and place, whether using devices derived from the land or culture in question or wholly imagined ones, and regardless of power relationship."[79]

Musicologists like Head and Chung not only continue the movement inaugurated by Said of placing politics and ideology at the center of interpretation, but they also magnify it. Those who interpret artistic experience through a purely ideological lens by necessity must abandon all questions of compositional method for fear of perpetuating an imperialistic tradition of cultural exploitation. While some may interpret my lack of emphasis on power relationships as indifference, if not blindness, a full-blown political commentary on the imperialist implications of Griffes's music would ultimately be deaf to his genuine artistic contribution. Why not embrace multiple perspectives? If Said's critique "affirms music's cultural multivalence by venturing far beyond [the] . . . essentially binary framework" of postcolonial criticism, my analysis also aims to uncover the musical "multivalence" of Griffes's overall style (for more details on Griffes's exposure to non-Western musical traditions, see chap. 1).[80]

Finally, my understanding of exoticism in Griffes's works is highly influenced by Gilles de Van's psychological interpretation of late nineteenth-century French culture. In his essay "Fin de Siècle Exoticism and the Meaning of the Far Away," he presents an enlightening conception of exoticism as a series of paradoxes: (a) the search for the foreign that leads back home; (b) the quest to find the unfamiliar that leads back to the familiar; and (c) the impetus toward the Other that becomes a mirror of the Self.[81] Based on these assumptions, Griffes's reliance on an "exotic" conflict of opposites—whether as a hybrid form for the whole work or as a set of conflicting referents within an individual theme—reflects a propensity for paradox that he shared with an entire generation of artists.

Another critical strategy in the study of musical exoticism has been to assemble an empirical catalogue or lexicon. For example, Derek Scott, in his article "Orientalism and Musical Style," enumerated a list of twenty-five Orientalist devices but did not provide specific illustrations of all of them.[82] But, by far, the most exhaustive catalogue appeared in Ralph Locke's monograph entitled *Musical Exoticism: Images and Reflections*, in which he carefully defined and illustrated musical characteristics that evoke exoticism.[83]

While these lexicons clearly have a useful descriptive purpose, ultimately I wish to question the assumption that underpins such a project. It is a misconception to assume that by creating such a catalogue, one will be able to identify a general category that embraces all of the particular instances or manifestations of exotic music. It is a preliminary step, like collecting empirical data that are out of the ordinary, that depart in any way from the usual Western musical features. The problem is that there is too much conflicting information to create a single category and yet not enough detailed information to create separate, precise subcategories. Questions arise: How many features are required to create an exotic identity? What if three exotic works display various features in the list but have no features in common? Wittgenstein's insight about family resemblances comes into play here (see below). In short, as much as Locke and Scott aspire to develop an empirical way station toward an ethnological study of the influence of non-Western sources on Western musical experience, ultimately their exotic catalogues fall short.

There are two more questions to consider before addressing the role that exoticism plays in Griffes's vision of the pastoral: the authenticity of sources and the novelty of exoticism—that is, the loose boundary between what was familiar and unfamiliar to early twentieth-century audiences.

The concept of authenticity in the perception and interpretation of exotic music is largely a myth and, therefore, a source of confusion for the interpreter. At the turn of the century, exotic music was rarely an outcome of meticulous ethnological study of foreign culture, a scholarly project to understand a musical tradition and then to replicate it. But even if composers *had* closely imitated foreign cultures, the degree of resemblance would have been lost on their audiences since, by and large, Western listeners would have had no point of reference. For Griffes's American audiences, the music from inside the Arab peninsula would have been as unknown as that of Outer Mongolia. In that respect, the degree of authenticity is the wrong tool to use to explain the organization of Orientalist music or to measure its artistic value.

Most important, even if it were possible to compare the degree to which a Western composer's treatment departed from its non-Western source, such a comparison would either ignore or at the very least minimize the element of creativity or fantasy on the part of the composer. Early twentieth-century works that have an exotic character can be arranged as a spectrum: at one end would be imitations of non-Western sources; at the other end would be music that either freely adapts non-Western sources or imagines new ones altogether. Most of Griffes's exotic music falls somewhere in between. To assume otherwise is to treat the history of Western Orientalism as a collection of poor transcriptions of music that composers had never heard.

The rise of musical exoticism also introduces an element of ambiguity in how early twentieth-century audiences distinguished between what was familiar and what was novel. To explain this ambiguity, it is useful to consider Ralph Locke's opposition between "overt" and "submerged" exoticism. "Overt" exoticism is a conscious evocation of a non-Western musical tradition. By contrast, "submerged" exoticism is the tendency for a given Western composer to absorb scales, harmonies, orchestral colors, etc. with non-Western associations into his or her personal musical style.[84] But problems arise when the novelty of some sounds—such as non-Western scales, unusual rhythms, and/or instrumental colors—begins to wear off. If that occurs, how is it possible to still consider them as exotic? If there is no way to measure the degree to which the sense of novelty has faded, then at what point is the specific feature familiar (or submerged) and no longer exotic?

For example, when a French composer such as Debussy employed Western compositional materials to evoke a non-Western musical tradition such as Indonesian gamelan, audiences' perceptions of these passages changed over time. The initial public impression was primarily novelty. Eventually, however, audiences began to associate these unusual characteristics with the style of a specific composer (Debussy), a group of composers (Impressionists), or even a national tradition (French). In some cases, the associations that a new exotic work possessed were based entirely on other similar exotic music that the audience already knew. To paraphrase Lévi-Strauss, any musical symbol refers to a network of previous musical symbols. What was originally perceived as a source of novelty gradually transformed into its opposite: an element of familiarity—that is, a recognizable feature of a composer's style. Ultimately, the distinction is of limited use. The categories of overt and submerged exoticism are not opposites, like exotic and non-exotic, but instead differ by degrees.

A good illustration of this phenomenon in Griffes's music would be his use of the whole-tone scale. For audiences familiar with Debussy's music, this feature would suggest a Debussyan, or perhaps French, influence on the American composer's style, rather than the influence of Javanese gamelan. This orientalist work would initiate a three-dimensional musical kaleidoscope: a new American work that signifies a previous French composer's work that, in turn, loosely signifies a non-Western tradition (for instruments tuned in equal temperament, the whole-tone scale is, at best, a loose approximation of either the *slendro* or *pelog* scale). Above all, the three layers of this kaleidoscope would blend together to different degrees. Finally, for those listeners not familiar with either Debussy's music or Javanese gamelan, passages in Griffes's works that were based on the whole-tone scale would sound unfamiliar and thus would be clearly marked as exotic.

At this juncture, it is useful to consider all of Griffes's pastoral works that either employ non-Western musical elements or have texts with non-Western themes (table 2.1). Close scrutiny of this list raises the following questions: What specific cues present in the works on this list trigger exotic associations in the listener? Is the primary means by which Griffes achieved exotic associations the use of alternative scales such as the whole tone, pentatonic, octatonic, and hexatonic, or did other cues play a role such as the languid and tarantella styles (see below)? More important, what do those associations have to do with the pastoral? The evocation of distant or imaginary exotic realms was an essential aspect of many of Griffes's pastorals—indeed, it became part of his pastoral signature. The degree to which his pastoral vision was colored by some kind of exotic character will be more closely examined in the context of specific analyses in chapters 4, 5, and 7.

Table 2.1. List of Griffes's pastorals that employ non-Western musical elements or contain texts referring to non-Western traditions

Musical Work	Poet
Celtic	
Vocal	
3 *Poems by Fiona MacLeod,* Op. 11	
—"The Lament of Ian the Proud"	Fiona MacLeod
—"Thy Dark Eyes to Mine"	Fiona MacLeod
—"The Rose of the Night"	Fiona MacLeod
Incidental Music for Play	
The Kairn of Koridwen	Edouard Shuré
Japanese	
Vocal	
—"Sakura, Sakura"	Traditional
Incidental Music for Pantomime	
—*Sho-jo*	Traditional
Japanese/Chinese	
Vocal	
5 Songs of Ancient China and Japan	
—"So-fei Gathering Flowers"	Wang Chang-Ling
—"Landscape"	Sada-ihe
—"The Old Temple among the Mountains"	Chang Wen-Chang
—"Tears"	Wang Seng-Ju
—"A Feast of Lanterns"	Yuan Mei
Instrumental	
The Pleasure-Dome of Kubla Khan	Samuel Taylor Coleridge
Hawaiian/Polynesian	
Vocal	
—"Waikiki"	Ruppert Brooke
Javanese	
Vocal	
—"Hampelas"	Traditional
—"Kinanti"	Traditional
—"Djakoan"	Traditional
Other	
Instrumental	
—"The White Peacock," *Roman Sketches*	William Sharp
—Two Sketches based on Indian Themes	

Let us take stock of our exotic meditations. It is clear that there is no single "necessary" feature that is associated with every form of exoticism in early twentieth-century music; instead there are multiple musical features with exotic associations that can occur alone or in combination. However, instead of trying to define the underlying essence of this phenomenon, I will explore the ways in which so-called exotic musical features—that is, features that early twentieth-century audiences would likely perceive as foreign—contributed to the pastoral character in some of Griffes's works. While there is no strict causal link between the exotic and the pastoral, the degree of emotional overlap between the two suggests a kind of symbiotic relationship. In chapter 3, I will explore a wide range of musical cues that helped create the idiosyncratic pastoral character found in some of Griffes's mature works.

Wittgenstein's "Family" and Polythetic Classification

The next step toward developing a theoretical foundation for the ambivalent pastoral is to expand upon a key idea drawn from the late writings of the twentieth-century philosopher Ludwig Wittgenstein. While several semiotic scholars have cited the Austrian thinker, no one has integrated his ideas into the theoretical foundation of a new approach.[85] To fully appreciate his insight, we must reconsider a basic assumption of the concept of musical topic. Topical analysis has an inherent philosophical dimension that arises from the very act of identification. Interpreters who use the concept of musical topic must address the question of universals—that is, they must agree on what constitutes a general category or type to which an individual instance belongs.

The question of generality is unavoidable when one consults a lexicon of musical topics—what Ratner called a "thesaurus"—in order to determine whether a given topic is at work in a piece. The modus operandi for anyone equipped with such a lexicon is that a one-to-one mapping exists between a token and a general type, assuming that each type represents a preexisting musical tradition. The implicit assumption for any topical lexicon can be summarized as follows: the bigger, the better. In other words, the larger the lexicon, the more comprehensive the collection of topics and, presumably, the more precise the eventual topical analysis will be. While topical analysis of a musical work almost always involves more than simply recognizing what topic is in operation, identification is a necessary first stage of a larger interpretive process. As a result, the interpretation of musical topics becomes synonymous with lexical proficiency.

The problem with this lexical approach is that it assumes that any topic can be successfully identified in a given passage—that is, that there are clearly defined discovery procedures. Such an approach fails to take into account situations where there is some ambiguity about what particular topic is displayed in a given passage: either there are not enough cues to establish a specific topic or there are multiple cues that conflict with each other, thereby indicating multiple topics. Furthermore, additional problems arise when composers employ new characteristics (or cues) that are idiosyncratic to their versions of a given topic, that are tailor-made to their own musical style. If we assume that early twentieth-century composers were not only reviving old topics, creating new syntheses of old and new topics as well as inventing new ones altogether, then the number of entries in the topical lexicon increases by leaps and bounds and the aim of developing a comprehensive "thesaurus" becomes less and less tenable.

However, there is a second, more skeptical perspective in which the assumption that a topic is an overarching group or universal type is itself subject to question. The inspiration for this skeptical approach toward grouping is the twentieth-century Austrian philosopher Ludwig Wittgenstein, who, in his late work *Philosophical Investigations*, proposed a theory of loose family resemblance. It is worth summarizing his theory in some depth in order to explain how I will adapt it.

Wittgenstein's critique of universals focuses on the concept of a game. Let us imagine various examples including board games (Scrabble), video games (Tetris), Olympic games (curling), and children's games (hide-and-seek). Wittgenstein asks: What do they all have in common? His answer is that while some games share different kinds of similarities—from the same overall structure to an identical detail—there is no single element they all share in common. The various activities called "games" are united by virtue of "a complicated network of similarities overlapping and criss crossing [sic]."[86] This network could be likened to a long rope twisted together out of many shorter fibers. Wittgenstein concludes that "the strength of the [rope] does not reside in the fact that some one fibre runs through its whole length, but in the overlapping of many fibres."[87] Just as a rope contains many overlapping strands, but no strand continues for its entire length, likewise his concept of a group does not require that any single property be present in every member. In short, group membership does not depend on any necessary property, but rather is determined by a subset of sufficient properties that overlap or crisscross among various members.

Wittgenstein's insight warrants one additional comment. When the expression *family resemblance* is applied to a concept of a game, it invokes a metaphor that could potentially be confusing. Membership in a family can be defined in more than one way—by virtue of a common physical or mental property or by virtue of a shared genetic code. Yet Wittgenstein had no interest in the biological criterion of membership and, instead, focused entirely on the logical network of similarities that all depend on different criteria. In that respect, Wittgenstein is implicitly rejecting the traditional logical categories of necessary and sufficient conditions. For him, membership in a group relies on a multiplicity of resemblances, not on a single principle of unity.[88]

Finally, the point of reviving Wittgenstein's concept of "family resemblance" is certainly not to undermine completely the concept of a universal group. Rather, my purpose is to expand the category of pastoral so as to include a broader range of dissimilar works. While there is still a reason for distinguishing between works that are pastoral and non-pastoral, a Wittgenstein-inspired approach to classification blurs the boundaries of identity and loosens the notion of membership in a group.

It is important to emphasize that Wittgenstein's critique of the intrinsic problems in group membership does not constitute a direct analogy to the group of pastorals that are the subject of this study. Instead, it must be slightly adapted, and the process of adaptation will be divided into three steps: a summary of the philosophical concept of "openness" that provides an alternative to the logical standard of necessary and sufficient conditions; the method of polythetic classification; and the concept of a "frame," borrowed from cognitive psychology, as a means of blending characteristics that revive Baroque pastoral dances along with new characteristics that Griffes himself introduced.

Weitz's Aesthetic Theory

The philosophical landscape following World War II could be described as post-Wittgensteinian in that his brand of cynicism cast a long shadow over aesthetic inquiry during the rest of the century and after. Philosophers such as Morris Weitz, William Kennick, and Paul Ziff debated whether it was possible to develop a comprehensive definition of art.[89] In 1956, Weitz wrote a groundbreaking article in which he posed the following two questions: What is art? Can art be defined in terms of a set of essential properties? His response is telling: "Aesthetic theory is a logically vain attempt to define what cannot be defined, to state the necessary and sufficient properties of that which has no necessary and sufficient properties, to conceive the concept of art as closed when its very use reveals and demands its openness."[90] Weitz's argument consists of two parts: (1) a critique of any aesthetic theory that relies on the rules of logic; and (2) an alternative approach based on the concept of "openness." Weitz questions the assumption that the category of art has a logical basis, which can be understood as follows: if an object possesses specific essential properties, then it belongs to the category; if it does not, then it falls outside the category. Rather than debating why one property should belong on the list defining an artwork and another should not, instead he focuses on the motivation for a list in the first place. He questions the assumption that artistic identity must be binary or, in other words, determined by the presence or absence of a set of essential properties.

Weitz's insight is to offer an alternative model of artistic identity. In place of essential properties, he introduces a different criterion—namely, similarity: "There are no necessary and sufficient conditions but there are the strands of similarity conditions, i.e., bundles of properties, none of which need be present but most of which are, when we describe things as works of art. I shall call these the 'criteria of recognition' of works of art."[91]

It is worth considering the advantages and disadvantages of Weitz's proposals. First, I fully endorse his critique of the logical basis of aesthetic theory. His proposals offer a new perspective for understanding the wide variety of aesthetic theories that had been proposed at that juncture in history and for assessing their lack of success. Second, unfortunately, Weitz's critique falls short in regard to practicality, for he does not provide a detailed method of defining what a "strand of similarity" is and how many strands are required to establish an object's identity. One of the theoretical goals of my project is to devise such a method and to clarify what criteria of similarity are required to recognize one of Griffes's pastorals.

The second fundamental insight that Weitz offers is the notion of "openness." While this concept has a rich philosophical lineage, encompassing such figures as Friedrich Nietzsche and Friedrich Waismann (who used the term *open texture*), I will turn to a summary proposed by Lydia Goehr in her recent work *The Imaginary Museum of Musical Works: An Essay in the Philosophy of Music*.[92] She identifies three characteristics of an open concept:

1. It does not correspond to a fixed or static essence
2. It cannot be defined in terms of necessary and sufficient conditions
3. It is "intensionally incomplete or essentially contestable—because the possibility of an unforeseen situation arising which would lead us to modify our definition can never be eliminated."[93]

Since the first two characteristics restate the critique of logical necessity mentioned above, let us consider the third in more detail.

The feature of incompleteness applies to a situation of an object being classified under a given category, which, in Weitz's case, would be an artwork. Goehr leaves open the possibility that an object may possess some unforeseen or unimaginable feature that falls outside the list of properties given in the original definition. While the identity of an object is undeniable, it nevertheless must be understood as something flexible and subject to change. Weitz describes two scenarios in which either the original definition is modified or a new definition is invented altogether: "A concept is open if its conditions of application are emendable and corrigible; i.e., if a situation or case can be imagined or secured which would call for some sort of decision on our part to extend the use of the concept to cover this, or to close the concept and invent a new one to deal with the new case and its new property."[94] The hypothetical situation he describes is exactly the challenge faced by anyone who wishes to classify Griffes's unusual treatment of the musical pastoral.

Weitz then goes further and distinguishes in what disciplines open and closed concepts are appropriate: "If necessary and sufficient conditions for the application of a concept can be stated, the concept is a closed one. But this can happen only in logic or mathematics where concepts are constructed and completely defined. It cannot occur with empirically-descriptive and normative concepts unless we arbitrarily close them by stipulating the ranges of their uses."[95] In his view, all empirical concepts should be considered as open, which, in his case, includes any concept related to the arts.

Finally, the notion of openness is fundamentally connected to another feature: historical change. A point of departure in Goehr's book is to propose that our understanding of musical experience should be understood as intrinsically contingent—that is, subject to change. This proposal grows out of her critique of the traditional analytical Anglo-American approach to philosophy, or what she calls "essentialism." She rejects the assumption that our understanding of a musical object corresponds to a fixed and static essence as represented by a score. For example, she rejects Nelson Goodman's argument that a performance of a notated score that contains a single wrong note "does not count as a performance of the work."[96] Instead of treating a musical work as a kind of object, she urges us to consider a performance as an "open concept" that belongs to an ongoing practice in which multiple versions of a work are possible. Examples of "open" practices are the improvisatory traditions in the historical performance of Baroque music and in Jazz. While Griffes did not embrace these open practices per se, her assumption about history is fundamental to my argument about musical topics and, in particular, the musical pastoral.

Weitz's critique of a purely logical basis for a theory of art serves as the foundation for my objection to the ways in which musical topics have traditionally been defined. Fueled by the skepticism of Wittgenstein, Weitz, and Goehr, I offer an alternative approach to topical classification that primarily relies on a polythetic organization rather than a list of essential properties that a topical prototype must possess. In addition, the concept of openness is highly useful as a means of tracing the more traditional features associated with the pastoral tradition alongside the new musical features that Griffes introduced.

Polythetic Classification

My solution to Weitz's suggestion of "strands of similarity" is the concept of polythetic structure. As an introduction to this concept, let us begin by imagining a hypothetical example that helps justify the use of Wittgenstein's alternative notion of "family." The contents of the following four sets, numbered 1–4, are arranged in a horizontal format:

1	A	B	C	
2	A	B		D
3	A		C	D
4		B	C	D

Upon close inspection, two things are clear. First, there is no letter that belongs to all four sets; they all have no single feature in common. Second, all four letters appear three times; in other words, there is considerable overlap in the content of these four sets. One could ask: How can we explain the relationship among these sets? Do they all belong to a single group? In fact, there is a concept called *polythetic classification* that applies directly to this situation, and it is used in such diverse fields as anthropology, psychology, and religious studies.[97] This type of classification "places together organisms that have the greatest number of shared features, and no single feature is either essential to group membership or is sufficient to make an organism a member of the group."[98]

As it turns out, the characteristics present in Griffes's pastorals display a similar polythetic organization compared to the abstract sets in the above diagram. Although there is no feature that appears in all of them, many individual features recur in various subgroups of the entire collection of pastorals. The result can be likened to a musical embodiment of Wittgenstein's image of a rope, a "family" whose members are unified by different degrees of overlapping content.

Infinite Regress

At this juncture, it is appropriate to consider a possible objection that could be raised to my proposals thus far. There is a potential pitfall in focusing on a characteristic of a musical topic rather than the topic itself: the age-old problem of infinite regress. If I argue that the category of a topic cannot be defined by a fixed set of characteristics or cues, then would not the category of a pastoral cue itself be susceptible to the same argument? In that case, the individual cue would become synonymous with a mini-topic, and the problem of infinite regress would rear its head. In short, if a topic must be redefined as a fluid combination of cues, then, by extension, are we not compelled to define an individual cue in the same way, as something fluid without a fixed identity?

My response to this hypothetical objection is that the ambiguity surrounding the concept of a category arises from the assumption that there is a fixed combination of musical features that constitutes a topic, not from the ambiguity of each musical feature by itself. One must assume that the rhythm, meter, harmony, melody, etc. of a musical passage can be measured and described with a reasonable degree of objectivity. The ultimate interpretive question is to determine how these features cohere together and create some kind of musical meaning.

A similar problem arises when we consider the relationship between a specific pastoral feature and the topic itself—what might be called the part and the whole. The question is whether an individual feature that suggests a given topic possesses the same emotional associations normally correlated with the topic itself. For example, is it reasonable to assume that the feature of a recurring pedal tone or interval will always have traditional pastoral associations? Regardless of what other features a musical passage may possess, if it contains a static pitch or interval in the bass, then should it be associated with feelings of serenity and contentment?

The short answer to this question is that not all static bass lines are created equal. While it is possible to ascribe a traditional pastoral association such as serenity to a fixed bass pitch or interval, the combination of other musical features can affect or even modify those associations. The point is not that each cue aligned with pastoralism possesses all of its traditional psychological associations or none of them. Instead, each cue has a latent potential for the traditional pastoral associations, and that potential can be realized to different degrees depending on the combination of other cues. Thus, the challenge is to explore the different complexions of passages with bass pedals, and not simply identify them all as equivalent because they display the same harmonic property. The same would be the case for the musical lament. In other words, it would be a mistake to assume that all descending chromatic bass lines possess the traditional associations of grief and sadness of the lament topic. Instead, the bass line's emotional impact will depend on whether it traverses the usual perfect fourth span and what other musical features appear in conjunction with it. My goal is to find an interpretive strategy to discover the particular blend of emotional associations within a pastoral passage or movement. The next step in that strategy is to explore recent developments in cognitive psychology that involve the concepts of prototypes and frames.

Prototypes and Frames

In daily life, it is tempting to assume that the laws of Aristotelian logic that have been central in Western thought for centuries—the principles of non-contradiction and of the excluded middle—are the standard for all human knowledge. Recent developments in cognitive theory, however, provide a more open-ended method of determining the basis of membership in a category. Cognitive psychologists such as Eleanor Rosch and Lawrence Barsalou have shown that, in some situations, people do not always rely on these Aristotelian standards. In a series of articles in the 1970s, Rosch proposed a theory of graded categorization in which some members were perceived as more central than others:[99] "These categories have a somewhat more complicated structure: membership is by degrees; category boundaries are relatively fluid and often hazy; and category structure can change over time. In these cases, the process of categorization is a highly dynamic one, requiring that we evaluate potential category members relative to existing category members, which, together, define a standard of typicality."[100]

An example of something that blurs boundaries is a linguistic "hedge," or an expression that introduces ambiguity or contradiction into the definition of a category. The following sentence is an apt illustration: "Loosely speaking, a bat is a bird." Technically, the sentence raises doubts about the strict limits of the category of birds. In effect, the expression *loosely speaking* implies that the rules for membership in the group called *birds* are being expanded and that bats are provisional members.

An additional development in this expanded approach towards categorization is a theory of "frames" and prototypes as proposed by Barsalou and adapted by Lawrence Zbikowski. In his recent publications, Zbikowski has raised a wide range of questions about the intersection between musical experience and human knowledge, perception, memory, and consciousness.[101] In his pathbreaking book *Conceptualizing Music: Cognitive Structure, Theory, and Analysis,* he fashions his own intellectual blend of recent psychological and linguistic theories, as proposed by Barsalou, Rosch, Gilles Fauconnier, and Mark Turner, to create a theoretical triptych consisting of categorization, cross-domain mapping, and the conceptual model.[102]

Barsalou has shown that a simple category such as *bird* can be conceived as a frame or relational network consisting of a set of four abstract attributes: size, color, sound, and means of motion. Likewise, each attribute can be divided into a handful of possible values. Thus, a bird's size can be large, medium, or small; its sound can be chirping, clucking, cooing, etc. The only requirement for an animal to belong to this category is to have one value from each attribute; likewise, each individual case is defined by the composite pattern of values among all the attributes.[103]

One application of Barsalou's network is to arrive at a prototype, which can be defined as a particular configuration of values within the network that a majority of people prefer. This definition creates a means by which membership in a category can be graduated and potential members can be assessed by their degree of resemblance to the prototype: "Thus category membership is not an all-or-nothing affair, but rather is graded, and we can speak of an individual as [a] better or worse example of a given category."[104] The term *prototypicality effects* describes the phenomenon of graded membership by which an example is understood as being more or less typical based on the degree of resemblance to a prototype.[105]

A similar approach toward grouping emerged during the 1960s based on the concept of a "fuzzy set," which has applications in mathematics, systems theory, and information theory. In a seminal article, Lotfi Radeh introduced new mathematical entities called fuzzy sets that "are not classes or sets in the usual sense of these terms, since they do not dichotomize all objects into those that belong to the class and those that do not." In his mind, a fuzzy set is "a class in which there may be a continuous infinity of grades of membership, with the grade of membership of an object x in a fuzzy set A represented by a number $f_A(x)$ in the interval $[0, 1]$."[106]

However, regardless of whether one embraces fuzzy sets or prototypicality effects, my reason for summarizing these approaches is not to develop a single prototype of preferred values. Instead, I wish to use Barsalou's concept of a network to model multiple instances with different combinations of values rather than a single prototype of preferred values. I would argue that it is possible to have multiple cases that have some degree of overlapping values and yet still belong to the same category. As an illustration, let us imagine three examples drawn from ornithology:

> small, brown, chirps, flies
> medium, brown, clucks, runs
> medium, white, coos, flies

Note that although the attributes *brown*, *medium*, and *flies* appear in two of the three examples, no single attribute appears in all three. If we translate this scenario into a musical framework, I would replace these ornithological attributes with musical cues. Hence, instead of a single prototype, my goal is to develop a family of multiple types, each with different degrees of overlapping content.

At this point, the reader must be wondering what on earth a summary of birds and beaks has anything to do with musical bucolics. Equipped with this summary of Barsalouian frames and prototypes, we are now prepared to consider their relevance to our understanding of musical pastorals. The question is whether the model of a prototype and a varied collection of examples is preferable to the polythetic model of organization, described above, in which there is no standard or prototype. As we will see, the solution falls somewhere in the middle.

On the one hand, Griffes's pastorals do not display a strictly polythetic structure. Wittgenstein's image of a crisscrossing pattern is not equally distributed but instead is weighted more to some cues than to others, as will be shown below. However, the frequency of these cues falls short of creating a genuine prototype. On the other hand, I have objections to the implicit quantitative purpose of the prototype model. The fundamental motivation for isolating a prototype of a concept is twofold: to illustrate how examples displaying a wide range of diversity all belong to a given category and to determine, if not measure, the degree to which these examples converge to a single prototype. In some respects, it is an exercise in measuring conformity. On the contrary, while one can isolate the most common properties of a Griffes-based pastoral—the semblance of a prototype—I am more interested in studying the degree to which they diverge from a common point of reference.

The innovative character of Griffes's pastorals is that new cues appear alongside cues with traditional pastoral associations. My goal is to develop an approach to classification that focuses not only on identifying the most frequently occurring attributes in a composer's output—what some would call a prototype—but also on new experiments in which more and less common attributes coalesce and, thereby, create new pastoral possibilities. In short, an outlier pastoral, while less common statistically, may be just as interesting artistically.

Eighteenth-Century Dances

The next step in assembling a model to interpret Griffes's pastorals is to summarize the eighteenth-century pastoral dance tradition and to identify what traces it left in his works. My point of departure is Wye J. Allanbrook's masterful monograph *Rhythmic Gesture in Mozart: Le Nozze di Figaro and Don Giovanni*, in which she combines two projects: a comprehensive encyclopedia of eighteenth-century dance topics and an analytical commentary on two Mozart operas.[107] She summarizes all the diffuse information found in the composition and performance treatises by Koch,

Mattheson, Kirnberger, and Quantz about a broad spectrum of dances. In her detailed survey, she identifies four dances associated with the pastoral: gigue, pastorale, siciliano, and musette. Each dance type carries the traces of distinct choreographic steps, which are reflected in its meter as well as its characteristic rhythms and accents. These choreographic movements are a vital part of the dance's identity even if later musical audiences either forgot them or never learned them in the first place. Let us briefly consider each type.

Of the four dance types, the gigue is the most complex. While it initially consisted of four subtypes, eventually the subtle distinctions between them merged into a single category, which later served as the final movement of symphonies, sonatas, and string quartets alike.[108] The basic features of this generic gigue include a quick tempo, dotted rhythmic patterns on first and fourth beats, a regular phrase structure, and a disjunct melodic line.[109]

Of the three pastoral topics, the origin of the siciliano is the most elusive. Although the treatises on which Allanbrook relies claim that the type originated in Sicily, apparently this historical link is based more on fiction than fact. Monelle wryly notes that "it would be satisfying to show that composers adopted a dance measure from the traditional culture of Sicily, the birth place of pastoralism's leading poet Theocritus.... Unfortunately, it is extremely hard to trace the origin of this style, or to associate it reliably with Sicily. By the [Baroque] era ... everyone knew what constituted a siciliana [sic], but its emergence as a topical signifier is almost impossible to trace."[110] Nevertheless, by the end of the Baroque period, the central characteristics of this musical tradition were well established: compound duple meter, a slower tempo than either the gigue or pastorale, frequent dotted rhythmic patterns, and a minor mode.

The pastorale mediates between the gigue and the siciliano—a mean between two pastoral extremes. Like the siciliano, its relationship to a specific dance or a set of physical gestures is doubtful. It is characterized by a moderate tempo, a static harmonic texture (or bass pedal), and the absence of dotted rhythms found in the siciliano. Allanbrook concludes that "the telling catchword *innocente* and the musette-style tonic pedal catch the idealization of the shepherd world which is the hallmark of the dance called pastorale, and of the pastoral genre itself."[111]

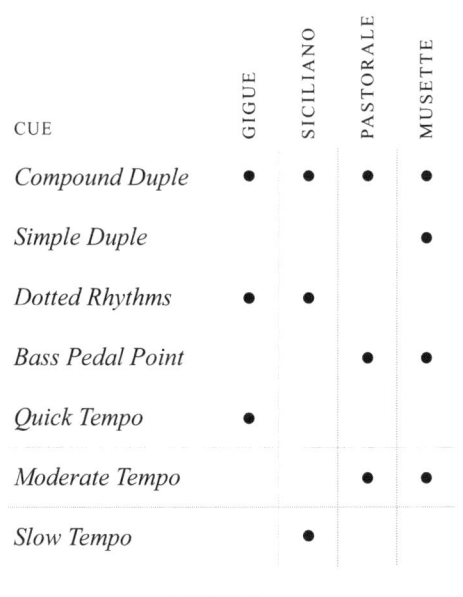

CUE	GIGUE	SICILIANO	PASTORALE	MUSETTE
Compound Duple	●	●	●	●
Simple Duple				●
Dotted Rhythms	●	●		
Bass Pedal Point			●	●
Quick Tempo	●			
Moderate Tempo			●	●
Slow Tempo		●		

FIGURE 2.1.

Matrix of cues for four Baroque dances (based on Allanbrook).

The musette, the final dance of the four, was named after a French version of the bagpipe; as a result, it had a characteristic harmonic texture—a drone bass, and a simple melodic line above it called a skirl. Most important, its meter was flexible—either simple duple (e.g., alla breve) or compound duple (e.g., 6/8). The musette resembled the pastorale to such a degree that Allanbrook concludes that "indeed any distinction between the two types is almost superfluous."[112] Of the four Baroque dances, Ratner regarded the pastorale and musette as quintessential examples of what he called the "pastoral style," and in his compendium *Classic Music: Expression, Form, and Style,* he illustrated them with excerpts drawn from Haydn's, Mozart's, and Beethoven's instrumental music.[113]

At this juncture, it is useful to provide a synopsis of the characteristic treatment of meter, rhythm, harmony, and tempo in each of the four pastoral dances, as described by Allanbrook (figure 2.1). This matrix deserves several comments. First, the idiosyncratic character of each dance is represented by the vertical arrangement of entries; each one has a unique fingerprint of cues. Second, there is no prototype, no subset of features that occurs in every dance. The closest thing to a prototypical feature is compound duple meter, which defines every dance except the musette. However, this time signature is so open-ended and recurs in so many different musical contexts that it can hardly be considered a genuine prototype. It functions more like a temporal framework or bare-boned temporal skeleton. Indeed, it would be more accurate to describe the structure of this diagram as polythetic, but with a strong predilection for one feature: compound duple. Overall, the model of Baroque dances is mostly polythetic but weighted toward a metric cue.

Finally, two other features of the matrix are noteworthy. Not only does no cue appear in all the dances, but, more important, no cue in the list is intrinsically pastoral. Instead, the pastoral character of each dance is collective in nature, which means that it is determined by a unique combination of cues drawn from a broader pastoral reservoir. As we will see below, Griffes's pastoral reservoir is deeper than the Baroque tradition summarized by Allanbrook in that it includes a wider range of cues, some inherited from eighteenth- and nineteenth-century composers, some of Griffes's own invention.

Allanbrook's catalogue also raises the question of stylistic influence. If there is no clear biographical support, one must rely on a preponderance of empirical evidence to confirm the strong likelihood that one composer influenced another. In this case, it is not a specific composer but rather the composite style of a previous generation of composers. On the whole, there is substantial empirical evidence that the late Baroque sensibility had some kind of influence on Griffes's musical style.

Next, let us consider a subset of cues from the above matrix. The list below includes the cues that occur most often in the four Baroque pastoral dances and that play an important role in Griffes's experimental pastorals.

- Meter: Compound (Duple, Triple, or Quadruple)
- Rhythm: Dotted Rhythms
- Harmony: Consonant Pedal Interval/Chord

The compound metric scheme reflects most of the pastoral dances (save the musette) but expands so as to include three and four beats per bar. In a number of his instrumental pastorals, Griffes had a predilection for using themes with dotted rhythms, a tendency that shows his attraction to the rhythmic textures of the siciliano and the gigue. In addition, the static bass and drone fifth found in the musette and pastorale became a central feature in many of Griffes's pastorals, although he often preferred to use a dissonant chord or interval as a pedal. Finally, it should be noted that I have omitted altogether the dimension of tempo from this Baroque amalgam. The reason for this omission is that Griffes's pastoral sensibility was not attuned to the subtle temporal differences between the siciliano, pastorale, and musette. In general, the tempi of his pastoral works and sections are either in the moderate range (e.g., andante) or improvisatory (e.g., languid, rubato).

This brief collection of musical features does not constitute an independent category. Rather, it is a distillation of the historical aspects of the musical pastoral legacy that Griffes inherited and then adapted in his own works. Even if some of these cues appeared in pastorals composed in the nineteenth century, they nevertheless represent a record of the collective musical influence that Baroque pastoral dances exerted on Griffes's imagination, a portrait of the historical traces that gave life to his pastoral inclinations.

The next step is to compile a checklist of attributes that occur at least twice in Griffes's experimental pastoral works.

- Meter: Compound (Duple, Triple, or Quadruple) *
- Temporality Ambiguity
- Rhythm: Dotted Rhythms *
- Rhythm: Ostinato
- Harmony: Bass Pedal/Consonant Interval or Chord *
- Harmony: Dissonant Pedal Interval/Chord *
- Harmony: Ambiguous Tonal Center
- Languid Style
- Tarantella Style
- Sacred Chorale Style
- Registral Expansion
- Cumulative Counterpoint
- Exotic Scales

Because these attributes are not based on their degree of frequency, it depicts the full palette of pastoral colors he had at his disposal rather than the combination of colors used in a single pastoral work. In short, it is a neutral composite, not a prototype, and therefore cannot be used as a basis for determining membership in a group. Also, three of the characteristics (i.e., meter, rhythm, and harmony) play a special role in that they echo the same three attributes isolated in the eighteenth-century amalgam presented above; they are marked with asterisks. But now two of the three have been transformed either by a difference in meter (compound triple or quadruple) or an increase in dissonance (dissonant pedal chord)—in short, by their context in Griffes's idiosyncratic style.

The list above also raises a logical question concerning the identity of pastoral cues that are idiomatic to Griffes. For example, do cues such as *temporal ambiguity* or *ambiguous tonal center* possess an intrinsically pastoral nature? Or is their pastoral character defined by their association with other more traditional pastoral cues in the same work? The answer is clearly the latter. Were one of these cues to appear in a work without any of the traditional pastoral cues such as a pedal point texture or recurring dotted rhythmic patterns, then there would be little reason to classify that work as a pastoral. Their identity as cues is determined partly by the broader pastoral environment within a work—that is, by the presence of cues with strong pastoral associations at the same time or in close proximity. One of Griffes's chief innovations was to introduce idiosyncratic cues such as registral expansion and cumulative counterpoint alongside traditional cues and, thereby, broaden his pastoral palette.

The next stage in the development of an interpretive framework is to compile a checklist, arranged as a matrix, of the frequency of cues, both traditional and idiosyncratic, in twelve of Griffes's pastoral works (figure 2.2). The matrix deserves several comments. It resembles the composite diagram of Baroque pastoral dances à la Allanbrook displayed in figure 2.1 except that now there are more cues in the rows and more pieces in the columns. The visual organization of the matrix invites two contrasting perspectives: the horizontal rows show the frequency of each cue in all twelve works, and the vertical columns provide a snapshot of the distribution of all cues in each work. It should be emphasized that the dot listed for any attribute in this matrix indicates that the given attribute appears in at least one section, not necessarily during the entire work. For example, although "The White Peacock" consists of a stunning array of contrasting rhythmic textures, it contains two short sections, mm. 27–33,

PASTORAL CUES	TR	KH	WP	LA	VA	BA	IA	EY	RO	TE	SY	PR
Compound Meter	•	•				•	•	•	•	•		
Temporal Ambiguity		•	•	•	•							
Dotted Rhythms	•	•	•	•	•		•	•			•	•
Rhythmic Ostinato		•	•	•	•				•	•	•	
Consonant Pedal	•	•		•		•	•					
Dissonant Pedal		•	•		•			•	•	•	•	•
Ambiguous Tonal Center		•	•		•				•			•
Languid Style	•	•	•	•	•	•	•	•			•	•
Tarantella Style		•				•						
Sacred Chorale	•	•	•		•					•		•
Registral Expansion		•	•	•	•	•		•	•			
Cumulative Counterpoint			•		•		•		•			•
Exotic Scales	•	•	•					•	•	•	•	

LAMENT CUES	TR	KH	WP	LA	VA	BA	IA	EY	RO	TE	SY	PR
Sigh Figure	•	•	•	•	•		•	•	•	•		•
Bass Tetrachord			•	•								

FIGURE 2.2.

Matrix of Pastoral and Lament cues in twelve of Griffes's works (abbreviations of titles from left to right are "Der traümende See," *The Pleasure-Dome of Kubla Khan,* "The White Peacock," "The Lake at Evening," "The Vale of Dreams," Scherzo/*Bacchanale,* "The Lament of Ian the Proud," "Thy Dark Eyes to Mine," "The Rose of the Night," "Tears," "Symphony in Yellow," Prelude #3).

37–40, eleven bars in all, in which a recurring rhythmic pattern serves as an ostinato. As a result, it is marked as containing a "Rhythmic Ostinato." Incidentally, in chapter 3 each of these cues will be discussed at greater length.

At this stage, the reader may well think that it is possible to form some general observations about the information displayed in the above matrix. For example, one could conclude that Griffes's pastoral works are characterized by a handful of properties: one of two types of pedal texture (consonant or dissonant) and the use of either compound meter or dotted rhythms. The aim of these two observations would be to determine an underlying essence of a Griffes pastoral, a set of properties that are necessary and sufficient to define its identity. While I can sympathize with this overall aim as a first impulse, ultimately I would reject it. A central philosophical goal of my overall project is to question the reliance on Aristotelian logic as the sole basis for determining group membership. Above all, for Griffes, pastoral identity embodies Wittgenstein's concept of family resemblance in that the frequency of cues resembles a crisscrossing pattern. Likewise, the failure of any single cue to appear in all the works in the list underlines that Griffes's pastoral character has an open character in the spirit of Weitz's aesthetic proposals, as described above.

Now let us consider the frequency of cues in the twelve Griffes pastorals to be discussed in this study.

Cue	Frequency
Languid Style	10
Sigh Figure	10
Dotted Rhythms	9
Dissonant Pedal (Interval/Chord)	8
Rhythmic Ostinato	7
Exotic Scales	7
Registral Expansion	7
Compound Meter	7
Sacred Chorale Style	6
Consonant Pedal (Interval/Chord)	5
Ambiguous Tonal Center	5
Cumulative Counterpoint	5
Temporal Ambiguity	4
Tarantella Style	2
Bass Tetrachord	2

It is easy to misinterpret the information presented in this list. For example, the number of times that a dissonant pedal interval or chord occurs in this collection of works—eight out of twelve—is, in itself, not particularly significant. What is more significant is that when one takes into consideration the number of works with either a consonant pedal pitch/interval (e.g., perfect fifth) or a dissonant interval/chord (e.g., V4/2), the total number of works displaying bass pedals increases to twelve (NB: in fact, the total is thirteen since *The Pleasure-Dome of Kubla Khan* includes both types of pedal textures). In this case, it is important to consider two cues as a pair, not each one in isolation. The conclusion to be drawn is that Griffes uniformly employs pedal textures—both consonant as well as dissonant—in his pastorals, a fact that underlines his desire to renew as well as inflect the tradition of the eighteenth-century musette. However, it should be emphasized that the cue that occurs most often, the pedal texture, appears in so many composers' styles and in so many different historical periods that it is too ubiquitous to be considered a prototype.

It should also be noted that the ordered list of cues above is weighted in terms of frequency. One pair of cues appears in all twelve works, two cues appear in ten, and various subsets of cues, pairs, and trios occur in either eight or nine pastorals.

Cue Combination	Frequency
Languid Style + Sigh Figure + Dotted Rhythms:	8
Languid Style + Sigh Figure:	8
Sigh Figure + Dotted Rhythms:	8
Languid Style + Dotted Rhythms:	9

Since no subset of cues occurs uniformly in all twelve pastorals, none of them constitutes a prototype as understood by cognitive psychologists such as Rosch and Barselou. Instead, a loose hierarchy exists among the cues. Although no cue by itself is inherently pastoral, it acquires a pastoral character by virtue of its simultaneous presence with a subset of other cues that together create a pastoral character.

There are two reasons that the pastoral cues are weighted differently. The first one is historical in nature. Some cues have greater pastoral potential because of the tradition of eighteenth-century dances that Griffes inherited; this group consists of compound meter, consonant pedal, and dotted rhythms. Audiences most likely had preconceived pastoral associations when hearing a texture that included some combination of these cues. The other reason is the pattern of frequency in Griffes's own works. The significance of the ordered list is that passages with pedal texture and the sigh figure have more pastoral potential in the context of Griffes's oeuvre and that cues like temporal ambiguity and tarantella style have less. In sum, his treatment of pastoral cues resembles Allanbrook's summary of Baroque dances in that both display a design that is mostly polythetic while still showing a preference for some cues more than others.

Throughout this book, I use Barsalou's conception of frame in order to provide a conceptual and visual basis for understanding how musical works can challenge the conventional notion of membership in a group—in this case, a musical topic. The concept of a frame helps explain how a piece can stretch the limits of topical identity and yet still be considered an example of that topical category. Barsalou's frame is also useful as a means of displaying characteristics of multiple topics, such as the pastoral and the lament. Creating a customized frame is the first step in explaining the range of meanings when two topics either intersect or conflict with one another.

Conclusion

Interpreting Griffes's various pastoral cues is like looking through a musical kaleidoscope in which some colors occur more often—the most common pairs or individual attributes—and other colors less often. In the pages that follow, my goal is to show that in each of the twelve works under consideration the pastoral cues interact with one another, sometimes in cooperation, other times in conflict, and that in each work they create a unique pastoral physiognomy. In this respect, I am taking to heart Zbikowski's own admonition about the inherent limitations of analytical approaches based strictly on the identification of dance topics. In a recent article devoted to the bourée of the *ancien régime* and its influence on later instrumental and vocal music, he observes,[114] "These last examples would seem to suggest that labels for different dance topics that some analysts have applied to music of the eighteenth century are less important than offering a careful account of the rhythmic and melodic features of the musical materials that a composer deploys, especially where the compositional strategies behind these materials seem to contrast with each other in marked ways." My strategy is to adopt a similar microscopic approach to music of the early twentieth century, but also to expand its parameters to include harmony, texture, dynamics, and form in addition to rhythm and melody. In the following chapter, I unveil a customized pastoral catalogue that explains in depth all of Griffes's musical cues and sets the stage for understanding his ambivalent vision of the pastoral in America during the early twentieth century.[115]

NOTES

1. Griffes composed a number of vocal settings of pastoral poems that I do not discuss, including "We'll to the Woods and Gather May" as well as his four settings of Wilde's poetry entitled *Four Impressions*. Examples of songs that are clearly not pastorals include "Cleopatra to the Asp," "Phantoms," "Song of the Dagger," and "War Song of the Vikings." For a complete list of Griffes's compositions, see Anderson, *Charles T. Griffes*, Appendix A.

2. The reason for the term *ontology* is that by raising questions about the usual constraints of a logical category—that is, necessary and jointly sufficient conditions—I also introduce questions about the ontological status of a musical work.

3. John Deely argues that the first thinker to propose that the study and interpretation of signs could be a separate "branch of inquiry" was the British Empiricist John Locke in his *Essay Concerning Human Understanding* (1689). See John Deely, *Why Semiotics?* (Brooklyn, NY: Legas, 2004), 11, 26.

4. Ferdinand de Saussure, *Cours de linguistique générale*, compiled by Charles Bally and Albert Sechehaye (Paris: Payot, 1962).

5. Other central dichotomies in his thought include: (a) synchronic (viewed at a single point in time) versus diachronic (viewed and compared at different points in time); and (b) syntagmatic (the relation between units within an utterance) versus paradigmatic (the relation between any single unit in an utterance and other substitute units for it based on association). For a detailed synopsis of this dichotomy, see Daniel Chandler, *Semiotics: The Basics*, 3rd ed. (Abingdon, UK: Routledge: 2017).

6. In order to distinguish his theories from those of James and Dewey, Peirce dubbed his approach as "pragmaticism." In addition, he referred to his theory of signs as "semeiotic." See Robert Burch, "Charles Sanders Peirce," *The Stanford Encyclopedia of Philosophy* (Summer 2022 Edition), Edward N. Zalta, ed., accessed June 22, 2022, https://plato .stanford.edu/archives/sum2022/entries/peirce.

7. Charles Sanders Peirce, *Collected Papers of Charles Sanders Peirce*, ed. Charles Hartshorne, Paul Weiss, and Arthur W. Burks, 8 vol. (Cambridge, MA: Belknap, 1931–66),

5:253–265 and 2:228. The former is referenced in Naomi Cumming, *The Sonic Self: Musical Subjectivity and Signification* (Bloomington: Indiana University Press, 2001), 60.

8. Technically, an interpretant is not limited to the individual who interprets but rather is the rule or habit of insight or relation by which the representaman is understood to stand as a sign for the object. The interpretant itself is a sign that leads to another act of interpretation—a fact that some have argued results in an infinite regression of interpretants. Also, Monelle argues that Peirce would define a musical work as a "rhematic indexical legisign" and the actual performance or a copy of the score as a "rhematic indexical sinsign." See Raymond Monelle, *Linguistics and Semiotics in Music* (Chur, Switzerland: Harwood Academic Publishers, 1992), 219.

9. For detailed accounts of these three stages, see Cumming, *The Sonic Self*; and Chandler, *Semiotics*.

10. David Lidov, *Elements of Semiotics* (New York: St. Martin's, 1999), 190–91.

11. Cumming, *The Sonic Self*, 104.

12. For example, Colapietro proposes an alternative triad of human knowledge: tacitly familiar, abstract definition, and pragmatic clarification. See "The Historical Past and the Dramatic Present: Toward a Pragmatic Clarification of Historical Consciousness," *European Journal of Pragmatism and American Philosophy* 8, no. 2 (2016), https://doi.org/10.4000/ejpap.627; and "The Pragmatic Spiral," *Relational Hermeneutics: Essays in Comparative Philosophy*, ed. Paul Fairfield and Saulius Geniusas (New York: Bloomsbury Academic, 2018).

13. See René Descartes, *Meditations on First Philosophy, with Selections from the Objections and Replies*, ed. John Cottingham, rev. edition (Cambridge, UK: Cambridge University Press, 1996).

14. See Alexander Miller, "Realism," *The Stanford Encyclopedia of Philosophy* (Winter 2019 Edition), ed. Edward N. Zalta, https://plato.stanford.edu/archives/win2019/entries/realism.

15. David Lidov, *Is Language a Music?: Writings on Musical Form and Signification* (Bloomington: Indiana University Press, 2005), 122.

16. Algirdas Julien Greimas and Jacques Fontanille, *The Semiotics of Passions: From States of Affairs to States of Feelings*, trans. Paul Perron and Paolo Fabbri (Minneapolis: University of Minnesota Press, 1993), xvii.

17. Peirce, *Collected Papers*, 5:172.

18. Vincent Colapietro, "Toward a Truly Pragmatic Theory of Signs: Reading Peirce's Semeiotic in Light of Dewey's Gloss," in *Peirce, Semiotics and Psychoanalysis*, ed. John Muller and Joseph Brent (Baltimore, MD and London: Johns Hopkins University Press, 2004).

19. Patrick McCreless, "Semiotics and Music: An End-of-Century Overview," *Musikkonzepte-Konzepte der Musik, Bericht über den internationalen Kongress für Musikforschung Halle (Saale) 1998* 1 (2000): 38.

20. Ibid.

21. See David Savan, *An Introduction to C. S. Peirce's Full System of Semeiotic* (Toronto: Toronto Semiotic Circle, 1988); and James Liszka, *A General Introduction to the Semeiotic of Charles S. Peirce* (Bloomington: Indiana University Press, 1996).

22. Stephen Rumph meticulously retraces the different stages in the development of Ratner's ideas about eighteenth-century composers' technique and listeners' sensibility. See *Mozart and Enlightenment Semiotics* (Berkeley: University of California Press, 2012).

23. Leonard G. Ratner, *Classic Music: Expression, Form, and Style* (New York: Schirmer, 1980).

24. For example, in his overview of Mozart's *Don Giovanni*, Ratner explores such issues as dramatic character expressed through dance types, symmetry of plot, and key associations based on contextual grounds rather than innate properties; see ibid., 397–411.

25. Kofi Agawu proposes that topical analysis should be incorporated into "a prior level of structure that is independent of topic. . . . Topics are always already auxiliary in application." "Topics and Form in Mozart's String Quintet in E Flat Major, K. 614/i," *The Oxford Handbook of Topic Theory*, ed. Danuta Mirka (Oxford, UK: Oxford University Press, 2014), 474.

26. Ratner, *Classic Music*, 9–27.

27. Kofi Agawu, *Playing with Signs: A Semiotic Interpretation of Classic Music* (Princeton, NJ: Princeton University Press, 1991), 30; and *Music as Discourse: Semiotic Adventures in Romantic Music* (Oxford, UK: Oxford University Press, 2009), 43–44.

28. Ratner concludes, "The topics themselves are drawn from various parts of the thesaurus—scoring, melodic styles and figures, characteristic bass progressions, and ornamentation." "Topical Content in Mozart's Keyboard Sonatas," *Early Music* 19, no. 4 (1991): 616.

29. In his article "Topics in Chamber Music," W. Dean Sutcliffe explains that a musical topic can encompass "a social dance, a ceremonial fanfare, or music for worship . . . [that is] then lifted out of that context. Thus a keyboard instrument can play a horn call or a string quartet can evoke sacred polyphony." See *The Oxford Handbook of Topic Theory*, 118. Danuta Mirka makes the same claim in her introduction; see *The Oxford Handbook of Topic Theory*, 2.

30. Raymond Monelle, *Linguistics and Semiotics in Music* (Abingdon, UK: Routledge, 1992); Nicholas McKay, "On Topics Today," *Zeitschrift der Gesellschaft für Musiktheorie* 4, no. 1 (2007); and Kofi Agawu, "Topic Theory: Achievement, Critique, Prospects" in *Passagen, IMS Kongress Zürich 2007: Fünf Hauptvorträge, Five Key Note Speeches*, ed. Laurenz Lütteken and Hans-Joachim Hinrichsen (Kassel: Bärenreiter, 2008). It is worth noting that the overarching themes in the history of music semiotics encompass systematic theories, close exegesis of historical sources, cultural histories of individual topics, broad philosophical meditations, and explorations of the limits of syntax in topical succession.

31. In his review of *The Oxford Handbook of Topic Theory*, Mark Ferraguto describes the lack of theoretical rigor as follows: "Indeed, the white whale—a concise, coherent theory of topical analysis—is not to be found in these waters. But there are other riches here. Drawing together music theorists, musicologists, and performers, this massive volume not only deftly historicizes the topical endeavour, but also foregrounds its interpretative potential through stimulating analyses and situated reflections." See "Review of *The Oxford Handbook of Topic Theory*," ed. Danuta Mirka, *Music and Letters* 96, no. 3 (2015): 473.

32. Leonard Ratner, *Romantic Music: Sound and Syntax* (New York: Schirmer Music, 1992).

33. See Janice Dickensheets, "Nineteenth-Century Topical Analysis: A Lexicon of Romantic Topoi," *Pendragon Review* 2, no. 1 (2003): 5–19; and "The Topical Vocabulary of the Nineteenth Century," *Journal of Musicological Research* 31, no. 2–3 (2012): 97–137.

34. Monelle echoes the same complaint against the lexical approach: "It is, perhaps, ill-advised to strive for a comprehensive dictionary of topics . . . because new topics

continually emerge from analysis." *The Musical Topic: Hunt, Military and Pastoral* (Bloomington: Indiana University Press, 2006), 7.

35. Márta Grabócz, *Morphologie des œuvres pour piano de Liszt: Influence du programme dur l'évolution des formes instrumentales* (Paris: Editions Kimé, 1986); Eero Tarasti, *Myth and Music: A Semiotic Approach to the Aesthetics of Myth in Music, Especially That of Wagner, Sibelius and Stravinsky* (The Hague: Mouton, 1979).

36. Keith T. Jones, *The Symphonic Poems of Franz Liszt* (Stuyvesant, NJ: Pendragon, 1997).

37. Julian Horton argues that the range of psychological meanings that the military topic signified in previous generations of listeners differs dramatically from its psychological significance today, which undermines the continuity that a musical topic is assumed to have. See "Listening to Topics in the Nineteenth Century," in *The Oxford Handbook of Topic Theory*, ed. Danuta Mirka (Oxford: Oxford University Press, 2014), 642–64.

38. Lawrence M. Zbikowski, "Music, Dance and Meaning in the Early Nineteenth Century," *Journal of Musicological Research* 31, no. 2–3 (2012): 164.

39. Ibid., 165.

40. Agawu, *Playing with Signs*, 137.

41. Agawu, *Music as Discourse*, 42–43.

42. Hatten, *Musical Meaning in Beethoven: Markedness, Correlation, and Interpretation* (Bloomington: Indiana University Press, 1994).

43. Ibid., 6. Hatten's use of the term *markedness* also deserves mention. It is a type of linguistic opposition in which one term has a broader, more generic referent, the other term a more limited one. In that respect, the two terms are asymmetrical. While acknowledging the critical value of this insight, I do not place it at the center of my theoretical project.

44. "Trope, v.," *Oxford English Dictionary*, accessed August 20, 2023 https://www.oed.com/dictionary/trope_n?tab=etymology#17639554.

45. Hatten, *Musical Meaning in Beethoven*, 166–70.

46. Robert Hatten, *Interpreting Musical Gestures, Topics, and Tropes: Mozart, Beethoven, Schubert* (Bloomington: Indiana University Press, 2004).

47. Robert Hatten, "The Troping of Topics in Mozart's Instrumental Music," in *The Oxford Handbook of Topical Theory*, ed. Danuta Mirka (Oxford, UK: Oxford University Press, 2014), 514–36.

48. In his most recent formulation, Hatten defines it as follows: "A topic is a *familiar style type with easily recognizable musical features* [italics his], ranging in complexity from a simple figure (fanfare, horn call), to a texture (learned style as polyphonic and/or imitative; chorale or hymn style as homophonic), a complete genre (various dance and march types; French overture), a style (*ombra, tempesta, Empfindsamkeit*), or some overlap of these categories." See ibid., 515.

49. Monelle, *The Musical Topic*, 185.

50. My fourfold classification is inspired by the approaches adopted in the following studies: Terry Gifford, *Pastoral* (London and New York: Routledge, 1999); "Introduction," in *The Pastoral Mode: A Casebook*, ed. Bryan Loughery (London: Macmillan, 1984); and Peter V. Marinelli, *Pastoral*, The Critical Idiom Series, No. 15 (London: Methuen and Co, 1971).

51. Loughery, *The Pastoral Mode: A Casebook*, 8.

52. See Theocritus, Idyll X, quoted in Gifford, *Pastoral*, 17.

53. Monelle, *The Musical Topic*, 186. Annabel Patterson even goes so far as to label this subtype "soft pastoralism." See *Pastoral and Ideology: Virgil to Valéry* (Berkeley: University of California Press, 1987), 279.

54. Examples of the realistic type include William Wordsworth's poem "Michael" (1800) and Matthew Arnold's "Dover Beach" (1867). It should be mentioned that Gifford interprets the latter poem as an instance of the "anti-pastoral"; see Gifford, *Pastoral*, 116–20.

55. Gifford includes a wide range of authors in this subtype, including Ted Hughes and David Craig as well as Heathcote Williams's recent poetry in which wild whales and dolphins have replaced domesticated sheep. See Heathcote Williams, *Falling for a Dolphin* (London: Jonathan Cape, 1988); cited in Gifford, *Pastoral*, 172.

56. William Empson, *Some Versions of Pastoral* (London: Chatto and Windus, 1935).

57. Paul Alpers, *What Is Pastoral?* (Chicago: University of Chicago Press, 1996).

58. Harold E. Toliver, *Pastoral Forms and Attitudes* (Berkeley: University of California Press, 1971), 1.

59. Toliver argues that "lyrics, odes, elegies, romances, and novels and epics with pastoral elements handle that tension [between the golden age and the normative world] quite differently, and every period interprets and reconstitutes them in its own ways." Ibid., 5.

60. Patterson, *Pastoral and Ideology.*

61. Ibid., 1–17.

62. Monelle, *The Musical Topic*, 185–228.

63. The following synopsis of the musical pastoral is based on two exhaustive surveys: Monelle, *The Musical Topic* and Geoffrey Chew, "Pastoral," *Grove Music Online* https://doi.org/10.1093/gmo/9781561592630.article.40091; In his article Chew adopts a similar dialogical approach, but without acknowledging his philosophical sources: "Pastoral depends upon the projection of a philosophical opposition, generally one between art and nature or between country and city."

64. Jeffrey Hopes, "The Sound of Early Eighteenth-Century Opera: Handel, Pope, Gay, and Hughes," *Revue Electronique d'Etudes sur le Monde Anglophone* 14, no. 2 (2017), https://doi.org/10.4000/erea.5741.

65. Monelle, *The Musical Topic*, 243.

66. Reinhold Brinkmann, *Late Idyll: The Second Symphony of Johannes Brahms*, Eng. trans. Peter Palmer (Cambridge, MA: Harvard University Press, 1995). His method of interpretation combines history and analysis: exegesis of a single work, Symphony No. 2 in D major, Op. 73; exhaustive study of archival resources, including a telling letter Brahms wrote about the symphony; and the author's magisterial view of the late Romantic period.

67. Ibid., 142.

68. Ibid., 200.

69. Frymoyer, "The Musical Topic in the Twentieth Century," 83–108. Also, in an unpublished paper she explored the pastoral topic in detail: "The Morphology of Musical Topoi: Topical Analysis and Stylistic Growth in Twentieth-Century Music," Joint American Musicological Society and Society for Music Theory Annual Meeting, Indianapolis, Indiana, November 4, 2010.

70. See Eric Saylor, *English Pastoral Music: From Arcadia to Utopia, 1900–1955* (Urbana: University of Illinois Press, 2017).

71. Ralph P. Locke, *Musical Exoticism: Images and Reflections* (Cambridge, UK: Cambridge University Press, 2009), 177.

72. Edward W. Said, *Orientalism* (New York: Vintage, 1978).

73. Jonathan Bellman, "Musical Voyages and Their Baggage," *Musical Quarterly* 94, no. 3 (Fall 2011): 417.

74. Jonathan Bellman, "Introduction," in *The Exotic in Western Music*, ed. Jonathan Bellman (Boston, MA: Northeastern University Press, 1998), xi.

75. The bibliography of recent scholarship devoted to the interface between Western and non-Western musical traditions is considerable and still growing. A representative example is Georgina Born and David Hesmondhalgh, eds., *Western Music and Its Others: Difference, Representation, and Appropriation in Music* (Berkeley: University of California Press, 2000).

76. Susan McClary, Review of Charles Rosen, *The Romantic Generation* (Cambridge, MA: Harvard University Press, 1995), in *Notes, Quarterly Journal of the Music Library Association* 52, no. 4 (June 1996): 1142.

77. Matthew Head, "Musicology on Safari: Orientalism and the Spectre of Postcolonial Theory," *Music Analysis* 22, no. 1–2 (March–July 2003): 211, 216.

78. Andrew Chung, Review Essay: "Music Theory Splintered Up, Not Broken Down," *Music Theory Spectrum* 44, no. 1 (Spring 2022): 175.

79. Bellman, "Musical Voyages," 420.

80. Ibid., 422.

81. Gilles de Van, "Fin de Siecle Exoticism and the Meaning of the Far Away," *Opera Quarterly* 11, no. 3 (1995): 77–94.

82. Derek B. Scott, "Orientalism and Musical Style," *Musical Quarterly* 82, no. 2 (1998): 309–35; reprinted in *From the Erotic to the Demonic: On Critical Musicology* (Oxford, UK: Oxford University Press, 2003).

83. See figure 3.1 in Locke, *Musical Exoticism*, 51–54.

84. Ibid., 217. Locke's central claim in this book is to broaden the criteria that interpreters use to identify musical exoticism. After exploring the traditional paradigm, which he calls the "Exotic Style Only," he suggests a more inclusive approach, which he dubs the "All the Music in Full Context" paradigm; see ibid., 48–65.

85. Hatten, *Musical Meaning in Beethoven*, 163, 295; Frymoyer, "The Musical Topic in the Twentieth Century," 83.

86. Ludwig Wittgenstein, *Philosophical Investigations*, 3rd edition, Eng. trans. G. E. M. Anscombe (Oxford, UK: Blackwell, 2001), 27.

87. Ibid., 28.

88. See Edward L. Zalta, ed., *The Stanford Encyclopedia of Philosophy*, s.v. "Ludwig Wittgenstein," accessed September 15, 2017, https://plato.stanford.edu/entries/wittgenstein/.

89. Noël Carroll, "Introduction," in *Theories of Art Today*, ed. Noël Carroll (Madison: University of Wisconsin, 2000), 3–24.

90. Morris Weitz, "The Role of Theory in Aesthetics," *The Journal of Aesthetics and Art Criticism* 15, no. 1 (September 1956): 30.

91. Ibid., 33.

92. Lydia Goehr, *The Imaginary Museum of Musical Works: An Essay in the Philosophy of Music*, rev. edition. (Oxford, UK: Oxford University Press, 2007); Friedrich Nietzsche, *Basic Writings of Nietzsche*, trans. and ed. W. Kaufmann (New York: Modern Library, 1968); and Friedrich Waismann, "Verifiability," *Proceedings of the Aristotelian Society*, Supplementary Volume 19 (1945): 119–50.

93. Goehr posits a fourth characteristic involving the concept of "vagueness," which is not relevant to my project. She writes that open concepts are "distinct from, though related to, vague concepts. According to Waismann a concept is vague if there are cases in which there is no definite answer whether the term applies ('Pink,' 'tall,' 'bald,' and 'middle-aged' are examples.)," Goehr, *The Imaginary Museum*, 91–92.

94. Weitz, "The Role of Theory in Aesthetics," 31.

95. Ibid.

96. Goehr, *The Imaginary Museum*, 40.

97. See Rodney Needham, "Polythetic Classification: Convergence and Consequences," *Man*, New Series 10, no. 3 (September 1975): 349–69; J. A. Silk, "What, If Anything, Is Mahayana Buddhism? Problems of Definitions and Classifications," *Numen-International Review for the History of Religions* 49, no. 5 (2002): 355–405; and Josef Parnas, "Differential Diagnosis and Current Polythetic Classification," *World Psychiatry* 14, no. 3 (2015): 284–87.

98. Sokal, Robert R., and Peter H. A. Sneath. *Principles of Numerical Taxonomy* (San Francisco & London: W. H. Freeman, 1963), 14. Quoted in Rodney Needham, "Polythetic Classification: Convergence and Consequences," *Man*, New Series 10, no. 3 (September 1975): 356.

99. Eleanor Rosch, Carolyn B. Mervis, Wayne D. Gray, David M. Johnson, and Penny Boyes-Braem, "Basic Objects in Natural Categories," *Cognitive Psychology* 8 (1976): 382–439; and Eleanor Rosch, "Principles of Categorization," in *Cognition and Categorization*, ed. Eleanor Rosch and Barbara B. Lloyd (Hillsdale, NJ: Erlbaum Associates, 1978), 27–48.

100. Ibid., 31.

101. A partial list of Zbikowski's recent articles includes "Dance Topoi, Sonic Analogues, and Musical Grammar" in *Communication in Eighteenth-Century Music*, ed. Kofi Agawu and Danuta Mirka (Cambridge, UK: Cambridge University Press, 2008), 283–309; and "Music, Emotion, Analysis," *Music Analysis* 29 (2011): 37–59.

102. Lawrence M. Zbikowski, *Conceptualizing Music: Cognitive Structure, Theory, and Analysis* (Oxford, UK: Oxford University Press, 2002).

103. For a detailed illustration of a frame, see ibid., 41–42.

104. Justin London, Review of Lawrence M. Zbikowski, *Conceptualizing Music: Cognitive Structure, Theory, and Analysis* in *Music Theory Spectrum* 29, no. 1 (Spring 2007): 117.

105. Zbikowski, *Conceptualizing Music*, 41–49.

106. Rudolf Seising, "Lotfi Zadeh: Fuzzy Sets and Systems," *Computer Aided Systems Theory—EUROCAST 2019*, vol. 12013: 101. Also, see Lotfi A. Zadeh, "Fuzzy Sets," *Information and Control* 8 (1965): 338–53.

107. Wye Jamison Allanbrook, *Rhythmic Gesture in Mozart: Le Nozze di Figaro and Don Giovanni* (Chicago: The University of Chicago Press, 1983).

108. These four subtypes are the ordinary gigue, loure, canarie, and giga.

109. Allanbrook, *Rhythmic Gesture*, 41–43. Her primary source for this pastoral quadripdych is Johann Mattheson's treatise *Der vollkommene Kapellmeister*.

110. Monelle, *The Musical Topic*, 215.

111. Ibid., 43.

112. Allanbrook, *Rhythmic Gesture*, 53.

113. Ratner, *Classic Music*, 21.

114. Lawrence M. Zbikowski, "Music and Dance in the *Ancien Régime*," in *The Oxford Handbook of Topic Theory*, ed. Danuta Mirka (Oxford, UK: Oxford University Press, 2014), 161.

115. Zbikowski offers a highly suggestive analogy for my conception of the pastoral category in his comprehensive study of the eighteenth-century *bourée*. He argues that the social and cultural functions of late eighteenth-century dance music could be arranged as three points along a continuum: (1) entire works explicitly designed for dancing; (2) passages of dance types within larger works; and finally (3) passages within larger works that employ rhythmic figurations of dance types "but whose meaning is largely dependent on the musical context within which they are embedded." His approach is highly suggestive in two respects: his notion of a continuum of functions underlines the absence of strictly defined categories, and his third function is contextually based, focusing on the particular combination of characteristics that constitute the musical complexion of an individual case, not on the identification of a general type. See ibid., 143–63.

3

Pastoral and Lament Cues

In this chapter, my aim is to investigate the musical ingredients or cues that appear in Griffes's pastorals and, thereby, provide a cross section of his treatment of this topic. My understanding of the pastoral is broader than a typical logical category in that it is based on a different philosophical foundation, which combines Wittgenstein's notion of family resemblance and Weitz's concept of openness (for more details, see chap. 2). Griffes's conception of the pastoral is open in two respects. The catalogue of cues includes those inherited from the eighteenth-century pastoral tradition such as a drone bass or dotted rhythm but also encompasses a subset of cues peculiar to Griffes—what I call *idiosyncratic*—such as cumulative counterpoint and registral expansion. In addition, some of his pastorals include elements of the lament topic such as the sigh motive and, occasionally, the descending chromatic bass line. Hence, his stylistic innovations include not only inventing his own pastoral characteristics but also borrowing elements from a different topic and, thereby, creating a new expressive synthesis. In order to appreciate Griffes's unusual pastoral taste, I will identify and describe in depth thirteen cues—eleven that signify the pastoral as well as two cues signifying the lament, each of which has its own historical, literary, and/or musical context. Taken together, these cues serve as a compositional palette that Griffes used to fashion a resplendent collection of pastoral canvases.

One may wonder how a list of pastoral cues differs from the copious topical lexicons developed by Agawu and Dickensheets about which I expressed reservations in chapter 2. The answer is that these lexicographical projects focus on a different level of the semiotic hierarchy than mine. To codify multiple topics that are shared by a generation of composers is entirely different from collecting and organizing multiple criteria that constitute an individual topic used by a single composer. While both projects involve defining and classifying groups, the purpose of assembling a list of specific cues is to broaden the category of a single topic, the pastoral, not to add more entries to the universe of strictly defined topics.

Let me begin with some initial observations about two topics that are central to this study: the pastoral and the lament. To begin with, if we rely on the ancient Greek literary models, then the two topical worlds clearly overlap in content. The emotions of grief, passion, and serenity all comingled together in the ancient pastoral mode; indeed, Theocritus's and Virgil's shepherds sang elegies about death almost as much as hymns to love. More important, at different junctures during the late Baroque and Classical periods, composers occasionally blended aspects of the lament with a pastoral dance such as the siciliano. Examples from Handel's operas include the arias "Son nata a lagrimar" from *Giulio Cesare* and "Se mi rivolgo al prato" from *Orlando*. Likewise, Mozart relied on the siciliano for some of his most melancholy slow movements such as the Andante movement from the Piano Concerto in A major, K. 488. Hence, there is potential for musical pastorals to acquire some emotional aspects of the lament, especially in the context of an appropriate dramatic or literary scenario.

The reason why the lament topic is not considered a strict subset of the pastoral is that, beginning in the early Baroque period, it developed into an independent musical tradition with its own characteristics, focusing on the expression of grief and loss. For example, it would be counterintuitive if a modern listener, critic, or performer described a Requiem mass as having an inherently pastoral character; likewise, to describe a recent instrumental or vocal piece as pastoral does not typically mean that the work evokes feelings of loss. Consequently, for the purposes of this study, I will treat the lament topic as an independent musical tradition that is characterized by either of two cues: the sigh figure (or *pianto*) and the descending bass tetrachord. Each of these will be discussed in depth below.

Another point of contrast between the two topics is that they are asymmetrical in scope. The musical pastoral is less a topic than what Hatten calls a "topical field," possessing a wide spectrum of emotional associations including serenity, spontaneity, nostalgia, and/or confessions of passion.[1] Conversely, the lament topic is more one-dimensional, possessing fewer musical cues and a more limited set of associations that often express grief due to unrequited love or death. One of Griffes's achievements was to expand the pastoral's emotional spectrum so as to include feelings such as aching lament, bacchanalian abandon, and deep spiritual longing.

In chapter 2, I investigated the question of whether a topic could be defined by alternative criteria—that is, something other than sufficient and necessary conditions. In this chapter, I will explore the scenario in which two topics recur in the same work and blend together to various degrees. In a recent article, Robert Hatten proposes four different axes to explain what he calls a "trope," the way one topic interacts with another topic as well as with its broader musical environment. One of his axes characterizes the relationship between two or more topics in terms of the "degree of dominance," which, in turn, depends on such issues as hierarchical weight, temporal order, and so forth.[2]

Instead of relying on his tetralogy of tropes, I propose the term *palimpsest* to denote the relationship between two or more topics that is defined in terms of a frontier with loose boundaries. For archaeologists, a palimpsest denotes a tablet or piece of parchment in ancient times on which layers of old and new messages were juxtaposed on top of one another. Reading a palimpsest, therefore, was an exercise in decoding messages written at different times and sometimes in different languages. For my purposes, a musical palimpsest is a passage or entire work in which multiple topics coexist without any predetermined hierarchy, which would be implied by such terms as *pastoral-lament* or a *lament-pastoral*. I prefer a concept in which elements from each type freely intermingle, the musical equivalent of a semipermeable membrane. Later in this chapter, I will explore a particular type of musical palimpsest, which I call cumulative counterpoint, in which the blending of elements coincides with a climax.

The palimpsest bears a strong resemblance to the *quodlibet* (a Latin phrase that means "whatever you wish"), in particular a subtype of this tradition in which multiple contrasting motives appear in the same texture.[3] However, there are two main differences between these two terms. First, a palimpsest refers to the combination of multiple musical topics, either in succession or as a simultaneity, that have predetermined psychological associations. It is not a question of quoting a single familiar work but rather of borrowing aspects of a familiar type of dance or style. Second, whereas the quodlibet is often associated with a playful or jovial tone, Griffes's use of layered textures is usually bereft of humor.[4]

Viewing Griffes's mature compositions as a whole, he clearly had a fascination with juxtaposing elements of the pastoral and lament topics together in a variety of musical contexts. The rest of this chapter is devoted to the specific cues associated with these topics either by exploring each cue's historical ties with previously established musical traditions or uncovering its connection to a new expressive tradition that began to emerge in Griffes's music. The final step in the hermeneutical process is a detailed analysis and commentary on the relationship between various pastoral cues within each work. Chapters 4–9 will be devoted to close readings of selected pastorals—both instrumental and vocal.

Finally, my reliance on a cognitive notion of "frame" is more than a mere metaphor of loose borders or vague boundaries. The evidence for the ambivalent pastoral consists of a set of examples that, while bearing some resemblances among each other, generally resist categorization and, hence, do not form a clearly defined group or family. A detailed study of the cues themselves will allow us to appreciate the pastoral physiognomy of each work in the collection.

Pastoral Cues

It will be useful to divide the pastoral cues into two groups: eighteenth-century cues, which symbolize Griffes's loyalty to previous pastoral traditions; and "idiosyncratic" cues, which represent his own unique musical style. As was shown in chapter 2, there is no single cue that appears in all twelve pastoral works, thereby uniting the collection as a whole. The end result is a nearly polythetic pattern of crisscrossing among the cues that resists the standard concept of a general type.

Eighteenth-Century Cues

Although there are many musical characteristics that are associated with pastoral dances, I will focus on only three:[5]

1. Meter: Compound duple or triple meter
2. Rhythm: Dotted rhythmic patterns
3. Harmony: Consonant Pedal (pitch, interval, or chord)

Many of Griffes's instrumental and vocal works pay homage to the eighteenth-century pastoral tradition. Even in the early twentieth century, such features as compound meter, dotted rhythms, and static harmony still possessed associations that could be traced back to older pastoral traditions. Let us briefly consider each one.

CUE #1: METER

The first cue involves meter. Griffes's pastorals, either within a section or over the entire piece, are often in compound duple, triple, or quadruple meter (e.g., 6/4, 6/8, 9/8, and 12/8). This tendency falls in line with the compound duple scheme of three of the four Baroque dances in Allanbrooks's survey; the only exception is the musette, which could be in either simple or compound duple (see chap. 2). Yet, as will be shown below, there are also pastorals among Griffes's mature works that are organized in other meters such as simple triple meter (e.g., 3/4) or occasionally irregular or changing meter. Consequently, meter alone is not a sufficient basis for determining a work's pastoral identity.

CUE #2: DOTTED RHYTHM

The next cue, also temporal in nature, consists of a recurring dotted rhythmic pattern that is usually organized by regular phrase grouping. This rhythmic profile is characteristic of at least two older dances: the siciliano and the gigue. In their compendiums, Allanbrook and Monelle provide numerous examples of sicilianos that employ such a rhythmic pattern.[6] The reason why this particular rhythm seems appropriate for depicting a pastoral lies not only in the repetition of the same durational pattern but also in its execution. By itself, a dotted rhythm might well evoke other emotions or associations far removed from the world of the pastoral such as a hero's bravado or a royal procession. The crucial elements are tempo and articulation. When a rhythmic pattern such as dotted eighth + sixteenth + eighth note is performed at a moderate tempo without any marcato or staccato articulation, there is an inclination to associate it with passive emotions such as peacefulness, languor, or even sadness. However, even though dotted rhythmic patterns appear in most of Griffes's pastorals (see the matrix of pastoral cues in chap. 2), it is difficult to establish a work's pastoral character solely on the basis of a single parameter—in this case, a melody's rhythmic durations.

CUE #3: CONSONANT PEDAL

The third cue traditionally associated with Baroque pastorals is derived from the characteristic sound of a family of folk instruments, or signifiers, such as the French musette, the Italian zampogna, and the hurdy-gurdy, which all generate a characteristic harmonic drone: either a pedal tone or a fixed interval such as a perfect fifth.[7] When a modern instrument or ensemble re-creates the drone beneath a melodic line, the resulting musical texture can be interpreted as an arrangement or adaptation of the typical sound from one of these folk instruments. The consonant pedal can be found in a number of Griffes's pastorals including the persistent drone fifth in his setting of "Tears" from the cycle *Songs of Ancient China and Japan*; the extended A♯–E♯ pedal in the *Poem for Flute and Piano*, Pio mosso section (mm. 116–31); and the tonic pedal in the opening and closing sections of "The Lake at Evening."

The frequency of all three cues in Griffes's works, whether alone or in combination, confirms the link between his experimental style and the musical pastoral tradition that stretches back into the eighteenth century.

In the following pages, we shall witness the degree to which he departed from that tradition and charted his own path through pastoral territory.

Idiosyncratic Pastoral Cues

The second list of cues is idiosyncratic in that it represents what is distinctive about Griffes's pastoral personality.

4. Dissonant Pedal: Interval or Chord
5. Rhythmic/Metric Ambiguity
6. Languid Style
7. Tarantella Style
8. Cumulative Counterpoint
9. Registral Expansion
10. Sacred Chorale Style
11. Alternative Scales

As a group, the idiosyncratic cues have a wide emotional scope, ranging from calm languor to wild frenzy. The first two are similar in that they both involve some form of ambiguity, either harmonic or rhythmic. Cues 6, 7, and 10 are designated as styles in that they are characterized by a distinctive approach to either tempo, texture, rhythm, melody, or dynamics. The following two cues are process-based, for each one participates in a given work's overall formal design. As a result, cues 8 and 9 highlight the difference between a local synchronic feature and a more encompassing diachronic process. In his book *Elements of Semiotics*, David Lidov generalizes this type of phenomenon across multiple artistic media (including music and the visual arts), dubbing them "processive signs."[8] The last cue refers to the use of alternative scales such as the pentatonic, whole tone, octatonic, and hexatonic types as well as the gamut of non-Western musical traditions they often signify. Because these collections have a broad range of potential associations, this cue is more open-ended than other entries in the list.

Finally, it should also be emphasized that each cue in this subset is not intrinsically pastoral in character. Instead, its pastoral identity is usually determined by the presence of other cues with more traditional associations in the same work such as a consonant pedal point or dotted rhythmic patterns. Ultimately, the pastoral profile of a given work could be likened to a mosaic in which traditional and idiosyncratic cues blend together, creating a unique pattern.

CUE #4: DISSONANT PEDAL: INTERVAL OR CHORD

In some of Griffes's pastorals, his treatment of harmony consists of the repetition of a dissonant sonority used either as a continuous ostinato or as a harmonic prolongation in the bass. The typical emotions associated with a dissonant pedal can vary, ranging from sensual pleasure and uncertainty (will the harmonic dissonance ever resolve?) to mystery. But it is safe to say that a common thread running through all instances of this cue is a feeling of ambiguity. To be sure, Griffes's use of static dissonant harmony is hardly revolutionary—previous nineteenth-century composers like Brahms had already exploited this feature to great effect.[9] What is unusual is his use of extended harmonic dissonance in the context of a pastoral.

An excellent illustration of this type of ambiguity occurs in "The Vale of Dreams," where a recurring ostinato chord, V4/2, permeates the initial and final sections. The listener becomes so mesmerized by the harmonic pedal that its dissonant quality gradually recedes. Other examples include a V9 chord that serves as a half cadence in the opening and closing sections of "The White Peacock," the tritone pedal in the prelude and postlude of *The Pleasure-Dome of Kubla Khan*, and the dissonant trichord in the opening section of Prelude #3. Each of these passages will be discussed in part II.

CUE #5: RHYTHMIC/METRIC AMBIGUITY

When the treatment of a single parameter such as rhythm presents two equally compelling interpretations, then it signifies a form of rhythmic/ metric ambiguity. There are two subtypes: polymeter created by the conflict between contrasting rhythmic *ostinati* sounding at the same time; and a confusion in grouping that leads to a conflict between the written and heard meter. While it is difficult to assign a specific emotional character to each of these subtypes, both contribute an element of rhythmic richness and unpredictability to Griffes's overall pastoral palette. Each one deserves a brief explanation.

The first subtype consists of the repetition of independent rhythmic and, sometimes, pitch patterns (or *ostinati*) in different voices of a texture; another term for this phenomenon is *extended hemiola*. A clear example of this type of rhythmic texture occurs at the beginning of "The Lake at Evening," where the bass repeats the pattern of two sixteenths + eighth as a pedal point on "A," thereby implying a 2/4 meter. By contrast, the upper part presents a melodic line that conforms to the notated 3/4 meter. Thus, the texture as a whole constitutes a hemiola or two voices implying conflicting meters (see ex. 8.1, chap. 8). A more complex illustration of this subtype of ambiguity occurs in the opening bars of the orchestral version of *The Pleasure-Dome of Kubla Khan* (mm. 7–14), where two separate musical layers with highly contrasting rhythms and implied meters are juxtaposed at the same time (see ex. 5.1, chap. 5). A similar example of metric/rhythmic ambiguity appears in the opening section of Griffes's "Nightfall," the second movement of *Roman Sketches*, Op. 7.

The second subtype of temporal ambiguity consists of a musical line that, due to a repeated rhythmic and pitch pattern, implies an alternative meter that conflicts with the notated meter. A clear example appears in "The White Peacock" in mm. 7–14, where Griffes introduces a lilting melodic theme with strong pastoral associations. This line consists of four statements of the same dotted rhythm arranged in two downward shapes (see ex. 4.2, chap. 4). However, the metric alignment of this melodic line is displaced. Even though the first pitch of this line arrives on beat five of the bar, the ascending flourish and slight crescendo on the immediately preceding beat gives it greater emphasis. Thus, although the $G\sharp_5$ is notated as an upbeat, it sounds like a downbeat. The ambiguity is metric in that the notated 5/4 time signature conflicts with the sounding 6/4 meter implied by the repeating rhythmic pattern, the treatment of dynamics, and the implied phrase structure.

CUE #6: LANGUID STYLE

The next two cues illustrate the idiosyncratic nature of Griffe's approach to the musical pastoral. The languid style grows out of his own performance directions, as he used the terms *languido* and *languidamente* in only a handful of works. Considering how seldom the term *languid* appears in nineteenth- and early twentieth-century scores, it is reasonable to speculate that examples by previous composers may have cast a historical shadow over Griffes, especially considering that he was aware of most of them. A partial list is below:

- Chopin, Frédéric, Nocturne in G minor, Op. 15/3: "languido e rubato" (1834)
- Wagner, Richard, *Tristan und Isolde*, Prelude: "schmachtend" (1865)
- Debussy, Claude, *Ariettes oubliées*, "C'est l'extase langoureuse" (1887)
- Scriabin, Alexander, Piano Sonata No. 9 ("Black Mass"), Op. 68: "avec une langueur naissante" (1913)
- Scriabin, Piano Sonata No. 10, Op. 70: "avec un douce langueur de plus en plus éteinte" (1913)

Taken together, the pieces on this list trace a long, sensual thread through the nineteenth and early twentieth century, encompassing some of the leading Polish, German, French, and Russian composers. Chopin occupies the top of the list since, beginning with Griffes's years in Berlin, he frequently performed the Polish composer's music.[10] But it is no exaggeration to conclude that the Prelude to Wagner's *Tristan und Isolde* played a major role in this history. The conflicting emotions that fuel the entire music drama—the competing imperatives of chivalric loyalty and a romantic love that must be but cannot be—are all encapsulated in the opening bars. The next chapter in this history is the voluptuous poem by Paul Verlaine, written in 1872, "C'est l'extase langoureuse," and the sumptuous settings by Fauré and Debussy that it inspired. Griffes was a devoted reader of Verlaine as early as 1912, when he purchased a volume of the Frenchman's poetry for his library.[11] Finally, the new element that Scriabin contributed was his unique mix of spiritual rapture and mystical wonder. In his diaries from fall 1916, Griffes expressed an interest in the Russian composer's music, mentioning that he had heard a student performance of Scriabin's Piano Sonata No. 8 and that he himself had practiced Two Poems, Op. 63.[12]

In sum, while there is no stylistic link shared by all members of this stunning collection, these works share a common fascination with emotional indulgence as indicated by the marking *languid*. In addition, there is evidence that they had at least an indirect influence on Griffes's style since, aside from the Chopin nocturne, he owned scores for all of them.[13]

Next, we must consider what role musical languor plays in a handful of Griffes's works and, most important, what psychological associations these pieces have in common. When he writes either the term *languido* or *languidamente* at the beginning of a work, it takes the place of a tempo indication or exact metronome marking. In this context, the term denotes a freedom in choice of tempo and perhaps an invitation to experiment with rubato, agogic accentuation, as well as changes in articulation, color, and tone quality. When the term *languid* (or its equivalent) appears in the middle of a work, it denotes a change in the prevailing emotional tone, coinciding with a sudden contrast in tempo, texture, and dynamic level or a division in the work's formal design.

There are four representative examples of this cue that share the same marking: two instrumental tone poems and two songs:[14]

- "The White Peacock"
- *The Pleasure-Dome of Kubla Khan* (an internal section)
- "Symphony in Yellow"
- "Cleopatra to the Asp"

Let us briefly consider what aspects these passages have in common: (a) all four works employ a free, improvisatory style of performance at a moderate tempo—an analogous term would be *liberamente*; and (b) three of the four employ a recurring rhythmic motive, sometimes as a continuous ostinato, that highlights a sense of freedom and improvisation in the melodic line above it (see "The White Peacock," "Symphony in Yellow," and "Cleopatra to the Asp"). Griffes's treatment of scale and harmony among these excerpts, however, is too diverse to permit any generalizations.

Finally, we turn to the question of what emotional or psychological character is associated with the term *languid*. First of all, there is a slight overlap in the associations with this marking and those of the traditional siciliano. What distinguishes Griffes's use of the term is the musical evocation of sensuality, not merely the simple or rustic life. These passages all suggest a sense of hedonism and timelessness and a desire for sensual pleasure. In the case of *The Pleasure-Dome*, the passage with this marking is evocative of the paradoxes of exoticism, the freedom from moral constraints, the ideal vision of a foreign land that ends up reflecting one's own country, and the ideal vision of the Other that also reflects the Self (see chap. 5).

This brief commentary on languor in Griffes's works illustrates that, to a limited extent, this cue relies on a historical foundation. Since the *languid* marking was used so rarely by previous composers, a given passage by Griffes that employs this marking also contains distant echoes of previous instances of musical languor. Ultimately, the justification for a distinct referent for this cue depends primarily on an empirical basis within Griffes's own oeuvre. Although there are only four scores that have the *languido* or *languidamente* marking, there are a number of other pieces marked *sognando* or *tranquillo* that share a similar emotional character. Any given work that contains a variant of the word *languid* shares a psychological kinship with other works that have the same marking—in short, a collective sense of languor. For example, when one hears a given passage from his song "Symphony in Yellow," it resonates with the sensual associations of his work for solo piano "The White Peacock." In sum, the sense of languor is essential to the psychological character of a subset of Griffes's experimental pastorals.

CUE #7: TARANTELLA STYLE

The tarantella style serves as the antipode of the languid style, and it appears in only two pastoral works: *The Pleasure-Dome of Kubla Kahn* and the Scherzo, *Fantasy Pieces*, Op. 6, no. 3. The source of inspiration for Griffes's tarantella style is an Italian folk dance by the same name that is associated with a tradition of abandon. This dance, most likely named after a city in southern Italy, Taranta, was usually a fast 6/8, performed by couples and conceived as a miming of courtship. There is a persistent legend that the name derives not from a city but from a spider, the tarantula.[15] The intensity of the dance was said to be a choreographic treatment to purge the spider's poison from a dancer's body. But whether the etymology of the tarantella is Italian or arachnidian, the association of a quick and repetitive dance in 6/8 with wild frenzy is still the same.

This Italian dance overlaps with another tradition of musical abandon: the bacchanal. The reason it is appropriate to use the term *bacchanalian* to refer to these works is biographical, for the composer himself used the word *Bacchanale* when he renamed the Scherzo and transcribed it for orchestra.[16]

The basic characteristics of the bacchanalian impulse expressed in music consist of a repeated rhythmic pattern and an increase in tempo combined with a climax in dynamics. If viewed in isolation, this treatment of rhythm, tempo, and dynamics is so widespread that it hardly deserves to be called a style. But in two of Griffes's pastorals, the confluence of these two parameters with motivic repetition becomes integrally connected to a large-scale formal design. The bacchanalian impulse also shares a similar character with another nineteenth-century topic, *stile appassionato*, as demonstrated in instrumental works by Beethoven and Schubert. The *appassionato* marking appears in slow tempos (e.g., lento, adagio) as well as faster markings (e.g., allegro). Both can be characterized by a gradual swelling of dynamics and increase in tempo, leading to a climax.

The psychological emotions associated with such an increase in tempo, rhythmic activity, and dynamics are varied, including freedom, intense desire, and even violent aggression. In this connection, Deborah Mawer proposes a striking analogy between the repetitive element of rhythmic ostinati and the repeating action of physical machines in the music of Ravel.[17]

This cue raises a historical question: to what earlier works with bacchanalian associations do the two Griffes pastorals refer? The etymology of the term can be traced back to the ancient Greek cult of Dionysus (or Bacchus in ancient Rome), where his followers were called *bachae* or *bacchantes*. However, there is no record of what music was played at the Dionysiac (or Bacchic) festivals. Another source of confusion is Dionysus himself, a mysterious divinity who was born twice and who symbolized four different attributes: not only the traditional association with wine and intoxication but also ritual ecstasy or madness, the world of the theater, and the mysterious realm of the dead.[18] Perhaps Griffes's propensity for ambiguity and paradox is less a commentary on late eighteenth-century aesthetic values than on those of the distant past in ancient Greece.

If one wonders how European composers before Griffes depicted the ideal of a musical bacchanal, there are a handful of historical precedents drawn from the nineteenth and early twentieth centuries:

- Wagner, Richard, *Tannhäuser* (Paris Version), Act I, Scene i, "Der Venusberg" (1862)
- Saint-Saëns, Camille, *Samson et Dalila,* Act III, "Bacchanale," (1877)
- Debussy, Claude, Premiere Suite d'orchestre, Piano Four-Hand Version: Movement 4, Bacchanale (1884)
- Glazunov, Alexander, "Autumn-Bacchanale," *The Seasons*, Op. 67, Tableau 4 (1899)
- Ravel, Maurice, *Daphnis et Chloé*, Suite No. 2, Scene iii, Bacchanale (1912)

Yet, a close examination of this list reveals that there are few common stylistic elements among its entries other than quick tempi and loud dynamics.

It should be emphasized that the tarantella style is not intrinsically pastoral in nature—that is, it does not constitute an independent cue denoting a pastoral mood or emotion. Instead, it arises in a larger framework where it serves as an antipode to the languid style. Consequently, it highlights by sheer contrast the traditional pastoral cues and their corresponding emotions.

The reason why I am including a musical feature associated with abandon in my list of idiosyncratic cues is that this feature always appears in works containing traditional pastoral cues. The emotional intensity and motivic repetition of the tarantella dance would not have been found in the idylls of Theocritus, the arias of Handel, or the gigues of Bach. Instead, the conflict between the languid and tarantella styles can be viewed as a musico-dramatic framework that organizes a particular piece in the early twentieth century. In two works, Griffes uses this framework in highly contrasting ways. In the Scherzo, Op. 6, musical textures displaying these two styles appear in alternation, first evoking wild abandon, then calm serenity. In *The Pleasure-Dome of Kubla Khan*, however, the section evoking wild abandon is abruptly interrupted, cutting short any sense of fulfillment. These passages are discussed in chapters 8 and 5, respectively.

CUE #8: CUMULATIVE COUNTERPOINT

This cue is an example of a musical palimpsest, as described above. It consists of the convergence of three distinct concepts: a contrapuntal texture in which melodic motives initially heard in succession now coincide along with an increase of register in the outer voices and a swelling of dynamics. Taken together, all three factors participate in a process that leads to a climax. The difference between a traditional concept of musical climax and cumulative counterpoint is that this passage is not merely high and loud—that is, based entirely on the treatment of register and dynamics. Instead, it is fundamentally linked to a piece's formal design in that it reflects the gradual accumulation of tension due to motivic development. An instance of cumulative counterpoint is more than merely a texture of polyphony; rather, it represents polyphony saturated with motivic significance. Since in most cases these motives have all appeared previously in the work, this passage serves as the culmination of a process of motivic development, the convergence of different temporal trajectories, all coinciding at a single moment. In Griffes's music, each pitch and/or rhythmic motive that appears in a passage of cumulative counterpoint carries its own referential history within the work. This linkage between motivic structure and emotional highpoint serves as a distinctive feature of his overall style.

To claim that a collection of American works from the turn of the century is organized around a climax is hardly news. What is new is that some of Griffes's pastorals stretch to the limit the conventions of the tradition. Taken by itself, the concept of climax at the very least suggests extreme emotions such as triumph and/or ecstasy, things not normally associated with sicilianos or musettes. Instead, in some of his musical pastorals, Griffes fashioned a crucible of contrasting emotions, a dramatic trajectory between contrasting affects, not the evocation of a single affect.

The history of the critical analysis of musical climax is abundant, including studies by William Newman, Ralph Kirkpatrick, Agawu, Hatten, and Zohar Eitan. All of these authors adopt either a different definition of climax from mine or a different method of measuring it.[19] A clear example of cumulative counterpoint occurs immediately before the climactic apex in "The White Peacock." To appreciate this juxtaposition, we must consider the opening measures where two highly contrasting themes appear: a complex rhythm implying the polonaise dance, which suggests 6/4, and a simpler pattern that suggests the siciliano, which implies 3/2 meter. In the initial section, these two rhythmic patterns (and implied meters) appear in immediate succession. However, in mm. 38–40, just before the climax, both rhythmic patterns appear simultaneously in counterpoint as a two-layer rhythmic ostinato. What was initially a texture of interruption and fragmentation eventually leads to synthesis and integration. Other examples of this feature appear in "The Vale of Dreams" and the song "The Lament of Ian the Proud."

Finally, it should be noted that there are some works by Griffes in which a convergence of motives occurs without being accompanied by an emotional climax. To understand this discrepancy, we must imagine a climax as the centerpiece of a two-part cycle, a balanced process marked by two opposite actions: a waxing and a waning. The waxing involves a slow buildup of tension, leading to an emotional climax that evokes physical pleasure or spiritual fulfilment. By contrast, the waning dimension is characterized by a gradual release of tension, or a dénouement. This entire process is represented musically by an overarching expressive trajectory: a gradual rise and fall in dynamics accompanied by an increase and decrease in rhythmic activity. The quintessential musical example of this type is "The White Peacock" (see chap. 4).

In some works, however, this two-part cycle is incomplete, and the waxing process is abruptly interrupted, never culminating in a genuine climax. This fissure in the work's expressive arc is characterized by such things as a sudden shift in dynamics, a change in tempo, a sharp descent in register, and/or an abrupt contrast in motivic material. Griffes seems to have been preoccupied with this process of interruption and its association with images such as a magical garden, the supernatural, and the fantasy of a bacchanal. The incomplete cycle with interrupted climax is found in two different works, one instrumental and one vocal: *The Pleasure-Dome of Kubla Khan* and "The Rose of the Night" (both are discussed in part II).

The psychological emotions that are associated with the two versions of this cycle show a great range—from spiritual ecstasy to the evocation of bacchanalian abandon and physical/sensual pleasure. Nevertheless, in both versions the initial structure of the cycle is the same: there is an increase in dynamics and emotional intensity. The difference is that in one cycle these feelings are fulfilled; in the other they are not.

CUE #9: REGISTRAL EXPANSION

Griffes's treatment of register in his pastorals is among the most unusual cue in the list. Griffes himself expressed curiosity about the spacing of dissonant harmonies in an interview in 1919: "When I went to Germany . . . I was of course ready to be swept under by the later Wagner and Strauss; it is only logical I suppose that when I began to write I wrote in the vein of Debussy and Stravinsky; those particular wide intervalled dissonances are the natural medium of the composer who writes to-day's [*sic*] music."[20] Though this quotation does not explicitly focus on the conjunction of registral expansion and motivic repetition, it confirms that he was highly attuned to the use of registral spacing.

Let us begin our introduction to Griffes's sensitivity to register change by considering an excerpt from his Scherzo, *Fantasy Pieces*, Op. 6, no. 3, which contains a sudden expansion in only one direction. The excerpt in question occurs at the end of the opening section: mm. 98–104 (see ex.3.1).

The passage serves a cadential role, for it brings the opening section to a close. But this is a cadence with a dramatic flair, for Griffes's treatment of harmony, dynamics, and register contributes to its effect. The harmony is utterly static—the same chord, B♭ minor, repeats sixteen times. To relieve this unrelenting harmonic repetition, Griffes lowers the bass voice by three octaves from B♭3 to B♭0 over the course of the passage. In addition, the dynamic level gradually increases from *mezzo forte* to *fortissimo*. The overall impact is a single musical gesture that builds to an enormous climax.[21]

When viewed in isolation, the formal function of this type of repetition may seem rather prosaic: to emphasize the end of a section. But when the change of register is taken into account along with chordal repetition, the passage's impact is magnified many times over. In some respects, it is more conclusive than the piece's actual ending—as if stealing the registral thunder of the final peroration.

EXAMPLE 3.1.

Griffes, Scherzo, mm. 98–104.

However, the situation changes dramatically when the expansion of register occurs over a longer time span and in more than one voice. There are two dimensions of this pastoral cue that together create a conjunction in the treatment of register and form: (1) a simultaneous outward registral expansion of the highest and lowest pitches in two statements of the same chord or polyphonic texture, a type of varied repetition that serves as a two-dimensional trajectory in musical space and time; and (2) the simultaneous presence of motivic/thematic repetition that heightens all the more this treatment of register.

The conjunction of registral magnification and thematic repetition has a significant impact on the overall formal plan of a work, depending on where the second statement(s) occurs. There are two patterns of spatial expansion in Griffes's works. If the second statement occurs somewhere in the middle of the work, the registral expansion coincides with the repetition of an entire section, thereby underlining and dramatizing an internal formal division. If the second statement occurs at the end of the work, however, the registral expansion will coincide with the final gesture, thereby reinforcing a circular character in the work's formal scheme.

Regardless of the work's overall repetition scheme, the confluence of registral expansion with motivic repetition becomes a new kind of musical signifier, which, when used in concert with other cues, helps distinguish Griffes's pastoral signature.

To better understand the second subtype of registral expansion, it is useful to borrow and adapt the rhetorical concept of *epanalepsis*. This ancient Greek term denotes the repetition of a word or phrase at the beginning and the end of a sentence for greater emphasis, as illustrated by the phrase[22] "Nothing is worse than doing nothing." A musical version of *epanalepsis* would be a work in which the opening texture repeats exactly at the end such as Beethoven's Piano Sonata in E major, Op. 109, movement 3.

In one of Griffes's most experimental pastorals, however, the analogy between music and Greek rhetoric must be adapted so that the second statement is not only a repetition in pitch—either a single note or harmony—but also a variation in register. The two statements of the same chord or phrase become the means by which a large-scale process of growth takes place. Ultimately, what is important is that the second statement of the opening sound has a different registral disposition than the first statement—the same pitches, but a different musical meaning. A literary analogy for this change in meaning can be found in the expression "The king is dead; long live the king!" The "king" referred to at the end of the sentence must be different from the one referred to at the beginning or else the sentence would be a mere redundancy. Instead, the second reference to the "king" could refer to either of two things: a particular person—that is, the new ruler who has taken the place of the old one; or the kingship itself—the institution of the monarchy. In either case, the word's connotation has shifted over the course of the sentence.[23] Likewise, the significance of the repetition of a work's initial chord or texture changes dramatically if its later statement is spread over a wider pitch space.

One may ask, Is there any inherent psychological response associated with this conjunction of motivic repetition and registral expansion? The answer involves both repetition and transformation. To begin with, the listener's memory of a previously heard harmony or harmonic interval between two melodic lines evokes the experience of restarting or resuming something familiar from the past. However, if the return of the initial harmony or harmonic interval is emphasized with a dramatic change of register, then this feature does not denote merely pitch repetition. Rather, the recurring pitches are linked to a pair of trajectories that serves as a musical analogue to the general concept of growth and a feeling of fulfillment. This two-dimensional expansion can also acquire other specific connotations, depending on the text associated with a given work. These connotations include a flower blossoming ("The White Peacock"), the echoes of a river flowing (*The Pleasure-Dome of Kubla Khan*), or the growth in a desire for spiritual deliverance ("The Rose of the Night"). Each of these associations will be discussed in the analytical commentaries in part II.

The most salient examples of registral expansion are summarized in the list below. Note that the principle of registral expansion is based on the transposition, often by twelve semitones, of an individual pitch, not a pitch class.

The Pleasure-Dome of Kubla Khan, Opening planing texture in piano → Postlude: Returns in celesta, mm. 215–17.

"The White Peacock," Opening V9 chord → Return of A Section, mm. 46–47.

"Lake at Evening," Opening tonic pedal + four-note motive → mm. 46–53 [NB: soprano and bass rhythmically displaced].

"The Vale of Dreams," Opening half-step motives: G♭–F, A–B♭ (mm. 4–5) → Climax in B section mm. 33–37.

Scherzo/Bacchanale, B section, Melody + accompaniment → Return of B Section, mm. 260–67.

"The Rose of the Night," Opening m9 between piano and voice, G♯–A → Climax, m. 49.

"Clouds," B section, Melody + accompaniment → Return of B Section, mm. 35–36.

CUE #10: SACRED CHORALE STYLE

As the name implies, this style originally took root in the church, in particular the sixteenth-century Lutheran liturgy where it was linked with vernacular German texts and the communal ritual of congregational singing.

Later it was appropriated into the Catholic liturgical tradition during the eighteenth century.[24] The chorale is typically characterized by a single melodic line supported by chordal texture in continuous rhythm (either quarter or eighth notes), usually at a moderate tempo and a continuous dynamic. The typical point of reference for this style is the four-part chorale settings of J. S. Bach, although they are characterized by frequent figuration in the lower voices.[25]

While some semiotic lexicons classify this type of texture as *religioso*,[26] recent scholars have tried to narrow its range of meaning using various subcategories. For example, in her dissertation on the music of Liszt, Marta Grabócz distinguishes two subtypes of pastoral: the traditional religioso, which features singing melody, diatonic harmonies, and arpeggiated accompaniment; and a pantheistic variant, which is colored by the pentatonic scale.[27] Even more suggestive is a recent article by Eric McKee where he isolates the "sacred chorale style," which initially appeared in eighteenth-century opera and was later exploited by Beethoven in his instrumental music.[28]

While sustained chordal textures with continuous rhythms occasionally appear in Griffes's music, he usually reserved his version of the "sacred chorale style" for very specific moments in a work's overall formal design. Griffes highlighted this style in two different ways: as both a processional and recessional—that is, the musical gesture that begins and ends a piece; and as a means of highlighting a work's climax. Examples of the former include *The Pleasure-Dome of Kubla Khan*; illustrations of the latter include "The White Peacock," "The Vale of Dreams," and Prelude #3. Each will be discussed in chapters 4, 5, 8, and 9.

CUE #11: ALTERNATIVE SCALES

This cue refers to the use of non-diatonic scales such as the pentatonic, whole tone, octatonic, and hexatonic. All four are displayed in example 3.2. It goes without saying that each of these scales has its own peculiar structure. While the pentatonic scale has an asymmetrical ordering of intervals, the other three are symmetrical, whether by a repeating interval (e.g., whole tone) or a repeating pair of intervals (e.g., octatonic and

EXAMPLE 3.2.

The Pentatonic, Whole-Tone, Octatonic, and Hexatonic Scales.

hexatonic). All four serve as referential collections in a wide variety of early twentieth-century works.[29]

However, Griffes also experimented with a more complex scale that has strong associations with either Arabic or Romani musical traditions. Example 3.3 presents two explanations of the same scale—one beginning on B, the other on F♯—that appears at a poignant moment in *The Pleasure-Dome of Kubla Khan*. The scale degrees listed above the staff are analogous to the Hijaz scale, a mode found in the Arabic maqamat system. In a fascinating article on Saint-Saëns's opera *Samson et Dalila*, Ralph Locke uses this scale to explain the exotic character of the oboe solo that initiates the "Bacchanale" dance in Act III.[30] Another interpretation is also possible, however, as illustrated by the scale degrees below the example that correspond to the Romani or so-called "Gypsy" scale, which Jonathan Bellman describes in his exhaustive study of the "style Hongrois."[31] The sequence of intervals is the same in both arrangements, but their tonal center is different. I would argue that each approach constitutes an equally legitimate framework for interpreting potential exotic associations. One may seem more authentic since Griffes himself admitted having borrowed an Arabic tune (for more information about this borrowing, see chap. 5). However,

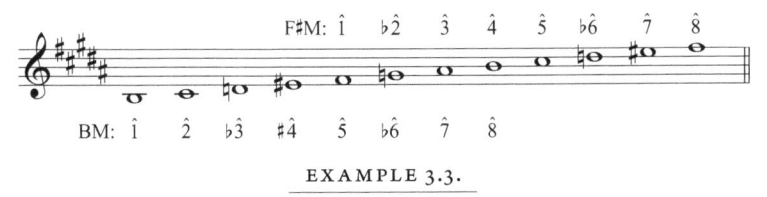

EXAMPLE 3.3.

Multiple Interpretations of Scale with Double Augmented Seconds:
"Hijaz" Scale above; Romani ("Gypsy") Scale below.

the question of "authenticity" remains elusive since it depends on whether the focus is on the compositional process itself or on the audience's perception of the end result of that process. It goes without saying that early twentieth-century audiences in Boston and New York would most likely have been more familiar with Western renditions of Romani music than with Arabic modes, especially if they had been exposed to the music of Liszt. While the scale is clearly "marked" in relation to the most common Western modes—major, minor, and the four church modes—the crucial point is that, in this case, there is an element of ambiguity present when trying to determine its tonal center and geographical origin.[32]

The use of alternative scales also introduces a much broader question regarding their associations with non-Western musical traditions and the role those traditions—what some call *musical exoticism*—played in Griffes's musical style. Indeed, exoticism in Western music is a rich confluence of political, philosophical, and musical issues that far exceeds a single topic or cue; I provide an overview of a handful of these issues in chapter 2. It is important to emphasize that most of Griffes's pastorals are associated with some kind of poetic text, either as an epigraph to an instrumental work or as the text of a song. As a result, the exotic associations of a given cue such as an alternative scale are inextricably bound up with the network of literary and musical significations within a given pastoral as a whole. My goal is to investigate the combination of pastoral cues that characterizes a given work, not to propose a general theory of musical exoticism and then elucidate the degree to which a given song or tone poem is or is not exotic.

Lament Cues

History

The lament is the human response to death, which in music can involve settings with voice alone, voice with instrumental accompaniment, or purely instrumental textures. When viewed from an ethnological perspective, there are a wide range of socio-psychological rituals and traditions associated with this response in various cultures around the world. While general expressions of grief include wailing, moaning, and crying, there is a distinction between the spontaneous wailing or grieving over the body itself, such as plantus or keening, and the more organized, poetic expression of grief. Musical titles in this funereal family include the elegy, threnody, lamentation, tombeau, funeral march, and requiem. Whether it be the death of an individual person or the abstract phenomenon of mortality, these works evoke a variety of emotions ranging from grief and loss to a broader spirit of meditation and resignation. In this study, I will focus on a small subset of this group: Griffes's revival and adaptation of the musical lament, which originated in the Italian *lamento* during the early Baroque period.

The lamento initially appeared during the mid-sixteenth century in the context of Italian secular madrigals.[33] But at the turn of the seventeenth century, it played a crucial role in the emergence of a new dramatic genre (opera) and a new monodic style of singing as well as an outpouring of theoretical speculation within the Florentine Camerata. The leading composers associated with this new form of musical expression were Monteverdi, Bonini, Possenti, and later Cavalli. Beginning as a loosely organized vocal work—whether in an opera or a free-standing monody with continuo—the tradition eventually crystalized as a highly structured vocal work with a repetitive accompaniment. In her detailed study of laments during the Baroque period, Ellen Rosand observes that the "lament is self-contained but it is not closed; it is not an aria."[34] The lament had a specific dramatic function in the context of a larger operatic narrative: a moment of highly concentrated expression of emotion. Its association with grief and loss derived not only from the specific text itself but also from the larger trajectory of the plot. Rosand calls it "the central affective climax of an opera."[35]

The crucial juncture in this brief history is the shift between music with text—that is, the genres of opera and madrigal—to purely instrumental music during the seventeenth and eighteenth centuries. The concept of a lament *topos*, or topic, depends on the tradition of associating a set of emotions and/or psychological states with a specific musical gesture regardless of title, genre, or text. References to laments appear in the titles of suites, sonatas, and capriccios by such composers as Froberger, Biber, Kuhnau, and J. S. Bach. For the purposes of this study, I will explore two musical characteristics that became inseparable from the lament tradition: one melodic, the sigh melodic figure; and the other harmonic, the descending bass tetrachord or the lament bass.

CUE #12: SIGH MOTIVE

The first characteristic feature is the descending half-step melodic motive. Monelle explores in detail the semiotic evolution of the correspondence between physical action and musical gesture. He describes the historical evolution among musical laments by using Peircian terminology, a process of semiotic transformation from *icon* to *index* and, eventually, to *symbol*. He observes that a genuine human cry or wail would be perceived as an icon, an expression of an intense emotion. But eventually the musical representation of weeping, the descending half-step, acquired the same emotional association with grief and personal loss, but without the actual sound of crying. The reason for this association is the ubiquity of dramatic and textual contexts in which this figure was associated with grief. It appears in madrigals by Wert and Marenzio to accompany words like *pianto* and *lagrime* as well as in vocal works by Caccini and Dowland. Its harmonic support could be dissonant, as an appoggiatura, or consonant. At this point, the falling half-step became an index. The final step in this semiotic progression occurs when the half-step appeared without any morbid or funereal context—that is, in instrumental music without text. The dark emotions associated with this melodic gesture have been culturally predetermined, and the melodic gesture has become a symbol.[36]

However, there is a second association with the same gesture that arose during the eighteenth century: sighing as an expression of pain and sorrow. Monelle concludes, "It is very doubtful that modern listeners recall the association of the *pianto* with actual weeping; indeed, the later assumption that this figure signified sighing, not weeping, suggests that its origin was forgotten. It is now heard with all the force of [a] ... symbol."[37] Ultimately, despite the physical differences between weeping and sighing, the common element amid the evolution of this melodic gesture is its association with dark human emotions such as pain, grief, and suffering.

One problem with identifying a half-step melodic motive in isolation is that this interval is ubiquitous in many different styles and textures. In Griffes's pastorals, this descending half-step gesture in an upper voice is usually accompanied by a fixed pitch in the bass, thereby suggesting an appoggiatura function. Most important, the emotional associations of the gesture prevail in instrumental as well as vocal works—that is, the meaning of the topic does not depend on the presence of a text that expresses lament. In both cases, the emotional associations with grief and loss are essential to appreciate the blend and ambiguity of topics that are characteristic of his style. However, as will become clear in the discussion of "The Rose of the Night," the third song in the Macleod cycle, in some works Griffes invests this same falling gesture with other associations that complicate, if not conflict with, the idea of lament such as the desire for sensual pleasure and the yearning for spiritual ecstasy.[38]

CUE #13: DESCENDING TETRACHORD

The other characteristic feature of the musical lament is the basso ostinato, usually descending between scale degrees 8 and 5, which can be either diatonic or chromatic. Rosand observes, "The most significant, potentially affective, feature of the pattern is its strong harmonic direction, reinforced by stepwise melody, steady unarticulated rhythm, and brevity. . . . Two other features of the tetrachord ostinato ... further establish the appropriateness of its association with the lament. Its strongly minor configuration ... invokes the full range of somber affects traditionally associated with minor . . . and, in its unremitting descent, its gravity, the pattern offers an analogue of obsession, perceptible as an expression of hopeless suffering."[39] The chromatic version was also identified as *passus duriusculus* (*harsh passage*), a term invented by Christoph Bernhard in his *Tractatus compositionis augmentatus* (1649). Although Bernhard used the term to refer to a wide range of musical gestures, such as an ascending chromatic line or even a dissonant interval, now it usually refers to the descending line in the bass.[40]

Regarding the emotional associations of this chromatic version, there has recently been some controversy. In 1997, Peter Williams wrote a meticulous study of the recurring bass pattern, a rich compendium of chromatic practice from Cipriano de Rore in the Renaissance to Richard Strauss and Art Tatum in the twentieth century.[41] Although Williams examines both the grammar and rhetoric of this pattern in detail, his goals are twofold: to challenge the argument that any compositional procedure—in particular, the chromatic fourth—has an intrinsic emotional association; and to promote the logic behind artistic technique for its own sake. Monelle objects strongly to Williams's skepticism, claiming that it would strip away all emotional associations with the gesture. Instead, Monelle argues that "in practice [the figure's] meaning is almost aways dysphoric."[42]

It is important to consider Griffes's revival of the lament bass in the context of his fascination with chromatic harmony. First of all, lament basses in Griffes's pastorals are few in number. If we include his *Poem for Flute and Orchestra* (which was arranged for flute and piano after his death), there are only three examples of this cue, all of which are slight adaptations of the traditional bass pattern; the other two appear in "The White Peacock" (see chap. 4) and "The Lake at Evening" (see chap. 8). Nevertheless, two questions arise.

First, does every descending chromatic bass in Griffes's music possess the same emotional associations that are characteristic of the entire lament tradition, beginning with the descending lines in early Baroque opera? The short answer to this question is no. If a given descending bass line is merely chromatic, it does not automatically express emotions of loss and grief. The emotional associations of the lament depend on the presence of multiple cues in a given passage—that is, the sigh figure plus the descending chromatic bass line.

Second, if a bass line has the contour and chromatic structure of the lament tetrachord but does not traverse the intervallic span between scale degrees 8 and 5, does it still evoke the same emotional associations? The answer is the same as above. While a chromatic bass line by itself may not carry the full impact of a traditional lament, if it appears either simultaneously or in close proximity to the other characteristic cue, the sigh figure, then it may well evoke the emotional associations of grief.

An excerpt from the opening section of Griffes's *Poem for Flute and Orchestra* illustrates the nuances of this particular cue. In example 3.4, the ensemble is in a harmonic transition, pivoting away from one key area towards another. As a result, the bass's chromatic descent—F♯, E, D♯, D, C, G♯, A—can be interpreted as scale steps in either of two keys: C♯ minor, the initial tonal center, or A minor. Taken by itself, this bass line is tonally ambiguous and, more important, does not fill in a perfect fourth melodic span in either key. But what confirms the connection with the lament and its psychological associations is the shape of the flute's melody, a sinuous line suffused with half steps: C♯–B♯–C♯–D–C♯. Each descending half step can be interpreted as a sigh figure that resolves to a harmonic consonance.[43]

EXAMPLE 3.4.

Griffes, Poem for Flute and Piano, mm. 16–21.

It is worth taking stock of the two cues for the musical lament. The sigh (or weeping) motive has much greater significance in Griffes's music than the descending bass tetrachord. Since many instances of the descending half step accompany a text, it is reasonable to assume that the composer was aware of its expressive power. Although he never uses a repeating bass ostinato to organize the harmonic structure of his pastorals, he occasionally employs a single instance of the chromatic variant for dramatic effect. In sum, the musical lament can be represented by characteristic treatments of meter, rhythm, tempo, key, melody, and harmony, which are summarized below.

Attribute	Value
Meter	Triple Meter
Rhythm	Rhythmic Ostinato
Tempo	Slow
Mode	Minor Key
Harmony	Descending Bass Tetrachord (diatonic or chromatic)
Melody	Sigh Figure

The next step is to display the two frames of Griffes's Pastoral and the Lament side by side, as shown in figure 3.1. It should be emphasized that this diagram is an abstraction, a cumulative record of all possible cues that appear in at least one of the pastoral works considered in my study (note the redundancy of "rhythmic ostinato"). This comparison of the pastoral and lament topics is more encyclopedic than exegetic—that is, whereas figure 3.1 displays the sum total of all possible topical intersections, no single piece nor any analytical interpretation will put them all into practice. Rather, this comprehensive scheme is the point of departure for studying the process by which an individual work brings this abstract collection of cues to life.

At this juncture, it is appropriate to draw some conclusions about the two lists of pastoral cues when viewed as a whole. On the one hand, Griffes expanded the traditional conception of the musical pastoral by heightening the tensions that are inherent in Toliver's and Patterson's conception of the literary pastoral, as described in chapter 2. These tensions are evident

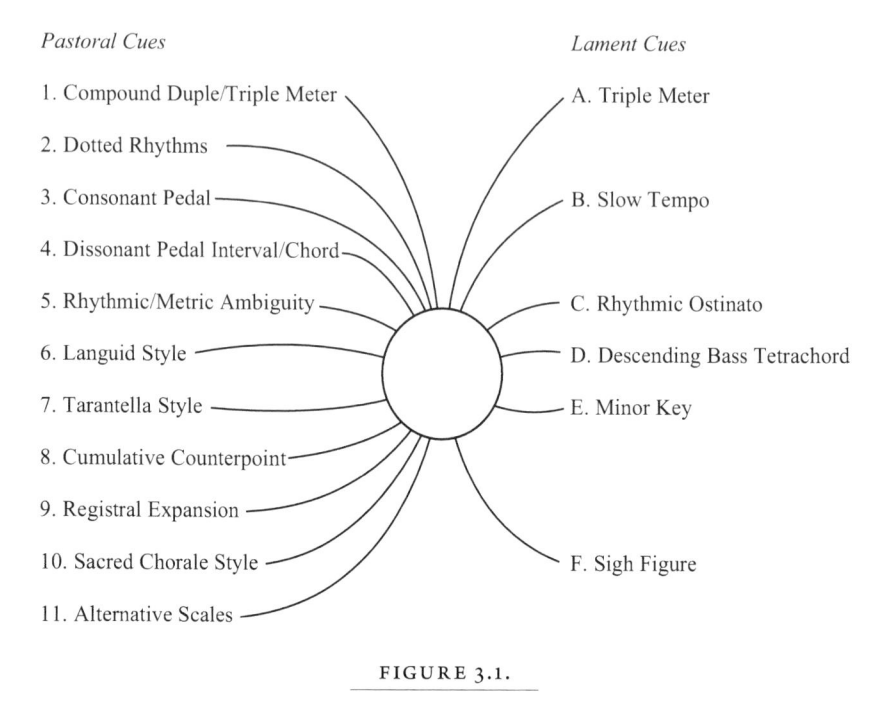

Pastoral Cues

1. Compound Duple/Triple Meter
2. Dotted Rhythms
3. Consonant Pedal
4. Dissonant Pedal Interval/Chord
5. Rhythmic/Metric Ambiguity
6. Languid Style
7. Tarantella Style
8. Cumulative Counterpoint
9. Registral Expansion
10. Sacred Chorale Style
11. Alternative Scales

Lament Cues

A. Triple Meter
B. Slow Tempo
C. Rhythmic Ostinato
D. Descending Bass Tetrachord
E. Minor Key
F. Sigh Figure

FIGURE 3.1.

Aggregate of Pastoral and Lament Cues.

in various oppositions present among different cues and within individual cues on these lists. These conflicts are one of the reasons that Griffes's pastorals resist membership in a unified group or genre. Yet, on the other hand, each individual work possesses a certain degree of aesthetic integrity that mitigates against these oppositions. In this connection, it is useful to posit two opposing aesthetic impulses at work in these cues and in Griffes's style as a whole: fragmentation and cohesion.

Fragmentation of Cues

Some cues have a fragmented character in and of themselves. Examples include the two subtypes of temporal ambiguity: the suggestion of multiple meters sounding simultaneously, and the discrepancy between the sounding meter and the notated time signature. Music that displays ambiguous meter, while rather commonplace during the nineteenth century, is highly unusual for a pastoral. What is striking is that a given pastoral work in Griffes's oeuvre rarely maintains temporal ambiguity in its entirety, but rather shifts in and out of various kinds of rhythmic and/or metric irregularity. In that sense, the opposition between a clear and an ambiguous sense of meter receives pride of place in his rhythmic palette.

Another example of a fragmented cue is the dissonant pedal chord. A passage with a continuous dissonant sonority evokes vastly different emotional associations compared to those of a passage with a pedal point of a single pitch or a consonant interval. Thus, it is reasonable to conclude that passages displaying either of these cues would have a conflicting set of associations.

In addition, the impulse toward fragmentation emerges when multiple cues are in conflict with one another. The opposition between languorous calm and tarantella frenzy is another vivid source of ambiguity and conflict that characterizes Griffes's vision of the pastoral. Although usually only one of these cues appears in a given work, in *The Pleasure-Dome of Kubla Khan* both styles appear at different junctures, helping to shape Griffes's musical portrayal of the poem. Also, two corollaries that grow out of the same opposition would be rhythmic freedom versus insistent rhythmic repetition as well as the contrasting rhythmic patterns associated with the siciliano and tarantella dances.

As an aside, a similar opposition between the languid style and tarantella style plays a central role in Michael Puri's compelling study of Ravel's aesthetic sensibility, which he calls the idyllic versus the bacchanalian.[44] Despite the broad interdisciplinary scope of his work, which embraces psychological, philosophical, historical, literary, and musical analysis, at many junctures he seems intent on confirming a preordained conclusion about Freud's and Lacan's view of the unconscious. My approach differs from Puri's in that I do not rely on a systematic theory of the human unconscious to account for the rich complexity of musical phenomena.[45]

Cohesion of Cues

There are various ways in which the impulse of cohesion is evident in the lists of pastoral and lament characteristics. First and foremost, it is significant that cues such as static harmony, compound meter, and dotted rhythmic patterns have preserved their associations with simplicity and serenity for such a long time. In short, the compositional means of evoking musical serenity have been persistent. The same can be said for passages that display the languid style. While Griffes tests the limits of this tradition in a limited number of experimental pastorals, he by no means overturns it. There are also individual cues with cohesive characteristics that are composite in nature. The conjunction of registral expansion and motivic repetition, which I define as a single cue, often highlights a work's forward trajectory, thereby demonstrating a cohesive character. In addition, the cumulative counterpoint cue exhibits cohesion in that individual motives initially presented by themselves are later juxtaposed at the same time, thereby embodying an organic sense of development, leading to thematic integration.

Conclusion

Now that we have fully investigated all of the pastoral and the lament cues, we are in a position to draw some overall conclusions. The question arises: Is Griffes's personal style, as represented by the sum total of these cues, what Agawu calls an "idiolect" or a "dialect"?[46] These two terms occupy opposite ends of a hypothetical spectrum of cultural and psychological associations. At one end, the pastoral and lament cues serve as a cipher for a highly personal artistic code, a private musical idiom in which each new work becomes a virtual sui generis or a one-of-a-kind. It seems as though some of the styles and cues that I have isolated are Griffes-specific—that is, the musical signature of a single composer. In that case, the concept of topic would merge with autobiography, and in each piece the composer would re-create himself or herself anew. An example of such an extreme would be the musical irony present in Prelude #3 (see chap, 9).[47]

At the other end of the spectrum, the lists isolate a subset of cues that can be found in pastoral works by Griffes's contemporaries as well as by himself. These cues are linked with a set of psychological and cultural associations shared by a whole generation of composers and their audiences—for example, the tarantella style in Ravel.[48] Does the aggregate of cues also aspire to the status of a dialect, a preliminary step toward reconstructing a broader expressive language common to a group of composers? David Lidov believes these two dimensions are complementary and essential to the process of interpretation. In his collection of essays *Is Language a Music?* Lidov explains their reciprocity in terms of "grammar" and "design": "Grammar and design are reciprocal in that a repertoire of related designs will serve to validate a grammar . . . and that a reiterated grammatical rule will produce symmetries of structure. In such cases the results of the two principles converge."[49]

Agawu also offers some insight into the difference between a shared compositional language and an individual act of composition. He argues that there are elements of continuity and discontinuity in the ways that eighteenth- and nineteenth-century composers employed topics in their music. "On one hand, the largely public-oriented and conventional topics of the eighteenth century often exhibit a similar orientation in the nineteenth century. . . . On the other hand, the ascendancy in the nineteenth century of figures born of a private realm, figures that bear the marks of individual composerly idiolects, speaks to a new context for topic."[50] Agawu implies that there is an unavoidable tension between Romantic composers' tendency to preserve traditional dances and styles and their desire to develop a uniquely personal compositional voice. The opposition between dialect and idiolect takes on special importance when contemplating the works by Griffes that qualify as pastorals. While there is always a distinction between the properties that a group of works share and the properties that are unique to an individual work, in the case of Griffes that distinction takes on greater importance. The reason for this is an underlying protean character in his musical personality—what might be called an aesthetic restlessness—that led him to experiment constantly with different styles and national traditions while still maintaining his own integrity. For Griffes, the concept of personal musical style must be understood as more open-ended than that of other composers, analogous to a semipermeable membrane.

An inevitable response to the diversity present in the list of cues is to reiterate the observation first made by critics during Griffes's lifetime and repeated ever since—that his personal style was eclectic. Yet it is one thing to recognize this eclecticism and another thing altogether to calibrate it. In this chapter, my goal has been to provide a first step in the process of calibration.

Ultimately, I hope that this study reveals how the aesthetic threads of one composer's work helped weave the artistic tapestry of a generation of experimental composers at the turn of the century. In addition to the usual oppositions such as city versus country, nature versus civilization, and subjective versus objective, Griffes introduced the musical equivalent of new colors and shapes in his pastoral kaleidoscope. In many works, these new colors converge into a single coherent aesthetic vision; in a few works, they diverge, creating a heterogeneous artistic result. In order to fully understand Griffes's contribution to the pastoral tradition, we must examine closely how the conflicting impulses of convergence and divergence come into play within a specific musical context—and that is the goal of the analyses in part II.

NOTES

1. In his book on Beethoven, Robert Hatten defines the pastoral as a "topical field," which is characterized by various polarities such as simple versus complex and major versus minor mode—see *Musical Meaning in Beethoven*, 76–84. In his later study of Mozart, Beethoven, and Schubert he describes the pastoral as a "mode"—see *Interpreting Musical Gestures, Topics, and Tropes*, 53–58.

2. Robert Hatten, "The Troping of Topics in Mozart's Instrumental Music," *The Oxford Handbook of Topical Theory*, ed. Danuta Mirka (Oxford, UK: Oxford University Press, 2014), 515, 519–21.

3. *Grove Music Online* defines "quodlibet" as "a composition in which well-known melodies and texts appear in successive or simultaneous combinations. Generally the quolibet serves no higher purpose than that of humour or technical virtuosity." https://doi.org/10.1093/gmo/9781561592630.article.22748, accessed August 20, 2023.

4. Peter Burkholder explores the quodlibet procedure in depth along with a host of other types of quotation in the music of Charles Ives. See *All Made of Tunes: Charles Ives and the Uses of Musical Borrowing* (New Haven, CT: Yale University Press, 1995), 369–79.

5. In his first book, Hatten lists ten pastoral cues found in the opening theme of Beethoven's Piano Sonata in A major, Op. 101, first movement, many of which typify the eighteenth-century tradition: compound meter, major modality, parallel voice leading (e.g. thirds), rocking accompaniment patterns, contrary motion between outer voices, static harmony (e.g. pedal points, drone fifths), diatonic and slow moving harmonic texture, simple melodic contour, use of consonant appoggiatura, elaborated resolution of dissonance; see *Musical Meaning in Beethoven*, 97–99.

6. See Raymond Monelle, *The Musical Topic: Hunt, Military and Pastoral* (Bloomington: Indiana University Press, 2006), 215–18; and Wye Jamison Allanbrook, *Rhythmic Gesture in Mozart: La Nozze di Figaro and Don Giovanni* (Chicago: University of Chicago Press, 1983), 41–43.

7. Monelle, *The Musical Topic*, 210–14.

8. Lidov defines them as follows: "a process involves [a] sustained engagement in environment, orientation, feeling, and/or disposition.... A processive sign is a sign in which the representamen, the object, or the interpretant is a process." *Elements of Semiotics* (New York: St. Martin's, 1999), 182.

9. An example of an extended dissonant pedal chord appears in Johannes Brahms, Intermezzo in B♭ major, Op. 76, no. 4. Robert Schumann ends two of his works with a half cadence: "Im wunderschönen Monat Mai," *Dichterliebe*, Op. 48, and "Bittendes Kind," *Kinderszenen*, Op. 15.

10. Anderson, *Charles T. Griffes*, 79.

11. See Anderson, *The Works of Charles T. Griffes*, 509.

12. Maisel, *Charles T. Griffes*, 179, 181. Scriabin was fond of using the term *languid* or *langueur* in other scores such as his tone poem *Le Poème de l'extase* (*The Poem of Ecstasy*), Op. 54, and the Four Preludes, Op. 39, no. 3.

13. My thanks to Donna Anderson for sharing with me a copy of the inventory of Griffes's library prepared by Harold E. Wands.

14. This term also appears at an internal transition in two other works: Barcarolle, Fantasy Pieces, Op. 6, no. 1, mm. 98–105; and the *Kairn of Koridwen* (chamber ballet), "Priestesses' Religious Dance" (Rehearsal No. 18).

15. *Grove Music Online*, "Tarantella," accessed August 20, 2023 https://doi.org/10.1093/gmo/9781561592630.article.27507.

16. He also penned a brief program for this rechristened work on the occasion of its orchestral premiere in 1919. For more details, see chapter 8.

17. Deborah Mawer explores the role that musical machines and mechanisms play in Ravel's music. See "Musical Objects and Machines," in *The Cambridge Companion to Ravel*, ed. Deborah Mawer (Cambridge, UK: Cambridge University Press, 2000), 47–67.

18. Simon Hornblower and A. Spawforth, ed., *Oxford Companion to Classical Civilization* (Oxford, UK: Oxford University Press, 1998), 232–35.

19. The history of the critical analysis of musical climax is abundant, including studies by William Newman, Ralph Kirkpatrick, Agawu, Hatten, and Zohar Eitan. Kirkpatrick's concept of "crux," the juncture in Scarlatti's keyboard sonatas immediately before the reprise of the opening material where the musical drama reaches its peak, is often analogous to that of Griffes's pastoral climax. In his study of Schumann songs, Agawu adopts the term *highpoint* rather than *climax* to denote a point of culmination in one or more individual musical parameters such as register, dynamics, harmony, and/or interval succession. The difference between his notion of highpoint and mine is that in Griffes's pastorals the climax is created by a convergence of intensity in multiple parameters. Regarding the other studies of climax, all differ significantly from mine. On the one hand, Zohar focuses exclusively on the melodic dimension, whereas Hatten defines two independent concepts, the crux and the apex, which in practice could occur separately or coincide. In my approach, the apex and climax coincide and, more important, are always distinct from the final reversal. See William S. Newman, "The Climax of Music," *The Music Review* 13 (1952):

283–93; Ralph Kirkpatrick, *Domenico Scarlatti* (Princeton, NJ: Princeton University Press, 1953); V. Kofi Agawu, "Structural 'Highpoints' in Schumann's *Dichterliebe*," *Music Analysis* 3, no. 2 (1984): 159–80; Zohar Eitan, *Highpoints: A Study of Melodic Peaks* (Philadelphia: University of Pennsylvania Press, 1997). For a perceptive study of Rachmaninov's use of climax, see Jason T. Stell, "Rachmaninov's Expressive Strategies in Selected Piano Preludes: Highpoints, Dramatic Models, and Dynamic Curves," Unpublished Master's Thesis, Pennsylvania State University, 1999.

20. "Artist Needs No Patriotic Aid: Compositions of Charles Griffes, Brought to Attention Here by Boston Symphony, Able to Stand without Label of 'American,'" *Evening Sun* [New York], December 19, 1919, 10; quoted in Donna Anderson, *Charles T. Griffes*, 186.

21. In the Piano Sonata, a similar treatment of registral space occurs twice during the reiteration of a single chord: mm. 121–23 and mm. 234–37. The difference is that in these two cases the register is contracting instead of expanding.

22. This form of repetition differs from the antimetabole in that it is not based on a pair of words or phrases that recur in reverse order (e.g., A B B A).

23. However, the sentence could also have an ironic interpretation in which case the speaker says one thing and means the opposite.

24. During the nineteenth century, the chorale texture began to acquire nationalistic associations in the piano music of Chopin; see Jeffrey Kallberg, "The Rhetoric of Genre: Chopin's Nocturne in G minor," *Nineteenth-Century Music* 11, no. 3 (Spring 1988): 238–61; and Halina Goldberg, *The Age of Chopin: Interdisciplinary Inquiries* (Bloomington: Indiana University Press, 2004).

25. The chorale can easily be confused with the hymn, which dates back to ancient Greek pagan religious song, but which is now usually applied to choral ensemble songs for Christian worship, written in metrical verse in lines of regular length; see Warren Anderson, T. Mathiesen, S. Boynton, et al, "Hymn," *Grove Music Online*, accessed August 20, 2023, https://doi.org/10.1093/gmo/9781561592630.article.13648.

26. Kofi Agawu, *Music as Discourse: Semiotic Adventures in Romantic Music* (Oxford, UK: Oxford University Press, 2009), 41–50.

27. Marta Grabocz, *Morphologie des Oeuvres pour Piano de Liszt: Influence du Programme sur l'Evolution des formes Instrumentales* (Paris: Editions Kimé, 1986), 41–43.

28. After enumerating the usual features such as texture, mode, meter, tempo, and the like, McKee argues that the most distinctive quality of this style is a recurring harmonic idiom, the deceptive cadence, and the associations of weightlessness and transcendent spirituality that it evokes; see "The Topic of the Sacred Hymn in Beethoven's Instrumental Music," *College Music Symposium* 47 (2008): 1–30.

29. For a concise introduction to these referential collections as well as copious musical examples, see Joseph N. Straus, *Introduction to Post-Tonal Theory*, 4th edition (New York: W. W. Norton, 2016), 228–60.

30. Ralph P. Locke, "Constructing the Oriental 'Other': Saint-Saens's "Samson et Dalila," *Cambridge Opera Journal* 3, no. 3 (November 1991): 266–68.

31. Jonathan Bellman, "Toward a Lexicon of the Style Hongrois," *Journal of Musicology* 9, no. 2 (Spring 1991): 214–37.

32. In a fascinating essay, Serge Gut considers a range of questions arising from two different arrangements of the double augmented-second scale—what he calls "la gamme tzigane" and the "la gamme orientale." He catalogues a number of examples from Russian,

French (who adopt a Spanish style), and Hungarian composers, focusing on their harmonic treatment of this scale. See "L'Echelle à double seconde augmentée: Origines et utilization dans la musique occidentale," *Musurgia* 7, no. 2 (2000): 41–60.

33. This summary relies on two sources: Ellen Rosand, "Lamento," *Grove Music Online*, accessed August 20, 2023, https://doi.org/10.1093/gmo/9781561592630.article.15904; and Raymond Monelle, *The Sense of Music: Semiotic Essays* (Princeton, NJ: Princeton University Press, 2000).

34. Ellen Rosand, "The Descending Tetrachord: An Emblem of Lament," *Musical Quarterly* 65, no. 3 (1987): 348.

35. Ibid., 356.

36. Monelle writes, "The sighing appoggiatura no longer means 'sigh' for the listener to Classical music; it has become a 'system-bound expression,' a lexical unit, its signification limited to the indexicality or associations of the sigh." *The Sense of Music*, 67.

37. Ibid., 73.

38. It should be emphasized that the emotional impulse of lament was already present in the earliest literary pastorals by the Greek poet Theocritus. The outpouring of grief in the context of the daily life of shepherds earned its own subtype: the pastoral elegy. However, as the literary and musical traditions became entwined over time, the pastoral associations with grief and loss gradually disappeared and associations with serenity, innocence, and indulgence became more prominent.

39. Rosand, "The Descending Tetrachord," 349–50.

40. The term is discussed in Monelle, *The Sense of Music*, 73–76; and William Caplin, "Topics and Formal Functions: The Case of the Lament," *The Oxford Handbook of Topic Theory*, ed. Danuta Mirka (Oxford, UK: Oxford University Press, 2014), 415–52.

41. Peter Williams, *The Chromatic Fourth During Four Centuries of Music* (Oxford, UK: Clarendon Press, 1997).

42. Monelle, *The Sense of Music*, 74. At the end of his book, Williams softens the strict distinction between grammar and rhetoric, observing that a passage of non-texted music may convey a fixed emotional meaning. "It also seems that context will tend to show the chromatic fourth as being either primarily grammatical or primarily rhetorical, though of course neither to the exclusion of the other." Williams, *The Chromatic Fourth*, 249.

43. It is telling that right before the flute's sinuous line, Griffes introduces a pair of chords in which the ascending and descending half steps fuse into a unison: G/A–G#/G# (mm. 17–18).

44. Puri defines this opposition as a dialectic between the idyll and the bacchanal. See *Ravel the Decadent: Memory, Sublimation, and Desire* (Oxford, UK: Oxford University Press, 2011), 121–39.

45. For Puri, all human behavior can be explained by the interaction of a trio of psychological forces: memory, sublimation, and desire.

46. Agawu, *Music as Discourse: Semiotic Adventures in Romantic Music* (Oxford, UK: Oxford University Press, 2009), 42–43.

47. One way of conceiving of the idiosyncratic cues in the matrix is the dramatic metaphor of "mask" as conceived by Arthur Wenk. Although three of the five masks can be found in other early twentieth-century music ("pastoral," "ragtime," "Spanish"), two are unique to Debussy—namely, "flute" and "ancient." Wenk argues that Debussy's highly personal style can be understood in terms of his unusual treatment of three parameters:

the pentatonic scale, characteristic dance rhythms, and unusual harmonic textures (e.g., the added-sixth chord and planing). See *Claude Debussy and Twentieth Century Music* (Boston, MA: G. K. Hall, 1983), 93–109.

48. Puri discusses this style at length in Ravel's *Daphnis et Chloé*; see *Ravel the Decadent: Memory, Sublimation, and Desire.*

49. David Lidov, *Is Language a Music? Writings on Musical Form and Signification* (Bloomington: Indiana University Press, 2005), 44.

50. Agawu, *Music as Discourse*, 42–43.

PART II
COMMENTARIES AND ANALYSES

4

"The Dreamy Lake" and the Unfolding Tale of "The White Peacock"

O ne of Griffes's greatest achievements was to develop a new approach to the pastoral topic—what I call the *ambivalent pastoral*, which transformed the dance-based tradition he had inherited from his predecessors into a new and vibrant means of expression. He expanded the psychological landscape of the pastoral by not only evoking the usual associations of serenity and a fascination with nature but also introducing new elements such as grief and spiritual longing.

In this chapter, I will investigate two pastoral works: one from early in his career, an accompanied song entitled "Der träumende See" ("The Dreamy Lake"); the other near the end, "The White Peacock," which is a solo piano work that he later set for orchestra. There are two reasons for juxtaposing this pair. First, the song serves as a kind of prelude to my set of commentaries on Griffes's mature pastorals since it displays more traditional features such as compound meter and an initial tonic pedal in the bass. This fact is understandable considering that he most likely composed it in Germany or immediately afterward. By contrast, "The White Peacock" is among his most innovative pastorals in that it displays more idiosyncratic cues such as temporal ambiguity, non-Western scales, registral expansion, and the languid style. The second reason is that these two genres, an accompanied song and a work for solo piano, are not only the heart and soul of Griffes's compositional oeuvre, but they also serve as the empirical basis of my interpretive study.

"Der träumende See"

"Der träumende See" dates from Griffes's early period and was most likely composed either in Germany or soon after he returned to New York in 1907; it was published in 1909. The complete score is reproduced in example 4.1.[1] The author of the text, like most of the poems Griffes set in his early songs, is German—in this case, Julius Mosen.[2] An English translation of the poem reads as follows.[3]

Der See ruht tief im blauen Traum	The lake rests deep in a blue dream
Von Wasserblumen zugedeckt.	Covered by water lilies.
Ihr Vöglein hoch im Fichtenbaum,	You, little bird high in the tree,
Dass ihr mir nicht den Schläfer weckt!	Do not wake the sleeper!
Doch leise weht das Schilf und wiegt	But the reeds quietly blow and balance
Das Haupt mit leichtem Sinn,	Their tops with easy sense,
Ein blauer Falter aber fliegt	But a blue moth flies
Darüber einsam hin.	Over, alone, towards them.

In this two-stanza lyric, the narrator describes an idyllic outdoor scene in which a lake, filled with water lilies and surrounded by reeds, is visited by a bird and a moth. Overall, the musical setting can be divided into three parts: mm. 1–12, the opening thematic material; mm. 13–16, a brief interjection marked by a dramatic shift in the piano's accompanying texture; and mm. 17–23, a slightly adapted return of the opening material.

Four musical features of this song reflect the poem's pastoral character: meter, rhythm, scales, and harmony. Let me consider each one in turn. The 6/4 time signature at a slow tempo (*tranquillo ma non troppo*) conforms to the metrical tradition of compound duple found in most Baroque pastoral dances. In her comprehensive study of dance topics in Mozart's operas, Wye J. Allanbrook explains that the gigue, pastorale, and siciliano all share the same compound meter, which she calls triple (see chap. 2 for a detailed summary of these dances).[4] In addition, the *tranquillo ma non troppo* marking underlines the song's overall serene character.

The song's rhythmic texture also resonates with eighteenth-century pastoral traditions, for the voice's trochaic rhythmic patterns (half +

EXAMPLE 4.1.

(ABOVE AND FOLLOWING PAGES)

Griffes, "Der träumende See," complete score.

quarter note) and especially the dotted quarter + eighth note pattern are both reminiscent of the siciliano dance. In many of his works, instrumental as well as vocal, Griffes relies on these rhythmic patterns to evoke some kind of pastoral mood. By contrast, the piano has its own distinct rhythmic texture: a stately chordal motto in syncopated rhythms that repeats throughout the first and third sections. At m. 13 the initial tranquility

disappears in favor of a more effervescent mood; now the stately chords are supplanted by rippling arpeggios, ascending and descending in regular cycles.

A brief comment is in order about the role of text painting in this song. Griffes's sensitivity to the text is evident in his depiction of two specific poetic images: the swaying reeds as a quick arpeggiated texture in the piano (m. 13) and the arrival of the flying moth (m. 19) as a long duration (whole note), a chromatic chord (D6 superimposed above C♯) plus a hint of a descending sigh figure in piano and elaborated in the voice: D–C♯.

The song also exhibits non-Western scales, some of which reinforce the song's pastoral dimension. For example, in mm. 3–6 the vocal line is almost entirely in F♯-pentatonic, which contributes to the melody's folk-like character. Later two whole-tone segments appear in the vocal line in the form of a melodic sequence: G–A–B–C♯ and D–E–F♯–G♯ (mm. 13–14 and mm. 15–16). As we will see below, several of Griffes's mature pastoral works are characterized by his use of the whole-tone, octatonic, and hexa-tonic scales—an outgrowth of his fascination for exoticism.

But it is the harmonic language where the song's pastoral dimension is most evident. In the opening section, the piano's harmonies are static—the low F♯ pedal tolling on alternate bars. This type of ongoing bass pedal is highly reminiscent of several eighteenth-century dances including the musette and the pastorale. Although this pedal ends at m. 8, where the piano briefly modulates to the dominant, it nevertheless establishes a strong harmonic reference to an older pastoral tradition. Then, at m. 13, the rolled chord heralds a change of mood and a new harmonic language. The piano's chordal vocabulary abruptly becomes more chromatic and less functional: c♯ø4/2–C♯4/2–D4/3–C♯4/3. Griffes's interest in harmonic color here shows a strong kinship with that of French composers such as Debussy and Ravel.[5] Indeed, Griffes's sympathy with a French musical sensibility at the fin de siècle is central to his eclectic musical style as well as to his treatment of the pastoral.

The evocation of the pastoral in "Der träumende See" has two dimen-sions. On the one hand, his setting in the opening and closing sections preserves key elements of the eighteenth-century tradition—meter, rhythm, and harmony—and shows the degree to which in his early works he absorbed the musical pastoral traditions of the late Baroque period. Although my overall investigation will reveal a wide range of musical fea-tures that signify the pastoral, both traditional and more Griffes-specific, his revival and adaptation of these three elements will play a central role in his expressive language.

On the other hand, it also contains the seeds of pastoral innovation. Griffes's treatment of rhythm and harmony in the brief middle section is an early indication of the stylistic eclecticism that would become even more pronounced in his later works.

"The White Peacock"

Soon after arriving in Berlin in August 1903, Charles Tomlinson Griffes visited the Zoological Garden and in a letter described his discovery: "Among the peacocks . . . a pure white one—very curious."[6] According to his first biographer, "Since his first glimpse of the bird in Germany Griffes seems to have been stirred by some symbolic dimension in it. . . . He clipped pictures of white peacocks from wherever discovered, and there is one large awkward photograph that he may have taken himself."[7] In 1915, this personal fascination turned into artistic inspiration when he composed his most well-known piano work, "The White Peacock," a musical tribute to a poem by the same name written by the Scottish poet William Sharp. Apparently, Griffes kept the poem "on his piano all the while he composed on that theme."[8] The circumstances in which he composed the opening gesture—while gazing at a sunset on a train between Tarrytown, where he worked at the Hackley Boys School, and New York City—is a microcosm of the two dimensions of his personal life, poised between the country and the city. The orchestral transcription of this work received its premiere in 1919 in the form of a ballet choreographed by Adolph Bolm at the Rivoli Theater in New York. Its performance that same year by the Philadelphia Orchestra under Leopold Stokowski as well as the abundant critical praise it received was one of the high points of Griffes's career.

"The White Peacock" is a compelling example of the ambivalent pastoral. It is also a vivid testament to the composer's preoccupation with gardens, for the instrumental and vocal works associated with garden themes were some of the most experimental pastorals within his overall output. There are two distinct pastoral moods in this tone poem that directly correspond with the structure of the poem. The first one, evoking emotions such as languor and sensual pleasure, appears in the introduction amid a constant parade of new themes, topics, rhythmic ambiguity, and changes in tempo. By contrast, the second mood emerges in the gradual approach to an enormous climax, evoking spiritual ecstasy, and it is achieved through Griffes's treatment of counterpoint, rhythm, scales, and dynamics as well as the magnificent expansion of registral space in the outer two voices. The conflict between these two pastoral moods embodies a garden full of sensuality, ambiguity, and paradox.

Finally, "The White Peacock," whether for solo piano or full orchestra, confirms Griffes's ties to the late nineteenth-century Aesthetic movement in Great Britain by reviving and celebrating one of its most vivid symbols: the peacock. The work also underlines his affinity with the Scottish poet William Sharp, who wrote the poem upon which the work was based. In the pages that follow, I will explore the ways in which the assumptions of Aestheticism as well as Sharp's unique artistic approach shed light on Griffes's work.

Literary History of the Peacock

The image of the peacock belongs to a rich history of exotic and even supernatural associations, stretching from ancient China through the Roman Empire to nineteenth-century Europe. For example, the Romans associated the bird with Juno, the queen of the gods and the personification of pride and, most important, immortality, for the animal's cooked flesh was believed to resist decay. In more recent times, the peacock became one of the most characteristic visual symbols of Aestheticism, one of the leading artistic movement in late-Victorian England. This movement began among writers and painters in Great Britain during the 1870s and 1880s such as Dante Gabriel Rossetti, Algernon Swinburne, and William Morris and later was adapted in America within the fine and decorative arts and architecture.[9] In his celebrated *Studies in the History of the Renaissance*, the English critic Walter Pater helped justify this new ideal of beauty and the sheer pleasure to be derived from it.[10] Other characteristics of this movement include an attraction to synaesthesia as well as a belief in the power of suggestion rather than exact statement—the latter of which reveals no small debt to the French Symbolist poets. For artists of this aestheticist persuasion, the peacock signified not only their passion for sensuous pleasure but also their common fascination with East Asian culture. Its images were ubiquitous, adorning canvases, wallpaper, clothing, furniture, stained glass, and porcelain alike (for more details on Aestheticism, see chap. 2).

A stunning illustration of the impact that peacock themes had on the Victorian artistic landscape is the infamous "Peacock Room," the private dining room of Frederick Leyland that the American expatriate painter, James McNeil Whistler, lavishly decorated in 1877 (its official title is *Harmony in Blue and Gold: The Peacock Room*). The room already proudly displayed one of Whistler's paintings entitled *Rose and Silver: The Princess from the Land of Porcelain* amid the owner's extensive Chinese porcelain collection. Yet Whistler completely changed the room's design, using countless variations of peacocks and feathers and, in the process, transforming it into "a veritable land of porcelain embody[ing] a fantasy view of 'the Orient' deeply embedded in European taste." (Incidentally, this book's cover is a derived and "whitened" version of one wall of Leyland's dining room.).[11]

The literary history of this pale peafowl encompasses several other leading British writers at the turn of the century including D. H. Lawrence and Oscar Wilde. To begin with, Lawrence named his first novel after the white bird.[12] By contrast, the case of Wilde is more complex. Although he is traditionally described as one of the leaders of Aestheticism, in his writings he playfully mocked this literary movement as well as traditional assumptions about gender, social class, and artistic expression itself. Wilde's preoccupation with satire and paradox often had a philosophical cast. In one of his best-known essays, entitled "The Decay of Lying," for example, he introduces the image of a white peacock as the epilogue to his argument that nature should imitate art rather than vice versa.[13] In addition, the same image of a white bird, now multiplied, appears at a pivotal moment in his controversial play *Salome*—when King Herod offers his stepdaughter a gift of one hundred white peacocks if she would withdraw her request for John the Baptist's head, an offer she refuses. In both cases, Wilde relied on the image of a white peafowl to underline a dramatic moment.

Poetic Interpretation of "The White Peacock"

The poem that serves as the basis for Griffes's instrumental work "The White Peacock" belongs to a collection of poetry entitled *Sospiri di Roma* (*Sighs of Rome*); the text is reproduced below.[14]

      Here where the sunlight
      Floodeth the garden,
      Where the pomegranate
      Reareth its glory
5   Of gorgeous blossom;
      Where the oleanders
      Dream through the noontides;
      And, like surf o' the sea
      Round cliffs of basalt,
10 The thick magnolias
      In billowy masses
      Front the sombre green of the ilexes:
      Here where the heat lies
      Pale blue in the hollows,
15 Where blue are the shadows
      On the fronds of the cactus,
      Where pale blue the gleaming
      Of fir and cypress,
      With the cones upon them
20 Amber or glowing
      With virgin gold:
      Here where the honey-flower
      Makes the heat fragrant,
      As though from the gardens
25 Of Gulistan,
      Where the bulbul singeth
      Through a mist of roses
      A breath were borne:
      Here where the dream-flowers,
30 The cream-white poppies
      Silently waver,
      And where the Scirocco,
      Faint in the hollows,
      Foldeth his soft white wings in the sunlight,
35 And lieth sleeping

Deep in the heart of
A sea of white violets:
Here, as the breath, as the soul of this beauty
Moveth in silence, and dreamlike, and slowly,
40 White as a snow-drift in mountain-valleys
When softly upon it the gold light lingers:
White as the foam o' the sea that is driven
O'er billows of azure agleam with sun yellow:
Cream-white and soft as the breasts of a girl,
45 Moves the White Peacock, as though through the noontide
A dream of the moonlight were real for a moment.
Dim on the beautiful fan that he spreadeth,
Foldeth and spreadeth abroad in the sunlight,
Dim on the cream-white are blue adumbrations,
50 Shadows so pale in their delicate blueness
That visions they seem as of vanishing violets,
The fragrant white violets veined with azure,
Pale, pale as the breath of blue smoke in far woodlands.
Here, as the breath, as the soul of this beauty,
55 White as a cloud through the heats of the noontide
Moves the White Peacock.

Sharp's poem is a catalogue of sensual delight, a litany of sumptuous images that celebrates the visual extravagance in a Roman garden. The narrator meticulously describes specific varieties in this visual feast, including such exotica as oleander, pomegranate, and ilex, each with its own unique color. But the most wondrous sight of all is a white peacock that emerges towards the end of the poem and unfolds its tail. The narrator's tone throughout is breathless, as though he or she were overwhelmed by such a magnificent display of Italian flowers and feathers. The poem is written in free verse, on the verge of being a prose poem, and its overall structure is episodic; each of the poem's five sections begins with the words "Here where the . . ."[15]

There are two aspects of this cultivated catalogue that are important for understanding Griffes's musical work. First, the poem highlights the contrast between the pure white color of the bird and the stunning variety of colorful flowers blooming in the garden. Curiously, when describing either the bird or a flower, Sharp often employs a pair of images, juxtaposing white with at least one contrasting color:

"white as a snow-drift in mountain-valleys when softly upon it the gold light lingers" (lines 20–21)
"white as the foam o' the sea that is driven o'er billows of azure agleam with sunyellow" (lines 22–23)

By describing the bird's white plumage in terms of a wide range of other colors, Sharp transforms the bird into a kind of magical living mirror. The absence of color in the bird somehow intensifies the abundance of colors around it. Griffes himself alludes to this dichotomy in the program notes he prepared for a performance of the orchestral version of the work by the Philadelphia Orchestra in 1919: "The music tries to evoke the thousand colors of the garden and the almost weird beauty of the peacock amid these surroundings."[16]

Second, a close reading of the poem reveals that the narrator, in his ecstatic effusions, presents two opposing portraits of the garden. The first portrait is a state of absolute calm, a stillness signified by the image of a sleeping "scirocco"—what is normally a mercurial Mediterranean wind. Silence reigns supreme in this depiction of the garden, allowing the reader to savor all the more the profusion of colors and perfumes. The second portrait appears at the moment when the peacock, the only animal present, folds and unfolds its tail. The grammatical structure of the poem emphasizes the significance of this action; two of the three independent clauses (ending with a period) coincide with the bird's movement (lines 25–26 and 34–36). Most important, the bird opens its tail twice: "that he spreadeth, foldeth, and spreadeth." Thus, the exact repetition toward the end of the poem creates the expectation that the peacock may continue opening and closing its tail, as though it were finally revealing the immortal powers that the ancient Romans believed it possessed. This new portrait is the exact opposite of the first, the stillness serving as a mere backdrop or prelude to the revelation of this bird's spiritual presence. By the poem's end, these contradictory impulses—one of calm associated with the garden itself, the other of action associated with the peacock—somehow unite into a single vision of paradise. As we will see below, this equilibrium between opposites must have stirred Griffes's aural imagination.

There is yet another element of intrigue surrounding the genesis of these poems. During an extended visit to Rome in the winter of 1891, Sharp met an English writer named Edith Wingate Rinder with whom he fell deeply in love and who fully supported his newfound female persona. This biographical detail is significant for the *Sospiri de Roma* collection because the theme of romantic love is established in the initial poem, called "Preface." Thus, in the genesis of these poems Sharp's dual identity was inseparable from romance. The following excerpt from the preface clearly establishes the degree to which the color white and romantic love are deeply intertwined in the poet's mind.[17]

> Few that shall see it,
> Fewer still/ Those that shall pluck it:
> But whoso gathers/ That snow-white blossom
> Shall love for ever,/ For the passionate breath
> Of the Shadow-Lily/ Is Deathless Joy:
> And whoso plucks it, keeps it, treasures it,
> Has sunshine ever/ About the heart,
> Deep in the heart immortal sunshine:
> For this is the gift of the snow-white blossom,
> This is the gift of the Flower of Dream.

Sharp inaugurates his collection of poems by describing a white blossom, a flower with mysterious if not magical powers. Anyone who plucks this flower receives eternal love as well as the power to dream and, by extension, to write. It also hints at the gift of immortality. For readers who begin with the initial poem, any subsequent reference to objects that are white reawakens all of these associations. Hence, even though a particular poem like "The White Peacock" does not refer directly to the "Flower of Dream," the continual references to the color white recall the same associations with romantic love and immortality. This reference to immortality will become important when we consider two conflicting interpretations of the piece's overall formal plan.

It is significant that in a number of poems of the collection, a single color confers special powers and/or significance to people or objects in the gardens, fields, and cities outside of Rome. In poems such as "Susurro," "The Swimmer of Nemi," "la Velia," "The Bather," "The Wild Mare," "Ultimo Sospiro," and "Epilogue, Il Basco Sacro," a wide range of characters—two swimmers (one male, one female), a seagull, a wild horse—all develop a special aura and become bigger than life. In Sharp's mind, to be white is to be pure, innocent, beautiful, and immortal. It is curious that two years earlier the French author Emile Zola used the same color to paint a magical scene in his novel *The Ladies' Paradise*.[18] As a result, when Griffes set "The White Peacock" to music, he inherited a text highly charged with amorous and magical as well as spiritual overtones.

Analytical Commentary

It is significant that Griffes's pastoral vision in this tone poem, like Sharp's poem itself, has two opposing emotional characters, one born of calm and languor, the other of growing intensity, eventually leading to ecstasy. Most important, the second character far exceeds the dramatic scope of the original text. The tension between these emotional characters also can be seen in Griffes's treatment of such features as musical topics, harmony, rhythm/meter, counterpoint, dynamics, and register, as well as two different ways of interpreting the work's large-scale form. Together, all of these factors create one of the richest portrayals of a garden in all of his oeuvre. To appreciate this contrast in character, I will examine two sections in detail: the Introduction (mm. 1–18) and the approach to the climax (mm. 37–47). The score for part of the Introduction is reproduced in example 4.2.

It is useful to display as a network the wide range of pastoral cues that appear in the Introduction.

Eighteenth-century Dance Types

- Polonaise
- Sarabande
- Minuet

Pastoral Cues

- Languid Style
- Dissonant Pedal Chord
- Rhythmic/Metric Ambiguity

The marking for this section, *languidamente e molto rubato*, serves as an apt introduction to Griffes's mature approach to the pastoral. The initial tempo is as slow as the rubato is indulgent. This languishing character, which I call the languid style, is characterized by an occasional fermata

To Rudolph Ganz

The White Peacock
Op. 7, No. 1 (1915)

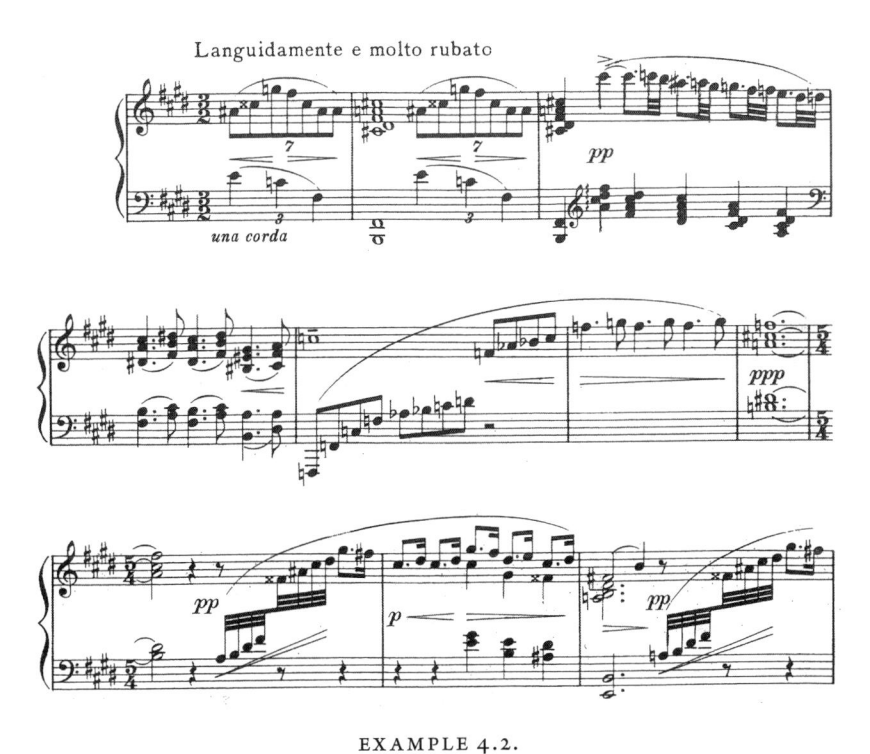

EXAMPLE 4.2.

Griffes, "The White Peacock," mm. 1–9.

and/or rubato as well as a continuous succession of contrasting themes and textures. This evocation of musical languor is so common among the selected pastoral works (ten out of twelve) that it becomes a customized cue for his personal signature.

Even more striking is Griffes's treatment of rhythm and meter in this opening section, which goes hand in hand with the indulgent tempo changes. In the space of seventeen bars, he introduces two different meters, a handful of contrasting rhythmic motives each with its own distinct texture. The overall effect is pure caprice, a stunning display of spontaneity that suggests an instrumental fantasy or rhapsody. Let us consider each one briefly.

The opening section witnesses two different sources of rhythmic/metric conflict. The first grows out of a sharp dichotomy between two different rhythm patterns associated with dance topics in triple meter: the polonaise and the sarabande. Though the polonaise is usually characterized by majestic rhythmic patterns, emphasizing the second beat, in m. 2 the rhythm is syncopated and irregular, suggesting a kind of temporal deformation. By contrast, the rhythmic pattern immediately following (m. 3) is utterly regular, a dotted quarter plus eighth note, repeated three times. This recurring pattern sounds processional and is reminiscent of the sarabande dance.[19] Due to the melody's slow tempo, shape, and brevity, this bar almost sounds like an abstraction or memory of a Baroque dance, but without the usual emphasis on beat two. Each rhythm is displayed in example 4.3.

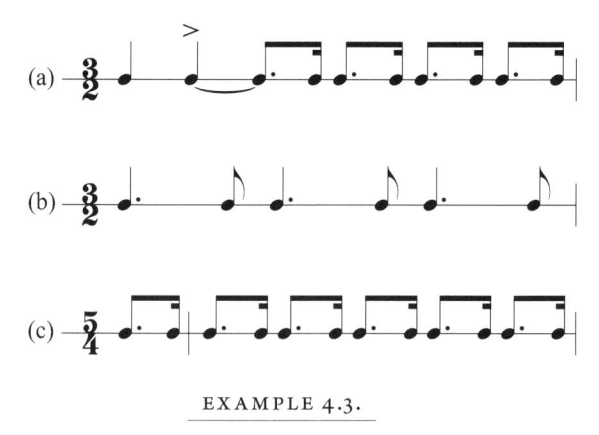

EXAMPLE 4.3.

Griffes, "The White Peacock": Three rhythmic motives: (a) polonaise rhythm; (b) sarabande rhythm; and (c) minuet rhythm.

Griffes's use of these two rhythmic patterns is significant in two respects. First, despite the occasional rubato, both patterns in (a) and (b) strongly reinforce a triple meter (3/2) at moderate tempo. The slow triple time signature could be associated with either the sarabande or the polonaise. But when Griffes changes the meter to 5/4, it could be likened to a type of rhythmic deformation. Since the sections in this quintuple meter always follow extended sections in 3/2, it often sounds as though the melodic material is missing one quarter note.[20] Second, these two dance rhythms reappear in two-part counterpoint right before the climax, thereby contributing to the work's large-scale motivic unity (mm. 38–40); this passage will be discussed below in greater detail.

The other source of rhythmic/metric ambiguity in this section involves notation. Beginning at m. 7, Griffes suggests a new pastoral dance rhythm in the form of a continuous stream of dotted eighth plus sixteenth notes: the minuet. Here, the same continuous dotted rhythms of m. 3 reappear, but now there are six instead of three iterations. Although the Classical minuet does not have a single characteristic rhythm, this repeating dotted pattern occasionally appears as a cadential gesture, as in Mozart's Redoutensäle minuets.[21] To compound the temporal confusion, this new rhythmic motive is notated in an irregular meter: 5/4. Despite its notation, the melody's crescendo to the anacrusis coupled with the overall circular melodic shape strongly suggest a 6/4 meter, which would be appropriate for a slow minuet. This discrepancy between written and heard meter creates a kind of temporal ambiguity that persists throughout most of the opening section (mm. 7–14) as well as its return in mm. 50–56.

In all, this opening section suggests three different dance rhythms: the polonaise, the sarabande, and the minuet—a virtual festival of topical allusion. In addition to this temporal diversity, the two sources of rhythmic/metric tension described above underline the spontaneous and fragmentary character of this passage. For Griffes, musical languor translates into temporal uncertainty.

It is also worth considering Griffes's unusual treatment of melodic motives in the opening measures. The soprano voice highlights the descending chromatic motive, Cx–C♯, which later expands to a turn figure, moving by parallel thirds, A♯/Cx–A/C♯–A♭/C–A/C♯. While the shape of this descending half step is identical to that of the lament sigh figure, its harmonic support—a different chord beneath each pitch—turns it into a traditional chromatic gesture. Later, in mm. 27–30, Griffes develops the sinuous turn shape as parallel thirds, slightly rearranged, in the inner voices (A/C♯–A♯/Cx–A/C♯–A♭/C).

Next, we turn to his treatment of harmony. In contrast to the early song, the opening section of "The White Peacock" is suffused by a highly chromatic harmonic idiom. Yet amid this display of chromaticism, the section is united by a single B9 chord that resounds over and over again, alternating with contrasting contrapuntal, homophonic, or monophonic textures (see example 4.2). Eventually, the chord's traditional harmonic function begins to recede in favor of its role as pure sonority, as a source of instrumental and timbral color. It is as if the recurring sonority evokes a meditative atmosphere, a tolling B9 bell that becomes the object of our musical contemplation. While this opening passage does not contain an extended bass pedal, as we saw in the opening passage of the song, the overall effect is a kind of harmonic stasis in which the sense of forward motion has been nearly suspended.

When this chord is considered along with the anacrusis that precedes m. 1, the passage as a whole becomes a musical aphorism, standing apart from the rest of the piece—as if the peacock were intoning some kind of musical mantra. This aphorism, like the garden itself, is a mixture of opposites: two-part counterpoint in short rhythms (3 against 7) versus a sustained seven-note chord (see example 4.2); polyphony versus harmony. The pitch material of these two textures is also highly contrasting— the whole-tone scale followed by a more diatonic collection. Finally, the roots of the two implied chords create descending fifth motion: F♯ and B. Throughout much of the "A" section (mm. 1–17), Griffes employs variants of this gesture, a panorama of half cadences, combining half-step motions with common tones.

Another unusual feature of the opening passage is the texture that appears in the piano's left hand in mm. 2–3. Griffes repeats the same five-note sonority, B9, eight times in succession, but in each statement, he rotates the vertical arrangement of pitches. In addition, each chord is a four-note subset of the original five-note sonority: A, C♯, D♯, F♯; then F♯, A, C♯, D♯; and so on. This type of textural repetition creates a kaleidoscopic effect while still prolonging the original B9 chord. Griffes must have been fond of this unusual rotating texture, for he recycled it at two crucial moments in his final work, Prelude #3 (see chap. 9).

At this juncture, it is appropriate to draw some preliminary conclusions. The watchwords for Griffes's treatment of harmony, rhythm, and musical topics in this passage are *multiplicity* and *ambivalence*. Overall, the harmonic vocabulary is at cross purposes: intensely chromatic as well as organized around a recurring point of stability—a dominant ninth chord. In this passage, we witness one of the central tensions of Griffes's harmonic style: a joint fascination with stasis and chromatic experimentation. Although the opening of "The White Peacock" is an extreme case, the ambiguity that results from the tight juxtaposition of so many contrasting dance rhythmic patterns and their attendant associations is common in many of his pastorals. Likewise, there are two other sources of temporal ambiguity present in the passage: the tension between triple and compound duple meter; and the conflict between the notated 5/4 and the perceived meter of 6/4. The cumulative effect of all these ambiguities is a form of temporal tension that persists throughout the opening section and returns later in the work.

The overall impact of this opening section is a fantasy-like texture with a strong improvisatory nature that can be described as the languid style. Three distinct dance rhythms appear in this opening section, but none prevails as the dominant theme or dance topic. The distinctive pastoral character grows out of the constant parade of contrasting melodic themes and textures, the changes in tempo, and the persistent rhythmic ambiguity. Initially, the opening section of "The White Peacock" invokes our expectations for pastoral spontaneity and sensual pleasure. But, as will become clear below, by the end of the work, they are called into question.

It is worth mentioning that the work resounds with historical references, for its aphoristic opening pays homage to two iconic nineteenth-century preludes: the initial bars of Wagner's Prelude to *Tristan und Isolde* as well as the opening section of Debussy's *Prélude à l'après-midi d'un faune*. The reference to Wagner is twofold. First, the initial *languido* marking is the same in both works; the lackadaisical musical character is a recurring feature in many of Griffes's pastoral works, what I call the languid style. Second, the initial gesture in both works ends on a half cadence.[22] There are also direct parallels between the opening passage in "The White

Peacock" and the initial flute solo in Debussy's *Prélude à l'après-midi d'un faune*. Both employ a chromatic melodic gesture descending from C♯, both begin by repeating the opening aphorism twice, and both are inspired by a mystical poem. Ultimately, the strongest reference to Debussy consists in the sheer act of repetition: each composer indulges in repeating a sweeping gesture twice, which contributes to the improvisatory character of both works.[23] Overall, the homage to Wagner and Debussy underlines the rich blend of German and French sensibilities present in "The White Peacock"—an overlap in the stylistic periods discussed in chapter 1. Finally, it should be stressed that while there is no direct evidence that Griffes was influenced by either work in this passage, the composer possessed both scores in his personal library.[24]

Following the Introduction, two short sections appear in which the minuet and the polonaise rhythmic themes are briefly developed. In the first section, mm. 18–26, marked *con languor*, the irregular minuet in 5/4 meter continues, progressing between different keys, initially B major and then shifting to B♭ major. Towards the end of this section, Griffes introduces one of his characteristic filigree melodic textures, in this case a voice in the high treble (played by flute in the orchestral arrangement) spinning around the slower moving lines below.

Beginning at m. 27, a new rhythmic theme appears in A major, which includes a hint of lament amid a slightly altered version of the polonaise-like descending theme of m. 2. It is the longest section up to this point with a recurring rhythmic texture. Griffes retains the intensely chromatic profile of the melody, except that this time there are two undulating chromatic lines: an ascending gesture in the soprano, D♯–E–F; and a descending line in the inner voice, doubled in parallel thirds, Cx–C♯–B♯–C♯. The sudden change of register within the F–E motive also suggests the lament character of an appoggiatura (the same half step appears in the soprano in mm. 31–32). The harmonic accompaniment is uncharacteristically diatonic, alternating between I and V7 in A major. Towards the end, the passage transitions to F major, to prepare for a return of the initial minuet theme in 5/4.

At a crucial moment in the work, mm. 37–47, Griffes evokes an entirely new emotion associated with ecstasy or bacchanalian excess that strongly conflicts with the opening evocation of languor; see example 4.4 for the

EXAMPLE 4.4.

(ABOVE AND NEXT PAGE)

Griffes, "The White Peacock," mm. 38–47.

score of this passage. Seven musical elements coincide to create this ecstatic effect, most of which are recurring cues in Griffes's pastoral works.
They are all displayed below. Let us consider each one in turn.

- Cumulative Counterpoint
- Repetition of Rhythm Motives
- Exotic Scales
- Sacred Chorale Style
- Increase in Dynamics
- Unfolding of a Motivic Bass Intervallic Span
- Expansion of Registral Space

First of all, this passage displays a stunning example of "cumulative counterpoint"—that is, a two-part contrapuntal texture that synthesizes two dance rhythms presented in the opening section, suggesting the polonaise and sarabande, respectively. But when these motives reappear, instead of sounding in succession, now they are combined in contrary motion, and, in the process, they take on a new character. The falling chromatic line descends much further than before—three octaves instead of one—and, thereby, evokes a dramatic sweeping gesture. By contrast, the ascending line rises only one octave within the same two bars. Furthermore, since the ascending line consists of slower dotted rhythms, it rises at a slower rate. Thus, an essential element of this motivic synthesis is its rhythmic dimension. The recurring rhythmic patterns and melodic sequences in both outer voices create a brief but relentless texture that builds up to an impressive climax.

At the end of the excerpt, mm. 43–46, an expanded if somewhat disguised statement of the opening motivic material occurs. An important feature of the passage's underlying harmonic structure is the bass's half-step motive, C–B, as shown in the upper two staves of the Schenkerian reduction in example 4.5(a). When compared to the opening bars, the voice leading has been redistributed among the voices: for example, the tenor part now resides in the bass. Example 4.5(b) shows how Griffes develops the bass's half-step motion by employing a rising third leap, C–E, which he then fills in with a chromatic descent derived from the soprano's chromatic scale in m. 2. The harmonic progression in this passage highlights the tritone, C and F♯, for these two triads appear prominently in the bass's composed-out third—either in root position or inverted with added seventh.

Another distinctive feature of this passage is the way that Griffes fuses different non-Western scales into a single climactic gesture. First is the soprano's fragment, F♯–E–D–C, which is drawn from the same whole-tone collection that made its initial appearance in the opening aphorism. Although the pitch material of this melodic descent soon becomes more chromatic, the reference to the opening whole-tone arabesque is unmistakable. Also, the arpeggiated chord at the end of m. 45 is a revoicing of the same pitches from the pick-up to m. 1.

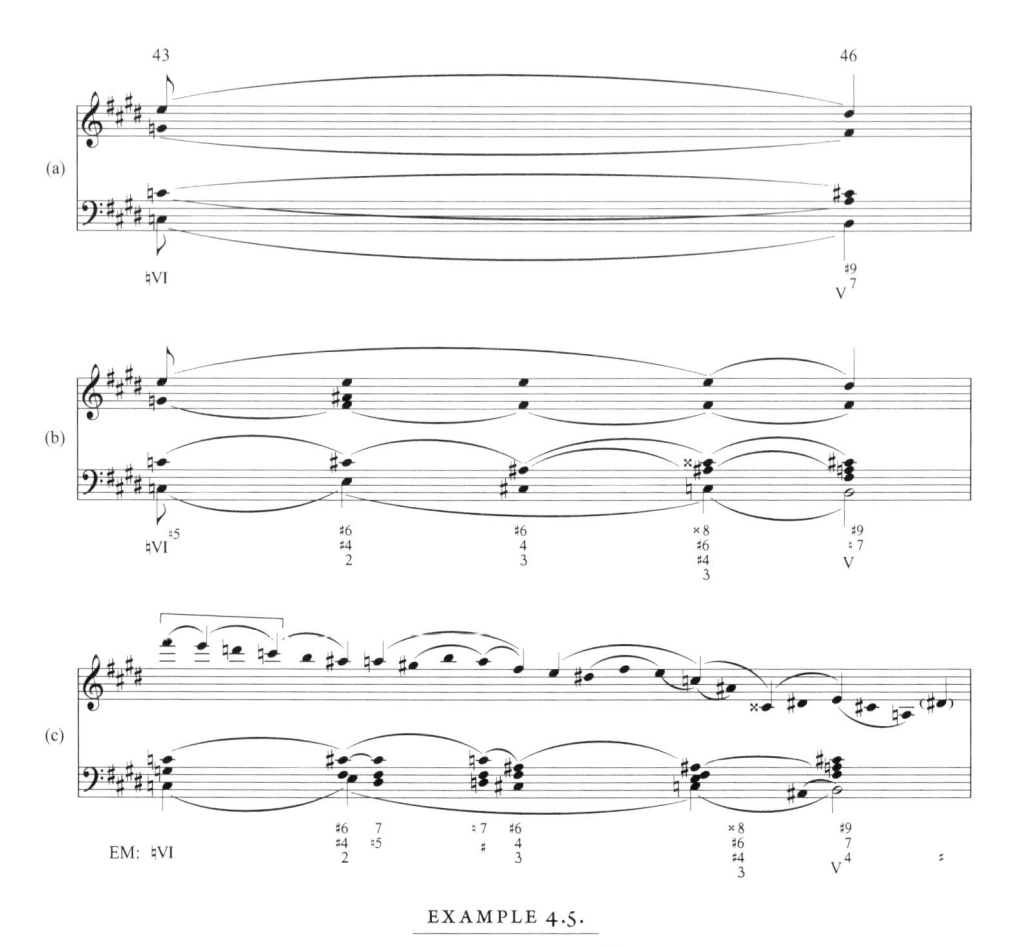

EXAMPLE 4.5.

Griffes, "The White Peacock," mm. 43–46: (a) upper middleground
reduction; (b) lower middleground reduction; and (c) foreground
summary with the whole-tone motive marked by a bracket.

The role that the octatonic collection plays in this passage is somewhat
more subtle. The pitch content of the most prominent chords of this passage, C and F♯7, includes six of the eight pitches from an octatonic scale
beginning on C. A similar octatonic scale with the opposite pattern of
half and whole steps already appeared in mm. 3–4: B9 followed by an F
minor chord with added sixth. Example 4.5(c) displays both scales. Finally, in mm. 38–40 Griffes helps prepare for the climax by using the same

octatonic collection (missing only a "D") but now as a melodic motive. Here the two voices move in contrary motion, one twice as fast as the other, all above a fixed D in the bass. Whereas the right hand ascends from E♭4–E♭5, traversing an octatonic path, the left hand descends through three octaves, E♭6–E♭3, repeating a chromatic motive derived from m. 2. The overall effect is an explosion of exotic scales and chromatic harmony, a fitting prelude to the unveiling of the bird's glorious tail.

Another crucial feature of the evocation of ecstasy in this passage is Griffes's use of dynamics, which resembles that of the opening gesture. The gradual crescendo and sudden decrescendo in mm. 37–47 mirror the precise tapering of dynamics found at the beginning. There are two differences between these passages: in the former, the duration of the passage is longer, ten measures instead of one and a half; more important, the extremes in dynamics are greater, from *pianissimo* to *fortissimo* and back to triple *piano* compared to a crescendo and decrescendo marked *una corda*.

In Griffes's setting, there are several instances of motivic magnification. Two bass prolongations occur, one embedded inside the other. I will focus on a major ninth span that initially appears as the outer pitches in the vertical sonority (mm. 1–2): B–C♯. A composed-out version of this same intervallic span encompasses the entire "B" and Development sections, beginning at m. 18 and culminating at m. 46. The large-scale melodic/harmonic structure of this passage can be seen in the Schenkerian middleground reduction displayed in example 4.6.

The source for this magnified gesture can be traced to the harmonic material of the "A" section—as if the B9 chord were a motivic seed and the unfolding were its germination. Of course, throughout the opening measures there are a profusion of B9 chords that saturate the harmonic texture (mm. 1–3, 6, and 15–17). However, one chromatically inflected variant in particular, a B9 with raised eleventh (or raised fifth)—B, D♯, F, A, C♯—found in m. 6, serves as a harmonic premonition of the overarching ninth span and its division into thirds. Example 4.7 displays a middleground reduction of the entire work.[25]

The final element that contributes to the impact of this passage is Griffes's treatment of register. In this work, the point of departure for any discussion of register is the opening B9 chord. What is striking is not

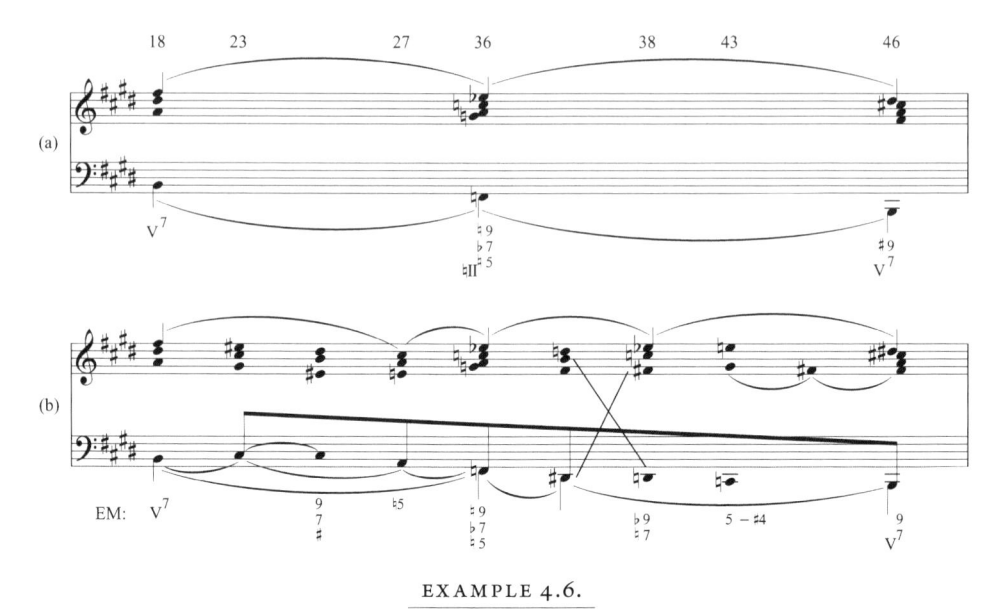

EXAMPLE 4.6.

Griffes, "The White Peacock," mm. 18–46: (a) upper middleground
reduction; (b) major ninth span, C♯3–B1, unfolded in the bass.

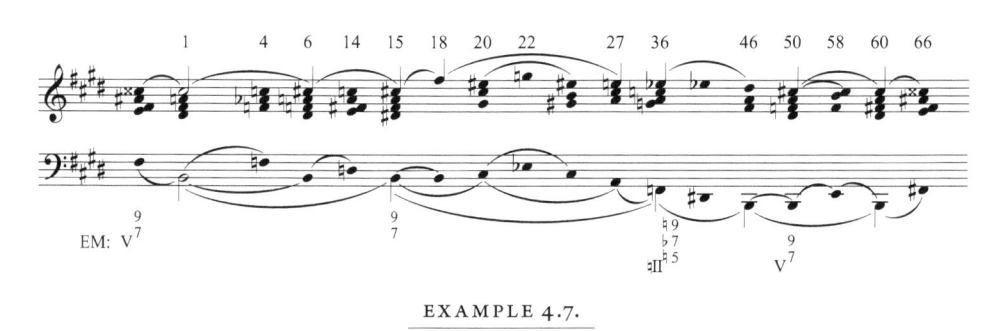

EXAMPLE 4.7.

Griffes, "The White Peacock": Middleground reading of the entire piece.

only its overall range (just over three octaves) but also the open space in
the middle between the two hands. Throughout the "B" section, Griffes
employs sweeping scales and arpeggios that quickly change register (e.g.,
mm. 39–42). But he saves the ultimate expansion in pitch space for the
climactic section in mm. 43–46. The soprano's largely stepwise descent

in constant quarter notes is truly breathtaking, traversing over two and half octaves: F♯6–A4. Beneath this stately descent, the lower part reaches down to C2 amid its frenzied arpeggiated figures. At m. 46, the familiar B9 sonority returns but now inhabiting six octaves: B1 to C♯7. Example 4.8 displays these two chords along with the C major triad in m. 44, which reaches even higher. By repeating the initial lush sonority at the recapitulation and increasing its register in both directions, Griffes uses an expansion of space to portray the unveiling of the peacock's tail in all its white glory.

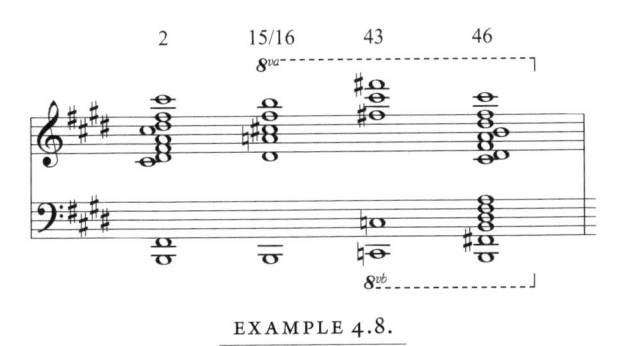

EXAMPLE 4.8.

Griffes, "The White Peacock": Expansion of register, mm. 2–46.

It is worth taking stock of the various ingredients that give rise to the climactic passage. Seven different features participate in this outburst of emotional intensity: cumulative counterpoint, motivic repetition, non-Western scales, sacred chorale style, a gradual crescendo, and an unfolding of a bass intervallic span as well as an expansion of registral space. Such a multidimensional confluence not only portrays the poem's central image—the opening of the peacock's tail; it magnifies it. In short, by expanding the dramatic scale of his musical setting, Griffes creates a different kind of musical pastoral.

Ternary Form

The final parameter that reflects the two dimensions of Griffes's musical response to Sharp's poem is the contrast between two formal designs:

modified ternary versus perpetual. Each design has a distinct emotional trajectory—one is balanced and conventional, the other is open-ended. Since there is evidence to support both plans and their corresponding emotional associations, the work's formal organization possesses an element of paradox. Each interpretation will be discussed in turn.

The work's overall formal design is a modified ternary plan with a truncated recapitulation (the "B" material, mm. 18–34, does not reappear); the lower level shows different subsections within each larger section.

mm.	o	2	7	18	27	35	46	50	60
section	Intro	A1		B		Dev	A2		Coda
subsection	a1	a2	a3	b1	b2	c/a	a2	a3	a1

The principal analytical criteria for making these formal divisions are repetition and thematic contrast. Each of the three subsections in A1 has its own distinct thematic material. The a1 subsection is open-ended, ending on a dominant-ninth chord. The overall effect is a fusion between the introduction and the following subsection. It is curious that when the opening motivic material returns in m. 46 (labeled as A2 on the diagram), the initial bars are omitted. In the a2 subsection at m. 2, the soprano unfolds a descending chromatic theme that emphasizes a diminished-seventh arpeggio: C♯, A♯, G, E. The third subsection, a3, introduces yet another contrasting theme, largely pentatonic, employing a diminution of the dotted rhythm first heard in m. 3.

It is worth briefly exploring the thematic material in the Coda (mm. 60–66). Two statements of the opening melodic gesture appear, followed by a third statement that is interrupted when the bass slowly descends into a whole-tone abyss. At this juncture, the initial half-step motive, Cx–C♯, is also left incomplete. While the harmonic support of this half-step gesture is not as static as that of a sigh figure, the motivic interruption bears a strong resemblance to Griffes's treatment of a genuine lament motive in "The Rose of the Night" (see chap. 6).

Perpetual Repetition

The second approach to the piece's form is technically not a different scheme altogether but rather a different way of interpreting the ternary scheme. According to this interpretation, the "Development section" (mm. 35–46) coincides with the end of the first part of this two-part dramatic framework. The A2 section and Coda serve as the first stage in the next progression. In this section, Griffes not only repeats earlier motivic material, he transforms it: new harmonic support for the pentatonic theme (e.g., F#9 in m. 56) and a new chordal theme, unfolding a ninth span in the soprano voice, B4–C#6. These motivic transformations suggest that the intensification process witnessed in A1 is beginning anew. The overall form would now be expressed as A B A' (B), the symbol (B) indicating a continuation of the two-part progression that is implied but never heard. The final measures also reinforce this perception, for in mm. 62–66 Griffes inverts the order of the two parts in the opening gesture: the coda closes on a predominant instead of a dominant chord, a fragmented arpeggio instead of a sustained sonority. The entire work ends on a note of uncertainty: Will the tail unfold one more time? Has the postlude become a new prelude, the musical tail turning into a new head? Will the tail keep opening and closing forever, a prophecy to be fulfilled? Or is it or a promise to be broken?

There is yet another layer to add to our interpretive process: the inaugural poem of the entire *Sospiri* collection. The title and the preponderant white imagery of "The White Peacock" all refer to the central images found in Sharp's "Preface": the "snow white blossom" and "the Shadow-Lily." According to the narrator, whoever discovers and plucks this flower will have perpetual sunshine and immortal love and be enchanted by the "Flower of Dream." The question is how to interpret the open-ended quality of Griffes's coda with its descending tritones in the soprano and bass (mm. 63–64). Does it foreshadow another revelation in which the bird opens its magical tail again? Or rather does it portray the promise of spiritual rapture mixed with romantic passion found in the "Preface"? In short, does it evoke spiritual fulfillment or emotional uncertainty?

In the end, we are left with a vision of floral paradise that is suffused by paradox.

An additional feature of Griffes's ambiguous and paradoxical musical garden is that it embodies Michel Foucault's concept of "heterotopia." A musical heterotopia is more than a mere poetic backdrop, providing atmosphere or color for a work's title or program; rather, it is an interdisciplinary artistic design that allows contradictory forms of musical expression to intermix with layers of literary associations (for more discussion of this concept, see chap. 5).

In the context of Griffes's musical peacock, the various types of paradox, though essential in the initial stages of interpretation, must finally be placed within a larger critical framework where reconciliation is possible. The peacock and garden together create a vision of spirituality, an epiphany of natural beauty, where stasis and action are mutually dependent. In the end, the paradox arises from the listener being able to perceive the final "A" section (mm. 46–66) as both closed and open at the same time—closed in that it completes a familiar pattern and open in that it inaugurates a new pattern that remains unfulfilled. The music beckons listeners to contemplate this formal paradox and then transcend it. The work affords the potential for the audience not only to perceive the conflict between opposites but ultimately to reconcile it into a new synthesis: open and closed, the ternary as well as the perpetual conception of form. While Sharp's original poem evokes the mystery of a white bird opening its tail amid an extravagant garden, Griffes's setting magnifies and enhances this mystery, giving the poem's spiritual character a new dimension.[26]

It is possible to interpret Sharp's poem and Griffes's musical response to it through a double autobiographical lens. The opening of the bird's glorious tail would express the poet's discovery of his own dual genders. In addition to the ornithological mating ritual based on revelation, the opening of the tail would become a gender transformation in which the poet expresses his newfound feminine sensibility. In fact, Sharp's own letters from Italy and the account in his wife's biography support this interpretation.[27]

> That moment began, he declared, 'my spiritual regeneration. I was a New Man, a mystic, where before I had been only a mechanic-in-art.

> Carried away by my passion, my pen wrote as if dipped in fire, and when I sat down to write prose, a spirit-hand would seize my pen and guide into inspired verse.

When we consider Griffes's musical response to the poem, its intensity and sensuality may seem like a perfect reflection of Sharp's remark about his "pen dipped in fire." As a result, it may be tempting to interpret the musical setting of the poem as an expression of the division in Griffes's own personal life: homosexual in his private affairs and heterosexual in his professional teaching position. However, to draw such a one-to-one correspondence between the biographical circumstances of the author in the 1890s and of the composer in the 1910s seems premature. What lingers in Griffes's tone poem is the musical portrayal of spiritual ecstasy and the multiple interpretations of the final gesture. The difference between the text and its musical setting is that while the poem coincided with a profound shift in the poet's sexuality, the musical setting participates in a larger artistic process that expresses the composer's deep ambivalence toward the pastoral.

Ekphrastic Coda

My portrait of "The White Peacock" would not be complete without exploring a remarkable embodiment of ekphrasis, which this work brings to life.[28] Ekphrasis can be defined as an artistic work in one medium that is inspired by a work in another medium. In ancient Greece, the term denoted a linguistic response to a non-linguistic work such as a verbal description of a painting or sculpture. The earliest examples can be found in Homer's *Iliad* and Virgil's *Aeneid*. Siglind Bruhn refers to ekphrasis as interartistic transformation or "transmedialization."[29] In reviving this concept of blending, artists in the Aesthetic movement were borrowing a page from early Romantic writers in France like Théophile Gautier (and later Symbolists like Charles Baudelaire) who had during the 1830s advocated a synthesis or "transposition" of different artistic traditions in which sonnets would be called pastels and pastels sonnets. Later in the century, the American painter James Whistler himself exemplified this idea when he regularly borrowed musical themes as titles for his paintings including

FIGURE 4.1.

"Pierrot en Pieds, Portrait of the Lady A. C.," Théodore
Roussel, Etching. Rosenwald Collection, National
Gallery of Art, Washington, DC, Open Access.

harmony, note, symphony, and *nocturne.* Among his most famous works are a series of works entitled *Symphony in White,* each of which is a portrait of a woman (or women), clothed in picturesque costumes and rendered in various shades of white (these works will be discussed in greater depth in chap. 7).

In the case of Griffes's peacock, the blending of senses is like a miniature genealogy of artistic culture at the turn of the century, spanning nearly thirty years and encompassing four different media: music, poetry, art, and drama. Griffes was inspired by a poem that itself had two previous sources of inspiration of which he was most likely unaware. According to Sharp's wife, Elizabeth, "The White Peacock" was intended as a literary tribute to Théodore Roussel, a French artist and student of Whistler, whose work Sharp had admired. In her biography of her husband, Elizabeth reports an entry in his diary dated February 1891: "In forenoon wrote 'The White Peacock' (56 lines)—a study in Whites for Théodore Roussel."[30] This reference is most likely to one of several art works by Roussel, who lived near the Sharps in Chelsea during the early 1890s. In the summer of 1888, Roussel fashioned four works—a pastel entitled *Ma fonction est d'être blanc* and three etchings—that were all inspired by Théodore de Banville's play *Le Baiser* (*The Kiss*), performed outdoors in Wimbledon, outside of London. All four depict the lead actress, Lady Archibald Campbell, who had donned the traditional white costume of Pierrot; the etching entitled "Pierrot en Pied, Portrait of the Lady A.C." is reproduced in figure 4.1.[31] Although in his poem Sharp makes no mention of the commedia dell'arte character, he shares with the French artist a fascination for subtle variations in white. It also suggests that a renewed interest in experimentation with color helped unite painters and poets as well as composers at the turn of the century. In sum, Griffes's peacock has a four-dimensional artistic heritage that traverses five countries and four different media: a play written by a French playwright inspired a pastel by a French painter living in England, which in turn inspired a poem by a Scottish writer visiting Italy, which in turn inspired a piano work by an American composer living in New York.

NOTES

1. Donna Anderson concludes that "Der träumende See" was completed sometime in the period between 1903 and 1909, when it was published by G. Schirmer; see Anderson, *Charles T. Griffes*, 235. The score in example 1 is drawn from the following reprint: *The Songs of Charles Griffes*, vol. 3, Medium Voice, ed. Donna Anderson (New York: G. Schirmer, 1995).

2. Robert Schumann also set same poem for four-part male choir as Op. 33, no. 1.

3. The English translation is by Laura Prichard, available on The LiederNet Archive, accessed January 6, 2021, https://www.lieder.net/lieder/get_text.html?TextId=113581.

4. "Although the word 'triple' is not found in the label of 6/8 meter, 'tripleness' is central to the definition of 6/8 and of the other compound duple meters and makes a decisive contribution to its movement and affect. . . . For this reason the dances written in 6/8 meter—the gigue, pastorale, and siciliano—are classed with the meters in triple time." Wye J. Allanbrook, *Rhythmic Gesture in Mozart: Le Nozze di Figaro and Don Giovanni* (Chicago and London: University of Chicago Press, 1983), 40–41.

5. The harmonic progression in mm. 12–15 is reminiscent of passages in Debussy's "Reflets dans l'eau," *Images*, Book I (1905) and Ravel's Sonatine: III (1905).

6. Edward Maisel, *Charles T. Griffes: Life of an American Composer*, 2nd edition (New York: Alfred A. Knopf, 1984), 36.

7. Ibid., 154.

8. Ibid.

9. See *Dictionary of Art* in 34 vols., ed. Jane Turner (Long: Macmillan, 1996), I: 170–71. For a sweeping overview of the influence of this movement in American culture, see Doreen Bolger Burke, ed., *In Pursuit of Beauty: Americans and the Aesthetic Movement* (New York: Metropolitan Museum of Art, 1986).

10. *Studies in the History of the Renaissance* (London: Macmillan, 1873). This definition of beauty was partly a reaction against the Victorian conception of art as an instrument of moral education. Swinburne, a leading figure in the Aesthetic movement, penned a virtual credo for this approach: "Art can never be the handmaid of religion, exponent of duty, servant of fact, pioneer of morality." Quoted in Lionel Lambourne, *The Aesthetic Movement* (London: Phaidon, 1996), 11.

11. When Leyland discovered what Whistler had done without his permission, he initially refused to compensate him, but later insulted him by paying a smaller fee in pounds, a currency meant for trade, instead of guineas, which was customary for professionals. But eventually Whistler got the last word by repainting one interior wall with two birds quarreling, surrounded by coins. See Linda Merrill, *The Peacock Room: A Cultural Biography* (Washington, D. C.: Smithsonian Institution, 1998), 9, 230–32. Upon Leyland's death, the entire room was acquired by Charles Freer, an industrialist in Detroit, who later gifted it to the Smithsonian in Washington, D.C. For a detailed survey of other nineteenth-century depictions of peacocks, see Lambourne, *Aesthetic Movement*, 50–65.

12. See D. H. Lawrence, *The White Peacock* (London: Heinemann, 1911).

13. In the final paragraph of Wilde's essay "The Decay of Lying," the narrator says, "The final revelation is that Lying, the telling of beautiful untrue things, is the proper aim of Art. . . . And now let us go out on the terrace, where 'droops the milk-white peacock like a ghost,' while the evening star 'washes the dusk with silver.'" See *The Complete Works of Oscar Wilde*, ed. G. F. Maine (London: Collins, 1948), 931.

14. The text is drawn from a subset of the original collection in William Sharp, *Poems*, selected and arranged by Mrs. William Sharp (New York: Duffield, 1912), 156–58. In the notebook that Griffes himself kept of books he purchased during the years 1903–14, the following entry appears: "1914, Poems, Wm. Sharp, 1.50." For a representative sampling from this list, see Anderson, *The Works of Charles T. Griffes*, 509.

15. As in much of his poetry in the collection, Sharp adopts an archaic mannerism, employing the suffix *-eth* for most verbs conjugated in the third singular.

16. Anderson, *Charles T. Griffes*, 164.

17. The excerpt is drawn from William Sharp, *Poems*. Incidentally, the full title of this poem is even more suggestive: "Prelude: to ———," *Sospiri de Roma*, (Roma: La Societá Laziale, 1891), accessed July 6, 2020, https://books.google.com/books?id=jT9DAQAAM AAJ&pg=PA9&source=gbs_selected_pages&cad=2#v=onepage&q&f=false.

18. Quoted in Lawrence Kramer, "Consuming the Exotic: Ravel's *Daphnis and Chloe*," in *Classical Music and Postmodern Knowledge* (Berkeley: University of California Press, 1995), 202:

> [A] tide of white assumed wings, hurried off and lost itself, like a flight of swans. And the white hung from the arches, a fall of down, a snowy sheet of large flakes; white counterpanes, white coverlets floated about in the air, suspended like banners in a church; long jets of Maltese lace hung across, seeming to suspend swarms of butterflies; other lace fluttered on all sides, floating like fleecy clouds in a summer sky, filling the air with their clear breath. And the marvel, the altar of this religion of white was, above the silk counter, in the great hall, a tent formed of white curtains, which fell from the glazed roof. . . . It made one think of a broad white bed, awaiting in its virginal immensity the white princess, as in the legend, she who was to come one day, all powerful, with the bride's white veil.

19. Examples of this rhythmic pattern appear in the sarabande movements of J. S. Bach's Partitas for Clavier, No. 5 in G major (BWV 829) and No. 6 in E minor (BWV 830).

20. Indeed, one could draw an analogy with the second movement of Tchaikovsky's Symphony No. 6: Allegro con grazia, which has been dubbed the "limping waltz."

21. See Eric McKee, *Decorum of the Minuet, Delirium of the Waltz: A Study of Dance-Music Relations in ¾ Time* (Bloomington: Indiana University Press, 2012), 51–55, 79–81.

22. The difference between the two passages is that, following the initial cadential gesture in Wagner's Prelude, he repeats and transposes the gesture two more times, creating a trio of half cadences, none of which resolves. Griffes merely repeats his initial gesture.

23. In a fascinating study of Debussy's compositional technique and its broader aesthetic context, James Hepokoski explores the French composer's reliance on aphoristic openings in a wide variety of works. Although Griffes's two-part gesture does not fit neatly into any of Hepokoski's three categories, it belongs unmistakably to the late nineteenth-century tradition of non-periodicity, mystery, and the ritual of art substituting for religion. Hepokoski concludes, "Once art has thus been sacrilized, even as an aesthetic fiction, the mode of entry into a work suggests *ipso facto* a corridor or vehicle of passage from one experiential realm to another"; it becomes an entrance rite from the profane to the sacred." See James A. Hepokoski, "Formulaic Openings in Debussy," *19th Century Music* 8, no. 1 (Summer 1984): 44–59.

24. See the comprehensive appraisal of Griffes's personal library by Harold Ernest Wands, Box 70, Series III, Donna K. Anderson Research Files on Charles Griffes, New York Public Library: Manuscripts and Archives, Music Division.

25. For a more detailed Schenkerian interpretation of the entire work, see Taylor A. Greer, "The Unfolding Tale of Griffes's 'White Peacock,'" *Gamut: The Online Journal of the Music Theory Society of the Mid-Atlantic* 3, Issue 1, Article 7.

26. For more information about this formal interpretation, see ibid.

27. William F. Halloran, "W. B. Yeats, William Sharp, and Fiona Macleod: A Celtic Drama: 1887 to 1897," *Yeats Annual* 13, ed. Warwick Gould (London: Macmillan, 1998), 68–69. For a general introduction to Sharp's life and work see Alaya, Flavia. *William Sharp—"Fiona Macleod," 1855–1905* (Cambridge, Massachusetts: Harvard University Press, 1970).

28. In "The Unfolding Tale of Griffes's 'White Peacock,'" I refer to this type of interartistic expression as a form of synaesthesia rather than ekphrasis. The latter can be understood as a subset of the former.

29. Siglund Bruhn, "Musical Ekphrasis: The Evolution of the Concept and the Breadth of Its Application," in *The Routledge Handbook of Music Signification*, ed. Esti Sheinberg and William P. Dougherty (London and New York: Routledge, 2020).

30. Sharp, *William Sharp*, 179.

31. Multiple versions of the etching "Pierrot en Pied, Portrait of the Lady A.C." exist, both in red as well as black and white, and are housed in various collections: the British Museum; Hunterian Art Gallery, University of Glasgow; Rijksprentenkabinet, Rijksmuseum, Amsterdam; Metropolitan Museum of Art, New York City; National Gallery of Art, Washington, DC; and Victoria and Albert Museum, London. See Margaret Dunwoody Hausberg, *The Prints of Theodore Roussel: A Catalogue Raisonné* (Bronxville, NY: M. Hausberg, , 1991), 46.

5

The Pleasure-Dome, *Paradox in Paradise*

In June 1912, after reading an excerpt from a novel by the late nineteenth-century French author Pierre Loti, Charles Griffes confided to his diary, "Read 'Fleurs d'ennui'. . . . Loti has here written a highly-coloured and strangely exotic tale of one Arab quarter of Algiers. Every word breathes Oriental perfumes. The preceding pages describing their cart-trip in [Ghinea] and entrance into the village and inn have also Loti's peculiar faculty of transporting the reader at once into a strange and exotic atmosphere."[1] It is significant that at this juncture Griffes was immersed in reading a stimulating novel about northern Africa, for throughout his artistic career he was inspired as much by literary as by musical sources (for more information about his broad literary tastes, see chap. 1). Indeed, Griffes would spend the next five years composing and revising his own sonic brand of "Oriental perfume" in his tone poem *The Pleasure-Dome of Kubla Khan*, based on the emperor's ancient garden, as imagined by Samuel Taylor Coleridge.[2] When the work was premiered in 1919, the critics agreed. A Boston music critic wrote, "This is a work intoxicating in color and exotic imagination, written with a boldness and an enthusiasm irresistible to the listener."[3]

The Pleasure-Dome[4] combines the conventional emotions found in Virgil's literary tradition—the evocation of serenity amid the contemplation of nature—with other emotions such as the expression of grief, aggression, and harbingers of war. Griffes's musical vision of Coleridge's garden is a conflict of opposites: a host of languid melodies versus a tarantella section, evoking bacchanalian frenzy; and two contrasting formal designs—one teleological, a dramatic buildup to a climax that is interrupted, the other circular, beginning and ending with the same mysterious chorale texture. Griffes's tone poem also expands the topic of the pastoral by combining traditional musical cues such as compound duple meter, dotted rhythmic patterns, and static bass lines with cues of his own making including the languid style, rhythmic/metric ambiguity, and the expansion of registral space. Finally, Michel Foucault's notion of "heterotopia" provides a rich interpretive framework for understanding one of Griffes's most challenging pastorals—in this case, the musical evocation of an ancient Chinese garden.

> In Xanadu did Kubla Khan
> A stately pleasure-dome decree:
> Where Alph, the sacred river, ran
> Through caverns measureless to man
> Down to a sunless sea.
> So twice five miles of fertile ground
> With walls and towers were girdled round:
> And there were gardens bright with sinuous rills,
> Where blossomed many an incense-bearing tree;
> 10   And here were forests ancient as the hills,
> Enfolding sunny spots of greenery.
>
> But oh! that deep romantic chasm which slanted
> Down the green hill athwart a cedarn cover!
> A savage place! as holy and enchanted
> As e'er beneath a waning moon was haunted
> By woman wailing for her demon-lover!
> And from this chasm, with ceaseless turmoil seething,
> As if this earth in fast thick pants were breathing,
> A mighty fountain momently was forced:
> 20   Amid whose swift half-intermitted burst
> Huge fragments vaulted like rebounding hail,
> Or chaffy grain beneath the thresher's flail:
> And 'mid these dancing rocks at once and ever
> It flung up momently the sacred river.
> Five miles meandering with a mazy motion
> Through wood and dale the sacred river ran,

Then reached the caverns measureless to man,
And sank in tumult to a lifeless ocean:
And 'mid this tumult Kubla heard from far
30　Ancestral voices prophesying war!
The shadow of the dome of pleasure
Floated midway on the waves;
Where was heard the mingled measure
From the fountain and the caves.
It was a miracle of rare device,
A sunny pleasure-dome with caves of ice!

A damsel with a dulcimer
In a vision once I saw:
It was an Abyssinian maid,
40　And on her dulcimer she played,
Singing of Mount Abora.
Could I revive within me
Her symphony and song,
To such a deep delight 'twould win me
That with music loud and long
I would build that dome in air,
That sunny dome! those caves of ice!
And all who heard should see them there,
And all should cry, Beware! Beware!
50　His flashing eyes, his floating hair!
Weave a circle round him thrice,
And close your eyes with holy dread,
For he on honey-dew hath fed
And drunk the milk of Paradise.

Poem and Tone Poem

The source of inspiration for Griffes's work was one of the most famous poems of the English Romantic school, Samuel Taylor Coleridge's "Kubla Khan, or a Vision in a Dream. A Fragment" (the text is reproduced above). Written in 1797, this poem is unusual in that its genesis, as described by the author, is inextricably bound up with its historical reception.[5] According to Coleridge's own preface, before falling asleep, he had been reading Marco Polo's account of the palace of Kubla Khan, the medieval Chinese emperor, as described in Samuel Purchas's collection of stories *Purchas his Pilgrimes.* Immediately upon awakening from a vivid dream or hallucination induced by an "anodyne" (most likely opium) he had taken, he furiously began writing. But in the middle of trying to capture this dream in words, he was interrupted by an extended appointment with a mysterious man from Porlock. Having lost his earlier inspiration, he struggled to finish the poem, what had now become a mere fragment compared to the extravagant dream he had begun to record.

There are two conclusions to be drawn from this elaborate autobiographical anecdote. First, Coleridge's fantastic poetic vision was fueled as much by a genuine historical source as by a hallucinogenic drug. Second, assessing the degree of truth in this confession is less important than focusing on the inherent two-part structure of the text—the poem reads as though the narrator had been interrupted. As will be shown below, the concept of interruption ends up playing an essential role in Griffes's musical evocation of the poem.

The opening two stanzas are devoted to a description of an extraordinary garden, full of stark opposites: sunny fields and verdant forests suspended above endless icy caverns, all of which are enclosed by a vast dome. Beneath this "savage" place lies a sacred river called "Alph" that flows to the sea. In the final stanza, an abrupt change occurs when the narrator describes a new character, the "Abyssinian maiden," who sings and plays a dulcimer. It is as if, in the final lines, the narrator is trying to recall the magic of this mysterious maiden, her music, and the imperial garden yet cannot quite recapture the original intensity of any of them. There is also a shift in temporality—from the present to the past—and, more important, a shift in tone: from the wonder of pure sensual pleasure to a kind of nostalgia. This shift is even reflected in the extended title Coleridge settled upon: he called it a "fragment" as well as a "vision of a dream," which leads the reader to infer that the poem is not a whole but rather a partial vision, an interrupted dream.

In Western European history, the garden myth has a long and abundant history, embracing natural beauty, emotional and physical respite, and, most of all, sensual pleasure. For Homer, Theocritus, and Virgil the garden was a *locus amoenus*, a pleasant place, whether understood in sacred or secular terms. In his exhaustive compendium *The History of Gardens*, Christopher Thacker defines six principal types of gardens that have recurred throughout the history of human civilization: *locus amoenus* garden, sacred grove garden, farm garden, garden associated with specific Greek and Roman gods, private garden, and paradise garden.[6] Of the six, the most relevant for my study of Griffes's tone poem is the paradise type. The significance of this garden for my study is that Griffes took liberties with Coleridge's original vision, crossing the serenity of paradise with the fury of bacchanalian passion, which leads us to the concept of a "heterotopic" garden.

Heterotopia is a concept initially described in the late writings of the twentieth-century French philosopher Michel Foucault, denoting a phenomenon that had multiple characteristics—hence the prefix *hetero*—and was not limited to utopia or its negation, dystopia. In Foucault's mind, a "heterotopia is capable of juxtaposing in a single real place several spaces ... that are in themselves incompatible."[7] Examples include ancient Persian gardens and Jesuit colonies in South America as well as modern museums and cemeteries. In recent years, Foucault's notion of heterotopia has inspired a surge of scholarly inquiry in such fields as literary criticism, architecture, landscape architecture, and geography.[8] For example, Luke Morgan uses this concept to explain a peculiar type of garden that emerged during the Renaissance, a so-called "monster garden," in which wildly conflicting iconography and emotional associations were juxtaposed together, including fear and violence alongside sensual beauty and serenity.[9]

The genesis of Griffes's musical response to the poem is one long labor of ambivalent love. It is not clear how he came in contact with Coleridge's text, but he began a piano work based on the poem sometime in 1912 and continued revising it until 1915. In a diary entry he confessed that "never before have I changed and changed a piece as much as this one."[10] Later, he initiated an orchestral version of the solo piano work by the same name and continued revising it until 1917. However, the version for orchestra differs so much from its piano counterpart that it should be considered an independent work, not a mere transcription. Two years later, when the orchestral piece was premiered in Boston, Griffes included brief excerpts from Coleridge's poem (lines 1–8, 11, 31–36). The composer himself pre-pared the following program notes for the concert:[11] "I have taken as the basis for my work those lines of Coleridge's poem describing the 'stately pleasure-dome,' the 'sunny pleasure-dome with caves of ice' the 'miracle of rare device.' Therefore, I call the work 'The Pleasure-Dome of Kubla Khan' rather than 'Kubla Khan'. . . . As to argument, I have given my imagina-tion free rein in the description of this strange palace as well as of purely imaginative revelry which might have taken place there."

These remarks are particularly telling about Griffes's aesthetic ap-proach in this work. First of all, he explains that he focused on the garden itself—hence, the different titles of the poem and the tone poem. More important, he admits that in his composition he invented something that was not in Coleridge's original dream: a scene of "imaginative revelry" inside the palace. This sensual supplement serves as the basis of a new kind of pastoral genre, a conflict of opposites that combines the peaceful contemplation of nature with the eruption of primal energy. This fusion

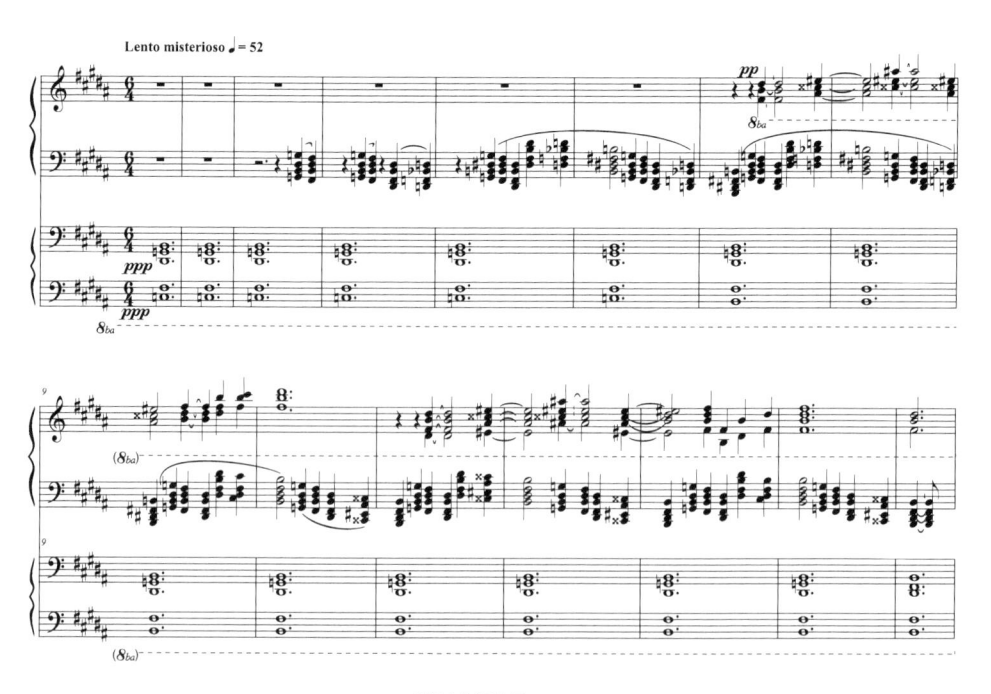

EXAMPLE 5.1.

Griffes, *The Pleasure-Dome*: Two-piano reduction, mm. 1–14.

of opposites—Apollonian calm and Dionysian abandon, which I have dubbed the heterotopic garden—was the product of a new aesthetic vision, a bold literary and musical collaboration, initially fueled by Coleridge but ultimately brought to fruition by Griffes alone.

The remainder of the chapter is devoted to exploring the wide range of conflicts and oppositions found in *The Pleasure-Dome*. My point of departure is a detailed examination of the work's Introduction, for this section displays a rich juxtaposition of contrasting topics that contain the seeds of Griffes's peculiar pastoral vision. Next, I will focus on three oppositions: (1) episodic form versus circular form; (2) the languid style, as exemplified in the initial oboe solo and the later so-called "Arabian" theme, versus the tarantella style, as illustrated in the sudden arrival of a dance section towards the end; and (3) the complete versus the incomplete psychological cycle. Each will be discussed in turn.

Introduction

As a whole, the Introduction in mm. 1–14, shown as a two-piano reduction in example 5.1, is a dialogue between conflicting musical topics that are associated with the river Alph, slowly passing under Coleridge's imaginary garden. The first one is a lament that gradually emerges from an unworldly tremolo, barely audible in the lowest reaches of the orchestra—cellos and double basses. The tremolo consists of a tritone juxtaposed against an augmented triad: D♯, G, B. Next, the solo piano presents the same augmented triad as a chordal sonority, which then resolves to a B-major triad. The moving voice presents the first melodic activity so far, a falling half step, G–F♯, a gesture strongly associated with suffering and grief. All of the salient cues found in this passage are displayed below.

Pastoral Cues

- Dissonant Pedal Chord
- Hunting Fanfare in Long Rhythmic Durations
- Rhythmic/Metric Ambiguity
- Sacred Chorale Style

Lament Cue

- Sigh Figure

It is noteworthy that the harmonic foundation for the entire passage, mm. 1–14, also has topical implications. The harmonies are largely static, an augmented triad, juxtaposed above a fixed interval, a tritone, which later changes to a perfect fifth. This initial dissonant pedal chord creates an unworldly effect—mysterious and foreboding. Though far removed from the consonant drone of a musette, the dissonant pedal nevertheless serves as one of Griffes's personal cues to signify the pastoral.

This opening section also illustrates Griffes's fascination with rhythm/ metric ambiguity in that two independent musical layers are juxtaposed at the same time. The first layer is a mysterious "sacred chorale" ostinato played by the piano, mostly in parallel counterpoint that repeats five times in all between mm. 3–14.[12] The harmonic pattern is twelve chords long, beginning on an offbeat, moving mostly by quarter notes, and subdivided as 7 + 5. By contrast, an additional contrapuntal layer occurs in the trombones and tuba: a three-voice chorale texture, suggesting a hunting fanfare in slow motion. But this layer contains a different form of syncopation, consisting of rhythmic attacks on beats 3 and 6. The combination of these two distinct layers, highlighted by contrasting instrumental textures, creates a stunning mosaic of rhythmic/metric ambiguity.

In addition, since each of these layers is a chordal texture, most of the Introduction is a celebration of the "sacred chorale style." Here Griffes combines rhythmic ambiguity with topical abundance, blending the associations of a solemn chorale with those of a plaintive lament and memories of the hunting horn. Even though the dynamic level throughout the opening section remains subdued, the gradual increase of voices and the eventual shift between a tritone pedal to a major triad creates a feeling of blossoming, as if the garden were slowly coming to life after winter.

It is also worth noting the unusual nature of the pitch collection in this passage. The top voice in the chorale texture presents five of the six pitches in the hexatonic collection: (B♭), B, D, D♯, F♯, G; note that the sixth pitch, the B♭, appears in the tuba/trombone theme (mm. 7–10). This symmetrical collection is significant for several reasons. First, it possesses an inherent tonal ambiguity in that it consists of two augmented triad subsets, separated by a half step. In this passage, Griffes fully exploits this potential for tonal uncertainty by implying two keys at the same time: B major in the ostinato pattern and B♭ major in the brass chorale. Second, this collection has the capacity for creating harmonic progressions that are linked by major third motion (or four half steps). In the section immediately following this Introduction, the composer includes two such rotational progressions: BM–GM6/5–BM (m. 16); and BM–D♯M–BM (mm. 23–25).

Now let us consider the emotional profile of the Introduction. Two features suggest that the passage should be identified as some kind of pastoral: the dissonant pedal chord and the hunting fanfare theme. Yet several factors make this topical identification problematic. First of all, the slower tempo of the hunting fanfare gesture dilutes the usual associations—suggesting either a distant memory of or a commentary on the hunt. In addition, the continuous presence of the lament gesture introduces an element of grief that conflicts with the usual positive associations of the hunt. The result is a combination of mystery, sadness, and ambiguity, an emotional palette that, due to the extreme variety of its constituent features, does not easily cohere into a whole. While there are other passages in the work that have clearer and more positive psychological associations, this initial feeling of ambiguity hovers over the entire work.

Formal Design

One of the most curious characteristics of Griffes's *Pleasure-Dome* is its formal design, for two different principles of large-scale structure are present: an episodic plan and a circular plan. The episodic design is evident in the constant variety of motivic material throughout much of the work, beginning at the B section and continuing to the H section (see the formal diagram below).

mm.	1	15	28	47	57	72	89	106	125	139	169	210
section	A	B	C	D	E	D₁	D₂	E₂	F	G	H	A'

In mm. 15–209, the formal plan is mostly additive, consisting of a series of diverse textures and motives, almost like a musical travelogue, and evoking a wide spectrum of emotions, ranging from placid to impassioned. It should be emphasized that there is a small element of repetition in this section of the work, as indicated by the recurring themes marked as "D" (the so-called "Arabian" theme) and "E." For a brief section, Griffes develops these musical ideas with new instrumentation and accompanying textures. Thus, while there is some brief repetition among subsections, the most distinctive feature of this plan is its unpredictability, the constant parade of contrast mirroring the breathless series of paradoxical images in Coleridge's poetic rhapsody.

The other notable aspect of the composition's form is its circular character, for in mm. 210–20 a truncated version of the opening section appears as a Coda (indicated by the recurring A' symbol). In this final section, Griffes repeats the opening chorale material but also introduces several changes. First, the overall passage is shorter, a compact ten-bar epilogue. Next, the same three-bar excerpt of the chorale appears twice in succession and at different registers—one octave lower in the piano and two octaves higher in the celesta. This type of motivic repetition accompanied by an expansion of register in two directions is one of the unique cues that characterizes Griffes's most experimental pastorals. Finally, the slow hunting fanfare theme has disappeared, and instead the mournful lament gesture returns, now highlighted in the viola and English horn parts (see the list below for the various cues at work in this passage).

Pastoral Cues

- Dissonant Pedal Chord
- Sacred Chorale Texture
- Expansion of Register

Lament Cue

- Sigh Figure

Ultimately, the piece's form can be understood in two different ways. On the one hand, the continuous contrast in theme and texture suggests an episodic design based on improvisation with a small degree of internal repetition. On the other hand, the return of the opening chorale texture, now shortened and rearranged, serves a narrative function, as if dramatizing the listener's arrival and departure from the garden—a horticultural ceremony with its own processional and recessional.

Languid Style

In a handful of pastoral works, Griffes employs markings such as *languidamente* or *con languore* to indicate the overall mood to be conveyed (for more details about the significance of this marking, see chap. 3). However, there are several passages in his works that, despite the absence of the specific Italian term, share many of the same characteristics. *The Pleasure-Dome* contains two of them.

The first example appears immediately after the Introduction at m. 15 (Rehearsal B); the relevant features of the passage are listed below.

Pastoral Cues

- Compound Duple Meter at Moderate Tempo
- Languid Style
- Bass Pedal Point
- Oboe Instrumentation (orchestral version only)

Three features are central to the pastoral character of this passage: meter, melody, and harmony. Griffes employs the compound duple meter (6/4) that is so characteristic of eighteenth-century pastoral dances. Next the melody itself has a lazy, idyllic quality due to its simple rhythms and slight chromaticism. That the melody is given to a double-reed instrument only enhances its languid character. Finally, the harmony in the first phrase is static, with a bass pedal on B. The combination of these features evokes a traditional pastoral character, and, in so doing, the passage dispels the ambiguity of the Introduction and replaces it with feelings of lethargy and serenity.[13]

Arabian Theme

The other passage that exemplifies the languid style also illustrates how complex Griffes's use of non-Western resources can be. In his hands, musical exoticism becomes a confluence of the unfamiliar and the familiar, a fusion between a non-Western scale and a rhythmic texture that strongly suggests an utterly Western dance: the waltz.

EXAMPLE 5.2.

Griffes, *The Pleasure-Dome*, mm. 47–57 (NB: the Horns in
F are playing two F♯s, tied from the previous measure). 1929

To set the stage for our interpretation of this section, we begin with the
so-called "Arabian" theme first heard at Rehearsal H + 2 (m. 47). In a diary
entry from 1912, Griffes confided that he discovered the tune in an anthol-
ogy of Arabian music from the New York Public Library (see ex. 5.2).[14]
The network of features and topics at work in the passage are listed below.

Pastoral Cues

- Compound Duple Meter at Moderate Tempo
- Languid Style: Expressive Melody

- Alternative Scales (double augmented 2nd's and implied hexatonic)
- Pedal Point
- Oboe Instrumentation (orchestral version only)

Lament Cue

- Sigh Figure

There are several features in this list worth noting. To begin with, the melody bears a strong resemblance to the stoic hexatonic theme of the Introduction. Example 5.3 presents the pitches from the piano's top voice in the opening bars juxtaposed against those from the oboe theme at m. 47 (slightly simplified). They are related by a T11 operation. This common hexatonic framework emphasizes an underlying motivic unity between the two passages. However, the melody includes more than six pitches, and, when they are taken into account, then the resulting collection has an unmistakable exotic character. This seven-note scale contains two augmented seconds: G–A♯ and D–E♯ (the G appears in the first violin, m. 54). Example 3.3 in chapter 3 provides two different explanations of the same scale—one beginning on B, the other on F♯—and each refers to a different ethnic tradition: Arabian and Romani, or so-called "Gypsy."

EXAMPLE 5.3.

Griffes, *The Pleasure-Dome*: Two hexatonic scales,
mm. 1–14 and mm. 47–57.

But there is more to this passage than merely identifying the starting pitch of a scale. Careful study of the passage's rhythmic pattern, phrase lengths, and harmonic support suggest that it possesses the underlying musical framework of a waltz, the most popular European dance in the nineteenth century. To appreciate this framework, it is useful to compare the orchestral work with the comparable passage in the original solo piano

EXAMPLE 5.4.

Griffes, *The Pleasure-Dome for Solo Piano*, mm. 53–58. 1984
© Permission by G. Schirmer. All rights reserved.

version, reproduced in example 5.4. Such a comparison reveals that the piano's accompaniment pattern has a strong waltz-like feel. Despite the 6/4 notated meter, the entire passage can be heard as if each measure were two bars of 3/4 or a two-bar hypermeter. Likewise, Viennese waltzes are typically notated in 3/4 but heard and danced in 6/4, which corresponds to the dancers' choreography: a rotation every two bars. Let us consider mm. 55–58 of the piano version. Here the piano's left hand plays a recurring ostinato rhythm in the bass accompaniment: two eighths followed by two quarters or short + short + long + long. Furthermore, the downbeat on every other measure is strongly emphasized in a low register by the pitch B1. Also, the melodic contour of the entire two-measure gesture is from low to high and then back down again. This type of accompaniment pattern is highly characteristic of Chopin's waltzes for solo piano.[15]

When the piano version of *The Pleasure-Dome* is compared to the orchestral version, the differences between the two are striking. Given that Griffes explicitly marks the piano excerpt as a "languorous dance rhythm," it is reasonable to interpret it as a slow, lyrical waltz. By contrast, the orchestral work contains a much simpler texture. Instead of the piano's rich accompaniment pattern, it maintains a continuous pedal on F♯, which highlights the profile and overall impact of the melodic line. Yet, enough similarities exist between the two versions to suggest that the orchestral work is a kind of disembodied yet exotic dance, the semblance of a spinning gesture that still evokes the distant memory of a waltz.

The section's waltz lineage is also evident in Griffes's treatment of phrase length in the orchestral version. Over the eight-bar passage, the phrase organization forms a regular pattern of 4 + 4. Furthermore, the cadence structure of the two phrases superimposed over a dominant pedal constitutes a parallel period—the first phrase ends on a half cadence, the second on an authentic cadence. However, there is a tension between the rhythmic shape of the melodic motive within each four-bar phrase and the rather square overall scheme. The sinuous arabesque motive falling through an octave span sounds indulgent, even unpredictable, due to the gradual rhythmic acceleration from the initial dotted quarter to the eighth-note triplets. This improvisational character is somewhat at odds with the regimented phrase rhythm.

Finally, the initial descending minor second in the melody, F♯–E♯, in slow rhythmic values over a pedal point in the bass strongly suggests the lament figure. The resemblance between this half-step gesture and that found in the Introduction underlines the similarity in scale type: the hexatonic. The emotional impact of this conjunct interval gives the oboe's theme an additional ambiance of mourning and melancholy.

It is worth taking stock of my observations about this passage. Griffes's use of an unorthodox scale in addition to utterly orthodox rhythmic patterns, phrase length, and harmonic plan creates a complex musical surface that is far more than a quotation from an Arabian source. As a seasoned pianist and composer, Griffes was certainly familiar with the nineteenth-century tradition of the waltz. The same could be said about contemporary audiences and critics who first heard the orchestral version when it was performed in Boston and New York City in the fall of 1919. Therefore, it is essential to interpret the passage beginning at m. 47 as a conflict of opposites having multiple interpretations, a blend of Middle Eastern and Western traditions that could be likened to a musical mosaic, displaying different evocations or, in semiotic terms, distinct significations. The result is a new musical synthesis, part Arabian, part Western, but altogether new.

Another curious dimension of Griffes's musical depiction of this ancient garden is his desire to briefly suggest elements of potential menace and aggression. The seed for this new dimension can be found in the poem itself, for the narrator mentions "a demon lover" and warns readers to beware "his flashing eyes, his floating hair." At m. 40 a new section is heralded by a bellicose ostinato in the tuba and timpani over a bass pedal on B♭. Though its quarter-note pulse is processional, its intervallic structure—replete with recurring tritones (B♭–D♭–E–B♭)—suggests something more sinister. Two bars later the horns and trombones present a military fanfare topic, but this one is slightly askew. The rhythms are syncopated and the melodic line highlights an octatonic mode. Altogether, we are left with either hints of war or whispers of woe.

Complete versus Incomplete Cycle

The final subject in my overview of *The Pleasure-Dome* is the concept of cycle that serves as an overarching psychological scaffolding for the work. Based on Coleridge's text, one may wonder whether in this work Griffes was trying to portray the different natural stages of growth and decay in a garden—that is, the change of seasons. A musical version of that cycle might consist of three parts: an initial a languid section; a more impassioned section that gradually approaches a climax; and then a final dénouement that releases tension. The quintessential example of such a complete cycle would be "The White Peacock."[16]

However, in several of Griffes's works this abstract cycle is incomplete. Here, the cyclic model is more personal, a large-scale psychological design formed by the interaction between the contrasting emotional associations of the languid and tarantella styles. The rupture in the work's expressive arc is characterized by a sudden shift in dynamics, a change in tempo, and/or an abrupt contrast in motivic material. He reserved this pattern of interruption for two works that are both associated with intense imagery such as a bacchanalian fantasy or a supernatural vision: *The Pleasure-Dome* and "The Rose of the Night," from *Three Poems of Fiona MacLeod* (see chap. 6). In the former case, the most radical departure from Coleridge's original poetic vision lies in the contrast between, on the one hand, the initial languid melodies and an exotic theme and, on the other hand, the gradual buildup to an enormous climax, which is suddenly subverted.[17] Let us consider how Griffes achieves this interruption.

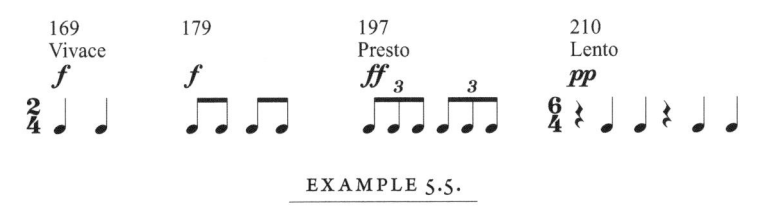

EXAMPLE 5.5.

Griffes, *The Pleasure-Dome*: Schema of interrupted Bacchanal.

Nothing in the opening 168 measures prepares the listener for the *Pleasure-Dome's* astonishing conclusion. Example 5.5 gives a synopsis of the musical evocation of debauchery and its interruption. At Rehearsal V (m. 169), the tempo, rhythm, dynamics, and phrase lengths all begin to change. Here, the tempo marking changes to vivace and later to presto (m. 197). Likewise, the dynamics increase to *fortissimo* and stay at that level until getting even louder at m. 201. The meter, which through most of the work has usually been 6/4 or 3/4, is now a spirited 2/4. Even more dramatic is the change in rhythmic values. Starting at Rehearsal W (m. 177), the music consists of either eighth notes, eight-note triplets, or sixteenth notes—creating a dramatic rhythmic acceleration. At rehearsal Y

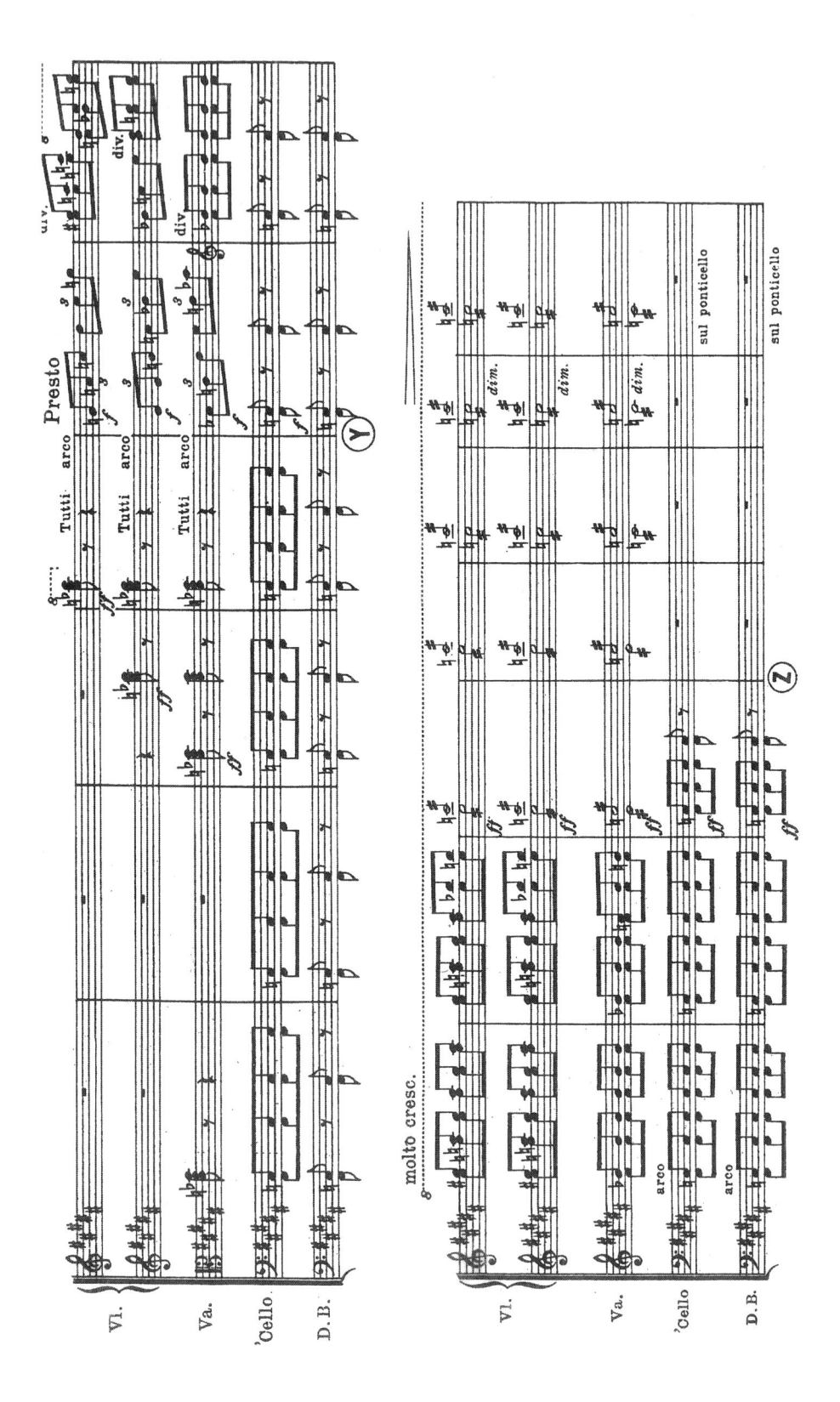

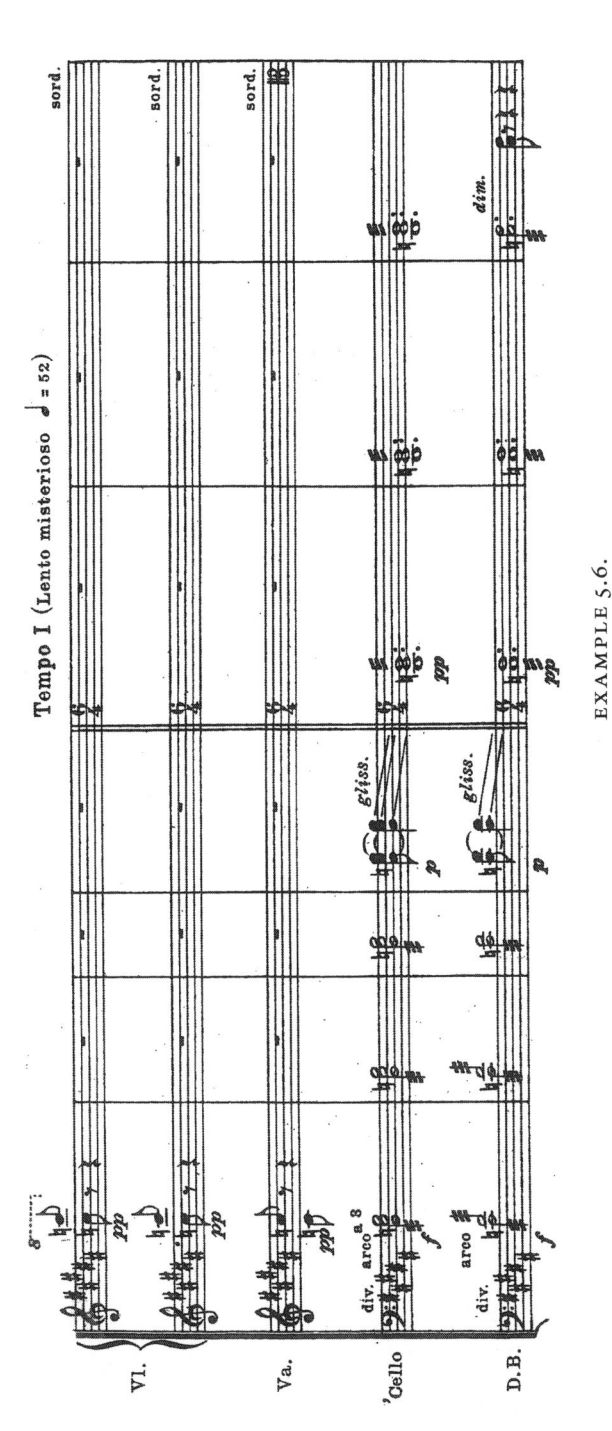

EXAMPLE 5.6.

Griffes, *The Pleasure-Dome*, String parts only, mm. 193–212.
1929 © Permission by G. Schirmer. All rights reserved.

(m. 197), the entire ensemble shifts to eighth-note triplets in 2/4, which is a notational equivalent to 6/8. For the next nine bars, the texture sounds like a tarantella raging out of control (the string parts are isolated in ex. 5.6). The phrase lengths change from six measures to two measures to a five-measure passage that leads to an extended tremolo at m. 202.

Everything up to this point suggests an impending musical climax. Yet the climax never arrives! Beginning at Rehearsal Z + 2 (m. 204), the dynamics suddenly die away from *ff* to *pp*. The ensemble thins out from a riotous tutti to a two-voice texture: a single melodic line in the tuba plus a muted tremolo in the low strings followed by a bizarre glissando in the low strings. Without warning, the musical "orgy" has expired, and the eruption of energy has come to an abrupt end. The overall effect is like an enormous interruption, a musical-dramatic purgation that never comes to fruition.

In some respects, this subverted climax could be interpreted as a musical analogy to the interruption of Coleridge's original burst of literary inspiration—the mysterious "knock on the door" that disrupted his creative process. Taken together, Coleridge's original dream and Griffe's musical response to it are both suspended in time—either in mid-stanza or in mid-tarantella. However, since what happens next in the orchestral work—an abbreviated repetition of the opening section—fails to reflect Coleridge's final lines, the correspondence between the musical and literary interruptions should be considered extremely loose.

Ultimately, there is a more persuasive interpretation. The three oppositions in form, style, and treatment of cycle serve a larger musico-dramatic purpose. Griffes's pastoral composite, part languid, part bacchanalian, is not a stable union of two equal partners. Instead, it functions more like a musico-rhetorical experiment, an unstable compound of two opposing and highly active ingredients. This conflict of opposites is less a strict formal category than a fluid formal process—one that changes from moderate to fast-paced, from soft to loud dynamics, from subdued sensual pleasure to wanton excess, from the spirit of Apollo to that of Dionysus. The only way that this musical work reaches some kind of fulfillment is in the return of the opening section. Thus, the reprise of the initial mysterious chorale and hexatonic melody at the end is like the mournful calm after the sensual storm, creating a semblance of closure.

Conclusion

At this juncture, it is worth taking stock of my reflections about Griffes's setting of Coleridge's poem. The question arises: what kind of a musical pastoral is *The Pleasure-Dome of Kubla Khan*? The answer is that it is less a unified aesthetic ideal than a forum of ambivalence in which different pastoral visions are in conflict with each other. In some ways, the work has a utopian character, especially in its expressive melodies and luxuriant textures. Yet in other ways, it evokes darker emotions, beginning in the mysterious introduction, continuing in the menacing ostinato passage, and culminating in the climax and its interruption. While the negative elements fall short of true dystopia, the whole is closer to being a musical paradox with a mixed emotional message—in short, it is a musical version of Foucault's heterotopia. This amalgam of opposites is evident in many ways.

First, the Arabian waltz passage is a fascinating portrait of musical exoticism at the fin de siècle in that it blends together Western and non-Western characteristics. This musical mosaic has contradictory elements that coincide, creating a new synthesis.

Second, what is striking about the work's overall dramatic trajectory is its hybrid and, ultimately, paradoxical character. Despite the multitude of marvels in the emperor's garden, Griffes adds yet one more—a musical evocation of a bacchanal. The result is an overarching conflict of opposites, a process of negation in which the idyllic languid theme near the beginning is transformed into its opposite: the tarantella. The two themes and their respective psychological worlds could not be more opposed: what begins in serenity and restraint leads to intensity and abandon.

But the ultimate power of the work is inseparable from the circularity in its form. The return of most of the introductory material at the end can be considered like a musical frame that encloses everything in between. *The Pleasure-Dome* belongs to a group of works that display a similar circular shape. Yet it is what happens immediately before this motivic return—the abrupt shift in rhythm, dynamics, and tempo—that determines the overall psychological impact of the work. As a result, this fissure in the musical fabric takes on a pseudo-narrative function, as if one were stepping outside the story or waking up from a dream. The initial parade of contrasting textures followed by the obsessive treatment of the Arabian theme all become things of the past, gradually fading from memory. What is left is the music from the entry into the garden—the slow methodical rhythms of the opening chorale, first in the piano's low register and then restated in the celesta's enchanting higher register.

The question arises: what does the motivic repetition at the beginning and the end mean? Does it suggest that nothing has changed, that the search for magical sights and sounds in a distant garden has come full circle and that we are back to where we started? There are two ways in which the return of the opening gesture is significant. On the one hand, the motivic repetition certainly reinforces Gilles de Van's paradoxical view of exoticism: "An impetus toward the other which becomes a mirror of the self."[18] In that respect, the listener has participated in a musical and horticultural journey that returns to its point of origin. The quarter-note rhythmic texture suggests a slow, mysterious processional, perhaps the evocation of human footsteps or the perpetual flow of the river Alph.

On the other hand, the slight variations in this motivic repetition also carry dramatic meaning. The changes in the musical procession's registral spacing and instrumental timbre signify some kind of expansion of the narrator's self-awareness. Also, the renewed emphasis of the lament gesture, G–F♯, adds an element of sadness and melancholy. In short, the journey itself suggests a process of self-awareness—that is, the process by which the listener proceeds through the entire work ensures that the final statement of the initial sighing motive has evolved since its appearance in the opening measures.

In one respect, Griffes's aesthetic aspirations for Kubla Khan's magical garden are even greater than those of Coleridge one hundred and twenty years earlier, for his vision encompasses greater emotional extremes— sensual pleasure, whispers of war, bacchanalian abandon—yet all under a shadow of mystery and grief. Perhaps the characteristics of ambiguity and paradox are the inevitable outcome of an aesthetic unity that is imagined but can never be achieved. In sum, Peter Marinelli's comment about the pastoral genre is as appropriate for collaborations between music and literature as it is for literature alone: the "entrance into the pastoral world represents . . . not an end but a beginning."[19]

NOTES

1. Diary entry June 29, 1912, Box 47, Folder 5-6, Series III, Donna K. Anderson Research Files on Charles Griffes, Music Division, New York Public Library for the Performing Arts. Pierre Loti (whose real name was Louis Marie-Julien Viaud) was a leading French author at the turn of the century, whose works explore themes of colonial life, romance, and melancholy. See Robin Anita White, "19th- and 20th-century Exoticism: Pierre Loti, Michel Leiris, and Simone Schwarz-Bart," PhD Dissertation, Louisiana State University, 2004.

2. In this connection, Griffes's comment about another prose fragment by Samuel Taylor Coleridge is relevant: "'The Wanderings of Cain' would be a good thing for a melodrama with piano.... The language is very dramatic and picturesque." Diary Entry, August 9, 1912, Box 47, Folder 5-6, Series III, Donna K. Anderson Research Files on Charles Griffes, New York Public Library: Manuscripts and Archives, Music Division.

3. Olin Downes, *Boston (Sunday) Post*, December 7, 1919, Special Section, quoted in Anderson, *The Works of Charles T. Griffes*, 32.

4. Hereafter, for convenience, I will abbreviate the full title of *The Pleasure-Dome of Kubla Khan* as simply *The Pleasure-Dome*.

5. The following summary and the text of the poem itself are based on this source: *Coleridge's Poetry and Prose: Authoritative Texts, Criticism*, ed. Nicholas Halmi, Paul Magnuson, and Raimonda Modiano (New York: W. W. Norton: 2004), 180–83.

6. Christopher Thacker, *The History of Gardens* (Berkeley: University of California Press, 1979), 9–17.

7. "Des Espaces autres, heterotopies," in *Dits et* Écrits: *1954–1988*, vol. 4 (Paris: Éditions Gallimard, 1967), 6. Published in English as "Of Other Spaces, Heterotopias," accessed on June 18, 2018, https://foucault.info/documents/heterotopia/foucault.heteroTopia.en/.

8. For a sampling of the breadth of influence that Foucault's concept of heterotopia has had, see the following bibliography: https://link.springer.com/referenceworkentry/10.1007/978-1-4614-5583-7_584.

9. Luke Morgan, *The Monster in the Garden: The Grotesque and Gigantic in Renaissance Landscape Design* (Philadelphia: University of Pennsylvania Press, 2016).

10. See Diary Entry, September 23, 1912, Box 47, Folder 5-6, Series III, Donna K. Anderson Research Files on Charles Griffes, Music Division, New York Public Library for the Performing Arts.

11. Anderson, *Charles T. Griffes*, 159.

12. For more information on the "sacred chorale," see Eric McKee, "The Topic of the Sacred Hymn in Beethoven's Instrumental Music," *College Music Symposium* 47 (2008): 1–30.

13. In m. 23, immediately after the oboe's theme, Griffes introduces a more spirited melodic idea in 6/4 meter, replete with dotted rhythms, that is reminiscent of the eighteenth-century siciliano dance.

14. "After lunch went to the Library and looked through all their works on Arabian music, in order to find something appropriate for use in 'Kubla Khan.' Copied out one rather good air." Diary entry, May 15, 1912, Box 47, Folder 5-6, Series III, Donna K. Anderson Research Files on Charles Griffes, Music Division, New York Public Library for the Performing Arts.

15. Examples of two-bar hypermeter in Chopin waltzes include Op. 34. No. 1, mm. 81–84, 97–100, 129–32; Op. 34, no. 3, mm. 93ff; Op. 64, no. 2, mm. 65ff; Op. 69, no. 1, mm. 65–80. I wish to thank Eric McKee for pointing out these analogies in Chopin's music.

16. For a detailed analysis and commentary of "The White Peacock," see Greer, "The Unfolding Tale of Griffes's 'White Peacock.'"

17. It should be emphasized that the overall psychological arc of *The Pleasure-Dome* is more complex than a progression from the initial languid melodies to the eventual bacchanalian outburst. For example, in mm. 40–46, immediately before the Arabian theme appears, Griffes introduces a more bellicose theme, suggesting some impending conflict: an octatonic military fanfare, marked *fortissimo*, in the horns and trombones that is accompanied by a dissonant ostinato in continuous half notes in the timpani, tuba, and piano (B♭, D♭, E).

18. Gilles de Van, "Fin de Siècle Exoticism and the Meaning of the Far Away," *Opera Quarterly* 11, no. 3 (1995): 78.

19. Marinelli, *Pastoral*, 73.

6

Songs of Lament and Spiritual Yearning

"To live in beauty—which is to put into four words all the dream and spiritual effort of the soul of man."

—Fiona Macleod[1]

"Your husband was a man of genius, who brought something wholly new into letters. ... He was certainly the most imaginative man—I use the word in its old & literal sense of image making—I have ever known, not like a man of this age at all."

—Letter from W. B. Yeats to Elizabeth Sharp[2]

Introduction

This chapter explores pastorals of a different color. Towards the end of his life, Charles Griffes composed a song cycle entitled *Three Poems of Fiona Macleod*, Op. 11 for voice and piano, which was premiered in the spring of 1919; that same month, the Philadelphia Orchestra performed a transcription for voice and orchestra.[3] The poetry was written by William Sharp, who also used a female pseudonym, Fiona Macleod, for the last thirteen years of his life. The combination of intensity and ambiguity in Macleod's poetry provided fertile artistic ground for Griffes's pastoral imagination. Indeed, theirs was a compelling partnership, for his musical settings magnify the psychological impact of the poetry, revealing ways in which emotions such as pastoral serenity are juxtaposed with various shades of grief, eroticism, and spiritual yearning. The result is an artistic expression of ambivalence that is unique in the composer's oeuvre.

The chapter will consist of three parts: (1) a brief comparison of the general artistic style and spiritual preoccupation of Sharp/Macleod with that of Griffes; (2) an analysis of the three poems in the cycle; and finally (3) a detailed exegesis of the composer's musical settings of them. My focus throughout will be on the ways in which Griffes not only revived the traditional musical pastoral but also transformed it.

William Sharp (1855–1905) was a controversial figure in English literature at the turn of the twentieth century. While his early works were closely aligned with the Pre-Raphaelite movement, a sojourn to Italy in 1891 served as the turning point in his literary career. Soon after that trip, he began writing under a different name, Fiona Macleod, while continuing to use his original name in some literary contexts. In short, he cultivated a double identity, one secret and female, the other public and male. Sharp's wife, Elizabeth, provides a meticulous but guarded account of her husband's double identity in her biography, including lengthy excerpts from his personal diary.[4] Inspired by this new persona, Sharp became prolific and in less than thirteen years penned two full-length novels, many short stories, over one hundred poems, and two stage plays, one of which, *The Immortal Hour*, was transformed into a popular opera by Rutland Boughton. She developed an enormous following in late-Victorian England, received several marriage proposals, and conducted an extensive correspondence of over one thousand letters that were transcribed by Sharp's sister, Mary, in order to conceal his own handwriting.[5]

This female persona not only renewed Sharp's literary passion, but it also changed his artistic orientation. Sharp/Macleod, along with such writers as W. B. Yeats, helped inaugurate the Celtic Revival, or Celtic Twilight, in turn-of-the-century England. The novels, plays, and poetry written under the name Macleod celebrated the folk tales and mythology of ancient Celtic culture and promoted a new awareness of nature, magic, and the supernatural.[6]

Sharp was among a small group of artists who felt the need to write us-ing some form of pseudonym.[7] In his output, there are two early examples of works in which he used a pseudonym other than Macleod. In 1892, he partnered with an American female writer, Blanche Willis Howard, to write *A Fellowe and His Wife*, an imaginary epistolary novel from the perspectives of a married couple. It comes as little surprise that the two authors reversed genders—Sharp wrote all the wife's letters and Howard wrote those of the husband. This joint project was a clear premonition of his later fascination with adopting a female perspective.

The other example was *The Pagan Review*, the first and only volume of a periodical also published in 1892, for which Sharp was the editor and sole contributor. The issue consisted of seven essays or short stories and an editorial preface, all written using different pseudonyms. The titles of these essays reflect Sharp's fascination with exoticism during this pe-riod; examples include "The Black Madonna" and "Dionysos in India."[8] It should be emphasized that by using the word *pagan* for this new journal, Sharp was by no means excluding all spiritual experience, but rather tra-ditional organized religion.[9]

Given the unusual nature of Sharp's fascination with dual artistic iden-tities, it is tempting to speculate that there is a one-to-one correspon-dence between those features of his biography and various dichotomies or dualities present in Griffes's music. But that would be a mistake. One thing is clear: it is almost certain that Griffes knew about Sharp's dual identities since the secret was revealed upon the author's death in 1905. But we cannot assume that his knowledge of and possible sympathy toward Sharp's artistic duality necessarily led him to create musical works that reflected this duality. To do so would constitute an interpretive "bed of Procrustes." Thus, while it is certainly possible to suggest a sympathetic resonance between Sharp's double literary persona and Griffes's personal circumstances, I will explore Griffes's settings of Macleod's poetry on their own merits, noting any dualities, oppositions, or paradoxes that ex-ist. Ultimately, the common element that linked the aesthetic sensibilities of William Sharp and Charles Griffes was a marriage of two passions: a love of evoking sensual pleasure and a longing for spiritual fulfillment (for more information on Sharp, see chap. 1).

It is worth considering the poems that Griffes chose for his cycle *Three Poems of Fiona Macleod,* Op. 11. The titles are "The Lament of Ian the Proud," "Thy Dark Eyes to Mine," and "The Rose of the Night." At first glance, there seems to be little that unites all three works. Whereas the first poem is an old man's outpouring of grief about a lost woman, the second and third poems are more spiritual in character, focusing on deliverance or transcendence from everyday life. There are different strategies for discovering correspondences between the poems. In some respects, the grief of the first poem stands alone, and the second and third belong together as a pair. Yet in terms of emotional character, the first and third poems are of the same high level of intensity, and the second one is more serene, less operatic. Considering the degree of contrast in this poetic trio, it would have been appropriate to give the entire set a pair of names. This would be in keeping with the title of another poem in the collection, "The Desire and the Lamentation of Coel," which is characterized more by dreamy desire than by lament.[10] With that in mind, a hypothetical title for the three poems in Op. 11 that reflects their sequence of emotions might have been "Three Poems about Lamentation and Desire."

But the question of unity—indeed, the very meaning of emotional lament or mystical faith—changes depending on whether the texts are viewed in isolation or within the larger context of Sharp/Macleod's entire oeuvre. First of all, the theme of lamentation is relatively common. For example, three other poems entitled "lament" appear in the collection *From the Hills of Dream*: "The Desire and Lamentation of Coel"; "The Lamentation of Balva the Monk"; and "The Lament of Darthoul." Furthermore, poems displaying a wide range of themes associated with mystical experience, such as ecstasy, dream, peace, and rebirth, can also be found in Macleod's collections.

There is another striking aspect of Macleod's conception of spirituality: the desire for romantic love fused with a dream of immortality. For example, in the poem "White Hands," another poem from the same collection, the narrator is obsessed with receiving a woman's kiss. She has eyes "like a doe" and a "honey-mouth" and, most important, the power "to take out the heart of me and grant me life or death." In another poem, the narrator is enraptured by the character Eilidh, who also appears in the second song of Op. 11, especially her golden hair, red lips, and white breasts.[11] Overall, this lyrical poetry highlights the same confluence of yearning found in the song cycle: the mutual desire for sensual pleasure and spiritual fulfillment. Thus, Griffes's choice of three sharply contrasting poems is truly representative of the broader tension between spirituality and sensuality found in Macleod's individual poems as well as in her writings as a whole.

"The Lament of Ian the Proud"

What is this crying that I hear in the wind?
Is it the old sorrow and the old grief?
Or is it a new thing coming, a whirling leaf
About the gray hair of me who am weary and blind?
I know not what it is, but on the moor above the shore
There is a stone which the purple nets of heather bind,
And thereon is writ: *She will return no more.*
O blown, whirling leaf, and the old grief,
And wind crying to me who am old and blind!

Let me begin by considering the text of "The Lament of Ian the Proud," the first poem in Macleod's song cycle, published in 1901 (see above).[12] It depicts an old man, alone on a windy moor, consumed by self-reflection and eventually overcome by grief. The poem's overall psychological design can be divided into three parts: a question, a poignant recollection, and an overwhelming recognition. The question the narrator initially poses to himself seems simple enough: What does the sound of the wind portend? However, the two answers he considers reveal something darker. The wind foretells either his "old grief" or something new, symbolized by a "whirling leaf." The remainder of the poem traces the process by which he arrives at an answer. First, he remembers a woman who is dead by recalling a stone inscription that "she will return no more"—presumably her gravestone. Then he is overwhelmed by the full impact of this memory. Whether the wind promises something old or new, the result is the same. He is old, blind, and heartbroken. The wind is merely the external projection of his own profound grief.

It is significant that the musical evocation of the narrator's pleas far exceeds the emotional scope of the poem. This musico-dramatic magnification is due to a number of factors. To begin with, in keeping with the poem's title, the musical setting combines elements of the lament along with those of the pastoral. More important, the song displays a gradual transformation from a simple musical texture at the beginning to an eruption of emotion near the end that coincides with four things: the apex in the voice's range, a climax in dynamics, a hint of a mode change, and, most of all, the simultaneous juxtaposition of previous melodic motives, which I call cumulative counterpoint. In Griffes's hands, the musical rendition of Macleod's text takes on operatic proportions.

The formal design of Griffes's musical setting not only honors the poem's three-part plan of question, memory, and recognition but also adds an instrumental prelude and postlude, making five sections in all.

mm.	1	8	25	37	47
Section	Prelude	Question	Memory	Recognition	Postlude

Despite occasional elements of motivic repetition, the song's overall formal design does not conform to a standard model and thus resembles a through-composed design. Let us briefly consider the topical complexion of each of these sections.

Prelude (mm. 1–7)

The song opens with an introduction for solo piano, evoking a nostalgic, even plaintive mood. This is due to several factors. First of all, there is a continuous open fifth interval in the bass, F♯–C♯, one of the hallmark cues of Griffes's pastoral works. Also, the piano's soprano voice presents a rising arpeggio, within a small range—mostly within the same perfect fifth span—that implies the Dorian mode.[13] Over the course of the song, this folk-like arpeggio figure and its chromatic variant serve as a recurring mantra that acquires different emotional associations. In the orchestral version, the composer underlines its initial plaintive character by scoring it for solo oboe. Finally, the rhythmic texture consists of a repeated pattern of pick-up triplets followed by a longer duration (dotted half note). Together, the melodic shape and rhythmic pattern evoke a somewhat fragmented, improvisational character.

The Lament of Ian the Proud

EXAMPLE 6.1.

Griffes, "The Lament of Ian the Proud," mm. 1–10.

Overall, it is difficult to draw any conclusions about the specific referent signified in the opening Prelude. It is not clear whether the rising arpeggio represents a specific person or memory, or rather evokes a general atmosphere of nostalgia. Furthermore, while the bass ostinato, the open fifth, coincides with one of the recurring cues present in Griffes's other pastoral works, here it contributes more to a mysterious and dolorous mood. Example 6.1 displays the piano prelude and the voice's initial phrase.

Question (mm. 8–25)

When the voice enters at m. 8, the overall scope of the musical drama changes. The passage as a whole (mm. 8–25) displays several key elements of the pastoral and lament, which are displayed below.

Pastoral Cues

- Compound Quadruple Meter
- Dotted Rhythmic Patterns
- Pedal Interval or Tonic Pitch

Lament Cues

- Sigh Figures

The pastoral identity of this section and the setting as a whole depends primarily on Griffes's treatment of meter and harmony. Though notated in 4/4, the piano's perpetual triplet accompaniment pattern implies a compound 12/8 meter, which is suggestive of an eighteenth-century pastoral dance.[14] However, there is a constant rhythmic tension between the vocal line and the accompaniment created by the opposition between simple and compound meter. The voice's square rhythmic patterns reinforce the notated meter while the triplet rhythmic groupings of the accompaniment suggest an alternative compound meter. In addition, in two short sections the piano's occasional offbeat, syncopated texture highlights the vocal line's simple rhythms: mm. 7–10 and mm. 37–39.

Throughout this section, the harmonic plan is nearly static, characterized by a tonic chord that arrives on most downbeats. The only true change of harmony, the subdominant at mm. 20–21, confirms the earlier hint of a plagal cadence: i–iv6/4–I (mm. 8–11). Another telling detail in this passage is the subtle change in texture. Now the piano accompaniment has multiple layers: one voice presents simple diatonic melodic motives, initially reminiscent of the opening arpeggio, while another voice has increasingly chromatic and rich florid textures that sound improvisatory. As we will see, this pattern of a gradual rise in tension will culminate at the climax in mm. 44–46.

The cue of the lament topic is also unmistakable in this passage. Although the vocal line is mostly diatonic (F♯ harmonic minor), the descending half step motive appears at critical moments in the text so as to highlight the words *sorrow* (D–C♯) and the *old grief* (F♯–E♯). In addition, Griffes introduces a whole step variant of the sigh, ♯6–5, which strongly suggests the Dorian mode—commonplace in Irish and Scottish folk traditions. Throughout the song, the opposition between these two descending motives—half step versus whole step—reflects the changing moods and events in the narrative.

Whereas the text portrays a soliloquy—a narrator posing questions to himself—the musical setting is more two-dimensional, as if the voice and piano were characters in an ongoing musical dialogue. The voice's entrance at m. 8 sounds as though it were responding to the immediately preceding material in the piano prelude. Questions abound: Does the initial rising arpeggio and its occasional repetition throughout the section (mm. 15–16) represent the "crying in the wind," the "old grief," or something altogether new, such as a sign of hope? While the music reveals no clear answer, its dialogical character transforms the original text. Another detail in the piano accompaniment is a foreshadowing of an important melodic motive, scale degrees 3–2–1 (mm. 12, 14) that will take on more importance in later sections.

Memory (mm. 25–37)

The next section of the song, which I call "Memory," is much more turbulent. It is immediately preceded by an instrumental transition, a return of the piano's opening arpeggio (mm. 24–25). In this section, there are few if any cues of the pastoral or lament topic. Instead, it is characterized by an increase in chromatic harmony, a new octatonic scale between the voice and piano, F♯, G♯, A, B, C, Cx, D♯, E♯; the development of various melodic motives; and a sudden swell in dynamics accompanied by rumbling bass tremolos.

Although the narrator is blind, he is troubled by his recollection of the words on a gravestone of a woman who "will return no more"; she is never named. Griffes's musical setting reflects this emotional change. To begin with, he emphasizes two poetic images—the gravestone as well as the woman who occupies the grave—with the same melodic third span, F♯–G♯–A, and its retrograde (mm. 29–30 and mm. 35–36). In addition, the harmonic language becomes more chromatic, dramatized by the appearance of a diminished-seventh chord, B♯, D♯, F♯, A, that persists throughout mm. 28–43. This vertical dissonance also shapes the song's melodic dimension, as there is a newfound emphasis of a dissonant melodic span, a diminished fifth, in the vocal line and the bass part. The sinuous vocal line emphasizes this interval, first as two ascents (F♯–C and B♯–F♯, mm. 26–28) and finally as a gradual descent between (mm. 31–32). Equally important is the large-scale pattern in the bass, connecting the same two pitches (mm. 28–37). This motion in the bass integrates the initial B minor chord (mm. 35–36), as if remembering the narrator's initial question about the wind.

Overall, the musical setting of this section underlines the poem's change in tone—from purely interrogatory to something more painful. It also highlights an intervallic and motivic opposition that prevails over the entire song: the diminished fifth, F♯–B♯ versus the perfect fifth, F♯–C♯.

Recognition (mm. 37–47)

The "Recognition" section is notable in that it is also saturated by the same diminished-fifth span from the previous two sections—as a descending gesture in the voice, F♯–B♯ (mm. 41–42) or an ascending one in the piano, B♯–F♯ (mm. 37–39). The material in mm. 37–40 serves as a powerful musical interjection between the lines of verse. Griffes recycles the same rising arpeggio from the initial Prelude, but now the chromatically inflected version sounds more sinister. This gesture serves as both a comment on the narrator's poignant recollection of the gravestone as well as a portent of the imminent feelings of despair, which are heralded by a crescendo and a wild rush of sixteenth notes in the piano (m. 40).

EXAMPLE 6.2.

Griffes, "The Lament of Ian the Proud," mm. 44–53.

At long last we arrive at the song's expressive crux (mm. 44–47), where prominent melodic themes previously heard all coincide in a texture of cumulative counterpoint—see the score in example 6.2. Griffes magnifies the narrator's emotional pain and grief in several ways. To begin with, the highest pitch in the vocal line, A#5, coincides with the accompaniment's highest pitch, the A# an octave higher. This pitch also introduces the opposition between A and A# (or scale degrees 3 and #3), which in turn signals the presence of modal ambiguity between two parallel keys. Deep emotional power resides in the opposition between the F# 6/4 in m. 44 and the f# minor 5/3 chord in m. 47, two chords that mark the beginning and end of the gesture. Finally, the arrival of the A# also coincides with a *fortissimo* marking in m. 44.

But this climax is far more than an exercise in modal mixture or a spike in dynamics. Three descending melodic motives appear in the accompaniment of mm. 46–47 that together create a parallel texture juxtaposed against sustained C#'s in the vocal line and the bass. In example 6.3, they are listed in vertical order from top to bottom: the texture of parallel counterpoint does more than simply emphasize a single word or phrase. Instead, it is a form of motivic magnification that highlights a single line— indeed, an essential melodic motive—by doubling it in parallel 4ths and 6ths and then embellishing it with continuous chromaticism. The narrator's emotions are considerably intensified by the vertical synthesis of different voice leading strands introduced earlier in the song.

EXAMPLE 6.3.

Griffes, "The Lament of Ian the Proud": Cumulative counterpoint of three melodic motives, mm. 46–47.

Each one of these lines has its own source of motivic resonance. First, the descending minor third span in the soprano, A–F♯, which was previously associated with the gravestone and the sobering reminder of the woman's death in mm. 35–37, returns but is now filled in chromatically. The second source of motivic resonance in this passage is the reference to the lament or half-step motives in the opening section. The opposition between D–C♯ and D♯–C♯ is now integrated into the passing motion through a minor third span in the piano's inner voice between scale degrees ♭7 and 5. What could be interpreted as a modal opposition between the Dorian and Aeolian modes now becomes transformed into a purely chromatic line. However, the "sighing" or "crying" motive does not completely disappear, for in mm. 44–45 the piano's soprano voice and the vocal line repeat the same half-step gesture, 6–5, in imitation (based on pitch, not rhythm). In addition, the bass voice presents an oscillating half-step motion between the same two pitches, C♯ and D. At this juncture, Griffes is indulging in what is traditionally called "word painting" of the singer's text: "crying to me who am old and blind!" Amid this interplay of motivic sighs, the voice ends by repeating the same pitch, C♯5, as if in an emotional trance. The lowest layer of the parallel texture is the minor third span, C♯–A. This motive is perhaps the most memorable of the entire song, for it is embedded in reverse order in the opening aphorism of the piano, the arpeggio, F♯–A–B–C♯, which also returns in the piano postlude. These three voice leading strands combine to create a planing texture, which is suffused with motivic significance.

The final element in this motivic confluence is a new melodic gesture: an augmented triad plus a descending half step: A♯–F♯–D–C♯ (mm. 44–45). The immediate harmonic function of this augmented triad is to embellish the prevailing V 6/4, not to serve as an independent chord. However, in the following two songs the same sonority reappears, each time acquiring a different harmonic function. In that respect, its initial appearance in "The Lament of Ian the Proud" heralds its role as a mega-motive that links all three songs into a unified cycle.

In sum, the emotions expressed in the poem are considerably intensified by the vertical synthesis of different voice leading strands introduced earlier in the song. The texture of cumulative counterpoint does more than simply emphasize a single word or phrase—or what Ratner defines as the third type of musical topic: "word painting." Instead, the gesture uses a form of motivic transformation, combining multiple melodic lines in parallel and enriching them with continuous chromaticism, as a means of magnifying the narrator's misery—in short, a chromatic cry for help.

Postlude

Although the postlude (mm. 47–53) is nearly an exact repeat of the piano prelude, it serves as a fitting dénouement to all of the previous Celtic sound and fury. The return of the opening mantra theme and static bass is now charged with the aftershock of the narrator's deep sense of loss. The element of repetition between the song's opening and ending helps emphasize that, on the whole, things are not the same as they were at the beginning and that there has been a significant shift in the narrator's self-awareness.

* * *

Considering the intense despair expressed in the poem, one wonders if it mirrors an aspect of the poet's own emotional life. In the prophecy "She will return no more," who is the woman? Is it some female Celtic divinity, such as Eilidh, who is highlighted in the poem of the following song? If the latter, then the narrator is pining for deliverance, for relief from his state of old age and blindness, and, finally, for transformation into a state of immortality. Or does the poem's female character refer in some way to the poet's own feminine persona that was awakened during his Italian sojourn in 1891? If so, the narrator may well be projecting in the future and imagining the loss of Sharp's newly emerging self.

Finally, the poem might in some way reflect a dramatic development in his relationship with Edith Wingate Rinder, for in his recent biography Blamires reveals that Edith gave birth to a daughter named Esther in July 1901 and that Sharp was her father. During the ensuing years, Edith raised the child with her husband, Frank, and William remained with his wife, Elizabeth, until his death in 1905.[15] In his biography of Sharp, William Halloran believes that William and Edith became more distant following the birth.[16] In sum, considering the whirlwind in Sharp's personal life at this juncture, it is difficult to attribute the suffering evoked in the poem to any specific biographical detail. Nevertheless, the narrator's reference to a gravestone and his own blindness inspired one of Griffes's most poignant musical settings.

Ultimately, the cumulative counterpoint in this song unites four musical dimensions—register, dynamics, harmony, and motive—all converging at a single point and reinforcing each other. The passage assumes epic proportions in several respects. On the one hand, the arrival at m. 44 of a major F♯ 6/4 chord at *fortissimo* dynamic suggests that this may be a moment of emotional triumph. Yet, on the other hand, the parallel counterpoint two bars later subverts this sense of triumph, instead fulfilling a large-scale psychological progression from the narrator's initial ignorance to the final realization of his own pitiful condition. This contrapuntal confluence synthesizes in a single gesture various melodic motives that signify different stages of the narrator's internal journey. In short, this song begins as a lament, includes a brief respite of triumph, and then culminates with self-pity. While the pastoral character of this song is less pronounced compared to that of the other two settings of the cycle, it still constitutes an expansion of the traditional conception of the genre. As we will see below, the psychological and spiritual conflicts expressed in the second and third songs will prove to be even more profound, exploring the boundary between life and death.

"Thy Dark Eyes to Mine"

The next stage in my study of *Three Poems of Fiona Macleod* is to consider the poetry of the second and the third songs in the cycle: "Thy Dark Eyes to Mine" and "The Rose of the Night." The central themes of both poems must be understood within the climate for alternative spiritual traditions such as Rosicrucianism and Theosophy, which was ripe in Europe and America during the fin de siècle. During this period, Sharp developed a close friendship with the Irish author and political activist W. B. Yeats. For example, Fiona wrote a heartfelt prose dedication to Yeats for a subset of poems in a later edition of the collection, *From the Hills of Dream*.[17] The two authors also shared a joint interest in spiritualism. In the early 1890s,

Yeats immersed himself in the Rosicrucian Order of the Golden Dawn and later invited Fiona numerous times to participate in a parallel order that focused exclusively on Celtic traditions.[18]

Most important, the rose is one of the central symbols of the Golden Dawn tradition, signifying such things as beauty, romance, and spiritual transformation. Both authors were inspired over and over again by the image of a rose in their poetry. For instance, not only do four poems by Sharp and Macleod include *rose* in the title, but three of their collections have strong floral connotations: *Flower o' the Vine, Flowers of Dream*, and *The Valley of Pale Blue Flowers*. Also, in 1893 Yeats authored an early collection of poetry entitled *The Rose*. In sum, the use of rose imagery in the final poem belongs to a broader artistic sensibility, shared by Macleod and Yeats, that celebrated the world of Celtic myths and folk tales as well as the Golden Order tradition.

Both poems reflect a deep mystical streak in Macleod's writing. She portrays mortals in two ways: those who touch immortality—that is, they enter the kingdom of the faeries—or those who wish they could. Her literary style mixes dream-like states of contemplation, subdued nostalgia along with outbursts of intense passion. Both texts are reproduced below.[19]

> Thy dark eyes to mine,
> Eilidh, Lamps of desire!
> O how my soul leaps
> Leaps to their fire!
> Sure, now, if I in heaven,
> Dreaming in bliss,
> Heard but a whisper,
> But the lost echo even
> Of one such kiss—
> All of the Soul of me
> Would leap afar—
> If that called me to thee Aye,
> I would leap afar
> A falling star!
> *
> There is an old mystical legend that when a soul among the dead woos a
> soul among the living, so that both may be reborn as one, the sign is a dark
> rose or a rose of flame, in the heart of the night.

The dark rose of thy mouth
Draw nigher, draw nigher!
Thy breath is the wind of the south,
A wind of fire,
The wind and the rose and darkness,
O Rose of my Desire!
Deep silence of the night,
Husht like a breathless lyre,
Save the sea's thunderous might,
Dim, menacing, dire,
Silence and wind and sea, they are thee,
O Rose of my Desire!
As a wind-eddying flame
Leaping higher and higher,
Thy soul, thy secret name,
Leaps thro' Death's blazing pyre,
Kiss me, Imperishable Fire, dark Rose,
O Rose of my Desire!

The two poems portray two types of spiritual transformation that are diametrically opposed to each other: (a) from divine to human; and (b) from human to divine. In the first type, an immortal being longs to be human again and to experience the look of a woman's eyes or the touch of her lips; this is the world of "Thy Dark Eyes to Mine." In the second type, "The Rose of the Night," the situation is reversed: a mortal fantasizes that he or she will transcend death by means of an immortal's kiss. Both poems are united by the spiritual significance of a physical gesture.

Let us take a closer look at the imagery in both poems. Apparently, the path to spiritual fulfillment relies on multiple senses; it is visual and tactile as well as aural. The poem "Thy Dark Eyes to Mine" initially focuses on the visual realm, depicting the narrator's obsession with eyes and a woman named Eilidh, which is a Gaelic form of the name Helen, and which also denotes the word *light*. In fact, in other poems from Macleod's collection she becomes a recurring character. Yet both poems also draw on the auditory dimension. While the first poem refers to a "whisper" and an "echo," in "The Rose of the Night" the sound of the sea is juxtaposed against the silence of a "breathless lyre." Finally, the sense of touch receives the greatest emphasis in that both poems highlight the physical act of kissing.[20]

The musical settings of these two poems are a study in contrast. The calm ambiance found in "Thy Dark Eyes" is the exact antipode to the operatic intensity of "The Rose of the Night." The extreme contrast of what might be called the "cold" and "hot" colors of spirituality creates a clear binary opposition. It is tempting to place these poems and their settings within a continuum of spiritual yearning—as if we were conducting a psychological study of the "varieties of religious experience," an addendum to William James's famous lecture series by the same name.[21] While both poems are born of the same desire for spiritual transcendence, the two musical settings differ dramatically in the way they portray and comment on the poetry.

When reflecting on the texts of these two songs, it is a mistake to ask whether the music actually portrays transcendence or a state of eternity. Indeed, it is difficult to identify a single musical feature that directly represents a divine being or the state of immortality in these songs. In this context, it is important to distinguish between two types of spirituality in music: the portrayal of immortality itself and the *psychological desire* for immortality and escape from death. In the second and third songs in the cycle, Griffes's artistic goal is clearly the latter. In both poems 2 and 3, the dramatic turning point is the narrator's intense plea for divine intervention—that is, an embrace from a Celtic spirit. Thus, the physical gesture of a kiss becomes infused with two layers: physical affection and the promise of immortality.

Now let us focus on the second song of the cycle, "Thy Dark Eyes to Mine," which he completed in 1918. This song provides a dramatic demonstration of how the concept of musical topic and its traditional associations must be adapted for the interpretation of Griffes's works. The categories of pastoral and lament along with their associations not only overlap with each other, but they also become infused with other contrasting associations. The result is an expression of musical ambivalence, an incongruous emotional composite, combining sadness with serenity and physical desire with spiritual yearning. Although the song is short in duration, it is long in topical ambiguity.

In particular, the repetition of a conventional musical gesture, a single falling half step located in different melodic and harmonic contexts, participates in a larger psychological process during which the narrator reveals the full spectrum of his emotions. This chromatic motive occurs numerous times in the voice and piano, and its significance slowly evolves in relation to the text that accompanies it. In the following pages, we will retrace that evolutionary process in order to fully appreciate one of the most unusual pastorals in Griffes's entire oeuvre.

The song's formal design is ternary—three short sections plus an instrumental prelude and postlude—which reflects the poem's three-part stanzaic structure.

mm.	1	4	12	24	31
Stanza		1	2	3	
Section	Prelude	A	B	A'	Postlude

The first section consists of two short phrases in the voice part, both of which are supported by a highly repetitive texture in the accompaniment. By contrast, the setting of the second stanza becomes increasingly passionate: the voice climbs higher in register, the dynamic briefly swells, and the accompaniment becomes more chromatic and contrapuntal. The setting of stanza 3 (section A') ends with a surprise. After returning to the voice's soaring motive and static harmonic support from the opening bars, Griffes introduces new material, concluding on a sustained half cadence (mm. 30–34) and a final chromatic twist in the accompaniment. Let us consider each section in greater detail.

Prelude

As we witnessed in the first song in the cycle, Griffes begins his setting of "Thy Dark Eyes" with a portrait of pastoral calm in the piano introduction. The idiosyncratic pastoral features are listed below.

Pastoral Cues

- Compound Quadruple Meter
- Rhythmic/Metric Ambiguity
- Moderate Tempo
- Major + Pentatonic Scales
- Pedal Interval

Lament Cue

- Sigh Figure

Thy Dark Eyes to Mine

EXAMPLE 6.4.

Griffes, "Thy Dark Eyes to Mine," mm. 1–7.

The pulsating rhythm in the accompaniment creates a soothing ambiance—see the musical excerpt in example 6.4. Whereas the repeating chordal pattern is duple, two eighth notes long, the underlying compound meter implies a grouping of three eighth notes, which together create a feeling of hemiola. In the bass, Griffes places an open fifth that recalls folk instruments such as the zampogna and the musette (for more details on these instruments, see chap. 2). Then, above this fifth, Griffes juxtaposes two four-note chords that combine to form an A♭ 13/9 or added sixth chord. While the overall collection is pentatonic, A♭, B♭, C, E♭, F, the voicing and doubling of these pitches combined with the hemiola rhythmic pattern evoke an initial hypnotic effect. Though this atmosphere of serenity soon disappears, it eventually returns in the coda.

Stanza 1

There are two central characteristics of Griffes's setting of Stanza 1 (mm. 4–11): its regular phrase structure and the introduction of a lament melodic figure. The phrase grouping in this section is based on two factors: the voice's long rhythmic durations and rests in every other bar, coupled with the piano's melodic responses: mm. 6–7 and 10–11. The voice takes the lead in this musical conversation, with the piano offering its own chromatic commentary. The ensuing musical dialogue establishes a regular rhythmic grouping of 2 + 2 (or question and answer) that later shifts to 4 + 4 pattern, culminating in the coda. Overall, the two-part dramatic structure and regularity of phrase organization in the setting of stanza 1 contribute to the perception of a traditional pastoral character.

The other remarkable feature of this opening section is the appearance of the lament motive, a descending half step, F♭–E♭, which appears twice (mm. 7, 10–11). In the context of the piano's subdued introduction, this gesture represents a harmonic and emotional shift. To begin with, this motive is steeped in associations awakened at the end of the previous song ("The Lament of Ian the Proud"). It is the first chromatic inflection so far, strongly suggesting the parallel minor. This melodic motive is supported by an augmented triad, A♭, C, E, that resolves to a major triad and, in the process, creates a chromatic appoggiatura. More important, the longer rhythmic pattern (half notes) implies a quietly pleading tone that conflicts with the serene atmosphere of the previous six bars. Finally, when the text is taken into account, this motive coincides with the introduction of a strong sensual dimension ("lamps of desire"). The result is a conflicting network of associations: hypnotic serenity in the piano, and sadness mixed with an expression of physical desire in the voice. As we will see, this curious emotional mixture only intensifies as the song continues.

Stanza 2

The second section witnesses several new developments. The piano accompaniment is more contrapuntal in that the initial rocking motion evolves into two or three independent melodic lines. Likewise, the initial diatonic character has long since disappeared, now supplanted by a chromatic harmonic vocabulary in the voice and piano. For example, the bass voice contains an ascending half-step motion, A♭–A–B♭–C♭.

But the most significant chromatic element appears in m. 18–19, where the same half-step motive from Stanza 1 returns in the bass voice as passing motion. Here the Fb supports a German augmented 6th chord (F♭, A♭, C♭, D), which resolves downward to a cadential 6/4 on E♭. The chromaticism acquires a new dimension in that the motive shapes the harmony as well as the melodic line. While the resolution of this chord is utterly conventional, the simultaneous presence of F♭ and D in the same chord nevertheless sets the stage for an instance of musical memory in the instrumental coda.

Most important, when the text is taken into account, the impact of the singer's plaintive lament takes on new proportions. The voice's rising half step, C♭–C, now coincides with the words "one such kiss." In the first two stanzas, the same melodic motive has now acquired a halo of associations that reflect the narrator's hunger for physical intimacy. Finally, Griffes marks the end of the stanza (mm. 19–22) with a swell of dynamics in the voice, climaxing on a V7 chord.

EXAMPLE 6.5.

Griffes, "Thy Dark Eyes to Mine," mm. 24–33.

Stanza 3

This section begins with a reprise of the voice's thematic material from stanza 1 but then evolves dramatically—see the score in example 6.5. The piano accompaniment, while still outlining the same A♭ chord, contains none of the rich hemiola from the opening section and instead is replete with eighth-note triplets. This section witnesses two different functions of the song's most important chromatic pitch, F♭. In the bass, it resolves downward as before, F♭–E♭ (mm. 28–30), and supports two different sonorities: ♭VI followed by a ii4/3 chord. By contrast, in the voice the same pitch proceeds in the opposite direction, climbing upward, F♭–F–A♭. This moment constitutes the third distinct treatment of the lament melodic shape. Here it is not only inverted, but it also acquires a new textual association, the narrator's "leap afar."

Another curious feature of this section occurs in Griffes's treatment of the vocal line. As the bass descends by half step, the voice ascends through a fourth, B♭–C♭–D♭–E♭ (mm. 29–31). The contradiction between the rising melodic contour and the words "a falling star" reflects more than a hint of irony.

Coda

In the Coda, Griffes recycles two pitches from the previous augmented-sixth chord, Fb and D (m. 18), transforming them into a chromatic ornament nested within the piano's continuous eighth-note accompaniment gesture: E♭–F♭–D–E♭ (mm. 32–33). This implied double neighbor figure is the final statement, now slightly embellished, of the chromatic lament motive.

An additional feature that confirms Griffes's pastoral signature is a recurring chord's expanded register in the piano prelude and postlude. To appreciate this gesture, it is necessary to ignore the opening pedal interval, A♭-E♭, and instead focus on the lowest pitch of the left hand's pulsating chord, E♭3 in mm. 1–5. At the other extreme, the highest pitch in this passage is E♭5, sounding in the vocal line and doubled in the piano. The difference between these two pitches constitutes a two-octave space.

Now, when the final pentatonic chord arrives at m. 30 (minus the B♭), the bass has descended to E♭1 and the soprano line rises to an E♭6. When these two chords are juxtaposed together, the expansion of register is dramatic—from two to five octaves.

Griffes's treatment of a half-step melodic motive in "Thy Dark Eyes" is significant in two ways. First, it is a source of motivic unity, not only within the song itself but also among all three songs, weaving an emotional thread through the entire cycle. Yet it is also a vehicle for variation and transformation. The simplest way to explain the differing interpretations of this melodic gesture is in the potential harmonic ambiguity of the augmented triad A♭, C, E, first heard in m. 7. In short, it can resolve by a half step in either direction. The descending version, E–E♭ (b6–5), has traditional associations of grief and loss. However, here it is also associated with the image of a "lamp of desire." The other version is an ascending half step, E–F (b6–6), which occurs near the end (mm. 26–27) and is used to set the image of "a leap from afar."

But the significance of the two different half steps is more than a one-to-one correspondence with particular images. These two opposite contours can also be correlated with the overarching theme of the poem: the narrator's fantasy of being transformed from divine to mortal. This transformation is strongly associated with physical gestures—from heavenly bliss to a human kiss. While Griffes uses the descending half step throughout most of the setting, he saves the ascending version of the motive for the setting of the final stanza where the narrator imagines becoming human again. Although the word coinciding with this motive, "to leap," has appeared throughout the poem, here it is infused with a new layer of meaning by the musical setting.

The final statement of the lament also endows the piano with the power of musical as well as linguistic memory. In short, it comments not only on all previous instances of the F♭–E♭ motive but also on the poem's final lines: "leap from afar, a falling star," as well as all previous junctures where the same chromatic lament appears such as the imagined intimacy of a kiss in bar 18. This simple musical gesture is suffused by three dramatic threads, each with its own temporal dimension: the present, as suggested by the speaker's narrative tone; the past, as suggested by the "lost echo of one such kiss" from Stanza 2; and the future as implied by the fantasy of reuniting with Eilidh, "leaping from afar."

Musical Topics

The unusual physiognomy of this song arises from the incongruity between Griffes's treatment of the pastoral and lament topics in relation to the conflicting emotions portrayed in Macleod's poem. The song begins and ends with the piano's evocation of pastoral serenity due largely to the continuity in rhythm, texture, and harmony. By contrast, in the body of the song the chromatic lament motive takes center stage as the same half-step gesture acquires a wide range of meanings including memories (or fantasies) of physical pleasure and longing for spiritual fulfillment. The words coinciding with the lament motive create a litany of emotions and textual associations: "desire" (m. 7); "kiss" (mm. 18–19); "leap" (mm. 26–27); and "falling star" (mm. 28–30). Finally, the piano's circular shape in the final bars (mm. 32–33) refers to the previous laments and, at the same time, leaves the question of fulfillment unanswered.

Ultimately, to appreciate the experimental nature of Griffes's setting of "Thy Dark Eyes" requires that the listener try to reconcile its constituent elements, however varied or contradictory they may be. The song raises questions about the very notion of a strict logical category that can be confirmed by necessary and sufficient conditions. It is not a matter of determining which topic has more constituent features present in the song and, therefore, is more dominant—either a lament-pastoral or pastoral-lament. Instead, we need a looser conception of the notion of category that relies less on the concept of unity and more on a new combination of unity and heterogeneity.

Text and Music

On the whole, there is a notable discrepancy between the emotional impact of the musical setting and the poetic text of "Thy Dark Eyes." When viewed in isolation, the lyrical yet subdued character of most of the vocal line seems out of step with the intensity of the narrator's fantasies of spiritual fulfillment and sensual pleasure. It is striking that the song never reaches a single climax in the duo—the swell in dynamics in the voice (m. 18) does not coincide with the *forte* marking in the piano (mm. 19–21).

However, this subdued character is not out of step if one focuses on an internal portion of the poem. The soothing, if not hypnotic, mood suggested by the prelude's intricate and continuous rhythmic texture evokes the character of an internal line from stanza 2: "Sure, now, if I in heaven/ Dreaming in bliss." Viewed from this perspective, the continuity in the rhythmic texture serves as a musical commentary on the text, expanding the emotional detachment from one section of the poem and muting the narrator's effusive fantasies and/or memories of a woman's eyes and, especially, of her kiss.

Likewise, the rhythmic continuity between the prelude and postlude might be interpreted as a return to the narrator's initial dreamlike state when he or she was obsessing on the eyes and lips of Eilidh. But when we consider the chromaticism of the final accompanying pattern, other possible interpretations come to mind. In mm. 32–33, the ornamented version of the chromatic lament motive can be interpreted in either of two ways: a chromatic confirmation that the narrator's wish for transcendence has come true, or an enigmatic musical gesture that neither confirms nor denies his wish. In either case, the song's postlude leaves the listener wanting more and, consequently, leads directly into the final song of the cycle.

The ultimate source of the song's disjointed emotional response is the juxtaposition of a musical gesture that has strong associations with grief and a text that contains overt references to the search for sensual pleasure as well as spiritual fulfillment. In the course of reflecting on his or her immortality, the narrator becomes overwhelmed by the look of a woman's eyes and the touch of her lips. The result is an unlikely blend of emotions: sadness mixed with serenity, and physical desire combined with spiritual longing. In particular, the memory of a physical kiss becomes infused with two layers of signification: romance between two lovers and the promise of immortality. By the end of the song, it is not clear if either has been fulfilled.

* * *

The ambiguity in this song's topical identity depends on the conflict between the pastoral elements found in the prelude and postlude and the frequent repetitions and transformations of a lament melodic motive in different harmonic contexts. In addition, the text coinciding with these statements of the lament adds several additional emotional layers—namely, the expression of physical desire as well as the search for spiritual fulfillment. In short, the intersection of rhythm, melody, harmony, and poetry creates an emotional trajectory that beguiles as much as it uplifts the listener.

When understood in the context of all three songs in the cycle, the composer's emotional restraint in this song also serves a larger dramatic purpose. "Thy Dark Eyes" is a psychological respite from the volcanic outpouring of sentiment in the poems and musical settings of the first and third songs.

Finally, we are left with several interpretive questions. First, how can a song that begins with a traditional pastoral texture but ends up evoking a wide range of conflicting associations still be considered a pastoral? The answer is that this song serves as a microcosm of Griffes's mature conception of this expressive genre; he renewed and at the same time expanded the pastoral musical/literary tradition. This unusual blend of topics and the curious mix of spirituality and sensuality underline why we need a new interpretive approach to do justice to his experimentation. Second, is the song a coherent whole, or is it fragmented and in conflict with itself? The best response to this question is that despite the song's multiple and sometimes conflicting associations, its overall integrity depends on its close relationship to the poem itself and on the group of poems as a whole. We will return to the question of artistic coherence when we consider the final song in the cycle.

"The Rose of the Night"

In the final song of the cycle, "The Rose of the Night," the aesthetic sensibilities of Charles Griffes and Fiona Macleod converge in an unlikely mix of conflicting emotions: erotic passion, vivid references to Nature, deep lamentation, and a yearning for spiritual deliverance. The overarching theme of the poem is the narrator's plea for a Celtic spirit's kiss, a physical gesture that is infused with the promise of immortality—as is evident in the epigraph preceding the poem. Griffes's musical setting magnifies the narrator's plea in various ways, leading to an enormous climax. Yet, as will become clear below, when the song comes to an end, the music leaves little room for ambiguity—the narrator's moment of spiritual transcendence has been interrupted and left unfulfilled.

Before embarking on an exegesis of Griffes's setting of "The Rose of the Night," I wish to briefly consider the origin of the epigraph that precedes the poem: "There is an old mystical legend that when a soul among the dead woos a soul among the living, so that both may be reborn as one, the sign is a dark rose or a rose of flame, in the heart of the night." The tone of this statement implies that Macleod is referring to a preexisting historical source. But it should be remembered that Sharp, when writing under the name of Macleod, was hardly an assiduous student of Celtic ethnography or literature. While she sometimes relied on genuine Celtic traditions such as mythological characters (e.g., "Deirdrê Is Dead") or places (e.g., "I-Brasil"), she seldom directly recounted a traditional folk tale. Instead, her poems are either tributes, laments, commentaries, etc. about these characters and places or rhapsodies drawn from her fertile imagination. A close inspection of the entire collection from which the poem is drawn reveals that Macleod includes epigraphs in a handful of other poems, some with attributions, others without.[22] Macleod also occasionally adopts multiple voices within the same poem, either as a preliminary epigraph or as a dialogue between characters (e.g., "The Desire and Lamentation of Coel" and "The Bandruidh"). In light of this evidence, it is reasonable to interpret the omniscient and anonymous narrator in the epigraph as a mannerism or technique in her general style rather than a genuine historical source.

It is worth exploring the remarkable range of imagery in Macleod's text, which appears in the previous section of the chapter. In short, three of the four elements in classical antiquity are present: wind, fire, and sea. The fourth one, earth, is implied by the image of the rose. Even a musical instrument, the lyre, makes a brief appearance, though it is silenced. Despite the sheer variety among these images, the most important one is the rose.

Not only does it appear at the end of each stanza, but somehow it serves a cumulative role, encompassing the emotions evoked in all the others.

This list of images prompts two comments. First, the sheer breadth of the imagery suggests that the narrator's spiritual desire is all-embracing, encompassing the entire physical world. The scope of this mystical union, if it occurs, will be universal. Second, the litany includes utter contradictions: the thundering sea alternates with silent night; then fire is juxtaposed against darkness. These contradictions underline that the spiritual deliverance the narrator hopes for is beyond reason.

Overall, Griffes's setting of "The Rose of the Night" reveals glimpses of his German musical heritage, in particular the shadow of Wagner, in its exaggerated outpouring of emotion and its reliance on chromatic harmony. But this shadow also overlaps with Griffes's own stylistic radiance including an idiosyncratic harmonic idiom based on an alternative scale and the traces of conflicting musical topics—namely, the lament and the pastoral.

It is useful to begin by considering the song's formal design. The poem consists of three short stanzas; by contrast, the song, while loosely reflecting the same structure, does not have a ternary repetition scheme. As in many of Griffes's songs, the same motivic and textural material occurs in the piano prelude and postlude. The resulting circular character plays a significant role in depicting the text. For convenience, I will refer to the music corresponding to each stanza by referring to Stanzas 1, 2, and 3.

mm.	1	6	22	37	54
Section	Prelude	Stanza 1	Stanza 2	Stanza 3	Postlude

As we saw in "Thy Dark Eyes," this song contains elements of conflicting musical topics, which contribute to an overall portrait of emotional ambiguity. The mix of pastoral and lament cues evident in the Prelude and Stanza 1 are indicated below.

Pastoral Cues

- Implied 9/8 Meter
- Dissonant Pedal Chord
- Double Augmented Scale

Lament Cue

- Sigh Figures

The Rose of The Night

There is an old mystical legend that when a soul among the dead woos a soul among the living, so that both may be reborn as one, the sign is a dark rose, or a rose of flame, in the heart of the night.

Poem by Fiona MacLeod*

Charles T. Griffes. Op.11, No.3

EXAMPLE 6.6.

(ABOVE AND FOLLOWING PAGE)

Griffes, "The Rose of the Night," mm. 1–15.

To begin with, the rhythmic and metric organization of the accompaniment are rather traditional. Although the initial time signature is notated as 3/4, the piano's continuous triplet texture sounds like 9/8, serving as an extension of the pastoral rhythmic texture from the previous song ("Thy Dark Eyes"). Although the notated meter occasionally changes to 4/4, Griffes retains the triplet subdivisions for most of the song—see the excerpt in example 6.6.

Despite the compound triple meter, the song's piano Introduction and the opening section are anything but pastoral, evoking a mysterious ambiance with hints of a haunting or foreboding character. The rich mix of emotions evoked in this section as well as in the entire setting can be traced to three sources: an alternative scale as well as his treatment of two melodic motives. Let me explore each one.

The experimental harmonic vocabulary in the song's opening section can be explained partly by the double augmented scale (sometimes referred to as the "Gypsy" scale), which contains two augmented seconds, marked in brackets on example 6.7. This double augmented scale has many subsets in common with other symmetrical scales, such as the octatonic, hexatonic, and whole tone, but none is present in its entirety. Instead, the scale is a repository of unusual combinations of half steps and augmented seconds, which the composer exploits at pivotal junctures in the song. In the prelude, the recurring left-hand pattern, a rocking pair of dyads (major seventh and major third), creates a striking pedal chord that derives from this scale: V b9/#7/#5. The combination of a static bass voice, the G♯ pedal, and a dissonant harmony built above it helps establish an unworldly atmosphere.

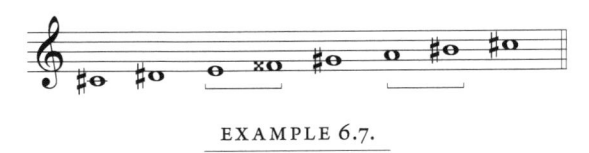

EXAMPLE 6.7.

Griffes, "The Rose of the Night": Double Augmented Scale.

Griffes must have been fond of this alternative collection, for he also uses it to construct a stunning exotic musical theme in his tone poem *The Pleasure-Dome of Kubla Khan* (see chap. 5). Whereas in *Kubla Khan* the scale's exotic associations grow out of Coleridge's fantastic vision of an ancient Chinese garden, in the final Macleod song the scale's associations belong to the spiritual realm. However, this unorthodox scale by no means generates all of the melodic and harmonic material in "The Rose of the Night." Instead, it creates an overarching sonic framework, permeating the piano prelude and postlude and serving as a point of reference for some aspects of the vocal line and the accompaniment in each stanza.

The second reason for the song's unusual character is Griffes's reliance on a recurring half-step motive or lament gesture. The first time this motive appears is within the piano's sweeping circular gesture, where it appears twice hidden within a longer melodic shape: A–G♯ and C♯–B♯. The same two pitch motives later appear in the vocal line either as a descending half step or as an interrupted gesture and, as a result, play a crucial role in commenting on the text.

What is significant about Griffes's treatment of this half-step motive is that the usual limited spectrum of emotions associated with the lament gesture has expanded enormously. His setting blends traditional associations of loss and sadness with new ones involving physical plea-sure ("mouth drawing nigher") and electrifying scenes of nature ("winds of fire"). Finally, when the narrator's yearning for spiritual fulfillment is taken into account, the end result is a descending melodic motive enliv-ened by a rich mix of conflicting emotions. This is a lament like no other.

The third source of mystery is the mercurial melodic motive in the piano, swirling above and below the vocal line, which covers an octave, either ascending or descending. In the context of the poem, this haunt-ing gesture can be interpreted as a musical incantation to attract the "soul among the dead." In all, the circular gesture repeats six times in the pre-lude and at the beginning of Stanza 3, where the same melodic shape and rhythm return but with slightly varied pitch content. One curious feature of the gesture is that it starts and stops on an A, creating a minor ninth dissonance with the bass's G♯.

It should be stressed that this gesture belongs to the overall fabric of the piano accompaniment, which is far more contrapuntal than the other two settings in the cycle. At several junctures in the song, the piano's increased rhythmic activity intensifies the message in the text, leading listeners to conclude that at these points the accompaniment is as much rhythmic as it is motivic.[23]

In Stanza 1, the vocal line highlights both half-step motives. The C♯–B♯ motive accompanies the narrator's plea for a divine mouth "to draw nigher." A few bars later, the singer presents a segment from the double augmented scale, descending from D♯ to G♯. Finally, the other half step, A–G♯, coincides with the first statement of a dominant (with added b9) in the song thus far (mm. 12–13).

The harmonic plan in this stanza is a descending line in the bass be-tween V and i that hints at a Phrygian mode: G♯–E–D–C♯ (mm. 12–22). This fifth motion is significant as a point of reference, for later in the setting Griffes begins a similar descending melodic line in the bass but stops on D, failing to continue to the tonic. Griffes also adds a touch of contrapuntal craft in that the bass's inflected third span (E–D–C♯) is imitated by the voice in a higher register several bars later.

In Stanza 2, the narrator's plea for deliverance gradually becomes more urgent, setting the stage for the eventual crisis, and Griffes's musical setting reflects it. The most important melodic motive in this section is another repetition of the lament motive, A–G♯, which occurs, now slightly embellished, at mm. 40–41. The second instance of the chromatic arabesque gesture occurs in the transition following Stanza 2, heralding the beginning of Stanza 3. Griffes alters two pitches compared to the first occurrence (A, D♯, F♯, G♯) and repeats the shape six times. The final iteration of this arabesque motive strongly suggests a C♯ 6/4 chord through which Griffes introduces a harmonic shift to the parallel major key.

Griffes's treatment of harmony in Stanza 2 also contributes to the accumulation of tension. Instead of a continuous dominant pedal, the bass line in this section becomes increasingly chromatic, descending by half step: F♯–F/E♯–E–D♯–D (mm. 29–37). There are two reasons why listeners expect the line to continue descending one more half step to C♯. First, the typical lament bass usually traverses a perfect fourth span, descending by half step. While the lament character in this passage is somewhat masked by the constant variety of motivic material in the voice and piano, the overall chromatic contour is unmistakable. The second reason is more contextual—the repetition of a striking chord at m. 37 that we have already heard: D, F♯, G♯, C. When this chord previously appeared in mm. 20–21, it resolved downward to the tonic, C♯ minor. At this juncture, however, the same French augmented-sixth chord ushers in the first statement of scale degree 5 in the bass, G♯, which persists until the end of the song. Thus, by avoiding harmonic closure at m. 41, Griffes links the settings of Stanzas 2 and 3 into a continuous musical statement.

Stanza 3 witnesses the expressive crux not only of the song but of the cycle as a whole—see example 6.8. Four different elements contribute to the section's expressive significance: (1) an enormous swell in dynamics; (2) a brief modal shift from predominantly minor to major; (3) an incomplete statement of a recurring lament motive; and (4) the registral expansion of a key vertical interval, a minor ninth, initially heard in the prelude. Let us consider each one more closely.

The first dimension of the climax is the most obvious—the volcanic surge in dynamics in mm. 41–49 between *mezzo forte* and *fortissimo*. Judging by dynamics alone, it is tempting to conclude that the incantation was successful and the deity has arrived. It goes without saying that in

EXAMPLE 6.8.

(ABOVE AND FACING)

Griffes, "The Rose of the Night," mm. 46–61.

Griffes's orchestral arrangement the aural impact of this swell is even more magnified. More important, however, is the *subito diminuendo* to piano in m. 50, which is the first indication of Griffes's poignant musical comment on the text.

It is worth noting that this song bears a striking resemblance to the final section of Griffes's tone poem *The Pleasure-Dome of Kubla Khan*, where, following the simultaneous surge in dynamics, increase in tempo, change in meter, and rhythmic acceleration, the ensemble suddenly collapses onto itself (see chap. 5). The interruption in "The Rose of the Night," though not

Rose,   O   Rose of my De - sire!

as exaggerated, nevertheless makes a telling commentary on the narrator's plea for deliverance.

The second aspect involves a brief shift between parallel modes. Since the opening prelude introduces an alternate scale, it is not possible to categorize the song's mode as strictly major or minor. But, based on the predominance of G♯ major chords and a C♯ minor chord at key junctures, it is reasonable to classify the work as closer to a minor modality. As a result, the arrival of a major C♯ 6/4 chord in m. 41 not only comes as a surprise, but the modal inflection (E–E♯) contributes to the expectation that the narrator's spiritual hopes will be fulfilled.

Griffes's use of an interrupted lament motive constitutes the expressive crux of the song, and to appreciate its full impact I must revisit earlier sections. In each of the three previous iterations of this motive in the vocal line, the half-step motive, A–G♯, is preserved. In m. 12, it coincides with the first clear statement of the dominant; in mm. 16–18, it initiates the approach to the first cadence in C♯ minor; and in mm. 40–41, a slightly ornamented version (A–Fx–G♯) heralds the arrival of the bass's G♯ pedal, which continues until the end. So when the voice climbs to A5 (m. 49), the highest note in the song, the listener clearly expects the line to descend by half step. But it does not.[24]

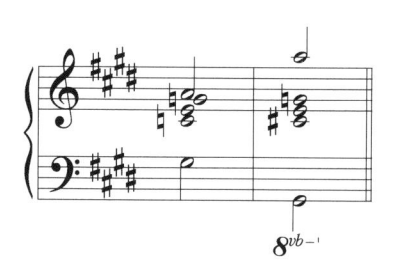

EXAMPLE 6.9.

Griffes, "The Rose of the Night": Registral Expansion, mm. 5–49.

This interrupted lament is made all the more poignant by the composer's treatment of registral expansion—one of the hallmarks of his unique approach to the musical pastoral. The vertical interval of a minor 9th between the voice and the piano's bass voice, G♯3–A4 in m. 5, returns at m. 49 but is now magnified in both directions: the soprano is one octave higher (A4–A5), the bass two octaves lower (G♯3–G♯1)—see example 6.9. Whereas in his instrumental works the expanding register often enhances a single sonority, in this case it not only highlights a chord, but it also subverts a melodic motive. Following this dramatic interruption, Griffes includes a musical aftershock where the tension briefly rises only to break off again. This second interruption relies on three factors, all converging at m. 58: an additional swell in dynamics, which is abruptly cut off; the completion of a prominent melodic motive, the rising octave line between B♯5 and B♯6 (spelled as C7); and finally, the immediate resumption of the opening piano texture with its haunting melodic motive. Hence, the potential release associated with the completion of the octave span is utterly subverted by the treatment of motive and dynamics.

Pastoral Cues

- Implied 12/8 and 9/8 Meter
- Bass Pedal and Dissonant Pedal Chord
- Registral Expansion

Lament Cue

- Sigh Figure (Interrupted)

The pastoral and lament cues at work in Stanza 3 and the Postlude are listed above. The piano postlude, mm. 58–61, is an abbreviated repetition of the piano's prelude with the same chromatic arabesque motive.

As a whole, Griffes's setting raises a significant question about the possibility of spiritual deliverance: how should the song's volcanic climax and its sudden interruption be interpreted?

- Do they represent the arrival of a supernatural being—a Celtic faery—who promises to unite with the narrator's soul and be reborn as one?
- Or are they a reflection of the narrator's own deep psychological desire for deliverance, a fantasy of spiritual fulfillment, that never comes to pass?

In short, is the song a miracle of spiritual revelation or a mirror of spiritual longing? The eventual return of the piano's mysterious incantation and rocking rhythmic texture strongly suggest the latter. Viewed as a whole, Griffes's musical commentary implies that the miracle of spiritual deliverance—heralded by images of fire, sea, thunder, wind, and a solitary rose—was nothing more than a mirage. Indeed, the narrator's (or singer's) impassioned pleas for deliverance have fallen on deaf immortal ears. Griffes's treatment of the incomplete lament motive at the climax also supports this interpretation. The juxtaposition of the desire for physical pleasure, the fascination with extreme forces of nature, and the yearning for spiritual deliverance creates a self-contradictory set of emotions. Yet, by the end, the other associations have dissolved, leaving only the traditional association of sadness and loss.

This book focuses on two different dimensions of the musical pastoral: the expansion of the tradition by virtue of a greater variety of musical cues associated with individual works; and the conflict and occasional confluence of two topical traditions: the pastoral and the lament. In many respects, this chapter illustrates both of these dimensions, showing especially how the two traditions intersect with each other in the song cycle. The reason they never truly merge together is that other emotions depicted in Macleod's poetry must be taken into account, and the end result is a profound psychological portrait of ambivalence. It is worthwhile considering what roles the pastoral and lament play in creating that portrait in each song.

"Ian the Proud"

The pastoral musical cues in the song's opening establish an emotional context for the narrator's internal journey. The emotions that Griffes portrays in his setting include tentative optimism and a much stronger sense of loss, initially forgotten (or denied) from the distant past and then re-experienced with fresh poignancy in the present. Most important, the pastoral is more than a neutral backdrop, an empty stage that the narrator occupies amid his self-reflections. Rather, it creates an emotional mirror, reflecting his initial guarded attempts at hope and optimism as well as his doubts and uncertainties, as represented by the recurring lament motives. Eventually, when the narrator finally realizes the darker, more repressed character of his emotions, the pastoral cues completely disappear and are replaced by an outcry of despair. The song closes with a return of the initial pastoral texture.

Overall, the lament motive's traditional associations of loss and grief that suffuse "Ian the Proud" influence the listener's perceptions in the following two songs. The blunt expression of physical desire and the longing for spiritual deliverance in Songs 2 and 3 are both colored by the expression of heartache and grief, still lingering from the previous song.

"Thy Dark Eyes to Mine"

Throughout the text of "Thy Dark Eyes," the narrator is experiencing two different emotions—physical desire and longing for spiritual deliverance—that he projects onto a single act: the promise of a kiss. In short, the poem consists of an elaborate fantasy in which the narrator, residing in heaven, reenters the mortal world in order to relive a memory from the past ("a lost echo of one such kiss") and to satisfy his physical desire.

Griffes locates this intersection of erotic fantasy and spiritual fulfillment within a topical framework that includes the pastoral and the lament. Indeed, this song is one of the most vivid examples in his entire oeuvre of a topical hybrid: part pastoral, part lament. But these two topical traditions do not unite into a coherent whole; instead, they participate in an ongoing process of emotional conflict, a dialogue between opposites in which the emotional character of the musical setting at times conflicts with the tone of the text. In Griffes's setting, the pastoral elements at the beginning and the end reflect the ideal setting of the narrator's initial musing in heaven, "dreaming in bliss." Yet the song's topical landscape also includes elements of the lament, which conflict with the otherwise serene atmosphere. When the narrator elaborates on his or her physical passion, the pastoral elements recede. The repetition in the postlude of the chromatic inflected lament motive leaves the listener hanging as to whether the narrator's hopes may well have been fulfilled. Finally, this poem bears a curious complementary relationship to the final poem in that the narrator's fantasy of an immortal returning from the afterlife to kiss a mortal is the reverse of what transpires in "The Rose of the Night."

"The Rose of the Night"

In this poem, not only do the same two emotions witnessed in "Thy Dark Eyes" reappear—physical desire and a longing for spiritual deliverance—but they are also projected onto the same physical action: a kiss. Yet here, the narrator's tone is more desperate than before, and the emotional stakes are higher.

Griffes introduces a new musical element in his setting of the poem, a mysterious melodic incantation that recurs throughout the song. This enchantment represents either the mortal or the immortal dimension of this strange encounter: if the former, it is associated with the narrator's heightened desire for erotic pleasure combined with spiritual fulfillment; if the latter, it is associated with the imminent arrival of a supernatural being. For the listener, what is remarkable about this setting is its operatic scale. The enormous swell in dynamics, the expansion of register between voice and piano, and the interruption of the falling lament motive all emphasize the same conclusion: the narrator's longings, erotic as well as spiritual, have not been fulfilled. Overall, Griffes's setting is a profound musical commentary that adds new dimensions to Macleod's poetic text.

In Griffes's setting of "The Rose of the Night," the pastoral plays a smaller role than in his settings of the other two songs in the cycle. Here, it is largely confined to the piano prelude and postlude, initially setting the emotional stage for the erotic and spiritual transformation and then later reflecting on the missed opportunity. By contrast, the lament topic plays a stronger role in the same two instrumental sections, either intensifying the initial musical incantation or later bemoaning the narrator's lack of fulfillment.

The conflict present in several songs in the cycle also introduces the broader question of his tendency to blend together different national styles—in this case, French and German. The fascination with harmonic and instrumental color among early twentieth-century French composers is evident in the piano prelude of "The Rose of the Night" as well as in later sections. However, the stylistic influence of Wagnerian opera—especially his treatment of the appoggiatura and the contrast in dynamics—is unmistakable in the third song's final stanza.

Our study of these three songs has revealed that the aesthetic sensibilities of Fiona Macleod and Charles Griffes intersect in two ways: a common love of sensual pleasure that borders on the erotic and a mutual yearning for spiritual deliverance. In the poems for the second and third songs, the dramatic turning point is the narrator's intense plea for divine intervention—that is, an embrace from a Celtic spirit. The physical gesture of a kiss becomes infused with two layers of signification: romantic intimacy and the promise of immortality. Whereas neither poem discloses whether the narrator's spiritual yearning has been satisfied, the codas of both musical settings reveal Griffes's interpretation. In the second song, the piano's final chromatic comment hints that the narrator's plea to savor Eilidh's kiss may have been answered. By contrast, in the third song, while the musical setting of the narrator's initial plea for deliverance seems promising, by the end the "rose" of his desire remains unfulfilled.

Overall, in these songs the pastoral and lament traditions are not only intertwined, but they are also incompatible. In each musical setting, the emotional balance between the two constantly shifts, creating an overall portrait of ambivalence. Griffes's innovative treatment of the lament motive in all three songs is especially remarkable in that the juxtaposition of the desire for physical pleasure, the fascination with extreme forces of nature, and the yearning for spiritual deliverance all create a contradictory set of emotions. The resulting emotional abundance is unique in his oeuvre.

NOTES

1. Sharp, *William*, 428.

2. Halloran, "W. B. Yeats," 65.

3. The version for voice and piano was premiered by Vera Janacopulos, soprano, and Griffes himself at the piano, March 22, 1919, Aeolian Hall, New York. The orchestral arrangement was first performed by the Philadelphia Orchestra, conductor Thaddeus Rich, March 24, 1919, Wilmington, Delaware; see Anderson, *Charles T. Griffes*, 229.

4. Sharp, *William Sharp*. Steve Blamires's recent biography of Sharp uncovers even more details about the origins of Fiona Macleod, Sharp's passion for Edith Wingate Rinder, and his fascination with the Celtic traditions of myth and magic. For example, Blamires speculates that origin of the name Fiona is a fusion of Sharp's favorite island in Western Scotland, Iona, and the great Gaelic hero Fionn; see *The Little Book of the Great Enchantment* (Cheltenham, UK: Skylight Press, 2013), 97. Other examples of multiple identities in the nineteenth century include the pair of opposites, "Eusebius" and

"Florestan," invented by Robert Schumann and the subject matter of Robert Louis Stevenson's novella *Strange Case of Dr. Jekyll and Mr. Hyde* (1886).

5. See the Introduction by Macleod's biographer in *Foam of the Past: Selected Writings of Fiona Macleod*, ed. Steve Blamires, (Cheltenham, UK: Skylight Press, 2014), 7.

6. For more information about William Sharp and his pseudonym, Fiona Macleod, consult Steve Blamires, *The Little Book of the Great Enchantment*, and the following online database, which includes numerous letters as well as various commentaries: https://www.ies.sas.ac.uk/research/william-sharp-fiona-macleod-archive/letters.

7. During the early twentieth century, this fascination with multiple identities was occasionally taken to extremes, as in the case of the Portuguese writer Fernando Pessoa (1888–1935), who invented nearly seventy-five alternative literary identities, which he called heteronyms—indeed, a virtuoso of multiplicity.

8. The first issue of the *Pagan Review*, edited by W. H. Brooks, consisted of the following essays and poems: "The Black Madonna," W. S. Fanshawe; "The Coming of Love," Geoffrey Gascoigne; "An Untold Story," Lionel Wingrave; "The Rape of the Sabines," James Marazion; "Dionysos in India (Opening Fragment of a Lyrical Drama)," William Windover; "La mort s'amuse," Charles Verlayne; and "The Pagans: An Untold Memory," unsigned; see *The Pagan Review* 1 (August 1892). For more background on late-Victorian cultural context, see *Yellow Nineties 2.0*, ed. Dennis Denisoff and Lorraine Janzen Kooistra, Ryerson University, 2010, accessed on February 6, 2023, https://1890s.ca/yb-v1-introduction.

9. According to the editor, the word *pagan* meant that the journal was questioning not only traditional religious traditions but also traditional gender roles within the concept of marriage. See Bénédicte Coste, "Late Victorian Paganism: The Case of the Pagan Review," *Cahiers victoriens et édouardiens* 80 (Fall 2014): 1–12.

10. In particular, that poem is a paeon to the goddess Macha of the Ruddy Hair.

11. The poem is entitled "The Love Chant of Cormac Conlingas."

12. "The Lament of Ian the Proud" initially appeared in *From the Hills of Dream: Threnodies, Songs and Other Poems* (Portland, ME: Thomas B. Mosher, 1901). Griffes most likely read it in a later collection he purchased in 1914—see Anderson, *The Works of Charles T. Griffes*, 509.

13. Griffes uses the same rising arpeggio as the initial theme in his Poem for Flute and Orchestra, which was arranged for flute and piano in 1922. However, in that work the harmonic language quickly becomes more chromatic.

14. There are continuous eighth-note triplets in the following sections: mm. 11–14, 17–19, 22–23, 29, 32–36, 41–44, 47–51.

15. Blamires, *The Little Book*, 185–86.

16. William F. Halloran, *William Sharp and "Fiona Macleod": A Life* (Cambridge, UK: Cambridge University Press, 2021). https://library.oapen.org/handle/20.500.12657/53190?show=full. Retrieved 8 July 2022.

17. Fiona Macleod, "To W. B. Yeats," in *From the Hills of Dream: Threnodies, Songs and Other Poems* (Portland, ME: Thomas B. Mosher, 1901), 81–85.

18. For more details about Yeats's ongoing interest in the Golden Order, see Richard Ellmann, *Yeats: The Man and the Masks* (New York: Macmillan, 1948): 91–98. William Halloran meticulously describes Yeats's solicitation of Macleod in *William Sharp and*

"*Fiona Macleod,*" 223–26. https://library. oapen.org/handle/20.500.12657/53190. Retrieved 26 June 2022.

19. It is difficult to determine the exact chronology of the three poems by Fiona Macleod that Griffes set to music. In his biography of Macleod, Steve Blamires observes that her writings were reprinted several times in different combinations and, in some cases, amended during Sharp's lifetime and immediately after his death. Foreign publishers (such as Thomas B. Mosher) also published editions that differ slightly from their British originals. The result, he concludes, is "a confusing mixture of editions and versions"; see *The Little Book of the Great Enchantment*, 241. In this study, I will assume that "Thy Dark Eyes to Mine" and "The Rose of the Night" first appeared in *From the Hills of Dream: Threnodies, Songs and Other Poems* (Portland, ME: Thomas B. Mosher, 1901) and were reprinted, following Sharp's death, as *From the Hills of Dream: Threnodies and Songs and Later Poems* (London: William Heinemann, 1907).

20. The act of kissing has a rich history in Danish literature that includes two fairy tales by Hans Christian Andersen: "The Swineherd" (1841) and "The Ice Maiden (1861). In both stories, the physical gesture of a kiss changes the course of a character's destiny. In the first tale, the princess is perfectly willing to offer her physical affection in exchange for an object; yet when she refuses the genuine love of a worthy suitor, the prince, she ends up being banished. In the second tale, the Ice Maiden's kiss has supernatural powers, and she becomes a harbinger of death. See *Hans Christian Andersen: The Complete Fairy Tales and Stories* (New York: Doubleday, 1974). However, there is no evidence that Griffes read or referred to these two stories.

21. William James, *The Varieties of Religious Experience: A Study in Human Nature, Being the Gifford Lecture Series on Natural Religion Delivered in Edinburgh 1901–02* (London: Longman, Green and Co, 1902).

22. Other poems by Macleod that begin with epigraphs include "The Bandruidh" (anonymous), "Oran-Bhroin" (anonymous), "Dream Fantasy" (attributed to William Drummond of Hawthornden), "Deirdrê Is Dead" (attributed to "The House of Usna"), and "The Dirge of the Four Cities" (attributed to "The Little Book of the Great Enchantment").

23. It is no surprise that in his orchestral transcription of "The Rose of the Night" Griffes assigns this motive to the flute.

24. However, the half step, A–G$\sharp$, does occur in the left hand of the piano in m. 49.

7

"Tears" and "Symphony in Yellow"

Went to "The Yellow Jacket" which I have wanted to see so long. Here is a real Chinese play done in Chinese fashion. One might call it a Chinese morality play or fairy tale for grown-ups, showing the hero as he goes through the temptations of life to attain his crown. The authors do not claim it to be a translation, but it is based closely on Chinese plays. The manner of performance is also entirely Chinese, the stage representing the old Chinese theatre stage in San Francisco. It shows a room with a door on one side through which the actors enter and another on the opposite side through which they leave. There is no change of scenery, but the stage-manager who all the time sits at the back of the stage, announces every new scene. The property man, a Chinaman, likewise sits at the side of the stage smoking cigarettes or eating rice, and changes around the few pieces of furniture as the new scene demands. But no new piece is added. There is not the slightest attempt at concealment or illusion and there is no desire for realism. The Chinamen wishes the scenery left to his imagination and looks upon the play merely as a skeleton foundation upon which his imagination can soar away and dream. So everything is mere suggestion and the means are often so crude and naïve as to be absurd. What saves it from a burlesque is the absolute seriousness of the actors of the realization of the Chinamen's standpoint. At the back of the stage is a round niche where sit 3 Chinamen with a row of Chinese instruments, upon which they play a good deal of the time a monotonous oriental music. This is most effective except at times when the arranger leaves the oriental modes and introduced chromatic scales in augmented 5th and other passages which are absurdly reminiscent of the "Fürchten" and Loge passages in the "Ring." But sometimes the music is most weirdly effective and

helpful to the imagination, as in a moonlight ride on the river where the combination
of the instruments and a few female voices behind the stage in the monotonous and
lulling repetition of a couple of distinctly Chinese motifs, has an almost uncanny
effect. I had to think of the boat-ride at the end of the Jardin des supplices.

The above quotation is drawn from Charles Griffes's diary about an eventful play that he witnessed in New York during December 1912.[1] It is significant in two respects. First, his first impression of Chinese theater with musical accompaniment is an excellent introduction to the role that non-Western music played in his creative life. Living in a cosmopolitan city afforded occasional exposure to musical traditions from China, Java, and India, and they continued to inspire him in various ways for the rest of his life (for more details about Griffes's interest in non-Western musical traditions, see chap. 1). Second, his aesthetic sensibility was truly interdisciplinary (or intermedial). His description of a new instrumental texture performed at a Chinese play has a literary rather than a musical point of reference—in particular, a scene from Octave Mirbeau's controversial novel *Le Jardin des Supplices (Torture Garden)*.[2]

This chapter will be divided into two parts. The first part reflects Griffes's fascination for exoticism, in particular the musical traditions of East Asia, as shown in one song from his cycle, *Five Poems of Ancient China and Japan*, op. 10. He combines elements from Asian and Western musical traditions in a new pastoral synthesis, fusing the pentatonic serenity of the folk melody, a restrained piano accompaniment with an unexpected outburst of chromaticism. In the second part, I will explore how his setting of Oscar Wilde's "Symphony in Yellow" reflects his attraction to the poet's literary style as well as to the general artistic principles of Aestheticism. This second song reflects the spirit of the ambivalent pastoral, combining traditional features, such as a drone fifth pedal, with a slow-moving kaleidoscope of harmonic colors in the piano and a gesture of irony at the final cadence.

"Tears"

The song cycle, *Five Poems of Ancient China and Japan*, Op. 10, was composed between 1916 and 1917.[3] The cycle demonstrates two approaches that

Griffes adopts toward non-Western musical traditions. One approach is to set or borrow a preexisting source. The first song, "So-fei Gathering Flowers," consists of an arrangement of a Chinese folk song that he had discovered—he recorded this fact on the verso of the manuscript of his setting.[4] The other approach is less appropriation than adaptation. The melodies of the remaining four songs are of Griffes's own design, which not only share the same pentatonic structure but also capture the spirit of the original folk song. The titles are as follows: "Landscape," a slow, doleful setting; "The Temple among the Mountains," a more upbeat treatment characterized by numerous pedal points; "Tears," a poignant musical lament, which will be discussed at length below; and finally "A Feast of Lanterns," which is the quickest in tempo and has the most uplifting effect in the entire collection

As a whole, the song cycle displays remarkable compositional discipline in Griffes's treatment of scale and rhythm: (1) all five songs are either purely or mostly pentatonic, which, in one case, means the song contains two extra pitches; (2) three of the five songs contain rhythmic ostinatos in the piano accompaniment; and (3) the accompaniments of two songs witness recurring rhythmic motives. He was quite forthright about his approach to pitch organization in that at the beginning of each song he identifies the scale to be employed. In several songs (1, 3, and 5), Griffes introduces a number of different ostinatos in succession, creating a slowly changing pattern of rhythmic repetition—in short, a large-scale temporal kaleidoscope. The accompaniments in the other two songs, "Landscape" and "Tears," though not organized by strict repetition, nevertheless contain recurring rhythmic and pitch motives that serve as a musical reminiscence as well as a commentary on the given text.

> High o'er the hill the moon-barque steers.
> The lantern lights depart,
> Dead springs are stirring in my heart;
> And there are tears.
> But that which makes my grief more deep,
> Is that you know not when I weep.

The above text is by a Chinese poet, Wang Seng-Ju, dating from the sixth century.[5] In a mere six lines, the poem recounts the narrator's despair, beginning with a description of nature, the moon above a hill, and a reference to the ritual of lighting lanterns (the final poem in the set includes the same two images but in a more optimistic vein). Then the narrator continues by confessing that he or she is weeping (the image of "dead springs in my heart") and that, even worse, the object of his or her affection is not aware of the grief. Overall, this short lyric grows in intensity until the final line, a feature Griffes evokes in his musical setting by means of a dramatic change of harmony, texture, and dynamics. It is also worth noting an uncanny resemblance between this ancient text and a poem by the late nineteenth-century French poet Paul Verlaine, "Il pleure dans mon coeur," from his collection *Romances sans parole*, a poem Griffes most likely had read.[6]

The song's two-part formal plan is loosely based on the poem's internal divisions—see below.

mm.	1	13	21
Section	A	B	Coda

His setting of this poem combines a traditional eighteenth-century pastoral with the lament, a historical thread that can be seen in his treatment of meter, rhythm, and harmony. The list of pastoral and lament features is displayed below:

Pastoral Cues

- Lento
- 6/4 Meter
- Perfect 5th Pedal Interval

Lament Cues

- Sigh Figure (Implied)
- Iambic Ostinato Pattern

The song's meter is mostly in 6/4 at a slow tempo (*Lento*), although there is a short section in 4/4 (mm. 17–20). More important, the piano's haunting iambic ostinato pattern (quarter note + half note) creates a stately but hypnotic character that persists throughout most of the song. By contrast, the voice's rhythms are less strict, often trochaic (complementing the piano), and are punctuated by long durations characteristic of wailing. The song's

EXAMPLE 7.1.

Griffes, "Tears," mm. 1–12.

phrase organization begins with an unrelentingly 4 + 4 scheme (assuming that one includes the one-bar piano introduction). However, at m. 16 a fermata interrupts the regular grouping and inaugurates a brief section in a contrasting meter and tempo. Then the final section parses into the original two four-bar phrases. Example 7.1 displays the score for mm. 1–12.

Griffes's treatment of pitch materials in "Tears" reveals his aspiration to unify elements from Western and non-Western musical traditions into a new synthesis. Although the pitch collection in the voice and piano is mostly pentatonic, a brief departure into chromatic harmony highlights an image in the text and underlines a lament gesture in the vocal line. Let us consider each of these elements in greater depth.

In "Tears," the pitch organization of the voice and piano differ dramatically. Whereas the vocal line is entirely in so-called G♯ "minor" pentatonic mode (G♯, A♯, C♯, D♯, F♯), at two junctures in the piano part—initially at m. 8 in the bass and again at m. 14—Griffes introduces a B♮ to expand the overall collection. Then at m. 14 he employs an additional new pitch, D♮, thereby expanding the scale from "pentatonic plus one" to "pentatonic plus two," making seven pitches in all. As a result, the pentatonic becomes heptatonic: G♯, A♯, B, C♯, D, D♯, F♯.

Measure 13 is one of the song's two emotional highpoints. The chord unfolded in the piano is not only dissonant—a B-minor triad with a major seventh—it departs radically from the harmonic vocabulary employed elsewhere in the song. It is difficult to overemphasize the expressive power such a harmonic interjection possesses—like throwing a chromatic stone into calm pentatonic waters. Griffes also highlights the word "tears" (which echoes the song's title) in three other musical dimensions: (a) the textural shift from austere block chords to upward sweeping arpeggios; (b) the apex in the piano's register, F♯6; and (c) a change in dynamics, from the opening *pianissimo* to *forte*. The treatment of all these parameters, harmony, rhythmic texture, range, and dynamics, suggests a blend of sensibilities: Chinese, French, and American.

In mm. 13–16, displayed in example 7.2, Griffes also underlines the song's lament character by introducing the half-step motive, D♯–D, between a pitch in the piano's rising arpeggio and an inner voice in the chord that immediately follows. It should be noted that if the singer had

EXAMPLE 7.2.

Griffes, "Tears," mm. 13–16.

presented the falling halfstep as a stepwise melodic motive, it would have disturbed the vocal line's purely pentatonic character. A melodic half-step motive does occur in the piano, but it ascends from C♯ to D (m. 15). Finally, beginning in m. 17, Griffes highlights the beginning of the final stanza with a brief episode of imitation in continuous quarter notes between voice and piano (mm. 17–20).

The song's harmonic language is almost entirely pentatonic, consisting of rich concatenations of fourths, fifths, and occasionally thirds, which reflects Griffes's summary of his harmonic palette in the setting of *Sho-Jo* (see chap. 1). The chord density is generally thick, varying between 4-, 5-, and 6-note sonorities. More important, the collection of pentatonic chords not only rotates in the distribution of fifths and fourths, it also slowly accumulates momentum, finally climaxing at m. 21 with a 7-note chord that consists of all five pitches in the G♯ pentatonic scale plus doubling, shown in example 7.3.

This pentatonic cluster assumes an important role in the song in four respects: (1) motivic—it verticalizes an important melodic gesture in the vocal line from the previous three bars, a succession of perfect fourths, D♯, G♯, C♯; (2) the breadth of register—at nearly three octaves, it is one of several junctures where the piano harmonic gesture covers a wide range (the

EXAMPLE 7.3.

Griffes, "Tears": Pentatonic sonority, m. 21.

others are mm. 14–16 and m. 17); (3) the dynamic marking, one of three *forte* markings in the song; and (4) text painting, as the chord emphasizes the word "you," the object of the narrator's grief.

* * *

For Griffes, musical exoticism, or what his generation referred to as Orientalism, was much more than a passing artistic fad that he briefly entertained and eventually outgrew. Indeed, it touched his aesthetic core. Although not all of the music he composed during his final thirteen years contained overt references to non-Western musical traditions, the study of the music and literature of foreign cultures began during his stay in Berlin and became a constant preoccupation during his later years.[7]

My reason for focusing on Griffes's setting of "Tears" is that it is a microcosm of several aspects of his fascination with what he called a "modified contact" with non-Western musical traditions in a 1917 interview (for more details, see chap. 1).[8] In this song, he blends two different sensibilities: a fascination with Chinese folk music, as shown in his arrangement of a folk melody ("So-fei Gathering Flowers"), the folklike contours of his own melody ("Tears"), and a more impassioned approach to text painting. Griffes's creative treatment of scale, harmony, rhythm, and texture all coalesce to reflect the poem's poignant emotions. In short, the dramatic evocation of the narrator's grief in "Tears" could be described as a form of aesthetic ambivalence, poised between restraint and indulgence.

What is significant for this study is the degree to which Griffes's passion for exoticism ultimately impacted his overall pastoral sensibility. Three of the other songs in the cycle contain more overt pastoral references, which include a strictly pentatonic pitch collection and frequent rhythmic ostinatos in the piano accompaniment. As a whole, the cycle serves as a microcosm of two conflicting aspects of his artistic temperament: the collector's obsession to gather new exotic mysteries and the artist's urge to experiment and make those mysteries his own. Ultimately, *Five Poems of Ancient China and Japan* reveals one way in which he reconciled these two impulses.

"Symphony in Yellow"

The second half of this chapter focuses on one of Griffes's most striking songs, "Symphony in Yellow," which was published in 1915 and is based on an early poem by the Irish poet Oscar Wilde. The question arises: why should Griffes's setting of a poem by Wilde be included in a chapter devoted to musical exoticism? The answer lies not only in the song's unusual pastoral character but also in the deep sympathy that Griffes held for the artistic principles shared by artists of the Aesthetic movement. His setting not only mirrors Wilde's love of sensuous beauty, but with its use of non-Western scales and harmonic color, it also adds a touch of musical irony.

Although Wilde is widely known as a late-Victorian playwright, novelist, and flamboyant personality, his initial writings were as a poet. In 1881, he published his first and only book of poetry at his own expense. It was autobiographical, mirroring his devotion to the study of ancient Greek and Latin classics as well as his immersion in contemporary English and French literature. The topics of these poems were conventional, ranging from "beauty, love, faith, decorated stories in the Romantic tradition, rapt self-analysis and self-reproach."[9]

Critical reaction to his poetry was mixed, mostly negative among the literati, though positive for the poems that he presented during his American tour the following year. Among early critics, the overwhelming objection was plagiarism. Anne Warty describes it as if he were "sorting through a wardrobe of different poetic styles, trying on one after another to see what suits him best and always wearing his erudition on his sleeve."[10] A critic in the magazine *Punch* wrote that "Mr. Wilde may be aesthetic, but he is not original. This is a volume of echoes, it is Swinburne and water."

> "Aesthete of aesthetes!
> What's in a name?
> The poet is Wilde,
> But his poetry's tame"[11]

Later critics were more generous, opining that since Wilde was open about his sources, "to describe a young poet's work as derivative is not the same as to condemn it."[12]

Another way of interpreting Wilde's early poetry is not only as a reflection of the past, but also as a form of refraction, viewing the literary tradition through the philosophical lens of his professor at Oxford, Walter Pater. Pater was one of the principal muses of the Aestheticist credo. In a series of essays, he proposed a nonsystematic approach to aesthetic thought, rejecting all general formulas. His approach is a philosophical brand of relativism with neither a fixed set of artistic principles nor any underlying belief in Truth in art or reality. Instead, Pater embraces multiplicity instead of unity and highly discriminating examples of individual beauty—in short, the sum of the parts instead of a whole (See chap. 1). The enormous breadth of beautiful phenomena that Pater considered artistic helps explain the diversity of styles in Wilde's poetry and, as we will see below, the wealth of musical inspiration found in Griffes's mature songs.

"Symphony in Yellow" stands apart from Wilde's other poems for a number of reasons. To begin with, it was written in 1889, eight years after his first volume of poetry. It not only displays a precise and economical style, suffused by metaphors of color, but it is also permeated with references to multiple art forms including painting, literature, and music. Finally, its title has more than a hint of irony.

The poem's title has a rich archaeological history that encompasses references to a wide range of events in popular culture as well as to the leading painters and writers in late-Victorian England. The first layer is a well-known "sensation" novel—that is, a precursor to the detective novel by Wilkie Collins entitled *The Woman in White* (1859). The novel was so popular that it became the subject of a play, a perfume line, two dances (a gallop and a waltz), and a parody play by Watts Phillips entitled *The Woman in Mauve*.[13] The second layer revolves around James McNeil Whistler, an expatriate American painter who built a stunning career, straddled between France and England. One of his earliest successes was a work entitled *The Woman in White*, completed in 1862, which was exhibited at the original Salon des Refusés in Paris along with other controversial Impressionist paintings such as Manet's *Déjeuner sur l'herbe*. Months after it was exhibited, Whistler renamed it *Symphony in White No. 1: The White Girl*. The motivation for the change of title was most likely due to Paul Mantz, an art critic, who in his review in the *Gazette Des Beaux Arts* (1863) called the painting a "symphonie du blanc."[14] Whistler was so enamored of this title that he recycled it over and over again, creating a series of eight visual "symphonies."[15] One of them, *Symphony in White, No. 2: The Little White Girl* (1864), inspired a short tribute by the English poet Algernon Swinburne, which Whistler later pasted onto the frame.

Wilde's decision to substitute a different color in his own literary "symphony" was hardly accidental since yellow images are ubiquitous in his poetry. The color reappears in six of the seven poems by Wilde that Griffes eventually set to music. Typical images include "ochre-colored hay," "a yellow silken scarf," "thin threads of yellow foam," and "a long wave of yellow light."[16] Beginning in 1894, the color yellow also became strongly associated with the Aestheticist and Decadent movements, in general due to the emergence of the British literary periodical *The Yellow Book* and its art editor, Aubrey Beardsley. But Wilde had already penned his own yellow tribute five years earlier.

Another explicit connection that links Wilde's poetry with late-Victorian paintings can be found in his poem "Impression du matin," which Griffes also set to music and which, despite its French title, was written in English. Here, the reference to Whistler is less in the title than in the imagery of the text itself. The poem opens as follows: "The Thames nocturne of blue and gold / Changed to a Harmony in Grey." In only two lines, Wilde manages to quote the titles of two different Whistler paintings: *Nocturne: Blue and Gold—Old Battersea Bridge* (1872–75) and *Harmony in Grey and Green* (1872–74). Considering that Wilde knew Whistler's work during this period and later had a series of encounters with him, it is difficult to believe that these references to his paintings were arbitrary. In short, the significance of "symphonies" and "nocturnes" in Wilde's poetry was as much visual as it was musical.

Griffes's fascination with Wilde encompassed all of his writings, including the poems, plays, and essays, for he owned the complete works in his personal library.[17] In a diary entry from 1912, Griffes reveals the depth of his curiosity:[18]

> Read interesting things about Oscar Wilde, including two good essays by Carl Dietz from the Preuss Fahrbinder and Sherard's Biography [*The Life of Oscar Wilde*]. Dietz says that Wilde was a combination of Wotton, Dorian and Basil in Dorian Gray—an explanation which I like. He thinks the man will be remembered for his search for beauty and connection with the esthetic movement long after his works are forgotten. He calls them "hot house plants," though perfect in form and containing most wonderful and beautiful language. He gives the comedies a good place in English literature. He mentions *Salome* as having been composed in some kind of dream. What kind?

Clearly, Griffes appreciated these "hot house plants," for, in all, he set seven of Wilde's poems to music: four as a set entitled *Four Impressions*, "Le Jardin," "Impression du matin," "La Mer," "Le Réveillon" (published in 1970); two in the set, *Tone-Images*, Op. 3: "La Fuite de la Lune" and "Symphony in Yellow" (1915); and one separately, "Les Ballons" (published in 1984). Also, in 1916 he composed an additional setting of "La Mer." Together, these settings reveal a different facet of Griffes's gifts as a song composer. They eschew the intense emotions found in the Macleod cycle with its inimitable blend of deep lament, erotic fantasy, and spiritual yearning. Instead, these songs evoke Wilde's taste for nuanced description of sensuous beauty by means of rich harmonic color, simple melody, and a wide range of rhythmic textures.

It is also worth mentioning that Griffes himself was keenly aware of James Whistler's innovations in the disciplines of painting and engraving. In an interview in 1917 regarding the compositional approach he adopted in *Sho-Jo*, his arrangement of Japanese folk melodies, he said the following: "Whistler's learned engraving from Japanese prints without sacrificing his own individuality."[19] Two things are noteworthy in this quotation. First, in his mind it was perfectly natural to use the example of a painter to explain a composer's relationship to his source of musical inspiration. Second, and more important, Griffes was as much a student of Whistler's visual symphonies as he was of Wilde's poems that quoted them—two of the leading artists in the Aesthetic movement.

Finally, the author and composer shared a similar passion for color. Not only was Griffes fascinated during his entire life by the visual world of painting and photography, but for some reason he was obsessed with the color orange. According to Donna Anderson, "From early childhood Charles exhibited an acute awareness of color. Orange was among his favorite colors." Griffes once remarked "that a beautiful color is lovely in itself quite aside from any part it plays in the design of the picture."[20]

The text of "Symphony of Yellow" is as follows:[21]

> An omnibus across the bridge
> Crawls like a yellow butterfly
> And, here and there, a passer-by
> Shows like a little restless midge.
> Big barges full of yellow hay
> Are moored against the shadowy wharf,
> And, like a yellow silken scarf,
> The thick fog hangs along the quay.
> The yellow leaves begin to fade
> And flutter from the Temple elms.
> And at my feet the pale green Thames
> Lies like a rod of rippled jade.

This short lyric has no overarching narrative thread. Instead, it is a scrapbook of all things yellow that the narrator happens to encounter in downtown London, which include a bus, a load of hay, a layer of fog, and leaves falling from elm trees. Not only is each image in the series isolated, but the order in which they appear also seems arbitrary. In some respects, there is an inherent narrative power of a litany of objects in an urban landscape that all share the same color. But in the final two lines, the narrator introduces one last image that completely changes the subject—the river Thames. The reason is because the river has a different color, a green stripe running through this otherwise yellow mise-en-scène.[22] Seen as a whole, this "symphonic" scrapbook is fragmented—the individual parts sound alone, not together.

When we take into account the poem's title, the absence of linear narrative becomes slightly ironic in character. It is called a "symphony" and yet there are no literary images involving sound or music. The etymological history of the term can be traced to ancient Greece, where it meant sounding together or harmonious sounds.[23] By the eighteenth century, a symphony denoted a musical work with multiple movements that not only contained contrasting themes and textures but also possessed a unifying key as well as an upbeat, if not triumphant, ending. Based on the two definitions, the poem's three stanzas seem closer to a "symphony" in ancient Greece than in modern Germany. Considering the poem's brevity and neutral tone, it could have easily been called "Reverie" or a "Nocturne in Yellow." Hence, Wilde's title is less about the specific musical genre and more about the abstract analogy between poems and paintings that use color as a source of unity as well as of subtle variation. As we will see below, Griffes's musical setting adds a new layer of inter-artistic signification, uniting literature, painting, and music.

The song's date of composition is somewhat in doubt, as there is no mention of it in Griffes's diaries. Since Schirmer accepted the manuscript for publication in late 1914 along with two of his other settings of Wilde's poetry as a set entitled *Tone-Images*, op. 3, Anderson speculates that the song was completed in either 1912 or 1913.[24]

The musical setting of "Symphony in Yellow" is a blend of traditional and innovative conceptions of the musical pastoral. The song possesses several features traditionally associated with the eighteenth-century pastoral tradition such as the bass's recurring fifth pedal in the opening and closing sections that accompanies the voice's lilting pentatonic melodic line. However, Griffes also employs an expanded harmonic palette not associated with his eighteenth-century predecessors; the piano part is suffused by pentatonic clusters and added-note chords, unfolding in slow motion. The initial *Languidamente* marking indicates its serene character, linking it with Griffes's other experimental pastorals. Finally, there is an aspect of the song that exudes irony, a feature that is perfectly in keeping with the Aestheticist predilections of the poet.

The song's formal structure can be outlined as follows:[25]

mm.	1	19	34
Section	A	B	A'

The overall formal design is a traditional rounded binary (ABA'). This design is unique among Griffes's settings of Wilde's poetry, for he usually preferred through-composed formal plans, which allowed him to evoke the wide ranges of images in each poem. The third section (A') repeats the opening phrase in the vocal part, which Griffes complements with a minor pentatonic scale in the piano accompaniment. This section also possesses a strong element of finality, for it ends on an implied authentic cadence above a bass pedal on "B." His treatment of form and harmony lends a new sense of finality to the poem's introduction of green imagery; the initial "A" section is displayed in example 7.4.

Throughout the song, the vocal part has its own distinct rhythmic texture and phrase organization. The declamation is syllabic, and the rhythmic durations are simple, mostly quarter and half notes. Initially, there is a strong link between melody and harmony in that the opening five-note chord and the vocal line are both derived from the same B-pentatonic scale: B, C♯, D♯, F♯, G♯ (see ex. 7.5a). By contrast, the voice's phrase lengths, 5 + 7, diverge dramatically from the constant two-bar rhythmic ostinato in the piano.

The song's rhythm/metric organization is not typical of Griffes's other pastorals. It begins in 4/4, and in the middle section it shifts to 3/4 with an implied 2/4 (mm. 19–22) due to hemiola subdivisions in the piano. However, in the outer two sections he relies on a more traditional pastoral cue in the piano: a mantra-like rhythmic pattern, half + whole + half. Indeed, the first and third sections are less a symphony than a set of variations, for they both possess elements of a passacaglia with a striking rhythmic and harmonic ostinato in the accompaniment (mm. 1–6, mm. 34–40).

Symphony in Yellow

EXAMPLE 7.4.

Griffes, "Symphony in Yellow," mm. 1–18.

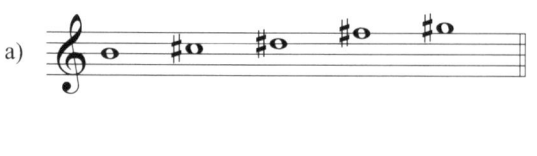

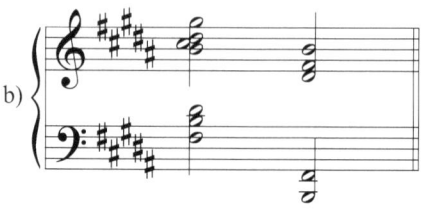

EXAMPLE 7.5.

Griffes, "Symphony in Yellow": Pentatonic collection
as (a) scale and (b) chord.

This rhythmic mantra not only suggests a slow duple meter, 2/2, but it also
serves as a form of text painting for the poem's vivid initial image—a "but-
terfly crawling." The same rhythmic pattern is also echoed in the registral
contour of the arpeggiated accompaniment pattern. In the opening section, a single five-note sonority is arpeggiated as a series of broken chords,
creating a recurring registral contour of high, low, and middle.

The song's harmonic texture possesses two conflicting dimensions,
which are emblematic of the ambivalent pastoral. On the one hand, the
pedal interval of a perfect fifth, acting as a recurring point of reference, is
utterly characteristic of the eighteenth-century pastoral tradition, based
on a recurring point of reference rather than a continuous drone. In the
outer two sections the interval, B–F♯, appears every other bar on beat
three, providing an element of continuity amid the continuous parade of
rich harmonies above it (see example 7.5b)

On the other hand, the harmonies built above the pedal in the first and
third sections transform a typical pastoral signifier, the pentatonic scale,
into a rich chromatic vocabulary, full of sevenths and added-note chords.
For one phrase in the final section, Griffes introduces a small but dramatic shift in the pentatonic collection, D♮ instead of D♯, which coincides
with "yellow leaves" in the text and implies an autumnal tone to the list

of images. Throughout the song, a tension exists between functional and nonfunctional harmony, since for much of the setting the succession of chords is used purely for color, departing from and returning to B major. Every two measures, he repeats the same sonority three times, B 13/9, by dividing it into its constituent parts—each iteration is either a different inversion or different subset of the chord. For example, since the referential chord contains five pitches, the piano presents different subsets of it, yet arranged for five or six voices, including doubling (see ex. 7.5b). It is as if the piano is a harmonic kaleidoscope, revealing the individual hues that make up the sonorous colors of each chord. Indeed, the musical setting is a showcase for contemplating chromatic harmony wherein listeners are invited to savor the intervallic ingredients of each sonority. Although individual chords in this pattern contain vertical dissonances, taken together, the cumulative effect is of a pentatonic haze. Overall, Griffes's treatment of harmony, rhythm, and register is utterly hypnotic.

It is worth noting the harmonic kinship between "Symphony in Yellow" and "The White Peacock," the latter of which was discussed in chapter 4. Although the genesis of this song preceded that of the piano work by several years, it is curious that both contain multiple statements of added-note chords above the same bass pitch. Although "The White Peacock" relies on a slightly different chord built on B, a dominant-ninth chord as opposed to a 13/9, both works reveal a fascination with a recurring rhythmic mantra and a rich spectrum of harmonic color.

Another source of kinship, the treatment of texture, helps unite this song with two other works by Griffes: "The White Peacock" and Prelude #3. The kaleidoscopic effect of replaying different constituent vertical intervals of the same chord also occurs in the opening section of "The White Peacock" (see chap. 4) as well as in Prelude #3 within the passages leading to the final cadences of each principal section (see chap. 9). In some respects, this synthesis of harmonic repetition and variation became a textural signature in some of his experimental pastoral works.

Two dimensions of irony exist in this musical setting, both of which arise from the striking conflict between the nonlinear poetic organization and the linear or teleological musical design. First of all, the setting culminates with an implied authentic cadence above the continuous drone fifth. Although the final B 13/9 sonority is the same as the initial chord, the composer's treatment of local tonal centers imparts a linear direction to the overall setting: B major, B♭ major, B minor, and B major. This sense of directed motion, beginning with, departing from, and finally returning to the same key, conflicts sharply with the purely episodic character of the text. In addition, a handful of other features—the slow tempo, the rhythmic ostinato composed of long durations, and the syllabic vocal setting—together create an expectation that some dramatic or prophetic message would be revealed. When the singer's parting words are merely that a green river is underfoot, an ironic disconnect emerges between the text and the musical setting. This discrepancy between music and text suggests either that the composer's taste is whimsical, aloof from the text, or that the disconnect is an ironic musical comment on Wilde's poem. In the context of Griffes's "final testament" to irony in Prelude #3, as will be shown in the following chapter, the evidence points to the latter.

* * *

Griffes's setting of "Symphony in Yellow" reveals his affinity for the world of British Aestheticism. Wilde's original poem embodies one principle shared by artists in the Aesthetic movement: the fascination with sensuous beauty for its own sake. The nonlinear nature of his litany of poetic images highlights this characteristic, allowing readers to savor each yellow image in the list. In his musical setting of the poem, Griffes translates the same principle into musical terms by means of a rich parade of scintillating harmonic colors. However, he adds an additional principle of Aestheticism, an ironic musical commentary on Wilde's text. The song's linear formal design, culminating with an authentic cadence that resolves in slow motion, conflicts with the predominantly nonlinear poetic design.

This song also reflects the confluence of multiple art forms that existed not only within late-Victorian England itself but also between England and America. By setting this particular poem, Griffes participated in a festival of senses that is comparable in scale to that found in "The White Peacock," as was discussed in chapter 4. The rich skein of references to painting, literature, and popular culture in this song is a direct reflection of the composer's own protean artistic voice.

"Symphony in Yellow" is a portrait of contrasts. There are elements in the song that suggest the serenity of a traditional pastoral such as a drone fifth in the piano, the hypnotic rhythmic repetition, and, at crucial junctures, a pentatonic pitch collection in the voice and piano. There are also elements that highlight Griffes's taste for experimentation. In particular, the revolving kaleidoscope of highly colorful, nonfunctional sonorities conflicts with the use of tonal function in the drive to the final cadence. Yet, when viewed together, these conflicts coalesce into a work that reveals a distinctly Aestheticist hue and, at the same time, embodies the character of the ambivalent pastoral.

NOTES

1. Diary entry, December 30, 1912, Box 47, Folder 5-6, Series III, Donna K. Anderson Research Files on Charles Griffes, Music Division, New York Public Library for the Performing Arts.

2. A young couple, Emma and the narrator, are gliding down a fictitious Chinese river at night, surrounded by the distant sounds of music, revelry, and debauchery. See Octave Mirbeau, *Torture Garden*, English trans. Alvah C. Bessie (New York: Citadel, 1948), 237–39.

3. See the list of works in Anderson, *Charles T. Griffes*, 227.

4. Anderson, *The Works of Charles T. Griffes*, 172.

5. The English version of Wang Seng-Ju's poem is drawn from *A Lute of Jade: Selections from the Classical Poets of China*, ed. and trans. Lancelot Cranmer-Byng, Wisdom of the East Series, ed. Cranmer-Byng and S. A. Kapadia (New York: E. P. Dutton, 1915), a volume that Griffes purchased in 1914. See ibid., xiv, 509, 534.

6. In 1912, Griffes purchased a collection of Verlaine poetry entitled *Choix de poésies*; Anderson provides a partial list of books Griffes purchased between 1907–14, ibid., 509–10.

7. Evidently, Griffes was fascinated with Japanese artwork as early as 1903–4, as indicated in the letters he wrote home; see Anderson, *The Works of Charles T. Griffes*, 174.

8. Frederick Martens, "Folk-Music in the 'Ballet Intime,'" *The New Music and Church Music Review* 16 (October 1917): 764–65.

9. Oscar Wilde, *Complete Poetry*, ed. Isobel Murray (Oxford, UK: Oxford University Press, 1997), x.

10. *Collected Poems of Oscar Wilde*, ed. Anne Varty (Hertfordshire, UK: Wordsworth Editions, 1994), ix.

11. *Punch*, June 25, 1881; quoted in *Collected Poems of Oscar Wilde*, viii.

12. Arthur Ransome, *Oscar Wilde: A Critical Study* (New York: Mitchell Kinnerley, 1913), 39.

13. The novel also inspired George Du Maurier's a satirical drawing entitled *Mokeanna, or The White Witness*, which appeared in the magazine *Punch* (1863); see Nicholas Daly, "The Woman in White: Whistler, Hiffernan, Courbet, Du Maurier," *Modernism/Modernity* 12, no. 1, Johns Hopkins University (January 2005): 6.

14. Ibid., 8.

15. The titles in this series share a common musical bond but diverge in color: *Symphony in White No. 1, The White Girl* (1862); *Symphony in White No. 2, The Little White Girl* (1864); *Symphony in White No. 3* (1865–67); *Symphony in Gray and Green: The Ocean* (1866); *The White Symphony: Three Girls* (1868); *Symphony in Blue and Pink* (1870); *Symphony in Flesh Color and Pink: Portrait of Mrs. Frances Leyland* (1871–73); and *Symphony in Gray: Early Morning Thames* (c. 1871).

16. For a complete list of Griffes's song settings, see Anderson, *Charles T. Griffes*, 226–31.

17. Anderson, *The Works of Charles T. Griffes*, 509.

18. Diary entry March 9, 1912, Charles Tomlinson Griffes Collection, 1884–1920, New York Public Library: Manuscripts and Archives, Music Division.

19. Martens, "Folk-Music in the 'Ballet Intime,'" 765.

20. Anderson, *Charles T. Griffes*, 31–32.

21. The text is drawn from *Collected Works of Oscar Wilde: Including the Poems, Novels, Plays, Essays and Fairy Tales* (New York: Greystone, 1920).

22. Another literary precursor for the theme of the color white that might have influenced Whistler as well as Wilde was a famous poem by Théophile Gautier entitled "La Symphonie en blanc majeur," published in 1849. Following a litany of white objects and settings throughout seventeen strophes, in the final lines Gautier introduces a new color—pink. This previous sudden shift at the poem's end may well have shaped Wilde's introduction of green in the final stanza of his "yellow symphony." See Calvin S. Brown, "The Color Symphony before and after Gautier," *Comparative Literature* 5, no. 4 (Autumn 1953): 289–309.

23. See https://www.etymonline.com/word/symphony, accessed on December 20, 2020.

24. See Anderson, *The Works of Charles T. Griffes*, 127–29.

25. The formal divisions are based on motivic repetition as well as on contrasts in meter and rhythmic texture.

8

Lake, Vale, and Bacchanale

In a diary entry on July 17, 1912, Charles Griffes recorded the following: "Had lunch with Arthur Farwell and then we went up to his rooms on 50th St. I played to him 'Kubla Kahn' [*sic*] and the little piece with the Poe lines as introduction ['The Vale of Dreams']. The latter he thought too exquisite and full of beauty of an ethereal and unearthly kind, but at the same time expressive of the poem."[1] This chapter provides a cross section of the "ethereal and unearthly beauty" that Farwell heard that day, by focusing on *Three Tone-Pictures*, Op. 5, a set of works that Griffes wrote for solo piano—"The Lake at Evening," "The Vale of Dreams," as well as Scherzo (also known as "Bacchanale")—from Fantasy Pieces, Op. 6 and later arranged for various instrumental combinations.[2] Composed between 1910 and 1913, this trio of works is a study in contrast, representing the broad musical and psychological palette of his middle period. While none of them relies on the garden-inspired programs found in "The White Peacock" and *The Pleasure-Dome of Kubla Khan* (see chaps. 4 and 5), each one is a rich blend of topical cues, demonstrating the breadth and depth of Griffes's vision of the ambivalent pastoral.

"Lake at Evening"

The point of departure for my analysis is to explore the significance of the titles and the texts that precede "The Lake at Evening," the first work in the set. Griffes recorded in his diary that he decided on the titles for all three works after he had composed them. For the first and third works in the set, he selected the epigraphs—that is, poetic excerpts preceding the scores—after the fact. By contrast, for the second work, "The Vale of Dreams," the poem was part and parcel of his creative process.[3] Since it also can be inferred that he added them at the recommendation of his publisher (Schirmer), some critics have dismissed the significance of these titles and epigraphs, treating them as whimsical layers of meaning added later for pure commercial gain.[4] In the case of the first work, Griffes chose an excerpt drawn from a highly atmospheric poem by William B. Yeats, "The Lake Isle of Innisfree," which celebrates the joys of nature and of living in peace and solitude. One of the central images in Yeats's poem is the sound of the lake water lapping up on the shore, a sound that haunts the narrator wherever he goes.

Even though Griffes selected the titles and the epigraphs after he had already composed the music, the impact of the three texts nevertheless creates emotional shadows that linger over each work in the collection. If we were to ignore the titles that Griffes happened upon and instead renamed all three works "impromptus" or "intermezzi," the sounds themselves display a strong sensitivity for evoking distinct musical colors, textures, and references to topics. In short, all three compositions reveal the composer's highly pictorial imagination and fully embody the spirit of the title of the collection, "tone-pictures." For example, while Griffes may not have originally tried to evoke the sound of water lapping against the shore in "Lake at Evening," the soothing texture resulting from two rhythmic ostinatos creates a calming, almost hypnotic effect that could be likened to almost any cyclical or pendular sound in nature. Hence, it is a mistake to focus on the fact that the titles do not represent his compositional process itself, and instead focus on what the music actually succeeds in representing.

In the context of Griffes's entire musical oeuvre, "The Lake at Evening" is an expressive amalgam, combining features of two highly contrasting topics: the pastoral and the lament. This unusual topical blend is indicated not only by traditional musical cues but also by those that are more idiosyncratic—that is, present in a number of his experimental pastoral works. To appreciate the particular nuances of this blend, we must look in depth at various passages in the work.

The first step in my exegesis of the work is to examine the work's large-scale formal structure, which is utterly conventional—a simple ternary or A B A′ structure (see table 8.1). The criteria for formal division are based on Griffes's treatment of (a) motivic structure and (b) dynamics/texture.

mm.	1	21	46
Section	A	B	A′

To fully grasp the subtleties of this work's pastoral character, it is useful to explore in detail the musical features and their psychological associations in each of the three sections.

The opening section of this work (mm. 1–22) evokes an unusual ambiance, the musical ingredients of which are listed below.

Pastoral Cues

- Expressive Marking: *Tranquillo e Dolce*
- Metric Ambiguity/Polymeter at Moderate Tempo
- Tonic Pedal Point (in the Bass or Inner Voice)
- *Piano* and *Pianissimo*

Lament Cues

- Sigh Figure
- Dactylic Ostinato Pattern

The expressive marking, *tranquillo e dolce,* is a conventional indication of the pastoral mood, which is also reflected in the subdued dynamics in the first as well as the third section (i.e., *piano* and *pianissimo*); the score for mm. 1–23 can be found in example 8.1.

One of the essential features of this opening passage is its unusual metric and rhythmic texture. First of all, the hypnotic rhythmic ostinato— a dactylic pattern of two eighth notes and one quarter note—implies a 2/4 meter. Then the phrase grouping of the soprano's melodic line in 6/4 and the notated triple meter (3/4) both suggest a waltz in slow motion.

The Lake at Evening
Op. 5, No. 1 (1910, later revised)

EXAMPLE 8.1.

Griffes, "The Lake at Evening," mm. 1–23.

Considered together, the two rhythmic layers and the resulting hemiola blur as well as enrich the passage's tranquil mood.

The soprano voice's phrase organization also contributes to the passage's impact. Although the melodic material in mm. 3–10 and mm. 14–21 is symmetrical, organized in 4 + 4 groupings, it lacks the weighted cadential structure of a period. This regular phrasing suggests simplicity and innocence, characteristics that act as a foil to the rhythmic complexity of the accompaniment.

The other salient pastoral feature is the static harmonic plan. The bass contains long sections of a fixed pitch, A, that eventually moves to a middle voice (mm. 15–20). Throughout this work, Griffes is obsessed with chromatic melodic lines, either as an inner voice(s) above a bass pedal point or as a descending bass line beneath a pedal in the middle voice. The resulting contrapuntal textures create a constant kaleidoscope of chromatic harmony interacting with a fixed voice.

Yet there is also a persistent source of ambiguity in Griffes's use of harmony within this work: his fascination with the augmented triad, usually expressed as a vertical sonority. He employs different forms of contrapuntal resolution, either as a neighbor to a root position triad or as a passing tone to an inverted triad. However, his chromatic vocabulary also encompasses a rich spectrum of extended dominants and other linear sonorities. Both short progressions summarized in example 8.2 begin with the same chord pair: an augmented triad built on A that resolves to an A6/4 chord. Yet each one ends differently. Whereas the progression at level (a) ends on a B #11/9 chord (m. 21), initiating the B section, the one at level (b) concludes on A add 6, ending the piece.

There are also several features in this work that suggest a lament topic. The sighing melodic gesture and its motivic offspring are suffused over the entire opening section. It initially appears in an inner voice, alternating between ascending and descending half steps: F–E (mm. 3–6); F–F♯ (inversion, mm. 7–10). Although the half-step motive is relegated to the accompaniment and not highlighted in the upper voice, the associations with grief and sadness are still present, if slightly muted.

In addition, when the dactylic rhythmic ostinato is reconsidered in the context of a lament, it adds a new layer of ambiguity to the rhythmic texture. The constant hemiola—the repetition of a duple rhythm in the notated 3/4 meter—is not merely an element of temporal serenity. It also evokes the hypnotic tolling of a church bell, which has strong associations with funerals or other religious rituals for the dead. Such unrelenting

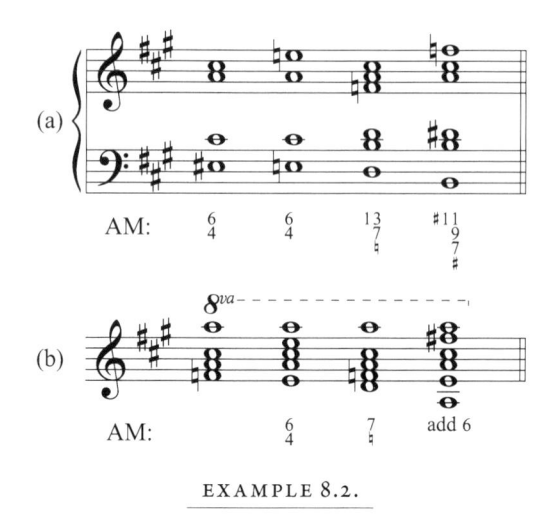

EXAMPLE 8.2.

Griffes, "The Lake at Evening," Harmonic reductions:
(a) mm. 15–22; (b) mm. 58–67.

rhythmic repetition in roughly two-thirds of the piece suggests an elegiac atmosphere. Although the "B" section of the piece (mm. 23–45) retains some elements found in the "A" section, it also has elements of contrast. These are displayed below.

Pastoral Cues

- Rhythmic/Metric Ambiguity

Lament Cues

- Sigh Figure
- Descending Chromatic Bass Line
- Dactylic Ostinato Pattern

To begin with, in this section Griffes continues juxtaposing the same duple rhythmic ostinato against a melody in triple meter, thereby preserving a similar element of metric/rhythmic ambiguity witnessed in the first section. The only passage where the ostinato is absent is mm. 37–39, where Griffes introduces sweeping bass arpeggios to help build tension.

    The defining feature of the middle section is the falling half-step motive, which now takes center stage in the bass and occasionally in the soprano voice (see mm. 35, 37, 38). For the first time in the piece, the bass line moves downward in a continuous stepwise descent, which in some ways evokes the traditional lament bass. Here, the traditional associations of grief and loss are unmistakable. However, Griffes abandons the familiar tetrachord span of a perfect fourth and, in its place, substitutes a chromatic descent through a major seventh, B3–C3 (mm. 22–40). Just when the listener expects the octave span to be completed, Griffes interrupts it and immediately initiates a new descent, beginning on G. In the Schenkerian middleground reduction displayed in example 8.3, the descending bass line possesses an overall coherence, prolonging the dominant of A major. However, at the foreground level this section's overall pitch structure sounds ambiguous, relying more on the sequential repetition of melodic motives than an overarching tonal center. Instead of reinforcing the balance between scale degrees 8 and 5 in the usual descending tetrachord, he subverts it. As a result, Griffes's treatment of chromaticism introduces a new element of ambiguity into the lament—an outpouring of harmonic grief that wanders without relief.

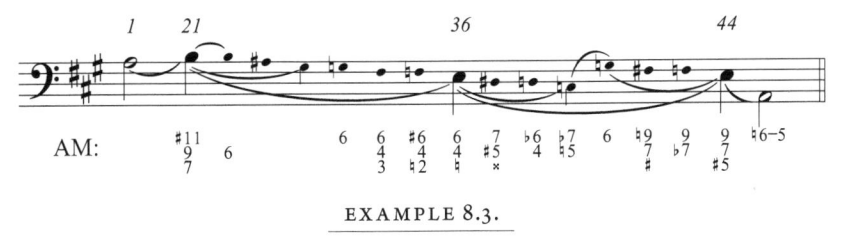

EXAMPLE 8.3.

Griffes, "The Lake at Evening": Middleground reading of bass, mm. 19–48.

The final section of the work is marked by a modified return of the opening motivic material. Likewise, the same mix of pastoral and lament cues from Section A (mm. 46–67) also returns, as shown below.

Pastoral Cues

- Expressive Markings: *Tranquillo e Dolce* + *Lontano* + *Morendo*
- Rhythmic/Metric Ambiguity
- Pedal Point (Bass + Soprano)
- Expansion of Register Using Pedal Point Motive

Lament Cues

- Sigh Figure
- Dactylic Ostinato Pattern

But in this section, there is one significant difference: Griffes's fascination with the expansion of register. This effect is achieved by means of an ostinato rhythmic motive, played on a single pitch, doubled at the octave, which begins in the middle register and at the end diverges in both directions by the same distance—two octaves higher and lower. These registral shifts are displaced in time, occurring in succession, rather than at the same time. One consequence of these registral shifts is an exercise in invertible counterpoint. At different junctures, he creates contrapuntal variety by repeating the same motivic material and rearranging the voices' vertical order.

"The Lake at Evening" serves as a showcase of the ambivalent conflict between the pastoral and lament in Griffes's aesthetic vision. On the one hand, many aspects of the piece suggest pastoral serenity: his initial marking, *tranquillo e dolce*, the moderate tempo, the hypnotic rhythmic ostinato, the soprano's simple melodic motives, the subdued dynamics in the first and third sections (marked *piano* and *pianissimo*), and, finally, the plagal cadence of iv7–I in mm. 62–67. In his initial depiction of the lake, serenity reigns supreme.

On the other hand, in the middle section his treatment of harmony is the antipode of serenity; instead it descends, meanders, and generally avoids closure. In this work, his treatment of a descending bass line reaches a chromatic extreme. Its avoidance of any harmonic arrival is a dramatic example of Wagnerian influence; indeed, the ghost of Tristan looms large over the central portion of Griffes's lake.

The role played by the lament motive changes dramatically over the course of the work. In the outer two sections, this expressive shape occurs in an inner voice, juxtaposed against a single prevailing harmony—an A major chord. By contrast, in the middle section (mm. 22–45), the falling half step is pervasive, now appearing as a continuous bass descent through a major seventh span and, along the way, creating a host of linear chromatic chords. By passing from an inner voice to the bass, it profoundly affects the piece's harmonic structure.

Ambivalence is also evident in his treatment of phrase structure. On the one hand, the phrase organization is uniformly regular, an unrelenting duple pattern of 2 + 2. On the other hand, he constantly subverts the listener's expectation for periodic harmonic structure by avoiding cadence and even subverting the very concept of cadential hierarchy within a period.

Finally, if nothing else, this work provides ample evidence of Griffes's interest in the transformation of pitch space. By shifting the register of the ostinato rhythmic figure higher and lower, he magnifies the listener's sense of musical space. Yet the registral expansion is staggered—the bass's descent fails to coincide with the soprano's ascent. The combination of relentless repetition and the overall gesture of spatial expansion creates a novel musical metaphor for the act of opening or blossoming.

In sum, as the earliest of the three works considered in this chapter, "The Lake at Evening" evokes a subtle combination of musical features and their respective psychological associations. Unlike the other two works in this chapter, it contains no genuine climax, instead relying on the cumulative emotional power of two contrasting musical topics engaged in a restless dialogue.

"The Vale of Dreams"

Introduction

The second work to be considered in the chapter, "The Vale of Dreams," also belongs to the set called *Three Tone-Pictures*, Op. 5. As we observed in "The Lake at Evening," this piece possesses features associated with two musical topics—the lament and the pastoral—as well as hints of an unusual Scottish dance, the strathspey. It also contains an impressive climax where melodic motives from previous sections coincide in a texture of cumulative counterpoint. Finally, he ends the work with a strong element of paradox, closing on an unexpected cadence. As a whole, the work is a rich composite of musical topics, combining features of multiple styles in a new expressive synthesis.

In this work, as in the other two of the collection, Griffes relies on a literary work for the title and epigraph. He precedes the score with a short excerpt from Edgar Allan Poe's poem entitled "The Sleeper," which is a passionate lament over the narrator's lost lover. The predominant images in the poem include the moonlight, a mountain valley, a lake, and, finally, a woman who is either sleeping or dead. Unlike "The Lake at Evening," Griffes discovered the title and epigraph of this poem while composing his piano work, and therefore each plays a role in its critical reception.[5]

The formal plan of "The Vale of Dreams" is conventional in nature, a simple ternary, with the following divisions.

mm.	1	23	43	57
Section	A	B	A'	Coda

The criteria for formal division are primarily based on contrast in texture and harmony; it is worth exploring each section in detail.

In Section "A" (mm. 1–22), Griffes combines elements of the pastoral as well as the lament.

Pastoral Cues

- Expressive Marking: *Sognando*
- Simple Triple Meter
- Ostinato Rhythmic Pattern
- Dissonant Pedal Chord

Lament Cues

- Sigh Figure (Soprano and Inner Voice)

The overarching expressive marking in the initial section, *sognando* (dreamy), suggests a tranquil mood. Although the 3/4 time signature is not common among eighteenth-century pastoral dances, the grouping of the soprano's melodic material suggests a slow 6/4 meter—that is, each four-bar phrase can be subdivided into two units, creating a 2 + 2 grouping. Example 8.4 displays mm. 1–16. In addition, the constant offbeat rhythmic ostinato in this section creates a soothing ambiance, highly appropriate for a pastoral. Though the rhythmic character of the accompaniment in the final section shifts from syncopated quarter notes into a continuous sixteenth-note pattern (beginning in m. 37), it still maintains the initial calming effect.

The opening bars also present a curious mixture of musical topics. To begin with, although Griffes includes an occasional low B♭ in the texture

The Vale of Dreams

Op. 5, No. 2 (ca. 1912)

EXAMPLE 8.4.

Griffes, "The Vale of Dreams," mm. 1–16.

(mm. 7, 11, 12, and 13), the harmonic foundation of the first and third sections is a recurring ostinato chord in a weak inversion: B♭4/2. This dissonant ostinato revives and adapts the static treatment of harmony found in some Baroque pastoral dances (e.g., musette). Juxtaposed against this syncopated ostinato pattern—pulsating in continuous quarter notes on offbeats—is a rich amalgam of rhythmic styles in the soprano including waltz-like rhythms (eighth-note triplets) and the traditional pastoral dotted patterns as well as a reverse dotted pattern that emphasizes the downbeat. The latter rhythm evokes memories of a popular Scottish dance known as the strathspey, in which the fiddler mixes dotted and reverse dotted rhythms in endless combinations within a duple or quadruple meter. The overall effect in this dance is the striking contrast between the different locations of the shorter rhythmic value—either on the beat or preceding the beat. Griffes's work, although in 3/4 meter, exploits a similar ambiguity between upbeat and downbeat since he simultaneously employs so many different types of rhythmic patterns. Finally, while the soprano voice's sinuous chromatic shape evokes a degree of tension, its jagged melodic contour is softened by the use of parallel third doublings.

The sigh (or *pianto*) figure, G♭–F, also plays an important role in Section A. It initially appears in two different voices but moving in opposite directions. In mm. 4–5, Griffes places it in the middle of the texture, accentuated by hairpin dynamics (incidentally, in his chamber arrangement of the work this gesture is highlighted by the French horn). Next, he also includes the same half-step motive as the lower voice in a texture of parallel thirds, now in retrograde, F–G♭. The first two times this occurs it confuses the ear, since, based on the prevailing B♭ 4/2 harmony, the G♭ would be a non-chord tone. The combination of two statements of the same half-step motive in reverse order—F–G♭ and G♭–F—creates an ambiguous contrapuntal texture. However, when a slightly varied version of the parallel thirds motive returns in mm. 8–10, it is less ambiguous because both voices present the same descending half-step motive, G♭–F. Overall, this slightly varied motivic repetition helps create a parallel period of 4 + 4.

The overall harmonic language in "The Vale of Dreams" has two distinct aspects that conflict with one another. For most of the work—the first and third sections—the harmonic dimension is largely static, based

EXAMPLE 8.5.

Griffes, "The Vale of Dreams," mm. 33–46.

on a recurring dissonant pedal chord. By contrast, in all three sections of the work, the harmonic palette is suffused by a late nineteenth-century style of chromaticism that bespeaks a German influence, specifically that of Wagner and Liszt. This is especially evident in Griffes's obsession with the augmented triad, which appears occasionally in the opening section (initially in m. 4) and is pervasive at the climax, occurring in sixteen of the piano's seventeen chords in mm. 33–36. In addition, the inner voice's descent in the same passage is an entire chromatic scale. Taken together, these two aspects lend a degree of ambiguity to the piece's pastoral character.

Yet the dissonant quality of the recurring pedal chord and later of the continuous arpeggiation figure also contributes to the work's ambiguous pastoral identity. On the one hand, a drone pitch in the bass is a fundamental characteristic of several eighteenth-century pastoral dances such as the musette and the pastorale. On the other hand, the actual harmony sounding through the A and A' sections, B♭ 4/2, is dissonant Although the constant repetition of the chord nearly mutes its dissonance, it still creates an unsettling emotional effect. Finally, due to its sheer reiteration, the root of this 4/2 chord, B♭, almost sounds like a tonal center.

What distinguishes the unusual character of the "B" section is the sudden intensity of the climax—the score of mm. 33–46 is displayed in example 8.5. The principal musical cues of this section are listed below.

Pastoral Cues

- Sacred Chorale Style
- Cumulative Counterpoint
- Expansion of Register

Lament Cue

- Sigh Figure (Bass)

In mm. 33–36, an emotional outburst occurs, releasing the tension that has accumulated in the opening section. It is characterized by a new marking, *inquietamente*, as well as an increase in tempo and in dynamic level. Also, Griffes magnifies the textural density of the opening section; in particular, the parallel thirds accompanying the soprano line expand into 7- and 8-note chords, moving in parallel above a fixed octave in the bass.

Most important, a striking instance of cumulative counterpoint occurs in this section. Griffes simultaneously combines three melodic themes previously heard in the opening section: the soprano's incomplete neighbor figure (initially heard in mm. 4–6), which occurs five times, decorating a descending Bb major arpeggio; a descending chromatic line in the inner voice now spanning an octave from F#4 to F#3; and, most important, an elongated lament motive in the bass, F#–F, which encompasses the entire descending gesture in the upper voices. The latter pitch motive is a repetition of the same lament gesture first heard in the inner voice in mm. 4–6, but now enharmonically respelled. The bass's arrival on "F" is a dramatic signal that the return of the opening motive is imminent. The confluence of all these elements in the same passage, combined with an increase in dynamics, creates an unusual type of polyphony, packed with motivic significance—see example 8.6.

EXAMPLE 8.6.

Griffes, "The Vale of Dreams": (a) middleground reading of
mm. 33–37; (b) summary of cumulative counterpoint.

The other pastoral cue that is specific to Griffes is his treatment of register. The augmented triad first heard in the opening section, G♭, B♭, D (m. 4), with closely stacked thirds now reappears in m. 33 with added dissonances and with its registral spacing expanded in two opposite directions: the soprano is two octaves higher (+24 half steps) and the bass is two octaves lower (-24 half steps)—see example 8.7. This magnification of register serves as a spatial metaphor of blossoming and is common to a handful of his most experimental pastorals.

EXAMPLE 8.7.

Griffes, "The Vale of Dreams," Expansion of register, mm. 4 and 33.

But it is the coda, mm. 57–60, where the most enigmatic passage of all appears—see the excerpt in example 8.8. Griffes heightens the piece's ambiguous character by introducing elements of motivic and harmonic paradox at the very end. As was shown above, the outer two sections are united by a recurring dissonant sonority, a B♭ 4/2—as either a pedal chord or a rolling arpeggio. Hence, by sheer repetition, B♭ major has acquired the status of a virtual tonic. Consequently, when the final E♭ 6/4 sonority appears, it catches the listener by surprise.

It is also worth mentioning that "The Vale of Dreams" includes a historical reference—whether conscious or unconscious—to a solo piano work by Robert Schumann. The work's final cadence is an unmistakable harmonic homage to the "Eusebius" movement from Schumann's *Carnaval*,

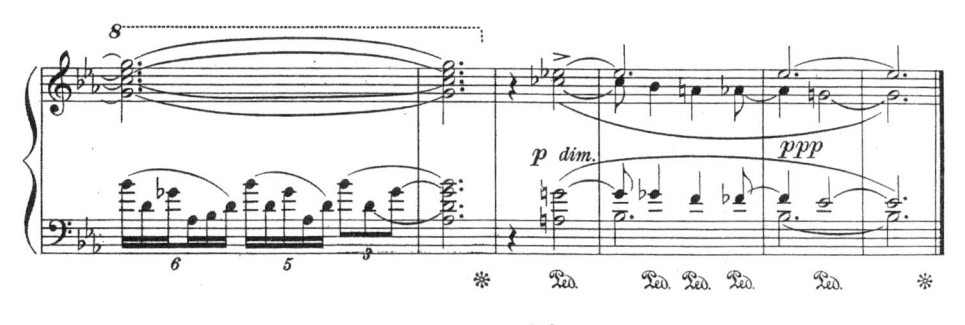

EXAMPLE 8.8.

Griffes, "The Vale of Dreams," mm. 55–60.

Op. 9. In Schumann's piece, the tempo is as slow as the character is expressive. Most important, the opening phrase and its three subsequent statements all end on the same chord: E♭ 6/4. This lack of closure in the same key points toward a harmonic form of homage (this excerpt will be discussed further in chap. 9).

A question arises: how do we interpret the final chord? In order to answer that question, it is necessary to explore the concept of closure in the work. The return of the opening material immediately after the climax suggests that the intensity of the climax has receded and that once again the opening equilibrium between serenity and lament has been restored. Considering that the emotional outburst in Section B is so sudden and intense, how should we interpret the return of the original motivic and harmonic material? Was the middle section a brief emotional storm that appeared and then passed? Or does its psychological impact linger?

On first impression, when one hears the initial combination of the sinuous chromatic melodic line, the lament gesture, and the strathspey rhythms, it is easy to assume that this return brings with it the initial emotional equilibrium. However, the enigmatic coda undercuts that interpretation and disrupts the formal balance of the ternary model. Not only does Griffes recycle and adapt earlier melodic motives, but he also introduces a new source of tension and harmonic uncertainty. One wonders: Does the inaugural appearance of E♭ major serve as confirmation of the tonic key? Or does this chord serve as a sudden harmonic detour, a subdominant aside, created by intersecting chromatic melodic motives? In short, does the final chord serve as an act of formal closure or rather as a sardonic comment on the expectation of closure? I argue that when the last chord dies away, tonal unity has been restored. Nevertheless, the passage's harmonic dimension embodies a striking display of musical irony that foreshadows an even more dramatic example in Griffes's final work, Prelude #3 (both works will be discussed in greater detail in chap. 9).

"The Vale of Dreams" is a testament to the power as well as the ambivalence of Griffes's pastoral vision. By combining features of two musical traditions, the pastoral and the lament, the piece achieves a fascinating topical blend. In the opening and closing sections, the ambivalent pastoral character is most evident in Griffes's treatment of harmony and rhythm. The ostinato chord, combined with its rhythmic character (initially repeating on the offbeats and later as continuous sixteenth-note arpeggios), conveys the traditional pastoral association of calmness. Yet the recurring harmony in these two sections is dissonant, which provides an uncertain foundation for the sinuous chromaticism of the upper voices.

The lament topic is evident in Griffes's fascination with the half-step sighing gesture, which appears in all three sections. While its initial appearance is quite subdued, confined to an inner voice, in the middle section it returns with a vengeance, now respelled in the bass and sounding at *forte*. By lengthening the rhythms and increasing the dynamics, Griffes highlights the bass's sigh figure. At the climax, the lament is writ large.

The piece also displays two of Griffes's idiosyncratic cues that involve the treatment of register and counterpoint. When the same augmented triad from the opening passage returns in section B with the soprano voice two octaves higher and the bass two octaves lower, this repetition becomes a stunning musical metaphor of blooming. Such a treatment of pitch space not only enriches the motivic repetition in this particular piece, but it also links it with a group of experimental pastorals from his mature period.

The other idiosyncratic cue associated with the pastoral is the texture of cumulative counterpoint that appears in mm. 33–36. This cue consists of the convergence of two distinct features: a contrapuntal texture in which multiple melodic motives from previous sections appear simultaneously, and a swelling of dynamics. Taken together, these factors not only enhance the piece's climax, but they also expand the scale of its pastoral character.

Scherzo/Bacchanale

The final work to be considered in this chapter is unusual in that it has two titles. Originally composed in 1913, the piece was published two years later, under the innocuous name "Scherzo," as the third member of the set called *Fantasy Pieces*, Op. 6.[6] Later, Griffes decided to transform the piano piece into an orchestral work that he renamed "Bacchanale." Its first performance in that version occurred on December 19, 1919 by the Philadelphia Orchestra under Leopold Stokowski in the Academy of Music during a marathon six-week period when a number of his works were performed by three major orchestras in Boston, Philadelphia, and New York City.

The title of the orchestral version of this work is somewhat misleading, for it is by no means a continuous exercise in bacchanalian excess—the musical portrait of a collective orgy. Rather, it is a dual portrait, a musical pendulum that alternates between contrasting dances and topics, between surges of intensity and interludes of mystery tinged with nostalgia. The piece begins with a tarantella dance pattern that evokes intense emotions, a musical fever running high; then, a contrasting section arrives, and the musical fever cools down. This pattern of alternation continues throughout the work, ending with a return of the tarantella theme, marked *con fuoco*. As a result, there is no overall prevailing emotional character but rather a constant shift in musical temperament.

Unlike the titles and epigraphs of the other two works, the source of the program for the Scherzo is Griffes himself. He penned a brief but colorful scene for this work when it was published in 1915 and then resurrected and slightly revised it as program notes for its later orchestral premiere:[7] "From the palace of Enchantment there issued into the night sounds of unearthly revelry. Troops of genii and other fantastic spirits danced grotesquely to a music now weird and mysterious, now wild and joyous. The piece is wholly fantastic as a fairy tale, with a wild climax at the end." Apparently, he invented this scenario himself, not relying on a preexistent poem or dramatic work. However, since he had already begun working on *The Pleasure-Dome of Kubla Khan*, a project in which he would end up immersing himself for nearly seven years, it is tempting to speculate that at least a whiff of Coleridge's poetic fantasy helped inspire the program for the Scherzo/Bacchanale.

Some might raise doubts about the significance of the epigraph since he penned it after he had begun composing the Scherzo and, most likely, in response to his publisher's demand for colorful titles. The simple answer to this objection is that if he had harbored any qualms about his earlier fantasy of grotesque dancing "now weird and mysterious, now wild and joyous," then he would have never included it in the program for the orchestral concert in 1919. These words belong to the historical record of the piece's reception and are not merely a post de facto layer of commercial marketing.

The overall formal plan of the entire piano work as well as the orchestral transcription is displayed below:

mm.	1	110	160	204	260	286
Section	A	B	C	A'	B'	A"

The three repetitions of the "A" section confirm that it is a slight variant on the conventional five-part rondo scheme. A significant factor in this scheme is the relative proportions between the various sections. Whereas the three "A" sections constitute one hundred and eighty bars of the total three hundred (or 3/5), the other two contrasting sections ("B" and "C") together add up to one hundred and twenty bars (or 2/5) of the entire work. The purpose of this sectional comparison is less to calculate the exact proportions than it is to show that, on the whole, there is almost as much non-bacchanalian as there is bacchanalian music.

As will become clear below, the most distinctive character of the work can be traced to the contrast between the two constituent elements of this topical hybrid: the crude intensity of the cadential sections as compared to the complex layering of associations, or what I call the cumulative counterpoint in the idyllic sections. Let us discover this contrast through a detailed examination of the work's three principal sections.

Scherzo

Op. 6, No. 3 (1913)

(orchestrated as "Bacchanale," ca. 1919)

EXAMPLE 8.9.

Griffes, Scherzo: mm. 1–26.

Section A

The opening section begins with a tarantella rhythmic pattern at a hushed dynamic, as if the listener were eavesdropping on a folk dance from afar—see example 8.9. The work's rhythm and meter express the most potency and, at the same time, the most subtlety. Example 8.10 displays the rhythmic values of the three main themes of Section A found in the accompaniment at mm. 1–4 and in the soprano line at mm. 5–8 and mm. 29–32.

The first two themes contain simple rhythms, mixing downbeat and occasional offbeat attacks that emphasize the quick 6/8 meter. Griffes even implies percussion instruments in this arrangement with his use of open fifth drumbeats sounding in a low register (mm. 9–10, 15–16). By contrast, Theme 3 begins with accented quarter-note attacks in the soprano line that strongly suggest a 3/4 meter, introducing an element of hemiola. The alternation between these two groupings is a central feature in this movement's rhythmic/metric profile. Another element of contrast in this theme is the melody's descending chromatic line. Finally, the texture explodes into ascending sixteenth-note scales (accented in the orchestral version by tambourines trills) that only add fuel to the tarantella fire (e.g., mm. 31–32).

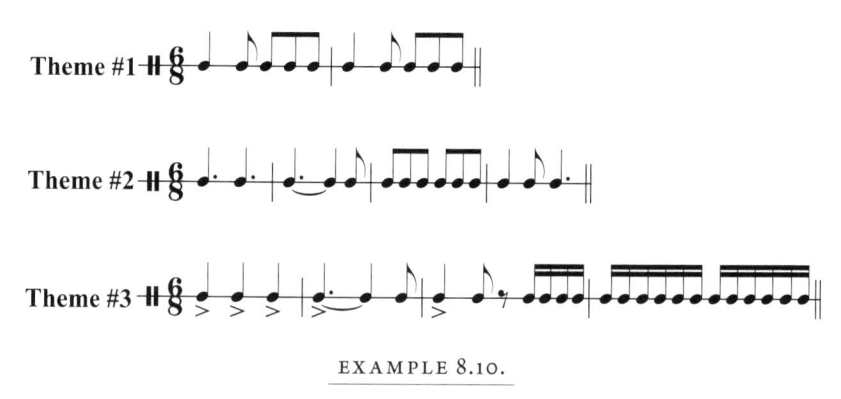

EXAMPLE 8.10.

Griffes, Scherzo: Rhythmic values of principal themes 1, 2, and 3.

Other musical dimensions of this opening section that contribute to its driving rhythmic momentum are harmony, phrasing, instrumentation, and dynamics. The overall harmonic plan is generally static, beginning with an extended tonic pedal. The theme in mm. 17–20 briefly suggests the Phrygian mode (e.g., an F♭ in E♭ minor), though it ends up confirming the tonic. While the harmonic plan (mm. 29–44) supporting Theme 2 is slightly more active—i–iv 6/4–V–i—and it is entirely appropriate for the folklike atmosphere. The phrase organization of the two opening themes is likewise simple, arranged in groups of either two or four. Another feature that contributes to the opening section's power is its instrumentation, for Griffes favors the oboe and flute—two woodwinds with a long history of pastoral associations. But it is his treatment of dynamics that most enhances the emotional impact of this section. Over the entire opening section, the dynamics expand and contract three times from *p* to *ff*—almost like an organic process. The recurring rhythmic patterns coupled with the increase in dynamics culminate in his treatment of cadence.

The closest thing to a climax in this section occurs in two short passages between mm. 90–104, where the composer repeats a single chord over and over again in a trochaic rhythm—that is, long + short, initially as an E♭9 chord (mm. 90–93) and then as an open fifth, B♭–F, in a six-voice texture (mm. 98–104). Here, the register expands dramatically: the soprano remains static while the bass falls three octaves. The formal function of this section is purely cadential—it brings section A to a close. However, its emotional effect is far more compelling: pure and sustained abandon, as if the repetitions could go on indefinitely.

The relentless rhythmic drive throughout this section, along with an occasional eruption of scalar passagework, strongly suggests that the work belongs to the class of nineteenth-century tarantella showpieces for piano or violin by such composers as Chopin and Wieniawski.[8] However, nothing prepares the listener for the emotional contrast and topical complexity that begins at m. 110.

Section B

Section B begins with a sudden contrast in texture that can be likened to a musical collage. There are three levels of activity—see example 8.11. On the one hand, the continuous eighth-note texture in the left-hand

EXAMPLE 8.11.

Griffes, Scherzo, mm. 94–125.

accompaniment affirms the notated 6/8 meter and character of the opening section. On the other hand, there is also a repeating pitch pattern in the accompaniment—a perfect fifth (G♭1-D♭2) alternating with a pitch an octave above the initial root (G♭2)—that implies a 3/4 meter. The conflict between the rhythmic groupings created by this pitch ostinato compared to the continuous eighth-note texture creates a mild undercurrent of hemiola. Technically, the combined rhythmic and pitch patterns found in the accompaniment can only loosely be considered a siciliano, especially considering the distinct melodic line.

Finally, the third level of activity in the soprano's melody is decidedly syncopated and always beginning on an upbeat. For the most part, the rhythmic values are much slower than in the initial section: dotted quarters, dotted halves, and dotted halves tied to dotted quarters. However, when heard in relation to a beat of a dotted quarter note, they have a strong kinship with ragtime, an early twentieth-century American popular style. To illustrate this analogy, in example 8.12 I juxtapose the melody's original rhythms in 6/8 at level (a) with a proportionally re-notated version in 2/4 at level (b)—the ratio of equivalence is one dotted quarter note equals one sixteenth note. The resulting set of rhythmic values and recurring syncopation are quite similar to those found in the opening melody of one of Scott Joplin's most lyrical and nostalgic works from 1909, "Solace (A Mexican Serenade)," the rhythms of which are notated at level (c).

There is some historical justification for drawing a rhythmic analogy between the middle section of the Scherzo and a ragtime tune. According to Griffes's biographer, Edward Maisel, Griffes himself was quite fond of Joplin's music, occasionally entertaining students at the Hackley School with uproarious renditions of the "Maple Leaf Rag."[9] While I have no biographical evidence that Griffes was quoting this particular ragtime melody, the strong resemblance between the rhythms of these two excerpts suggests that he was not immune to the ragged charms of this popular tradition.

The ultimate meaning of this three-level hierarchy is a kind of interpretive mosaic. The listener's first impression of this passage is a mixture of incompatible elements: general tranquility with an added element of tension simmering in the background. When the melody's relaxed rhythmic

EXAMPLE 8.12.

Griffes, Scherzo: (a) Original rhythmic values, mm. 120–34; (b) rhythmic
values, mm. 120–34 proportionally renotated in 2/4; and (c) rhythmic
values of a phrase from Scott Joplin's "Solace (A Mexican Serenade)."

character is taken into account, the combined effect exceeds Griffes's *tranquillo* and *espressivo* markings, instead expressing a nostalgic character. In some respects, this interlude evokes a dreamlike atmosphere, as though the listener were lost in a reverie between bacchanalian outbursts.

But there is an additional interpretive question in this passage: whether the transformation of a popular musical style suggests an element of parody. In other musical contexts, the rhythms of a popular dance played in slow motion could have a satirical or even grotesque character. A celebrated example from the nineteenth century is the "Tortues" ("Tortoises") movement from *Le Carnaval des animaux,* where Saint-Saëns playfully transforms the upbeat cancan dance from Offenbach's *Orphée aux enfers* (*Orpheus in the Underworld*) into an expressive aria, marked *andante maestoso,* for strings and piano. But in Griffes's Scherzo, the transformation is different. First of all, there is no exact quotation from a previous work but rather what might be called a rhythmic reference to a style of ragtime. Second and more important, the repetitive accompaniment texture lends this melodic theme a serious, even enigmatic quality that undermines any possible hint of humor.

Section C

The third principal section, mm. 160–204, is notable in three respects. First of all, it is suffused with harmonic uncertainty in that the same harmonic progression recurs and never cadences to the tonic: ii7–v7. This lack of resolution creates a tone of foreboding. Second, the overall texture utilizes a wider range than the previous two sections, from the falling fifth bass ostinato, F–B♭, to the soprano's rising and falling octave B♭'s. In the orchestral version, Griffes enhances these two ostinato patterns with colorful instrumentation. Finally, there is a thematic overlap at the juncture between Sections B and C (mm. 200–203), which can be dissected into three strands. The soprano at m. 200, marked *lontano*, repeats the opening theme an octave higher, strongly indicating a return. However, the harmonic accompaniment continues the same pair of chords and rhythmic patterns along with the same low bass ostinato heard throughout Section B. The effect is cinematographic, like a visual montage where one scene dissolves into the next.

Griffes's taste for musical quotation also extends to patriotic repertoire. To appreciate the significance of the second quote, we must consider the biographical context of his life in America before and during World War I. After having spent four years living in Berlin, where he came of age as a composer, for the rest of his life he maintained a deep tie to German culture. Nevertheless, when the specter of war appeared on the horizon, Griffes was touched by some kind of American patriotic fever. In early November 1918, he applied and was accepted to serve as an interpreter in the Interpreters' Corps in France—however, the US signed the armistice before he assumed his duties.[10] Another sign of his interest in nationalism is that he composed three works with overt patriotic aims: a setting for voice and piano of John Addington Symond's poem "These Things Shall Be" (1917); and two collections for solo piano composed and published in 1918 under the pseudonym Arthur Tomlinson: Six Bugle Call Pieces, and Six Patriotic Songs.[11] The final collection included such favorites as "America," "The Star-Spangled Banner," and, most important, "The Red, White, and Blue." The latter was an alternate name for the popular tune "Columbia, Gem of the Ocean."[12]

The reason why the song "The Red, White, and Blue" is important is that in the middle of the Scherzo/Bacchanale, Griffes quotes the opening phrase of that melody twice in minor toward the end of Section A—see example 8.11, bass voice, mm. 94–97. Although the first version of the Scherzo was originally composed between 1913–15 during the initial period of the European conflict, Griffes returned to this work in 1918, when he prepared the orchestral transcription.

The role that quotation plays in Griffes's output of pastorals is relatively small, for it is limited to a single piece: the Scherzo/Bacchanale. Nevertheless, the popular melodies that are quoted and adapted in this work constitute a striking musical collage: a phrase from an American patriotic song and the rhythms and phrase organization of one of Scott Joplin's rags crossed with an Argentinian tango. Suffice it to say that the presence of two popular melodies in the context of a spirited tarantella suggests a complex type of signification, an ambiguous blend of reverence and satire.

Griffes's treatment of musical topics in the Scherzo differs dramatically from that in the other two piano works. Its large-scale form, a modified rondo, determines the trajectory of musical topics. This miniature tone poem evokes an imaginary celebration with a range of contrasting moods: revelry, quiet reflection, and overflowing passion. The work begins with an evocation of a wild tarantella in high heat; at the end, Griffes turns up the temperature of the dance even higher. The interior "B" section combines features of two musical traditions: the pastoral in the form of a pedal chord and the ragtime in slow motion. The emotional impact of this combination is a respite from the previous fire and passion, a kind of syncopated serenity. For Griffes, the only way to reach closure is to bring the Bacchanale to a full boil.

Now that I have explored the entire work, the question arises: Since this work has only one section with overtly pastoral qualities, why is it included in a study of Griffes's pastorals? The simplest answer to this question is that the work consists of a constant dialogue between two emotional extremes: pastoral calm and bacchanalian frenzy. And one of these extremes bears a strong kinship with his most famous orchestral piece, *The Pleasure-Dome*.

There are two ways in which these works resemble one another. First and foremost, both works contain sections that are inspired by the fiery tarantella dance. In the case of *The Pleasure-Dome*, the tarantella passage, though brief in duration, is the culmination of an enormous buildup of tension. In the case of the *Bacchanale*, the tarantella sections are longer and more frequent. Second, Griffes himself provides a verbal guide to understanding the two works' associations with bacchanalian excess, either in terms of an excerpt from a poem (*The Pleasure-Dome*) or a personal program (Scherzo/Bacchanale). While it is difficult to explain his motivation for composing music that evokes wild abandon, at several junctures it became an essential part of his emotional and aesthetic palette.

Conclusion

The goal of this chapter has been to illuminate the ways in which Griffes's ambivalent pastoral sensibility is displayed in three instrumental works: "The Lake at Evening," "The Vale of Dreams," and Scherzo/Bacchanale. Each work embodies a unique musical physiognomy, blending traditional characteristics of the pastoral and lament topics as well as more customized cues.

In many passages, the interplay of contrasting musical topics either within a single section or between different sections seems contradictory, referring to opposite or contrasting emotional associations. Yet, at the same time, these references are also complementary, creating an emotional equilibrium in each work. In two pieces, he combines elements that evoke lament and suffering as well as pastoral serenity. Even though without a specific text or program the exact source of the lament is impossible to determine, the resulting musical evocation is nonetheless palpable. In one work Griffes introduces an element of paradox that raises questions about tonal closure. Finally, one piece relies on quotations of well-known American popular music while another work includes an unmistakable harmonic reference to a nineteenth-century character piece. The style of signification in these two works ranges from homage to parody. Overall, considered as a trio, "The Lake at Evening," "The Vale of Dreams," and

Scherzo/Bacchanale embody three different versions of the ambivalent pastoral, each offering a rich amalgam of emotional associations that conflict with as well as commingle with each other.

NOTES

1. Diary entry July 17, 1912, Box 47, Folder 5-6, Series III, Donna K. Anderson Research Files on Charles Griffes, Music Division, New York Public Library for the Performing Arts. Cited in Anderson, *The Works of Charles T. Griffes*, 538.

2. Griffes arranged "The Lake at Evening" and "The Vale of Dreams" twice in 1915 and 1919 for two different combinations of ten players: the first group consists of flute, two oboes, two clarinets, two horns, two bassoons, and harp; the second consists of two quintets—one of strings, the other of winds. When he transcribed the Scherzo for orchestra, he renamed it *Bacchanale*—see Anderson, *Charles T. Griffes*, 224–25.

3. Ibid., 199.

4. Ibid., 199–201.

5. Griffes was well acquainted with Edgar Allan Poe's writings since in 1912 he purchased the author's complete works. See Anderson, *The Works of Charles T. Griffes*, 509.

6. The other two works in the set are Barcarolle and Notturno.

7. In his diary, Griffes wrote, "Spent the day in New York. . . . Spent an hour in the Library looking for a poem for the 'Barcarolle'. The 'Notturno' has verses from Paul Verlaine and the 'Scherzo' a couple of prose sentences of my own." Quoted in Anderson, *The Works of Charles T. Griffes*, 256. Griffes used the same program he had already published with the piano work but added the final sentence for the premiere of the orchestral version.

8. Chopin, Tarantella, Op. 43; Wieniawski, Scherzo-Tarantelle, Op. 16.

9. Maisel, *Charles T. Griffes*, 116.

10. Anderson, *Charles T. Griffes*, 140.

11. Ibid., 232.

12. The provenance of this song is surrounded by controversy. It appears that the music was originally composed by David Shaw and the lyrics by Thomas a'Beckett in 1843. But after the song achieved some success, the latter artist claimed he had also composed the music.

9

Prelude #3, Irony Goes Wilde

Lying, the telling of beautiful untrue things, is the proper aim of art.
—Oscar Wilde, "The Decay of Lying"

I live in terror of not being misunderstood.
—Oscar Wilde, "The Critic as Artist"

Introduction

It is appropriate to begin this chapter with a pair of epigrams by Oscar Wilde, for in his hands the literary fragment became a genre unto itself. In his plays, essays, and novels, his thought was crystalized in the form of pithy phrases, combining wit, whimsy, and paradox. In this case, both epigrams address the world of art: how an artwork should be interpreted, whether it should be judged as true, and whether the artist has been fully understood. The second epigram is particularly striking in that the full impact of the message—the double negative—only becomes clear at the very end, with the last word. This literary design will have a direct analogy when we consider how a piece of music can possess an ironic character.

Wilde's literary epigrams are also appropriate as a way of introducing Griffes's own forays into musical irony. As was shown in chapter 1, there is considerable biographical evidence that Griffes held the Irish writer in high esteem. Although Griffes left no direct confirmation of his ironic intentions, the most convincing empirical evidence of their artistic affinity can be found in "The Vale of Dreams" and, especially, the Three Preludes, which was his last completed work. The third prelude of the set reflects many of the same characteristics that are found in Wilde's aphorisms: elegance, brevity, and paradox. Finally, this prelude displays a new dimension of Griffes's pastoral sensibility, for it is less a genuine pastoral than a *commentary* on his preoccupation with the pastoral tradition.

While Griffes's propensity for musical irony could never rival that of twentieth-century composers like Shostakovich or Prokofiev, in one work his fascination with paradox is undeniable.[1] Griffe's use of irony in Prelude #3 has a critical character in that he questions the underlying theoretical assumptions about scale-degree identity and, as a consequence, the traditional concepts of consonance and dissonance found in eighteenth- and nineteenth-century music. In addition, this work undermines the model of binary form and the aesthetic principles of balance and closure upon which that model is based. As a result, the third prelude constitutes a kind of musical-philosophical challenge, an aesthetic exclamation point that invites listeners to reconsider traditional definitions of interval quality, tonality, and formal closure.

The following chapter consists of four parts: (1) a brief introduction to the concepts of simple and double irony, including Heinrich Heine's notion of *Stimmungsbrechung*; (2) an episode in the history of punctuation that highlights the challenges of recognizing irony; (3) an analysis of the ironic character found in the coda of "The Vale of Dreams"; and (4) a detailed study of Griffes's Prelude #3 that reveals its reliance on simple as well as double irony.

Irony and Musical Irony

The tradition of rhetorical irony has a distinguished ancestry, beginning with the teachings of Socrates in ancient Greece, flourishing in the nineteenth century in the works of Friedrich Schlegel and Søren Kierkegaard, and continuing with the writings of Thomas Mann in the twentieth century.[2] There have been countless histories of literary irony, such as those by Douglas C. Muecke, Wayne Booth, and Joseph Dane.[3] The aim of all three authors is to collect various ironic examples, describe them in detail, and then develop a nuanced catalogue, like a modern-day Peterson Field Guide of Irony or what one writer described as a "cottage industry in taxonomy."[4] For example, Muecke enumerates nineteen different types of irony that have already been proposed and then identifies eight separate criteria on which these definitions depend—a terminological Tower of Babel. He even pokes fun at his own catalogue, calling it "ironiology" or "ironiotics."[5] More recently, Linda Hutcheon has written an exhaustive and perceptive compendium of the political and social context of irony.[6]

The tradition of irony embraces a wide range of concepts including ambiguity, incongruity, and paradox. In this chapter, I wish to focus on the musical counterpart of two types: simple irony and double irony. This distinction has been renamed at various times by different thinkers: simple versus double (Muecke); finite versus infinite (Sheinberg); and irony as stimulus versus irony as terminus (Kierkegaard). Simple irony amounts to saying one thing and meaning another, often for the purpose of ridicule. For the interpreter, this type of irony requires deciphering the true meaning that is hidden beneath the apparent one. In other words, one interpretation emerges as preferred and the other is rejected. As will be shown below, "The Vale of Dreams" is a musical realization of this type of irony. The reason why Kierkegaard calls it irony as stimulus is that the ironic statement "stimulates" or challenges the interpreter to discover which message is true. That said, the challenge of determining which message is preferred can be daunting. The literary critic Stanley Fish offers a provocative and entertaining inquiry into the historical controversy that arose over a popular song, "Short People Got No Reason to Live," and the broader problems that arise when trying to confirm which ironic message is true.[7]

When one imagines how this species of irony could be translated into musical experience, problems arise. It is difficult, if not impossible, to express simple irony in purely musical terms—that is, to express simultaneously a pair of messages and then to discover which one is true and which one is false. The most common musical analogy to this type of irony is the concept of enharmony. This concept arises when the same musical sound—such as an interval or chord—appears twice in a work and in each instance has a different tonal function and, usually, orthographic spelling. The multiple enharmonic interpretations are the musical equivalent of a pun. It should be emphasized that in these situations both harmonic functions are equal—neither one is preferred or rejected.[8] This type of harmonic sleight of hand was a virtual stock-in-trade for many nineteenth-century composers. In a fascinating study of enharmony entitled "Chopin and the In-F-able," Brian Hyer explores this question in one of Chopin's mazurkas.[9]

Double irony, by contrast, arises when the overall artistic context leads the interpreter to doubt whether either of the two messages is true. According to Muecke, in this type of irony "two equally invalid points of view cancel each other out."[10] One challenge raised by the concept of double irony is that it hovers between science and skepticism—that is, between a project of logical classification and a foray into philosophical doubt. Double irony occupies the frontier between rational and irrational thought, a frontier that can be encapsulated by the epigram "Neither either nor or."[11] This species of irony will take center stage in our discussion of Prelude #3 below.

It is worth briefly considering the relationship between double irony and the concept of paradox. Since the ancient Greeks, there have been a wide range of paradoxes, some more straightforward than others. One type is an apparently self-contradictory or strongly counterintuitive statement, which can be resolved by careful consideration of its internal terms or implicit assumptions. Examples would include Zeno's infamous paradoxes. This type is more accurately described as a puzzle since it often can be solved. Yet, there are also more profound paradoxes that are integrally connected to developments in logic, mathematics, and physics by such figures as Charles S. Peirce, Georg Cantor, and Bertrand Russell. For example, Peirce, at various junctures in his career, investigated a wide range of logical questions involving the principles of the excluded middle and of noncontradiction as well as the so-called Liar Paradox, attributed to the ancient thinker Epimenides.[12] Finally, there are paradoxes that arise in an artistic context, especially in literature, and that seem "on the

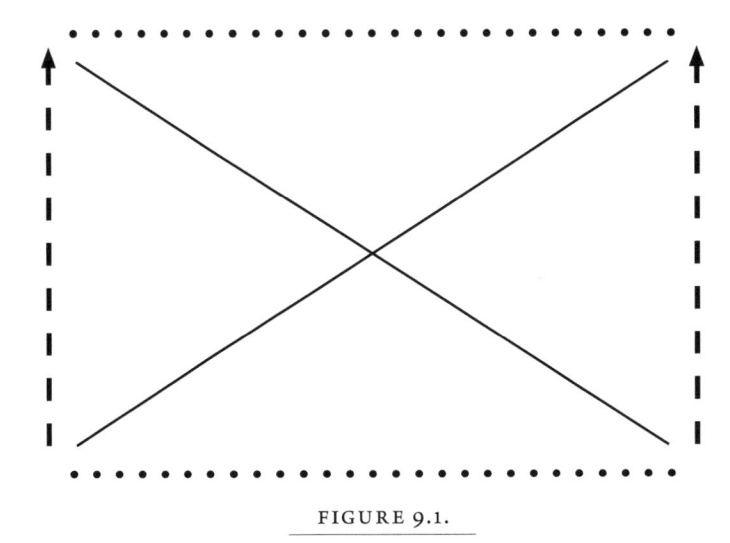

FIGURE 9.1.

The Greimas Semiotic Square.

surface contradictory, but which [involve] an element of truth. Because of the element of contrast between the form of the statement and its true implications, paradox is closely related to irony."[13] The contradiction and irony displayed in Griffes's Prelude #3 belong to this third type of paradox.

To better understand Griffes's use of double irony, it is instructive to consider a geometric analogy that is an integral part of the semiotic tradition and that has been used to explain irony: the Greimas square—see figure 9.1.[14] As is well known, the central building block of this model is binary opposition. Four terms are juxtaposed in three different pairings: contraries displayed as a horizontal pair; contradictories displayed at the diagonal; and complements (or implications) displayed as a vertical pair. One possible advantage of this model is that one of the pairings, the complements, may uncover new relationships among the four given terms—an oppositional light shining in the semantic darkness. In fact, Sheinberg uses the conceptual square as a means of investigating musical ambiguity and irony.[15]

I would like to raise a geometric protest against the semiotic fascination with the square. Why represent the concepts of ambiguity or irony

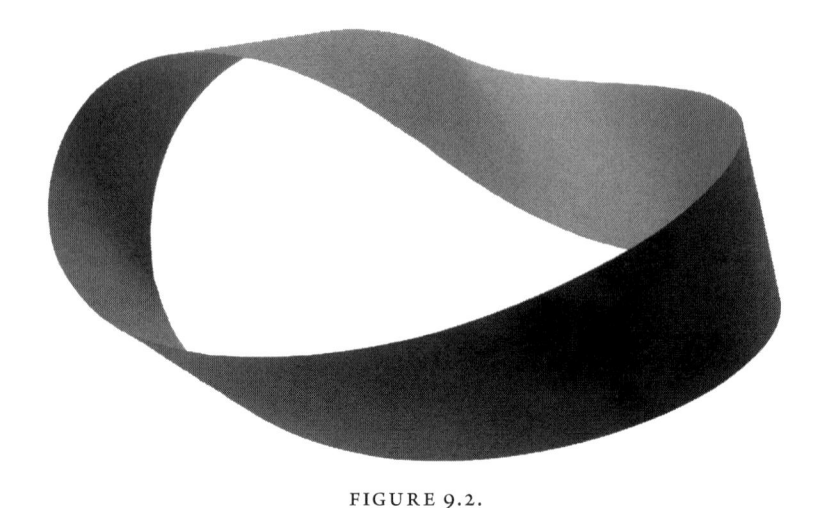

FIGURE 9.2.

Image of the Möbius Strip.

by using a visual metaphor of opposition? Rather than expressing pairs of opposites as different corners within a standard geometric shape, I argue that we should use an alternate visual model, the Möbius strip (the special case of the Klein bottle), to challenge the assumption of opposition—see figure 9.2.

The justification for this new model would be to *undermine* the notion of opposition, not *underline* it. The difference between the two sides of the strip, above and below, is called into question when one retraces its entire length. Indeed, a geometric shape that appears to have two sides, in fact, has only one. The concept of binary opposition cannot be taken at face value since what was assumed to be a familiar property of the shape, the difference between the upper and the lower side, is thrown into question. Hence, the relationship between these two sides—or, as we will later see, two musical characteristics—cannot always be represented as opposites and needs to be reconsidered. Rather than simply pouring old wine into new theoretical bottles, I am asking us to imagine irony as something that does not hold liquid in the first place.

In recent years, the field of musicology has witnessed a rebirth of interest in the tradition of musical irony, and there have been two prevailing approaches. The first approach is an inductive study of the empirical evidence itself. The goal in this venture is to establish a definition of irony based on language, and then to collect and classify many examples that depend on a loose analogy between linguistic irony and its various musical realizations. Examples include Ray Longyear's essay on Beethoven or Stephen Zank's book on Ravel.[16] A more recent compendium is Michael Cherlin's *Varieties of Musical Irony: From Mozart to Mahler,* where, after establishing a general framework that relies on Kenneth Burke's tetralogy of tropes, he identifies twelve different species of musical irony.[17] These studies focus on meticulous study of individual examples rather than proposing an overarching theory of how any piece of music can express irony.

A second group adopts a more theoretical approach. These scholars have systematic aspirations in that they initially develop a general theory of musical irony and then illustrate it with various excerpts. Representative examples include the following: Esti Sheinberg, who borrows Hatten's model of correlation to explore a wide range of ambiguity and irony in Shostakovich's music; Yayoi Uno Everett, who interprets Ligeti's music by blending Linda Hutcheon's social conception of parody with Sheinberg's concept of existential irony; and, finally, Michael Klein, whose revival of Northrup Frye's theory of narrative archetypes along with James Liszka's theory of transvaluation reveals new dimensions in works by Chopin and Brahms.[18] My study of musical irony is more inductive in character and, therefore, belongs to the first group.

Of all the various species and types of musical irony, I am particularly interested in cases that involve surprise endings—in short, epilogues that leave listeners hanging or codas with a kick. To appreciate this type of irony, it is necessary to briefly survey previous formulations by Aristotle and Heine.

Griffes's use of the ironic epilogue revives the Aristotelian concept of *peripeteia,* or turning point, but without the element of tragedy. In the *Poetics,* Aristotle defines the concept as "a change to the opposite in the actions being performed . . . in accordance with probability or necessity."[19] *Peripeteia* in conjunction with *anagnorisis*—that is, the central character's self-recognition—are both essential for the form of Greek tragedy. Griffes transforms the ancient Greek tradition by avoiding any sense of the tragic and, instead, relies purely on a moment of ironic reversal—in short, *peripeteia* without the *pathos*. In his hands, the ending contradicts what has already transpired in such a way that it raises questions about the music's underlying theoretical assumptions and, in one case, creates an irresolvable paradox.

An even closer analogy arose in the literary tradition of *Stimmungsbrechung* (or breaking of mood), made popular by the celebrated nineteenth-century German author Heinrich Heine, in which a poem's unexpected ending is central to its overall meaning. S. S. Prawer describes these endings as "a sting in the tail" or "a moral slap in the face."[20] Susan Youens provides a good introduction to this concept in her interpretation of Schubert's musical setting of one of Heine's poems: "'Das Fischermädchen' . . . constitutes a conundrum worthy of Heine at his most complicated because its ambiguities ultimately cannot be resolved. Is it a love song or a mockery of a love song? . . . The queasiness of meaning, the ambivalence, is surely deliberate. . . . Which of Janus's faces in this song is the 'real' song? I think it is both at once, in a deliberate, uneasy equipoise unavailable of resolution one way or the other."[21] Likewise, Griffes's compositional endings display different degrees of reversal, each with its own nuances. In the passages to be discussed, both succeed in "getting the last word," but only one creates an insoluble paradox.

Finally, it is appropriate to introduce Heine as a precedent for Griffes's treatment of musical irony since altogether he set eight of the German author's poems for voice and piano. However, Griffes composed these songs during his early period, 1903–11, and none of his settings shows a propensity for irony.

Point d'Ironie

A curious footnote in the history of grammar offers an insight into the sudden reversal in Griffes's musical epilogues: ironic punctuation. The authors of these bizarre graphic signs had genuine philosophical aspirations, for they tried to clarify the presence of irony or sarcasm in a text by using unorthodox types of punctuation. Beginning in England in 1575 and continuing all the way to the nineteenth century in France, the *point*

FIGURE 9.3.

Ironic Punctuation, Alcanter de Brahm, *L'ostensoir
des ironies*, based on Keith Houston.

d'ironie forms a fascinating thread in the history of grammar. A short
graphic history of ironic signifiers would include Henry Denham, who
initially proposed a reverse question mark to terminate rhetorical questions. Then, one hundred years later, John Wilkins, the brother-in-law of
Oliver Cromwell, suggested—or rather exclaimed—an alternative, an
inverted exclamation point: ¡. Finally, Alcanter de Brahm (nom de plume
for Marcel Bernhardt) revived the original reversal strategy in his book
L'ostensoir des ironies to indicate the presence of irony—see figure 9.3.[22]

This brief history deserves a few comments. To begin with, two of
the symbols are conventional punctuation marks that are reoriented in
space—that is, inverted horizontally or vertically. These graphic manipu-
lations serve as a metaphor for interpretation, since irony was usually
treated as a reversal of the conventional meaning of a word or message.
The hypothetical point d'ironie would no longer possess the usual grammatical function of punctuation—separating and organizing words in a
sentence. Instead, it would have a more philosophical purpose: to help the
reader understand what the words mean.

This brief typographical tour is designed to emphasize that, since ironic
messages are difficult to recognize in any medium, it is understandable
that authors at various junctures in history have tried to develop a specific
sign that clarifies when irony is present. However, in musical textures with
no text, there is nothing comparable. Instead, for Griffes, the presence of

irony is determined by the musical context itself—that is, by expectations that are developed within a given piece itself. In particular, the closest thing to an ironic punctuation sign would be a single chord or cadence that, because of its location at the end of a piece, provides a framework for determining whether and kind of irony may be present. The two works to be considered below embody different versions of musical irony. In "The Vale of Dreams," the final chord illustrates an ironic reversal of the listener's sense of overall tonal unity. By contrast, in Prelude #3 the moment of irony coincides with the second of a pair of cadences, or a *cadence d'ironie*. As we will see, in each work the final chord creates ironic meaning on a contextual basis. Indeed, each of these sonorities has a theatrical dimension, like a new character who enters the stage and throws all previous events into question.

Ultimately, however, there is a problem with the pursuit of ironic punctuation, for the very act of introducing such a sign implies that it is possible to determine objectively when this condition is or is not present. Indeed, the need for clarity and predictability in our ironic meditations betrays a scientific approach—as if we could ever know for certain that a work of art is ironic.

In short, "is there an unmistakable sign for irony in music or literature?" is the wrong question to ask. To try to confirm that irony is present is to treat the characteristics of ambiguity, paradox, and uncertainty as if they were empirical facts like a tempo marking or a tonal center. Irony signifies the potential for multiple interpretations of a work and, thereby, multiple critical orientations of the listener. In this semiotic territory, the quest to find the Holy Grail of absolute certainty is an epistemological mirage. Instead, the preferred solution is to embrace the uncertainty of interpretation for all it is worth.

"The Vale of Dreams"

The first work to be considered, "The Vale of Dreams," was composed in 1912 and published three years later as part of a small collection of pieces for solo piano called *Three Tone-Pictures*, Op. 5. The work possesses features associated with two musical topics—the lament and the pastoral— as well as hints of a popular Scottish dance, the strathspey. It also contains a stunning climax where melodic motives from previous sections coincide in a texture of cumulative counterpoint. Finally, he ends the work with a strong element of paradox, closing on an unexpected cadence (for a detailed commentary on the entire work, see chap. 8).

The overall harmonic language in "The Vale of Dreams" has two distinct aspects that conflict with one another. For most of the work—the first and third sections—the harmonic dimension is largely static, based on a recurring pedal. While the B♭4/2 pedal chord itself is dissonant, by sheer repetition it creates a continuous harmonic foundation, suggesting a tonal center of B♭ (see ex. 8.4 in chap. 8). The other aspect is the piece's harmonic vocabulary. Despite the static bass line, the harmonic palette in all three sections of the work displays a late nineteenth-century, post-Wagnerian style of chromaticism. This style is especially evident in Griffes's obsession with the augmented triad, which appears occasionally in the opening section (m. 4) and which returns with a vengeance at the climax in mm. 33–36. Taken together, these two aspects lend a degree of ambiguity to the piece's pastoral character.

Griffes further heightens the piece's ambiguous character by introducing a motivic and harmonic paradox at the very end—see example 8.8. It is worth reconstructing this passage (mm. 57–60) layer by layer. The bass voice contains a rising half-step motive: A–B♭. Then, the two inner voices descend chromatically in parallel thirds, each covering a major third span. Finally, the soprano voice sounds a single pitch, E♭5. The upper three voices initially create an augmented triad, G, C♭, E♭, which eventually resolves to an E♭ major chord in second inversion. The final sonority and rising chromatic bass line are highly reminiscent of a famous movement from Robert Schumann's *Carnaval*, Op. 9, entitled "Eusebius," which happens to be in the same key.[23]

Griffes's work belongs to a small group of nineteenth-century miniatures by such composers as Schumann, Chopin, Brahms, and Liszt that either delay or avoid cadential resolution.[24] In his essay "Liszt's Open Structures and the Romantic Fragment," Ramon Satyendra identifies four characteristics that a handful of works by Liszt all share: a recurring dominant-function harmony; the absence of a cadential confirmation of the tonic; a contrapuntal organization within a single major/minor mode; and traditional syntax of tonal harmony.[25] It is significant that until the final 6/4 chord arrives, "The Vale of Dreams" possesses all four of these properties.

Satyendra also argues that this group of pieces embodies the "Romantic Fragment" as defined by John Daverio and Charles Rosen. According to Rosen, such pieces are suffused by paradox in that they are closed and open at the same time.[26] They are closed because the dominant, by sheer repetition, acquires a degree of stability. For example, in Griffes's piece the B♭ 4/2 chord appears in the opening and closing sections—twenty-six out of a total of sixty bars. Yet these pieces are also open in that the same dominant sonority points toward another tonal center, in this case E♭.

When the final E♭ chord appears, it catches listeners by surprise. At that moment, the piece can be considered neither a member of the "dominant-based" works by Liszt nor an exemplar of Rosen's fragmentary ideal. This chord serves as a harmonic version of reversal or a musical *Stimmungsbrechung*. The source of irony is a fundamental shift in how listeners interpret the tonal function of the recurring dominant. Instead of hovering between stability and instability, poised between openness and closure, the B♭ 4/2 chord now functions as a traditional dominant—as if it had been waiting all along to reveal its true tonal identity. In short, the work's prevailing paradoxical character has been transformed by its final sonority, a *cadence d'ironie*.

Yet the final chord also has broader ironic implications. Does it serve as an act of formal closure, restoring tonal unity, or rather as a sardonic comment on the expectation of closure? Here, the evidence points toward the former interpretation. In "The Vale of Dreams," Griffes fashions an elaborate harmonic puzzle, and he delays the solution until the very last sonority. The ending embodies a striking display of ironic reversal that foreshadows an even more dramatic example in Griffes's final work.

Prelude #3

Preliminaries

Prelude #3 is a festival of musical signification, combining elements of the pastoral and the lament as well as musical ambiguity, simple irony, and double irony. No other work in his output exhibits the characteristics of

III

EXAMPLE 9.1.

(ABOVE AND FOLLOWING PAGE)

Griffes, Prelude #3. 1970 © Henmar Press Inc, New York.
Permission by C. F. Peters Corporation. All rights reserved.

irony to the same degree. Before exploring the means by which he achieves them, let me begin by considering the work's pitch content, overall form, and motivic structure. The entire score is reproduced in example 9.1.

In several of his late works, such as the Piano Sonata (1918) and the *Kairn of Koridwen* (1917), Griffes experimented with various synthetic scales. In her monograph on Griffes, Donna Anderson describes his continuing interest in alternative scales that vary in length (containing six, seven, eight, or nine pitches) and that often highlight the augmented second.[27] In example 9.2, the prelude's pitch materials are organized by individual subsection.[28] The scales he employs in mm. 1–10 share seven out of eight pitches in common; the only difference is the placement of an additional

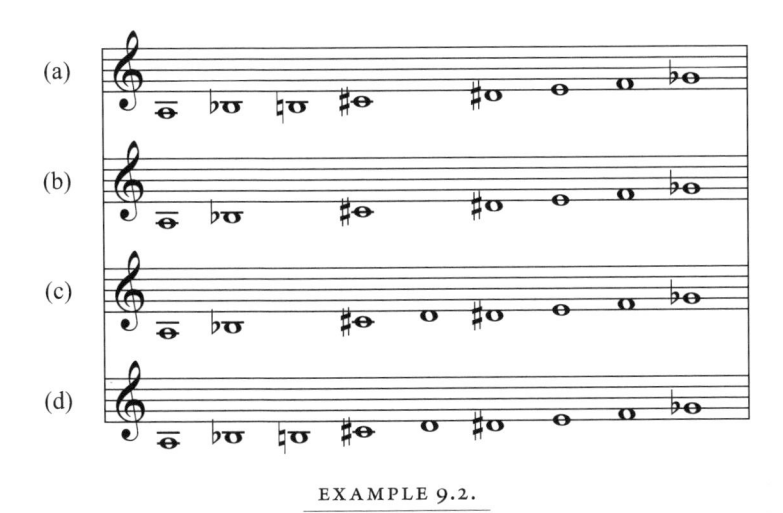

EXAMPLE 9.2.

Griffes, Prelude #3, Summary of pitch content: (a) subsection a1;
(b) subsections b1, c1, and c2; (c) subsection a2; and (d) total pitch content.

half step—C♯, D in place of B♭, B. Finally, at level (d) the scales found in
all the subsections are combined into a nine-note scale that serves as the
reservoir of pitch material for the entire work.

The prelude's overall formal scheme is binary, A A′, as shown below;
the primary criterion for determining the formal divisions is his motivic
treatment.

mm.	1	7	11	15	21
Section	A			A′	
Subsection	a1	b1	c1	a2	c2

The first principal section (mm. 1–14) can be likened to a musical collage
rather than a continuous musical utterance. It consists of a succession of
three contrasting musical ideas, each with its own distinctive texture,
rhythm, melodic shape, and harmony. In the above formal diagram, they
are labeled as a1, b1, and c1. Most important, these ideas have a strong
referential character in that they echo the meter and/or rhythmic patterns present in some of Griffes's own earlier experimental pastorals. As
such, they constitute a vivid musical commentary on the process of topical

identification in his music as well as on his pastoral sensibility as a whole. It is worth considering each one in brief.

The opening subsection (a1) possesses hints of a pastoral character, customized to Griffes's own aesthetic. This is due to his treatment of meter, rhythm, and harmony. First of all, the 5/4 meter is irregular, a type which can also be found in previous works such as "The White Peacock," the piano Introduction to "The Song of the Dagger," and Prelude #1 as well as "Clouds" (7/4). Not only does the meter have an odd number of beats but the rhythmic texture throughout is asymmetrical and unpredictable. In mm. 1–2, the melody's extended dotted rhythmic pattern creates a 2 + 3 grouping. Eventually, in m. 5, a quicker dotted pattern arrives, eighth + sixteenth, briefly suggesting a distorted minuet. Since the same combination of continuous dotted rhythms in 5/4 meter appears prominently in the opening section of "The White Peacock," this passage serves as a form of temporal self-quotation. Lastly, a fixed pedal chord in the upper register accompanies a lyrical melody in the piano's middle register. The offbeat pedal chord, D♯, A, E, creates a dissonant yet static harmonic foundation found in some of his other pastorals (*The Pleasure-Dome*, "The White Peacock," and "The Vale of Dreams"). Taken together, the opening section's unusual metric, rhythmic, and harmonic organization reflects that of a handful of Griffes's other pastoral experiments.

Subsection b1 witnesses a complete shift in terms of rhythm, tone, and texture. Here, the soprano line moves in continuous eighth notes and is doubled in two lower voices, creating monophony in three voices. This short passage can be likened to an insistent recitative, which consists of two phrases, ending on a half cadence in B♭ minor. Below, I will explore its harmonic structure in greater detail.

Finally, the third passage, subsection c1, witnesses the most dramatic shift of all. Here, Griffes introduces a six-voice chorale, a pungent yet ethereal procession of polychords, descending in quarter notes and possessing strong associations with the Sacred Chorale Style. As we will see below, the dense pitch material in these repeating hexachords is not new but rather grows out of the dissonant vertical sonorities that have already appeared in the previous two subsections. When the final hexachord in the procession occurs three times, it becomes a compelling cadence, as if Griffes were insisting that this chord can stand alone.

Viewed as a whole, the "A" section is highly fragmented, a curious assortment of contrasting motives and textures that lacks any unifying motive, key, or texture. The only way the listener knows that the section has come to an end is the insistent repetition and extended duration of the cadence chord. But, as will become clear below, this perception of finality is an essential ingredient of the work's ironic design.

The second principal section, A' (mm. 15–24), is an abbreviated statement of the opening fourteen bars. Griffes includes variants of the first and third subsections, a2 and c2, but omits b1 altogether. The most dramatic difference, however, is that he substitutes a new ostinato chord in the initial subsection—an A major triad. This change from a dissonant to a consonant pedal chord ends up playing a crucial role in the work's ironic character.

Overall, Prelude #3 is a portrait of profound contrast: within each principal section the contrast is motivic; between the two sections it is harmonic. The difference between the harmonic treatment of the same motivic material in two subsections, a1 and a2, falls short of being pure negation or contradiction: non-tonal versus tonal. Instead, the harmonic character of the opening subsection, a1, is best described as ambiguous, hovering between a persistent augmented triad, suggesting a tonal center of Bb, and an independent dissonant idiom without any clear tonal center. The contrasting cadences that end c1 and c2 reinforce the work's binary formal structure—as though an antecedent/consequent phrase pattern were reenacted at a global level—a kind of "post-tonal period" writ large.

Simple Irony

A crucial ingredient of the work's ironic character is the motivic parallelism between the initial two subsections. Example 9.3 isolates three melodic motives that initially appear in subsection a1. When each motive returns in the second section, Griffes preserves its rhythms, transposes and/or varies its intervals, and, most important, transforms its harmonic context. Whereas the underlying support for the melodic motives in the first subsection (a1) is an ambiguous augmented triad, in the restatement of this material, (a2) the harmonic texture is a recurring A-major pedal chord. This type of motivic parallelism reinforces the work's binary formal design.

EXAMPLE 9.3.

Griffes, Prelude #3: Recurring melodic motives in a1 and a2: (a) mm. 1 and 15; (b) mm. 2–3 and 16–17; and (c) mm. 5–6 and 19–20.

However, Griffes also employs another type of pitch repetition: the enharmonic pun, which can be understood as a restatement of a previous motive, either in its original order or in reverse order, but in a new harmonic context. There are two instances of this type of ironic commentary, both melodic in nature. The first musical pun is an ordered melodic motive in mm. 2–4, as displayed in example 9.4(a). Its original statement and later retrograde transformation at R4 (or R0, using "movable do" notation) underline the element of opposition at work in the prelude: E–F–G♭–F (mm. 2–4) becomes F–G♭–F–E (m. 17). In the first version, the arabesque melody circles around the pitch, F; in the second version, it ornaments the pitch, E, largely because of the ostinato A-major triad.

The second instance of an enharmonic pun is a five-note melodic motive first heard in m. 7, as shown in example 9.4(b). Although it initially

EXAMPLE 9.4.

Griffes, Prelude #3, Melodic puns: (a) mm. 2–4 and 17; (b) mm. 7 and 19.

appears within a purely melodic texture, the harmonic context is clearly B♭ minor. It is curious that Griffes retains the same pitch orthography from the a1 subsection—for example, spelling scale degree 3 as C♯ instead of D♭. By contrast, when the motive reappears in m. 17 in an embellished form (indicated by pitches in parentheses), the pitches' harmonic functions have changed—now heard in relation to the recurring A-major pedal chord. Here, the spelling of the pitch, C♯, is diatonic. In sum, by repeating the same melodic shape as well as pitch content in two vastly different harmonic contexts, Griffes engages in a form of ironic musical commentary. But, as mentioned above, neither version of the motive is preferred.

EXAMPLE 9.5.

Griffes, Prelude #3, mm. 3–6: (a) middleground reduction of lower voice; (b) foreground reduction of lower voice.

Harmonic Ambiguity

There is also an undercurrent of ambiguity present in subsection a1, which grows out of the conflict between the recurring pedal sonority and the melodic line. Taken by itself, the alto melody consistently outlines an augmented triad built on F, which suggests a dominant harmonic function in B♭ major/minor. Griffes's rhythmic treatment also reinforces F, A, and C♯ as structural pitches. Example 9.5 presents a loose Schenkerian reading of the lower voice in the opening passage. However, the three-note bell chord, D♯, A, E, recurring on the offbeat throughout the passage, clashes with this harmonic interpretation. It can be interpreted in either of two ways.

On the one hand, the perfect fifth, A–E, suggests that the implied harmonic point of reference is A, not B♭. According to this interpretation, the constant emphasis on the pitch, F, would be treated as an E♯ in that key. On the other hand, it can also suggest a more tonally neutral reading in which neither A nor B♭ is a tonal center. Such an approach would highlight the two constituent interval classes in the pedal chord, ic1 and ic5, and a family of set classes, such as (016) and (0167), that appear as vertical sonorities in

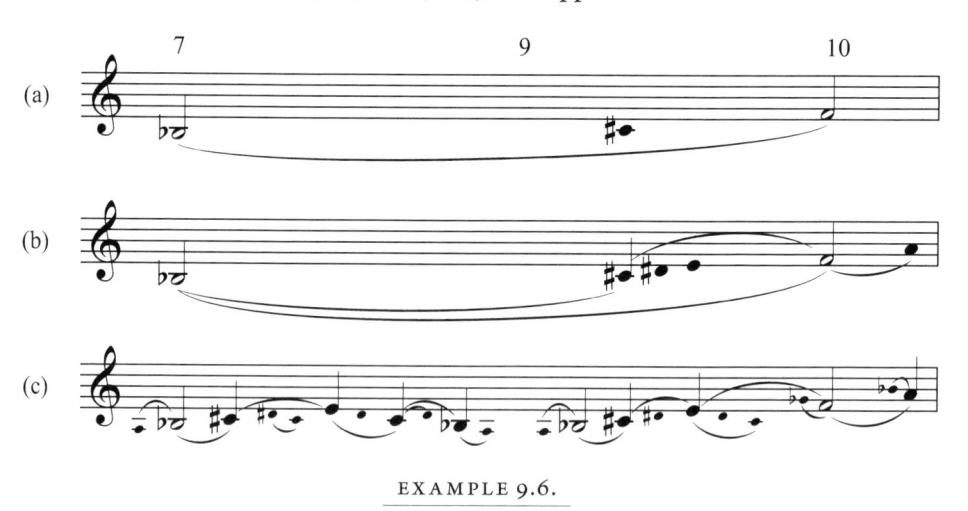

EXAMPLE 9.6.

Griffes, Prelude #3, mm. 7–10: (a) upper middleground
reduction; (b) lower middleground; and (c) foreground.

mm. 1–6. At various points in the following subsection (mm. 7–8) the set class (016) is also highlighted. We will discuss such an atonal interpretation in greater detail below—see Example 9.9.

The ambiguity present in the opening subsection continues in the b1 subsection, but here it grows more out of orthography than of tonality. Overall, the periodic phrase structure in mm. 7–10 reinforces a structural axis between B♭–F and, by extension, the key of B♭ minor—see example 9.6. Here, the source of ambiguity arises from Griffes's choice of spelling scale-degrees 3 and 4 as C♯ and D♯, respectively, and, by extension, the tonic chord as B♭, C♯, F. As will become evident below, the pitches traversed in this recitative serve as a reservoir for the chordal texture's pitch content in the following subsection.

Atonal Kaleidoscope

At m. 11, everything changes. The descending chorale in subsection c1 (mm. 11–13) and its slightly varied return in c2 (mm. 21–23) display a musical language altogether different from anything else in the work. In these two passages, the notion of scale degree recedes and eventually disappears—as if Griffes were intoning some kind of atonal commentary on the previous hints of tonality. Both sections are organized by a strict canon, which can be understood from either a horizontal or a vertical point of view. The recurring collection is Hexachord I, which unites five of the six voices of the texture, each line in m. 11 beginning on a different pitch. The remaining inner voice, the bottom voice in the right-hand part, presents another six-note collection, Hexachord II, that differs by only one pitch: E takes the place of F.[29] Both collections are shown in example 9.7.

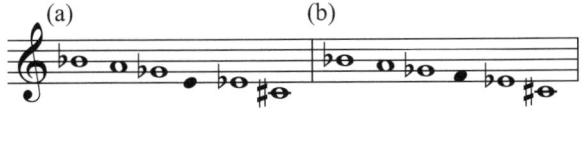

EXAMPLE 9.7.

Griffes, Prelude #3: (a) Hexachord I (6–z50); (b) Hexachord II (6–31).

The opposition between the two collections is somewhat masked since the hexachords are juxtaposed in a continuous rhythmic texture. This pattern of imitation could also be described in vertical terms. The left hand's succession of five three-note chords in m. 11 (E♭, G♭, B♭ then C♯, F, A and so on) recurs in the right hand one beat later and one octave higher—in short, a canonic procession of trichords. Likewise, every sixth chord interrupts this strict vertical imitation only to recommence on the following beat. Another pattern of pitch-class rotation occurs within every other trichord in each hand. This pattern is clearly evident below, where the two hexachords are represented as a series of integers (mod 12) within each vertical trichord.

1	10	9	6	5	3
9	6	5	3	1	10
4	3	1	10	9	6

10	9	6	5	3	1
6	5	3	1	10	9
3	1	10	9	6	5

Throughout this passage, there is a striking balance between opposites: a sense of stasis as well as of motion, a constant stream of repeating vertical intervals that nevertheless displays gradual kaleidoscopic shifts in harmonic color. The continuous revoicing of the same vertical chord is reminiscent of similar repetitive textures in three previous works: "The White Peacock" (see chap. 4), "The Symphony in Yellow" (see chap. 7), and the Piano Sonata.[30] Finally, there is a pedagogical aspect to this aural kaleidoscope. By attuning to these subtle harmonic nuances, the listener learns to hear each hexachord as an independent sonority.

A Tale of Two Cadences

Now we are prepared to consider how the piece manifests double or infinite irony. The rhetorical crux of the prelude and, indeed, its central source of irony arises from the cadence chords concluding c_1 and c_2. Two statements of the same collection—Hexachord II (A, C♯, F, E♭, G♭, B♭)—function in diametrically opposite ways: whereas in mm. 13–14 the pedal chord stands defiant, in no need of resolution, in mm. 23–24 the same chord resolves to a consonance. To put this another way, at the end of the first section the collection stands alone as a polychord, an independent, six-note sonority; at the end of the second section it is no longer independent, instead embellishing the triad that immediately follows with multiple appoggiaturas, as shown in example 9.8. This cadential gesture is another instance of cumulative counterpoint in that three voices have motivic significance in the work: F–E, reenacts the pitch inflection between the left-hand arpeggios in a1 and a2; E♭–C♯ reflects the difference between the ostinato chords in a1 and a2; and, finally, B♭ and A are the competing tonal centers throughout the work. In addition, two of these three motives have strong topical significance, for they are both a descending half step—in short, they are both sigh figures. Griffes waits for the final two bars to insert two contrapuntal motions that refer to grief or to a parody of it. By the end, the listener is still left wondering.

EXAMPLE 9.8.

Griffes, Prelude #3, mm. 23–24: Final cadence interpreted
as multiple appoggiaturas above a bass pedal.

Taken together, the contrasting ways in which Griffes treats Hexachord II create a framework of musical irony in that they raise fundamental theoretical questions: What constitutes a cadence? What constitutes a key? The difference between the chord's function at the end of c_1 and c_2 rests on the concept of scale-step identity. While there is some ambiguity about which tonal center is at work in subsections a₁ and b₁, at least there is a sense of tonal hierarchy among the pitches. Yet at m. 14, when the hexachordal chorale has completed its slow ethereal descent, any sense of key or tonal unity has long since disappeared . In the context of a piece suffused by enharmonic puns, the question at m. 14 is not *which* scale degree is present but rather *whether* the concept of scale degree exists at all.

EXAMPLE 9.9.

Griffes, Prelude #3, mm. 1–6: Three-, four-, and five-note subsets of Hexachord I.

To appreciate this opposition more fully, let us consider the first of the two hexachords found in c₁ in relation to the music of the preceding subsections. The perception of this dissonant chord's stability can be explained as a cumulative phenomenon whereby the listener is prepared for its arrival by the introduction of various vertical subsets between mm. 1–6. Example 9.9 isolates a diverse group of three-, four-, and five-note collections that appear in the opening passage. The first and perhaps the most important preparatory trichord is the right hand's "bell" or pedal chord, listed under m. 1 in the example (as is customary, the set structure isolated here assumes pitch-class inversional equivalence as well as enharmonic equivalence). The remaining tetrachords and pentachords in this example are created by juxtaposing selected pitches from the left hand's chromatic melodic line against the dissonant "bell" chiming in the right hand, thereby creating new vertical sonorities. Hence, when the dissonant six-note polychord arrives at m. 11, it has already been heard in bits and pieces during the previous ten bars. In essence, its harmonic stability has been contextually defined.

Such a cumulative listening approach also takes place at a more microscopic level within the c₁ subsection itself. Hexachord I is not immediately perceived as a nonfunctional sonority—that is, as an unordered pitch-class set. Rather, the shift between tonal function and the emergence of a new contextually based stability occurs gradually over the course of this kaleidoscopic chorale—thirteen iterations of the same two polychords in all. Most important, over the duration of this short passage the listener's perception of the same sonority evolves from traditional scale-step function to the complete absence of function.[31]

All this sets the stage for the prelude's ironic "second act." While the previous pedal chord resounding over and over again was dissonant, now there is nothing but consonance. Measures 15–20 sound like a middle range chromatic melody, meditating on the glories of the major triad suspended above it. When Griffes repeats every detail of c_1 and then changes the final chord, he invents a new, more traditional ending: an appoggiatura chord that resolves to a root-position triad. In the process, however, he casts doubt retrospectively on what made the previous ending at m. 14 sound cadential—that is, on the very notion of a contextually based cadence. According to this view, the final chord's rhetorical twist appears to be one-dimensional, a single degree of irony. The final triad now serves as a biting commentary on the previous dissonant textures, expressing nostalgia for the simplicity and clarity of a musical language that was largely absent in the opening section. What was initially perceived as closed at the end of section A is now shown to be open; what dissonances seemed stable and at rest in the middle of the prelude were in fact unstable and waiting for their final resolution ten bars later. What seemed true about the hexachord in m. 14 is proven false in the final measure. The lesson from this exercise in musical irony seems to be that dissonances can be deceiving, and that all's well that ends well—as long as it ends on a major triad.

But there is more to this musical story. Griffes's treatment of irony has a second dimension, leading us to reconsider all of our newfound interpretive discoveries. By ending the prelude on an A-major triad in m. 24, Griffes could just as well be poking fun at the listener's expectation of a final concord, mocking the traditional paradigm of dissonance resolving to consonance, tension leading to resolution. What is more, the stepwise motion of the various lines in mm. 23–24 could also be satirizing the very concept of appoggiatura and the underlying principle of chord identity on which it depends. In this reading, the prelude neither celebrates the pleasures of dissonance nor affirms the need for consonance, but instead undercuts them both. It is a harmonic version of yet another musical *Stimmungsbrechung*, but this time the degree of irony is even more profound.

This double-edged interpretation can be framed in relation to the prelude's pitch content. Accordingly, the material displayed in example 9.2 (d) could be interpreted in either of two ways: as a hierarchical collection (or scale) whose tonal center has priority over all other members or as a non-hierarchical collection in which no single pitch has inherent priority over any other. The prelude would perpetuate, not resolve, the tension between the two. By the same token, the foundation of binary form itself would also be shaken, as though such an expanded period, whether tonal or post-tonal, were no longer possible. Perhaps it is the sense of closure itself that is turned inside out, leaving the listener with yet more questions to ponder: Does the prelude underline or undermine tonal nostalgia? Does the final A major triad restore the countenance of tonality or thumb its nose at it? Instead of suggesting one alternative or the other, the music suggests both, a paradox that can be summarized as follows: *neither either nor or*.

Ultimately, the final cadence of Prelude #3 serves as a musical paradox, a kind of philosophical exercise that raises fundamental questions in the listener's mind. One of these questions is whether this paradox can be resolved by consulting Aristotle's famous Law of the Excluded Middle. According to that principle, a given proposition is either p or not p, which, in this case, translates into a given chord being either tonal or not tonal. If this principle were strictly applied to Prelude #3, then a dissonant chord either needs to resolve or does not need to resolve. As it turns out, the piece offers an alternative to such a strict binary opposition by challenging listeners to reevaluate their assumptions. Instead, the prelude constitutes a profound commentary on the limitations of logic and the artistic possibilities of paradox.

Conclusion

Let us return to one of Wilde's epigrams posed at the outset of the chapter: Art is the telling of "untrue things." Or is it? To reflect on irony is to contemplate the phenomena of puns, paradoxes, double entendres, deceptions—indeed, the entire spectrum of ambiguity. What could be the musical counterpart to this ambiguous spectrum? Although many answers to this question have been proposed, I would argue that the spatial model of a Möbius strip is an apt analogy to capture the musical paradoxes expressed in Prelude #3. In that work, Griffes raises questions about the usual music theoretical assumptions that Western listeners and performers take for granted—in short, whether every pitch in a particular chord has a scale-degree function or whether no pitch has a scale-degree function. Consequently, by the end of the prelude, Griffes not only underlines the difference between the presence and absence of tonal function, but he also undermines it.

At this juncture, we are left with three additional questions:

- Why should this prelude be considered a pastoral?
- Why did Griffes focus on tonality as a vehicle for expressing irony?
- What are the consequences of this statement of musical irony for the listener and for Griffes's oeuvre as a whole?

To begin with, one wonders if this miniature piano work is truly a pastoral. Why include it in a book that is devoted to the full gamut of Griffes's pastoral imagination? The answer is that his treatment of irregular meter, recurring dotted rhythmic patterns, and metric ambiguity is reminiscent of previous works with various pastoral associations. Thus, the piece's pastoral character is defined partly by its resemblance to other pieces that Griffes had already composed—in short, a contextual correspondence. But, since these rhythmic and metric features do not continue throughout the work, we must also take into account the piece's motivic fragmentation as a whole. The constant kaleidoscopic shifts in musical texture can be heard as a series of musical memories, some of which have pastoral or even religious associations. In short, Prelude #3 is less a pastoral per se than a *commentary* on Griffes's fascination for the pastoral tradition.

The second question raises the slippery question of intentionality. In short, in the absence of a detailed letter or diary entry about his compositional process, it is impossible to identify Griffes's motivation for writing the piece. That said, this prelude is not an isolated experiment but instead belongs to a small group of pieces that reflect a profound shift in his musical style toward the end of his career. Works like the Piano Sonata and the "Clouds" movement from *Roman Sketches*, Op. 7, reveal a new taste for a highly dissonant musical idiom. In this context, Prelude #3 not only serves as a commentary on the pastoral, but it also confirms his fascination with a new more abstract style. Hence, it is possible to infer in this work an underlying source of creative inspiration to explore and comment upon the nature of tonal coherence.

Finally, what if the listener fails to recognize both degrees of irony and instead focuses on the first stage where, in the final measure, consonance seems to triumph over dissonance? The answer to this question is that the prelude would still be an exercise in musical irony but now would be limited to one dimension. While such an interpretation is perfectly reasonable, this hypothetical listener would not realize the full rhetorical potential of this prelude and would savor fewer of its rich ironic colors. In addition, the striking motivic parallelism and binary structure serve a clear didactic function—as if the prelude were beckoning the listener to compare and reflect upon similar musical material being treated in radically different ways. Yet the piece is more of an aesthetic puzzle than a lecture on logic, and, in this case, the puzzle has more than one solution.

In Prelude #3, Griffes merges the worlds of pedagogy and philosophy. It is pedagogical because its motivic material is so repetitive, and its form is so simple. The philosophical dimension emerges because the piece raises questions about traditional theoretical assumptions concerning interval quality, tonality, and formal closure. Griffes's prelude provides no final answers, instead framing its critical questions in purely musical terms. It is neither a vision of a new compositional approach nor a manifesto of a new theory of interpretation, but rather it is a prelude to new musical meditations. It succeeds in fusing a work of art with a workshop about art.

In the Introduction to his book entitled *On Puns*, Jonathan Culler describes a view of irony that throws light on one way this prelude may be a stimulus for new forms of creativity. He argues that "puns show speakers intently or playfully working to reveal the structures of language, [and] allowing signifiers to affect meaning by generating new connections—in short, responding to the call of the phoneme, whose echoes tell of wild

realms beyond the code and suggest new configurations of meaning."[32]
If Culler is right about the potential for play in the tradition of linguistic
punning, then perhaps Griffes's treatment of pun and irony in this prelude
has a similar potential for generating new kinds of compositional experiments.

One final question arises: how are we to interpret this outburst of musical irony when viewed in the context of the composer's other pastorals?
Is this dramatic departure in style a mere accident, an uncharacteristic
digression—the equivalent of an aesthetic doodle or artistic hiccup? After
all, since Griffes began composing "The Vale of Dreams" as early as 1912,
his taste for irony had appeared and reappeared at different stages in his
musical career. I believe that Prelude #3 constitutes a provocative artistic
statement for Griffes that continues a thread of aesthetic experimentation first witnessed in his *Three Tone Pictures* and then magnifies it. As his
last completed work, Prelude #3 was not his ultimate artistic statement;
rather, it was the last work he happened to finish within a new artistic
trajectory. His final prelude is a musical and philosophical waystation
within a larger creative process that he never completed. If Griffes had
lived longer, one can only wonder what new visions of musical irony he
might have ventured.

NOTES

1. Esti Sheinberg has written an exhaustive and enlightening account of various species of irony in Shostakovich's music; see *Irony, Satire, Parody and the Grotesque in the Music of Shostakovich: A Theory of Musical Incongruities* (Burlington, VT: Ashgate, 2000).

2. Friedrich Schlegel, "On Incomprehensibility," in *Friedrich Schlegel's Lucinde and the Fragments*, trans. Peter Firchow (Minneapolis: University of Minnesota Press, 1971); Soren Kierkegaard, *The Concept of Irony, with a Continual Reference to Socrates*, ed. and trans. Howard V. Hong and Edna H. Hong (Princeton, NJ: Princeton University Press, 1989). For an excellent overview of their views on irony, see Sheinberg, *Irony, Satire, Parody*, 33–43.

3. Wayne C. Booth, *A Rhetoric of Irony* (Chicago: University of Chicago Press, 1975); Joseph Dane, *The Critical Mythology of Irony* (Athens and London: University of Georgia Press, 1991); Donald C. Muecke, *The Compass of Irony* (London: Methuen and Co. 1969).

4. D. A. Monson, "Andreas Capellanus and the Problem of Irony," *Speculum* 63, no. 3 (1988): 539–72.

5. The list includes the following: tragic irony, comic irony, irony of manner, irony of situation, philosophical irony, practical irony, dramatic irony, verbal irony, ingénue irony, double irony, rhetorical irony, self-irony, Socratic irony, Romantic irony, cosmic

irony, sentimental irony, irony of Fate, irony of chance, irony of character. See Donald C. Muecke, *The Compass of Irony* (London: Methuen, 1969), 4.

6. Linda Hutcheon, *Irony's Edge: The Theory and Politics of Irony* (London and New York: Routledge, 1994).

7. Stanley Fish, "Short People Got No Reason to Live: Reading Irony," *Daedalus* 112, No. 1 (Winter, 1983): 175–191.

8. Beethoven's treatment of the diminished-seventh chord in his Piano Sonata in C minor, Op. 13: I, mm. 134–135, illustrates how two instances of the same chord can be spelled differently and have different tonal functions: C, E♭, F♯, A and C, D♯, F♯, A. Incidentally, in typical rhetorical lexicons such instances of multiple meaning are categorized by a host of other names such as antanaclasis and paronomasia. See Richard A. Lanham, *A Handlist of Rhetorical Terms: A Guide for Students of English Literature* (Berkeley: University of California Press, 1968).

9. Brian Hyer, "Chopin and the In-F-able," *Musical Transformation and Musical Intuition: Eleven Essays in Honor of David Lewin*, ed. Brian Raphael Atlas and Michael Cherlin (Dedham, MA: Ovenbird, 1994).

10. Muecke, *The Compass of Irony*, 24.

11. This phrase is the title of Andrew Cross's perceptive study of Kierkegaard's tract on irony, "Neither Either Nor Or: The Perils of Reflexive Irony," in *The Cambridge Companion to Kierkegaard*, ed. Alastair Hannay and Gordon D. Marino (Cambridge, UK: Cambridge University Press, 1998), 125–53.

12. Robert Lane offers a comprehensive and imaginative interpretation of Peirce's multiple and often confusing proposals regarding Aristotle's foundational principles of the excluded middle and of noncontradiction; see "Peirce's 'Entanglement' with the Principles of Excluded Middle and Contradiction," *Transactions of the Charles S. Peirce Society* 33, no. 3 (Summer 1997): 680–703. For a detailed account of Peirce's writings on the Liar Paradox, see Richard Kenneth Atkins, "This Proposition is Not True: C. S. Peirce and the Liar Paradox," *Transactions of the Charles S. Peirce Society* 47, no. 4 (2011): 421–44.

13. See "paradox, n. and adj." *OED Online*, Oxford University Press, March 2023, www.oed.com/view/Entry/137353. Accessed March 28, 2023.

14. This heuristic approach is named after the distinguished linguist and semiotician A. J. Greimas.

15. Sheinberg, *Irony, Satire, Parody*, 10–12.

16. Ray Longyear, "Beethoven and Romantic Irony," in *The Creative World of Beethoven*, ed. Paul Henry Lang (New York: Norton, 1971), 145–62; and Stephen Zank, *Irony and Sound: The Music of Maurice Ravel* (Rochester, NY: University of Rochester Press, 2009).

17. In all, Cherlin explores twelve categories of musical irony: transition between movements or sections, contrapuntal juxtaposition, irruption or interruption, quotation or restatement, conflict between music and text, dramatic Irony, *peripeteia*, irony of reversal (often tragic), irony of distancing or detachment, irony of making repulsive attractive, irony in parody, irony in relation to a precursor, and irony of undecidables. See Michael Cherlin, *Varieties of Musical Irony: From Mozart to Mahler* (Cambridge, UK: Cambridge University Press, 2017), 20–103.

18. Sheinberg, *Irony, Satire, Parody*; Yayoi Uno Everett, "Signification of Parody and the Grotesque in György Ligeti's *Le Grand Macabre*," *Music Theory Spectrum* 31, No. 1

(Spring 2009), 26–56; and Michael L. Klein, "Ironic Narrative, Ironic Reading," *Journal of Music Theory* 53, no. 1 (Spring 2009): 95–136.

19. Aristotle, *Poetics*, trans. Malcolm Heath (London: Penguin, 1996), 18.

20. Cited in Kofi Agawu, "Structural 'Highpoints' in Schumann's 'Dichterliebe,'" *Music Analysis* 3, no. 2 (July 1984): 159–80.

21. Susan Youens, *Heinrich Heine and the Lied* (Cambridge, UK: Cambridge University Press, 2007), 53.

22. Keith Houston, *Shady Characters: The Secret Life of Punctuation* (New York: Norton: 2013), 213–19.

23. Both pieces end on the same E♭ 6/4 chord, which is preceded by a rising chromatic bass line. However, one significant difference between the two is that Schumann introduces an element of closure in his movement via a traditional authentic cadence at the end of a climactic internal phrase.

24. Examples include Chopin, Prelude no. 23 in F major, Op. 28; and Brahms, Intermezzo in Bb major, Op. 76, no. 4.

25. Ramon Satyendra, "Liszt's Open Structures and the Romantic Fragment," *Music Theory Spectrum* 29, no. 2 (Fall 1997): 184–205.

26. John Daverio, *Nineteenth-Century Music and the German Romantic Ideology* (New York: Schirmer Books, 1993). In Rosen's words, "the form is not fixed but is torn apart or exploded by paradox, by ambiguity, just as the opening song of *Dichterliebe* is a closed, circular form in which beginning and end are unstable—implying a past before the song begins and a future after its final chord." See Charles Rosen, *The Romantic Generation* (Cambridge, MA: Harvard University Press, 1998), 51.

27. Analysts differ as to the length and content of the synthetic scale exhibited in the Piano Sonata; Dean Luther Arlton argues for seven notes, Arthur Berger and Jonathan Lee Chenette for eight, and Gilbert Chase tops all with thirteen. See the summary in Anderson, *Charles T. Griffes*, 211–13.

28. It must be emphasized that the horizontal order of pitches in this example is somewhat arbitrary since over the course of the entire work multiple tonal centers are implied.

29. The respective set classes are 6–31 and 6–z50.

30. There is a similar passage in mm. 363–70 of the Piano Sonata, where three-note segments from a single scale appear as chords in ascending order. Though the scale is slightly different from that of Prelude #3—D, E♭, F, F♯, G♯, A, B♭, C♯—the effect is the same: an intervallic rotation that displays the properties of the synthetic scale.

31. It should be emphasized that such an interpretation assumes a composite model of pitch space—both tonal and so-called "atonal." For example, each of the trichord, tetrachord, and pentachord set classes listed in example 9.11 assumes pitch-class space and inversional equivalence. Some listeners may find it difficult to hear unordered pitch-class sets projected vertically at the same time that a B♭ minor tonality is implied by the left hand's melodic line in mm. 1–10. This interpretive approach is ex post facto and arises as a means of justifying why one of the two hexachords in m. 11–14 sounds so stable and so familiar.

32. Jonathan Culler, "The Call of the Phoneme," *On Puns: The Foundation of Letters*, ed. Jonathan Culler (Oxford, UK: Basil Blackwell, 1988), 3.

Pastoral Postlude

It seems fitting to end our journey through Griffes's pastoral imagination with his final composition, "Salut au Monde," which he left unfinished at his death in 1920. The work is based on a poem by the nineteenth-century visionary American poet Walt Whitman that appeared in the second edition of his magnum opus, *Leaves of Grass*, published in 1856. Beginning with twelve poems, the collection grew into a massive compilation of over four hundred works, encapsulating his philosophy of life. Originally titled "Poem of Salutation" and later renamed, the poem poses two rhetorical questions, one about sight, the other about sound.[1] It is a breathless litany of images, fantasies, and memories, overflowing with empathy and covering a wide swath of humanity including different races, genders, nationalities, and social classes. Whitman's literary salute has universal aspirations in that its pantheistic spirit touches all aspects of human experience.

The origin of this musical tribute to the "salute" can be traced to Alice and Irene Lewisohn, who owned the Neighborhood Playhouse, a small theater in Greenwich Village, and who shared a passion for Whitman's poetry. Griffes already had a long-standing relationship with the Lewisohns since in 1917 they had commissioned him to compose music for another dramatic collaboration, *The Kairn of Koridwen*. The difference is that while in the earlier piece he provided the incidental music for the entire production, in this work his music appears in only one section. Since Griffes had already read Whitman's *Leaves of Grass* as early as 1913, he was eager to participate.[2] Like Whitman's poem, the production assumed epic proportions, for it was modeled after Wagner's ideal of *Gesamtkunstwerk*, combining music, drama, singing, choral speech, narration, and dance pantomime as well as special lighting and color effects.

"Salut au Monde" can be divided into three parts:[3]

Part 1

- Musical prelude
- Scene 1: the Sphere
- Scene 1: the Sphere, the shaded part—chaos
- Scene 1: the Sphere, the lighted part—constructiveness

Part 2

- Musical prelude
- Five scenes of traditional ritualistic music, including Hebrew, Greek, Hindu, Mohammedan, and Christian

Part 3

- Social Orders of Civilization
- Epilogue

Although Griffes never completed his musical contribution, the entire work was premiered two years later thanks to Edmond Rickett, who reconstructed the score for Part 1 using the composer's sketchbooks and added his own newly composed music for Part 3. The most distinctive feature of Griffes's portion was a choral texture alternating between sung sections and passages "intoned without pitch with each voice seeking its natural pitch, although rhythm and inflection were carefully indicated."[4] In her book *Twentieth Century Music*, Marion Bauer concludes, "The result was a marvelous wealth of tone color, of a harmonious dissonance welded together by rhythmic definiteness."[5] His music in Part 1 sets the stage for the following section, a whirlwind tour of music from around the world— in short, a medley of exotic musical traditions.

"Salut au Monde" is neither Griffes's ultimate musical statement nor a culmination of his life's work. Rather, it was his final opportunity to celebrate Whitman's protean literary spirit by means of an intermedia collaboration between music, literature, drama, and dance. This extravaganza reflects the spirit of Griffes's overall style and artistic achievement in three ways: (1) his reliance on literary sources of inspiration, (2) his fascination with works in which multiple art forms intersect, and (3) his penchant for eclecticism as a means of expanding the pastoral tradition.

This tribute to Whitman demonstrates the enormous role that literature played in Griffes's artistic life. In every work I have explored in this study—whether for solo piano, voice and piano, or orchestra—poetry serves either as an epigraph preceding the score, a text to be sung, or a resource that gives new life to the music. Griffes had a voracious appetite not only for literature but also for transforming his literary muses into musical adventures. In addition, the episodic character of Whitman's ode echoes the structure of the poetic litanies by Coleridge and Sharp that inspired Griffes's most ambitious works for solo piano (later transcribed for orchestra).

"Salut au Monde" also illustrates Griffes's attraction for literary texts that refer to multiple artforms. For example, the titles of two of his pastoral works serve as miniature genealogies of artistic culture at the turn of the century. The history of his tone poem "The White Peacock," inspired by William Sharp's poem, covers a span of nearly thirty years and encompasses four different media: music, poetry, art, and drama. Likewise, Griffes's setting of Oscar Wilde's poem "Symphony in Yellow" comments upon a series of paintings by James Whistler and, thereby, participates in an intermedia festival, connecting music with literature and the visual arts.

The extreme variety in the ritualistic music in "Salut au Monde" raises the general question of eclecticism in Griffes's style. When contemplating the dazzling musical colors exhibited in his entire oeuvre, it is tempting to focus on the sheer variety in terms of contrasting dances (siciliano, minuet, and waltz), national styles (French and German), and non-Western traditions (Chinese, Javanese, and Native American folk melodies) that appear. The same thing could be said about the breadth of topical cues present in his music. When considering the various lists that I have compiled at different junctures in this book—whether the multiple styles in chapter 1 or the matrix of pastoral and lament cues in chapter 2—it may be tempting to interpret them as catalogues to be used for an exercise in topical identification. Nothing could be further from the truth. My primary purpose has been hermeneutical interpretation, not topical description. Each chapter in part II has been a case study of a different species of the ambivalent pastoral, revealing the subtle shades of meaning among the musical cues by themselves and in various combinations. It is worth briefly revisiting each work.

The dual nature of Griffes's tone poem "The White Peacock" grows directly out of William Sharp's poem. While the opening section expresses feelings of languor by the use of multiple dance topics and non-Western scales, the eventual climax evokes spiritual ecstasy by the strategic use of two-part counterpoint, an apex in dynamics, and an expansion of registral space in the outer voices. *The Pleasure-Dome of Kubla Khan*, based on Samuel Taylor Coleridge's poem, is a showcase of the deep conflicts found in Griffes's ambivalent vision of the pastoral, combining the conventional feelings portrayed in the literary tradition—serenity amid the contemplation of nature—with other darker emotions such as grief, aggression, and bacchanalian frenzy.

Each of the three works discussed in chapter 8, the two works drawn from *Three Tone-Pictures* and the Scherzo/Bacchanale, embodies a unique pastoral physiognomy, blending elements that evoke lament and suffering as well as pastoral serenity. Likewise, the songs in the Fiona Macleod cycle not only continue this pattern of opposition, but they also amplify it. Griffes's innovative treatment of the lament motive in all three songs is remarkable in that it accumulates multiple emotions: the desire for physical pleasure, the fascination with forces of nature, and the yearning for spiritual deliverance. The result is three contrasting yet compelling portraits of musical ambivalence.

As the last complete work Griffes finished before his untimely death, Prelude #3 for solo piano is less a pastoral per se then a *commentary* on Griffes's fascination with the pastoral tradition. This work is a musical-philosophical challenge that raises questions about the conventional assumptions regarding interval quality, tonality, and formal closure.

Perhaps the most telling insight into the origins of the ambivalent pastoral comes from the composer himself. Marion Bauer, a close friend and fellow composer, recalls him making this remark in "Charles Griffes as I

Remember Him": "I long to be in the city. The country does not inspire me especially; perhaps I take it too much for granted. I get much more inspiration from reading Oriental folk tales than I do from looking at a tree. At this season of the year I can hardly wait for school to be over so that I can get to New York for the summer. I love the skyscrapers and the pavements."[6] On first impression, Griffes sounds like a proud urbanite for whom the joys of the country—things like gardens, rivers, and forests—had lost all appeal. However, when we take into consideration the texts that inspired some of his most experimental music, a different story emerges.

> And there were gardens bright with sinuous rills/
> Where blossomed many an incense-bearing tree;
> And here were forests ancient as the hills,
> Enfolding sunny spots of greenery....
> Five miles meandering with a mazy motion
> Through wood and dale the sacred river ran.
>
> Here where the sunlight floodeth the garden
> Here as the breath, as the soul of this beauty ...
> Moves the white peacock.

Both excerpts are drawn from poems that he included as epigraphs to his published scores: the first is from Coleridge's "Kubla Khan," the second from Sharp's "The White Peacock." Clearly, Griffes was as fascinated with miraculous gardens and magical peacocks as he was with big-city "pavement."

Taken together, the quotation and the poetic excerpts are symptoms of a deep paradox that lies at the heart of Griffes's musical aesthetic. He was as eager to renew musical traditions of the past as he was to embrace new experiments in the present. The musical pastorals he composed during his final thirteen years are less "skyscrapers" than watercolors that reflect the cosmopolitan character of his artistic ambitions. These works reveal the degree to which he reflected the pastoral traditions of the eighteenth century as much as he refracted them through his own aesthetic lens. Terry Gifford describes the inherent potential for the pastoral to encompass various tensions and contradictions: "The pastoral can be a mode of political critique of present society ... or it can be a retreat from politics into an apparently aesthetic landscape that is devoid of conflict and tension. It is this very versatility of the pastoral to both contain and appear to evade tensions and contradiction—between country and city, art and nature, the human and the non-human, our social and our inner selves . . . that made the form so durable and so fascinating."[7]

* * *

Now that we have arrived at the end of this study, it is appropriate to raise one final question. In what ways can my study of Griffes's pastorals inform our understanding of other early twentieth-century composers' music? In other words, do the ideas expressed in this book have an afterlife?

It is convenient to divide my response into two parts that reflect some of the work's central themes: (a) a philosophical critique of the logical concept of a group; and (b) some final thoughts about whether and how to apply my approach to interpret the music of other early twentieth-century composers.

One of my goals in this study has been to show how the colors in Griffes's pastoral palette shifted among various works. To trace these colors, I developed a customized list of cues that not only captures the echoes of previous topical traditions still resonating with contemporary audiences but that also reflects new features that Griffes inaugurated himself. What is remarkable is that he introduced some new musical as well as psychological hues into his pastoral palette—such as the fusion of sensual desire and spiritual fulfillment. Were someone to develop a similar list of cues tailored to different composers from this period, such as Edvard Grieg or Jean Sibelius, it would contain a different collection of colors, some more nationalistic than others.

Most of the twelve pieces that I analyze in this book are associated with text in some way, whether it be a title, a program, or a poem that precedes an instrumental score or the lyrics of a song. In that respect, the nuanced readings I present do not rely exclusively on the traces of musical topics. Instead, I explore the intersection between topical cues (both historical and idiosyncratic); general musical features such as melody, harmony, rhythm, phrase structure, formal plan, etc.; and the network of imagery in a given text. Whether such an approach is appropriate for another early twentieth-century composer depends on the degree to which he or she relied on the printed word.

One source of inspiration for my interpretive approach has been the epistemological and aesthetic controversies that arose during the mid-twentieth century in the writings of Ludwig Wittgenstein and Morris Weitz. By reenacting a handful of arguments from their work, I hope to raise questions about the traditional notion of a musical topic as a strictly defined group, unified by necessary and sufficient conditions. Instead of merely proposing a critique, however, I also offer an alternative, an interpretive framework that has an "open" character, in Weitz's sense, and that blurs the logical boundaries of membership in a category. Wittgenstein's looser conception of a family leads directly to the polythetic approach to classification whereby no single property is common to every member of a group. Instead, the members of the group are unified by subsets of properties that overlap to various degrees. My aim has been to reveal the individual physiognomy of each work by Griffes while still preserving the continuity of the composer's overall style. For those who wish to use topic theory as a means of interpreting other composers' music, a rule of thumb would be to strike a balance between general principles and the unique complexion of an individual work. If we view the twelve pastorals in this study as an exercise in theme and variations, then at times the presence of the original pastoral theme may seem so faint that the work hardly qualifies as a variation. My approach to classification challenges the traditional assumption of thematic unity among different so-called "variations" and redefines what it means to be a member of a set.

The theoretical seed of my project has been to blur the boundaries between a general type such as a musical topic and particular instances that display characteristics associated with that type. As a result, I hesitate to generalize my interpretive approach or claim that it can be applied wholesale to understand another composer's music. Nevertheless, I humbly offer some initial speculations about how it might be adapted to explore the output of composers of the late nineteenth and early twentieth centuries who shared a similar pastoral sensibility.

Although it may sound paradoxical, the most likely general impact my approach would have on subsequent interpretations is to eschew generalization. While the style of many turn-of-the-century composers could be considered eclectic, the character of Griffes's eclecticism is unique. The point of departure for interpretating another composer's music during this period would be to develop a framework that grows out of the historical circumstances of the given composer's experience. For example, instead of merely concluding that Griffes's piano work Scherzo, op. 6 combines the pastoral ideal of serenity with a more aggressive style such as the tarantella, I revealed the deep opposition in his own life between urban adventure and rural escape and then explored how that opposition helped shape his artistic approach. Likewise, it is not enough merely to describe the innovative treatment of the pastoral tradition in his settings of Fiona Macleod's poetry. Instead, by exploring the complex artistic and personal journey of William Sharp as he embraced double literary personas, I tried to establish a historical context for the potential resonance they may have created within Griffes's musical aesthetic.

When one considers what turn-of-the-century composers would profit from an interpretive approach based on topical cues, Edward MacDowell and Frederick Delius come to mind. In some respects, the arcs of their musical careers are inversions of one another. MacDowell's many years of living in Europe (including Paris, Frankfurt, and Wiesbaden) fueled his own adaptation of German Romanticism before returning to Boston; by contrast, Frederick Delius's brief sojourns to a plantation in Florida ignited a passion for African American musical traditions that stayed with him long after he came back to France. That said, each of these composers had his own personal constellation of influences and motivations to guide him. As a result, to assemble a matrix of musical cues would also require developing a rich psychological portrait that places these musical cues in a biographical and historical context.

One point of departure for adapting my approach to classifying Griffes's pastorals can be found in a section of Agawu's book *Music as Discourse: Semiotic Adventures in Romantic Music*, where he juxtaposes a number of new topics—essentially addenda to Ratner's original topical catalogue—that have recently been proposed. These topics are designed to account for the musical styles of such composers as Liszt, Mahler, Bartók, and Stravinsky.[8] However, among the newly proposed topics he lists categories associated with ethnic groups and/or national styles including Jewish, Czech, Polish, Hungarian, Spanish, and Latin American as well as categories drawn from American traditions including spirituals and jazz. While positing such broad categories might be useful at an initial stage of investigation, eventually it would behoove any analyst to identify specific cues of rhythm, meter, scale type, harmony, texture, groove, etc. that are characteristic of each of these categories. It could well be that the cues found in a collection of one composer's works display a polythetic organization comparable to that displayed in Griffes's pastorals.

Another recent trend in musical scholarship could be perceived as having a kindred spirit to my focus on pastorals: the sense of place. In a recent essay entitled "Landscape and Ecology," Daniel Grimley surveys a wide range of instrumental works, from Beethoven's Pastoral Symphony to Delius's evocation of an exoticized American idyll, as a means of mapping nineteenth-century composers' obsession with the idea of landscape and place.[9] Likewise, in 2003 Denise Von Glahn wrote a book-length study of fourteen works (mostly instrumental) by nineteenth- and twentieth-century composers who were all inspired by particular spaces in America.[10] The physical places vary from dazzling cityscapes and verdant landscapes to barren deserts. In her view, these "place pieces" not only reflect the musical personality of a given composer but also portray the nation's identity and how it changed over time. Overall, Grimley and Von Glahn both pivot away from the pastoral per se and, in the process, introduce a new framework for understanding the complex relationship between a musical work, a physical space that inspired it, and the emotional world they both share.

In closing, I wish to consider three different ways in which this study serves as a postlude. The first involves "Salut au Monde." Since this mixed media work was left unfinished at Griffes's death in 1920, its subsequent performance two years later was a creative postlude and a musical tribute to his cumulative artistic achievement. In a real sense, I hope that my book helps continue the spirit of that tribute.

Considering that the final work Griffes completed was a set of preludes for solo piano, any analytical commentary of that work and, by extension, his other works can be considered an interpretive postlude. One wonders if it was merely a coincidence that one of his first compositions at the age of fifteen was a set of Four Preludes.[11]

Finally, my deepest hope is that one outcome of this book will be for performers and audiences to rediscover the music of Charles Tomlinson Griffes and to hear it anew—indeed, a postlude of performance.

NOTES

1. For the full text, see Walt Whitman, *Leaves of Grass, First and Death-Bed Editions*, ed. Karen Karbiener (New York: Barnes and Noble, 2004), 294–305.

2. Griffes Personal Diary, 1913; see table 1.1, chap. 1.

3. This summary of "Salut au Monde" can be found in Donna Anderson, *Charles T. Griffes: A Descriptive Catalogue,* (Ann Arbor: UMI Research Press, 1983), 376.

4. Marion Bauer, "Charles T. Griffes as I Remember Him," *The Musical Quarterly* 29, no. 3 (July 1943): 374.

5. Marion Bauer, *Twentieth Century Music* (New York: G. P. Putnam's Sons, 1947), 219.

6. Bauer, "Charles T. Griffes as I Remember Him," 356.

7. Terry Gifford, *Pastoral*, The New Critical Idiom, series ed. John Drakakis (London: Routledge, 1999), 11.

8. Kofi Agawu, *Music as Discourse: Semiotic Adventures in Romantic Music* (Oxford, UK: Oxford University Press, 2009), 43–50.

9. Daniel M. Grimley, "Landscape and Ecology," in *Oxford Handbook of Music and Intellectual Culture in the Nineteenth Century*, ed. Paul Watt, Sarah Collins, and Michael Allis (New York: Oxford University Press, 2020). Grimley avoids reference to musical topics, instead relying on literary, visual, and philosophical categories to develop an interpretive approach.

10. They include three nineteenth-century peans to Niagara Falls, two orchestral movements by Charles Ives, and various works by Aaron Copland, Edgar Varèse, Duke Ellington, Ellen Zwilich, and Steve Reich. See Denise Von Glahn, *The Sounds of Place: Music and the American Cultural Landscape* (Urbana: University of Illinois Press, 2021).

11. Donna Anderson includes Four Preludes in her list of works as Op. 40—see *Charles T. Griffes*, 235.

BIBLIOGRAPHY

Archival Sources

Burnet Corwin Tuthill Papers, Music Division, Library of Congress, Washington, DC.

Charles Tomlinson Griffes Collection, Gannett-Tripp Library, Elmira College, Elmira, New York.

Charles Tomlinson Griffes Collection, Library of Congress, Music Division, Heineman Collection, Washington, DC.

Charles Tomlinson Griffes Photographs of Hackley School and the Hudson Valley. [graphic], Music Division, New York Public Library for the Performing Arts, Dorothy and Lewis B. Cullman Center, New York City.

Donna K. Anderson Research Files on Charles Griffes, Music Division, New York Public Library for the Performing Arts, New York City.

Edward Maisel Research Files on Charles T. Griffes, JPB 14-22. Music Division, New York Public Library for the Performing Arts, New York City.

William Sharp "Fiona Macleod" Archive, Institute of English Studies, School of Advanced Study, University of London. https://www.ies.sas.ac.uk/research/william-sharp-fiona-macleod-archive/letters.

Books and Articles

Adajian, Thomas. "On the Prototype Theory of Concepts and the Definition of Art." *Journal of Aesthetics and Art Criticism* 63, no. 3 (Summer 2005): 231–36.

Agawu, Kofi. *Music as Discourse: Semiotic Adventures in Romantic Music.* Oxford, UK: Oxford University Press, 2009.

———. *Playing with Signs: A Semiotic Interpretation of Classic Music.* Princeton, NJ: Princeton University Press, 1991.

———. "Structural 'Highpoints' in Schumann's *Dichterliebe*." *Music Analysis* 3, no. 2 (1984): 159–80.

———. "Topics and Form in Mozart's String Quintet in E Flat Major, K. 614/i." In *The Oxford Handbook of Topic Theory*, edited by Danuta Mirka, 474–92. Oxford, UK: Oxford University Press, 2014.

———. "Topic Theory: Achievement, Critique, Prospects." In *Passagen, IMS Kongress Zürich 2007: Fünf Hauptvorträge, Five Key Note Speeches*, edited by Laurenz Lütteken and Hans-Joachim Hinrichsen, 38–69. Kassel: Bärenreiter, 2008.

Alaya, Flavia. *William Sharp—"Fiona Macleod," 1855–1905*. Cambridge, MA: Harvard University Press, 1970.

Allanbrook, Wye Jamieson. *Rhythmic Gesture in Mozart: Le Nozze di Figaro and Don Giovanni*. Chicago, IL: University of Chicago Press, 1983.

———. *The Secular Commedia: Comic Mimesis in Late Eighteenth-Century Music*. Edited by Mary Ann Smart and Richard Taruskin. Berkeley: University of California Press, 2014.

Alpers, Paul. *What Is Pastoral?* Chicago, IL: University of Chicago Press, 1996.

Andersen, Hans Christian. *Hans Christian Andersen: The Complete Fairy Tales and Stories*. New York: Doubleday, 1974.

Anderson, Donna K. *Charles T. Griffes: A Life in Music*. Washington, DC: Smithsonian Institution Press, 1993.

———. *Charles T. Griffes: An Annotated Bibliography-Discography*. Detroit, MI: Information Coordinators, 1977.

———. *The Works of Charles T. Griffes: A Descriptive Catalogue*. Ann Arbor, MI: UMI Research Press, 1983.

Aristotle. *Poetics*. Translated by Malcolm Heath. London: Penguin, 1996.

Atkins, Richard Kenneth. "This Proposition Is Not True: C. S. Peirce and the Liar Paradox." *Transactions of the Charles S. Peirce Society* 47, no. 4 (Fall 2011): 421–44.

Barrett, Constance Elizabeth. "Towards Development of a Critical Edition of the String Quartets of Charles Tomlinson Griffes," DMA diss., Ohio State University, 1994.

Bartoli, Jean-Pierre. "L'orientalisme dans la musique française du XIXe siècle: la *ponctuation*, la second augmentée et l'apparition de la modalité dans les procedures exotiques," *Revue belge de musicologie* 51 (1997): 137–70.

Bauer, Marion. "Charles T. Griffes as I Remember Him." *Musical Quarterly* 29, no. 3 (July 1943): 355–80.

———. "Impressionists in America." *Modern Music* 4, no. 2 (1927): 15–20.

———. *Twentieth Century Music*. New York: G. P. Putnam's Sons, 1947.

Bellman, Jonathan. "Musical Voyages and Their Baggage: Orientalism in Music and Critical Musicology." *Musical Quarterly* 94, no. 3 (Fall 2011): 417–38.

———. "Toward a Lexicon of the Style Hongrois." *Journal of Musicology* 9, no. 2 (Spring 1991): 214–37.

Bellman, Jonathan, ed. *The Exotic in Western Music*. Boston, MA: Northeastern University Press, 1998.

Bell-Villada, Gene H. *Art for Art's Sake & Literary Life: How Politics and Markets Helped Shape the Ideology & Culture of Aestheticism, 1790–1990*. Lincoln: University of Nebraska Press, 1996.

Bender, John W., and Gene Blocker, ed. *Contemporary Philosophy of Art: Readings in Analytic Aesthetics*. Englewood Cliffs, NJ: Prentice Hall, 1993.

Blake, Angela M. *How New York Became American, 1890–1924*. Baltimore, MDz: Johns Hopkins University Press, 2006.

Blamires, Steve. *The Little Book of the Great Enchantment*. Cheltenham, UK: Skylight Press, 2013.

Booth, Wayne C. *A Rhetoric of Irony*. Chicago, IL: University of Chicago Press, 1975.

Born, Georgina, and David Hesmondhalgh, eds. *Western Music and Its Others: Difference, Representation, and Appropriation in Music*. Berkeley: University of California Press, 2000.

Bothwell, Beau. "For Thee America! For Thee Syria?": Alexander Maloof, Orientalist Music, and the Politics of the Syrian Mahjar," *Journal of the Society for American Music* 14, no. 4 (November 2020): 383–418.

Bourne, Janet. "Perceiving Irony in Music: The Problem in Beethoven's String Quartets." *Music Theory Online* 22, no. 3 (Spring 2016): 1–26.

Brett, Philip, and Elizabeth Wood, ed. *Queering the Pitch: The New Gay and Lesbian Musicology*. New York: Routledge, 2006.

Brinkmann, Reinhold. *Late Idyll: The Second Symphony of Johannes Brahms*. Translated by Peter Palmer. Cambridge, UK: Cambridge University Press, 1995.

Brown, Calvin S. "The Color Symphony before and after Gautier." *Comparative Literature* 5, no. 4 (Autumn 1953): 289–309.

Brown, Jane. *The Pursuit of Pleasure: The Social History of Gardens and Gardening*. New York: Harper Collins, 2000.

Bruhn, Siglind. *Musical Ekphrasis: Composers Responding to Poetry and Painting*. Hillsdale, NY: Pendragon, 2000.

———. "Musical Ekphrasis: The Evolution of the Concept and the Breadth of Its Application." In *The Routledge Handbook of Music Signification*. Edited by Esti Sheinberg and William P. Dougherty. London: Routledge, 2020.

Burke, Doreen Bolger, ed. *In Pursuit of Beauty: Americans and the Aesthetic Movement*. New York: Metropolitan Museum of Art/Rizzoli, 1986.

Burke, Kenneth. *A Grammar of Motives*. New York: George Braziller, 1955.

Burkholder, Peter. *All Made of Tunes: Charles Ives and the Uses of Musical Borrowing*. New Haven, CT: Yale University Press, 1995.

Caldwell, Helen. "The Dance Poems of Michio Ito: The White Peacock, to Music by Griffes." In *Making Music for Modern Dance: Collaboration in the Formative Years of a New American Art*, edited by Katherine Teck, 18–22. New York: Oxford University Press, 2011.

Caplin, William. "Topics and Formal Functions: The Case of the Lament." In *The Oxford Handbook of Topic Theory*, edited by Danuta Mirka, 415–52. Oxford, UK: Oxford University Press, 2014.

Carroll, Noël. "Introduction." In *Theories of Art Today*, edited by Noël Carroll, 3–24. Madison: University of Wisconsin Press, 2000.

Chai, Leon. *Estheticism: The Religion of Art in Post-Romantic Literature*. New York: Columbia University Press, 1990.

Chandler, Daniel. *Semiotics: The Basics*, 3rd ed. Abingdon, UK: Routledge: 2017.

Chard, Chloe. *Pleasure and Guilt on the Grand Tour: Travel Writing and Imaginative Geography 1600–1830*. Manchester, UK: Manchester University Press, 1999.

Chauncey, George. *Gay New York: Gender, Urban Culture, and the Makings of the Gay Male World, 1890–1940*. New York: Basic Books, 1994.

Chen, Qi. "Aristocracy for the Common People: Chinese Commodities in Oscar Wilde's Aestheticism." *Victorian Network* 1, no. 1 (Summer 2009): 39–54.

Chenette, Jonathan Lee. "Synthetic Scales, Charles Griffes, and The Kairn of Koridwen." PhD diss., University of Chicago, 1984.

Cherlin, Michael. *Varieties of Music Irony: From Mozart to Mahler*. Cambridge, UK: Cambridge University Press, 2017.

Chung, Andrew. Review Essay: "Music Theory Splintered Up, Not Broken Down." *Music Theory Spectrum* 44, no. 1 (Spring 2022): 173–86.

Colapietro, Vincent M. "The Historical Past and the Dramatic Present: Toward a Pragmatic Clarification of Historical Consciousness." *European Journal of Pragmatism and American Philosophy* 8, no. 2 (2016). https://doi.org/10.4000/ejpap.627.

———. *Peirce's Approach to the Self: A Semiotic Perspective on Human Subjectivity*. Albany: State University of New York Press, 1989.

———. "The Pragmatic Spiral." In *Relational Hermeneutics: Essays in Comparative Philosophy*, edited by Paul Fairfield and Saulius Geniusas, 77–89. New York: Bloomsbury Academic, 2018.

———. "Toward a Truly Pragmatic Theory of Signs: Reading Peirce's Semeiotic in Light of Dewey's Gloss." In *Peirce, Semiotics and Psychoanalysis*, edited by John Muller and Joseph Brent, 102–29. Baltimore and London: Johns Hopkins University Press, 2004.

Collingwood, Robin G. *The Idea of History*. Oxford, UK: Clarendon Press, 1946.

Collins, Sarah, and Dana Gooley. "Music and the New Cosmopolitanism: Problems and Possibilities." *The Musical Quarterly* 99, no. 2 (Summer 2016): 139–65.

Cook, Nicholas, "Encountering the Other, Redefining the Self: Hindostannie Airs, Haydn's Folksong Settings, and the 'Common Practice' Style." In *Music and Orientalism in the British Empire, 1780s–1940s*, edited by Martin Clayton and Bennett Zon, 13–37. Aldershot, UK: Ashgate, 2007.

Cooper, David. *A Philosophy of Gardens*. New York: Oxford University Press, 2006.

Coste, Bénédicte. "Late Victorian Paganism: The Case of the Pagan Review." *Cahiers victoriens et édouardiens* 80 (Fall 2014): 1–12.

Cotkin, George. *Reluctant Modernism: American Thought and Culture, 1880–1900*. New York: Twayne, 1992.

Cousin, Victor. *Du Vrai, du beau et du bien*. Paris: Didier, 1836.

Cranmer-Byng, Lancelot. *A Lute of Jade: Selections from the Classical Poets of China*, Wisdom of the East Series. Edited and translated by Lancelot Cranmer-Byng and S. A. Kapadia. New York: E. P. Dutton, 1909.

Cross, Andrew. "Neither Either Nor Or: The Perils of Reflexive Irony." In *The Cambridge Companion to Kierkegaard*, edited by Alastair Hannay and Gordon D. Marino. Cambridge, UK: Cambridge University Press, 1998.

Culler, Jonathan. *Ferdinand de Saussure*, 2nd edition. Ithaca, NY: Cornell University Press, 1986.

———, ed. *On Puns: The Foundation of Letters*. Oxford, UK: Basil Blackwell, 1988.

Cumming, Naomi. *The Sonic Self: Musical Subjectivity and Signification*. Bloomington: Indiana University Press, 2001.

Curry, Ben. "Valency-Actuality-Meaning: A Peircean Semiotic Approach to Music." *Journal of the Royal Musical Association* 142, no. 2 (2017): 401–43.

Dahlhaus, Carl. *Between Romanticism and Modernism*. Translated by Mary Whittall. Berkeley: University of California Press, 1980.

———. *Nineteenth-Century Music*. Translated by J. Bradford Robinson. Berkeley: University of California Press, 1989.

Daly, Nicholas. "The Woman in White: Whistler, Hiffernan, Courbet, Du Maurier." *Modernism/Modernity* 12, no. 1 (January 2005): 1–22.

Dane, Joseph. *The Critical History of Irony*. Athens, GA: University of Georgia Press, 1991.

Daverio, John. *Nineteenth-Century Music and the German Romantic Ideology*. New York: Schirmer Books, 1993.

Day-O'Connell, Jeremy. *Pentatonicism from the Eighteenth Century to Debussy*. Rochester, NY: University of Rochester Press, 2007.

Deely, John. *Why Semiotics?* Brooklyn, NY: Legas, 2004.

Denisoff, Dennis, and Lorraine Janzen Kooistra, ed. *The Pagan Review* 1 (August 1892). *The Yellow Nineties Online*. Ryerson University, 2010. December 26, 2011.

Dickensheets, Janice. "Nineteenth-Century Topical Analysis: A Lexicon of Romantic Topoi." *Pendragon Review* 2, no. 1 (2003): 5–19.

———. "The Topical Vocabulary of the Nineteenth Century." *Journal of Musicological Research* 31, no. 2–3 (2012): 97–137.

Dowling, Linda C. *Aestheticism and Decadence: A Selective Annotated Bibliography*. Garland Reference Library of the Humanities 82. New York: Garland, 1977.

Dreyfus, Laurence. "The Hermeneutics of a Lament: A Neglected Paradigm in a Mozartian Trauermusik." *Music Analysis* 10, no. 3 (1991): 329–43.

Dubrow, Heather. *Genre*. London: Methuen, 1982.

Dusdieker, Carol. "Fiona Macleod: Poetic Genesis and the Song Settings of Arnold Bax and Charles Griffes." PhD diss., Indiana University, 2012.

Eggers, Beth Jennings. "Charles Tomlinson Griffes: Portrait of an American Impressionist." *American Music Teacher* 32, no. 1 (September–October 1982): 28–29.

Eitan, Zohar. *Highpoints: A Study of Melodic Peaks*. Philadelphia: University of Pennsylvania Press, 1997.

Ellestrom, Lars. *Divine Madness: On Interpreting Literature, Music, and the Visual Arts Ironically*. Lewisburg, PA: Bucknell University Press, 2002.

Ellmann, Richard. *Oscar Wilde*. New York: Alfred A. Knopf, 1988.

———. *Yeats: The Man and the Masks*. New York: Macmillan, 1948.

Emerson, Ralph Waldo. *Complete Writings of Ralph W. Emerson*. New York: W. H. Wise, 1929.

Empson, William. *Seven Types of Ambiguity*, 2nd edition. New York: New Directions, 1947.

———. *Some Versions of Pastoral*. London: Chatto and Windus, 1935.

Ertan, Deniz. "The Beginning of the End of Something." In *Over Here, Over There: Trans-atlantic Conversations on the Music of World War I*, edited by William Brooks, Christina Bashford, and Gayle Magee, 224–240. Champaign: University of Illinois Press, 2019.

Everett, Yayoi Uno. "Parody with an Ironic Edge: Dramatic Works by Kurt Weill, Peter Maxwell Davies, and Louis Andriessen." *Music Theory Online* 10, no. 4 (December 2004).

———. "Signification of Parody and the Grotesque in György Ligeti's *Le Grand Macabre*." *Music Theory Spectrum* 31, No. 1 (Spring 2009), 26–56.

Fallis, Richard. *The Irish Renaissance*. Syracuse, NY: Syracuse University Press, 1977.

Ferraguto, Mark. Review of *The Oxford Handbook of Topic Theory*, edited by Danuta Mirka. *Music and Letters* 96, no. 3 (2015): 473–76.

Fish, Stanley. "Short People Got No Reason to Live: Reading Irony." *Daedalus* 112, No. 1 (Winter 1983): 175–91.

Foucault, Michel. "Des Espaces autres, héterotopies" *Architecture/Mouvement/Continuité* 5 (October 1984): 46–49, "Of Other Spaces, Heterotopias." Accessed on March 24, 2021. https://foucault.info/documents/heterotopia/foucault.heteroTopia.en/.

———. *The Order of Things: An Archaeology of the Human Sciences*. (Eng. translation of *Les Mots et les Choses*. Paris: Editions Gallimard, 1966). New York: Random House, 1970.

Frisch, Walter. *German Modernism: Music and the Arts*. Berkeley: University of California Press, 2005.

Fritzsche, Peter. *Reading Berlin 1900*. Cambridge, MA: Harvard University Press, 1996.

Frye, Northrup. *Anatomy of Criticism: Four Essays*. Princeton, NJ: Princeton University Press, 1957.

Frymoyer, Johanna. "The Musical Topic in the Twentieth Century: A Case Study of Schoenberg's Ironic Waltzes." *Music Theory Spectrum* 39 no. 1 (Spring 2017): 83–108.

Galland, Joel. "Topics and Tonal Processes." In *The Oxford Handbook of Topic Theory*, edited by Danuta Mirka, 453–73. Oxford, UK: Oxford University Press, 2014.

Gaut, Berys. "Art as a Cluster Concept." In *Theories of Art Today*, edited by Noël Carroll. Madison: University of Wisconsin Press, 2000.

———. "The Cluster Account of Art Defended." *British Journal of Aesthetics* 45, no. 3 (July 2005): 273–88.

Gifford, Terry. *Pastoral*. London and New York: Routledge, 1999.

Goehr, Lydia. "Being True to the Work." *Journal of Art and Art Criticism* 47, no. 1 (Winter 1989): 55–67.

———. *The Imaginary Museum of Musical Works: An Essay in the Philosophy of Music*, rev. edition. Oxford, UK: Oxford University Press, 2007.

Goldberg, Halina. *The Age of Chopin: Interdisciplinary Inquiries*. Bloomington: Indiana University Press, 2004.

Gooley, Dana. "Cosmopolitanism in the Age of Nationalism, 1848–1914." *Journal of the American Musicological Society* 66, no. 2 (August 2013): 523–49.

Grabócz, Márta. *Morphologie des oeuvres pour piano de Liszt: Influence du programme sur l'evolution des formes instrumentales*. Paris: Editions Kimé, 1986.

Green, Miranda Jane. *Celtic Myths: The Legendary Past*. London: British Museum Press, 1993.

Greer, Taylor A. "Charles Griffes's Xanadu: A Musical Garden of Opposites." In *The Routledge Handbook of Signification*, edited by Esti Sheinberg and William P. Dougherty, 154–63. London and New York: Routledge, 2020.

———. "Peacocks, Paradox, and Peripeteia: Griffes's Transformation of the Pastoral." Online Conference Proceedings of the International Conference on Music Semiotics in Honor of Raymond Monelle, edited by N. Panos and V. Lympouridis. Publisher: International Project on Music and Dance Semiotics, 2013.

———. "A Tale of Two Cadences: Charles Griffes's Prelude to Musical Irony," *The American Journal of Semiotics* 39, no. 1–4 (2023): 47–70, https://doi.org/10.5840/ajs202372490.

———. "Tarantella in Arcadia: Charles Griffes's Scherzo as a Hybrid Pastoral." Virtual Identities, *Yearbook of the Semiotic Society of America* (2015): 35–43. https://doi.org/10.5840/cpsem20155.

———. "The Unfolding Tale of Charles Griffes's 'White Peacock.'" *Gamut, the Journal of the Music Theory Society of the Mid-Atlantic*, Volume 3/1 (2010), Festschrift issue, "A Music-Theoretical Matrix: Essays in Honor of Allen Forte," Article 7.

Greimas, Algirdas Julien, and Jacques Fontanille. *The Semiotics of Passions: From States of Affairs to States of Feelings*. Translated by Paul Perron and Paolo Fabbri. Minneapolis: University of Minnesota Press, 1993.

Griffes, Charles Tomlinson. *The Pleasure-Dome of Kubla Khan*, Piano Solo, ed. Donna Anderson. New York: G. Schirmer, 1984.

———. *The Pleasure-Dome of Kubla Khan*, Symphonic Poem for Grand Orchestra. New York: G. Schirmer, 1929.

———. *The Songs of Charles Griffes*, Volume 1, High Voice, edited by Paul Sperry. New York: G. Schirmer, 1989.

———. *The Songs of Charles Griffes*, Volume 2, Medium Voice, edited by Paul Sperry. New York: G. Schirmer, 1989.

———. *The Songs of Charles Griffes*, Volume 3, Medium Voice, edited by Donna Anderson. New York: G. Schirmer, 1995.

———. *Three Preludes for Piano*. New York: C. F. Peters, 1949.

———. *The White Peacock and Other Works for Solo Piano*. Mineola, NY: Dover Publications, 1999 (based on original editions published by G. Schirmer).

———. *The White Peacock for Orchestra*. New York: G. Schirmer, 1917.

Grimley, Daniel M. "Landscape and Ecology." In *Oxford Handbook of Music and Intellectual Culture in the Nineteenth Century*, edited by Paul Watt, Sarah Collins, and Michael Allis, 343–68. New York: Oxford University Press, 2020.

Gut, Serge. "L'Echelle à double seconde augmentée: Origines et utilization dans la musique occidentale." *Musurgia* 7, no. 2 (2000): 41–60.

Haché, Reginald. "Charles Tomlinson Griffes Revisited: An Essay on the Music of Charles Griffes." *The Journal of the American Liszt Society* 34 (July–December 1993): 32–42.

Halloran, William F. *The Life and Letters of William Sharp and "Fiona Macleod."* Cambridge, UK: Open Book, 2018.

———. "W. B. Yeats, William Sharp, and Fiona Macleod: A Celtic Drama: 1887 to 1897." *Yeats Annual* 13, edited by Warwick Gould. London: Macmillan, 1998.

———. *William Sharp and "Fiona Macleod": A Life.* Cambridge, UK: Open Book, 2022. https://library.oapen.org/handle/20.500.12657/53190. Accessed June 26, 2022.

Halmi, Nicholas, Paul Magnuson, and Raimonda Modiano, ed. *Coleridge's Poetry and Prose: Authoritative Texts, Criticism.* New York: W. W. Norton: 2004.

Hamilton, Walter. *The Aesthetic Movement in England.* Reprint of first edition. London: Pumpernickel Press, 2011.

Hatten, Robert S. *Interpreting Musical Gestures, Topics, and Tropes: Mozart, Beethoven, Schubert.* Bloomington: Indiana University Press, 2004.

———. *Musical Meaning in Beethoven: Markedness, Correlation, and Interpretation.* Bloomington: Indiana University Press, 1994.

———. *A Theory of Virtual Agency for Western Art Music.* Bloomington: Indiana University Press, 2018.

———. "Toward an Adequate Theoretical Framework for Interpreting Complex Signification in Music," *The American Journal of Semiotics* 39, no. 1–4 (2023): 135–48. https://doi.org/10.5840/ajs202372087.

———. "The Troping of Topics in Mozart's Instrumental Music." In *The Oxford Handbook of Topical Theory*, edited by Danuta Mirka, 514–36. Oxford, UK: Oxford University Press, 2014.

Hausberg, Margaret Dunwoody. *The Prints of Theodore Roussel: A Catalogue Raisonné.* Bronxville, NY: M. Hausberg, 1991.

———. "Whistler and Roussel: Linked Visions." The Art Institute of Chicago. Accessed January 18, 2023. https://publications.artic.edu/whistler/api/epub/406/412/print_view.

Head, Matthew. "Musicology on Safari: Orientalism and the Spectre of Postcolonial Theory." *Music Analysis* 22, no. 1–2 (March–July 2003): 211–30.

Helmreich, Anna. "Body and Soul: The Conundrum of the Aesthetic Garden." *Garden History* 36, no. 2 (Winter 2008): 273–88.

Hepokoski, James A. "Formulaic Openings in Debussy." *19th Century Music* 8, no. 1 (Summer 1984): 44–59.

Hill, Edward Burlingame. *Modern French Music.* New York: Da Capo, 1969. First printed Boston: Houghton Mifflin, 1924.

Holl, Herbert. "Some Versions of Pastoral in American Music." PhD diss., University of Texas, Austin, 1980.

Hooper, Giles. "A Sign of the Times: Semiotics in Anglo-American Musicology." *Twentieth-Century Music* 9, no. 1–2 (March 2012): 161–76.

Hopes, Jeffery. "The Sound of Early Eighteenth-Century Opera: Handel, Pope, Gay, and Hughes." *Revue Electronique d'Etudes sur le Monde Anglophone* 14, no. 2 (2017) https://doi.org/10.4000/erea.5741.

Hornblower, Simon, and A. Spawforth, ed. *Oxford Companion to Classical Civilization.* Oxford, UK: Oxford University Press, 1998.

Horton, Julian. "Listening to Topics in the Nineteenth Century." In *The Oxford Handbook of Topic Theory*, edited by Danuta Mirka, 642–64. Oxford, UK: Oxford University Press, 2014.

Houston, Keith. *Shady Characters: The Secret Life of Punctuation, Symbols, and Other Typographical Marks.* New York: W. W. Norton, 2013.

Hutcheon, Linda. *Irony's Edge: The Theory and Politics of Irony.* London: Routledge, 1994.

Hyer, Brian. "Chopin and the In-F-able." In *Musical Transformation and Musical Intuition: Eleven Essays in Honor of David Lewin*, edited by Brian Raphael Atlas and Michael Cherlin, 147–66. Dedham, MA: Ovenbird Press, 1994.

Jacobsen, Jens Peter. *Niels Lyhne.* London: Penguin, 2006.

James, William. *The Varieties of Religious Experience: A Study in Human Nature, Being the Gifford Lecture Series on Natural Religion Delivered in Edinburgh 1901–02.* London: Longman, Green and Co, 1902.

Janvier, Catherine A. "Fiona Macleod and her Creator William Sharp," *The North American Review* 184, no. 612 (April 5, 1907): 718–32.

Johnson, Mark. *The Body in the Mind: The Bodily Basis of Meaning.* Chicago: University of Chicago Press, 1987.

Jones, Keith T. *The Symphonic Poems of Franz Liszt.* Stuyvesant, NJ: Pendragon, 1997.

Kallberg, Jeffrey. *Chopin at the Boundaries: Sex, History, and Musical Genre.* Cambridge, MA: Harvard University Press, 1996.

———. "The Rhetoric of Genre: Chopin's Nocturne in G minor." *19th Century Music* 11, no. 3 (Spring 1988): 238–61.

Karácsony, Noémi. "The Evolution of French Musical Orientalism in the Works of Francisco Salvador-Daniel." *Bulletin of the Transilvania University of Brasov, Series VIII, Performing Arts* 12 (2019): 151–60.

Kierkegaard, Søren. *The Concept of Irony, with a Continual Reference to Socrates.* Edited and translated by Howard Hong and Edna Hong. Princeton, NJ: Princeton University Press, 1989.

Kirkpatrick, Ralph. *Domenico Scarlatti.* Princeton, NJ: Princeton University Press, 1953.

Kitzan, Laurence. *Victorian Writers and the Image of Empire: The Rose-Colored Vision.* Westport, CT: Greenwood, 2001.

Klein, Michael L. "Ironic Narrative, Ironic Reading." *Journal of Music Theory* 53, no. 1 (Spring 2009): 95–136.

Knight, Ellen. "Boston's 'French Connection' at the Turn of the Twentieth Century." In *Perspectives on American Music, 1900–1950*, edited by Michael Saffle, 1–18. New York: Garland, 2000.

Kohl, Norbert. *Oscar Wilde: The Works of a Conformist Rebel.* Translated by David Henry Wilson. Cambridge, UK: Cambridge University Press, 1989.

Kramer, Lawrence. "Consuming the Exotic: Ravel's Daphnis and Chloe." In *Classical Music and Postmodern Knowledge.* Berkeley: University of California Press, 1995.

Kreider, Noble. "The Story of 'The American Debussy.'" *Etude* 62, no. 7 (June 1944): 379–90.

Krom, Anna. "The East in the Works of Charles Griffes." *Vestnik of Saint Petersburg University. Arts* 10, no. 1 (2020): 3–16. https://doi.org/10.21638/spbu15.2020.101.

Lakoff, George, and Mark Johnson. *Metaphors We Live By*. Chicago: University of Chicago Press, 1980.

Lambourne, Lionel. *The Aesthetic Movement*. London: Phaidon, 1996.

Lanham, Richard A. *A Handlist of Rhetorical Terms: A Guide for Students of English Literature*. Berkeley: University of California Press, 1968.

Larson, Steve. *Musical Forces; Motion, Metaphor, and Meaning in Music*. Bloomington: Indiana University Press, 2012.

Lawrence, David H. *The White Peacock*. London: Heinemann, 1911.

Lears, T. J. Jackson. *No Place of Grace: Antimodernism and the Transformation of American Culture, 1880–1920*. Chicago: University of Chicago Press, 1981.

Lidov, David. *Elements of Semiotics*. New York: St. Martin's, 1999.

———. *Is Language a Music?: Writings on Musical Form and Signification*. Bloomington: Indiana University Press, 2005.

———. "Mind and Body in Music," *Semiotica* 66, no. 1–3 (1987): 69–97.

Lippman, Edward. *A History of Western Musical Aesthetics*. Lincoln, NE: University of Nebraska, 1992.

Liszka, James. *A General Introduction to the Semeiotic of Charles S. Peirce*. Bloomington: Indiana University Press, 1996.

———. *A Semiotic of Myth: A Critical Study of the Symbol*. Bloomington, IN: Indiana University Press, 1989.

Locke, Ralph P. "Beyond the Exotic: How 'Eastern' is *Aida*?" *Cambridge Opera Journal* 17, no. 2 (July 2005): 105–39.

———. "Constructing the Oriental 'Other': Saint-Saëns's *Samson et Dalila*." *Cambridge Opera Journal* 3 (1991): 261–302.

———. *Musical Exoticism: Images and Reflections*. Cambridge, UK: Cambridge University Press, 2009.

London, Justin. Review of Lawrence M. Zbikowski, *Conceptualizing Music: Cognitive Structure, Theory, and Analysis. Music Theory Spectrum* 29, no. 1 (Spring 2007): 115–25.

Longworth, Francis, and Andrea Scarantino. "The Disjunctive Theory of Art: The Cluster Account Reformulated." *The British Journal of Aesthetics* 50, no. 2 (March 2010): 1–17.

Longyear, Rey. "Beethoven and Romantic Irony." *The Musical Quarterly* 56, no. 4 (October 1970): 647–64.

Loughery, Bryan. "Introduction." In *The Pastoral Mode: A Casebook*, edited by Bryan Loughery, 8–24. London: Macmillan, 1984.

Lowe, Lisa. *Critical Terrains: French and British Orientalisms*. Ithaca, NY: Cornell University Press, 1991.

Machor, James. *Pastoral Cities: Urban Ideals and the Symbolic Landscape of America*. Madison: University of Wisconsin Press, 1987.

MacKenzie, John M. *Orientalism: History, Theory and the Arts*. Manchester, UK: Manchester University Press, 1995.

Macleod, Fiona. *Foam of the Past: Selected Writings of Fiona Macleod*. Edited by Steve Blamires. Cheltenham, UK: Skylight, 2014.

———. *From the Hills of Dream: Threnodies and Songs and Later Poems*. London: William Heinemann, 1907.

———. *From the Hills of Dream: Threnodies, Songs and Other Poems*. Portland, ME: Thomas B. Mosher, 1901.

Mahoney, Kristin. *Literature and the Post-Victorian Decadence*. Cambridge, UK: Cambridge University Press, 2015.

Maisel, Edward. *Charles T. Griffes: Life of an American Composer*. Rev. ed. New York: Alfred A. Knopf, 1984.

Marinelli, Peter V. *Pastoral* (The Critical Idiom Series, No. 15). London: Methuen, 1971.

Martens, Frederick. "Folk-Music in the 'Ballet Intime.'" *The New Music and Church Music Review* 16 (October 1917): 762–65.

Marx, Leo. *The Machine in the Garden: Technology and the Pastoral Ideal in America*. New York: Oxford Galaxy, 1967.

Mawer, Deborah. "Musical Objects and Machines." In *The Cambridge Companion to Ravel*, edited by Deborah Mawer, 47–67. Cambridge, UK: Cambridge University Press, 2000.

McClary, Susan. Review of Charles Rosen, *The Romantic Generation*. *Notes, Quarterly Journal of the Music Library Association* 52, no. 4 (June 1996): 1139–42. Cambridge, MA: Harvard University Press, 1995.

McCreless, Patrick. "Semiotics and Music: An End-of-Century Overview." *Musikkonzepte-Konzepte der Musik, Bericht über den internationalen Kongress für Musikforschung Halle (Saale) 1998*, no. 1 (2000): 36–47.

McGuire, Charles. "American Songs, Pastoral Nationalism, and the English Temperance Cantata." In *Music and Performance Culture in Nineteenth-Century Britain: Essays in Honour of Nicholas Temperley*. Farnham, UK: Ashgate, 2012.

McKay, Nicholas. "On Topics Today." *Zeitschrift der Gesellschaft für Musiktheorie* 4, no.1, 2007.

McKee, Eric. *Decorum of the Minuet, Delirium of the Waltz: A Study of Dance Music Relations in 3/4 Time*. Bloomington: Indiana University Press, 2012.

———. "The Topic of the Sacred Hymn in Beethoven's Instrumental Music." *College Music Symposium* 47 (2008): 1–30.

Mellers, Wilfred. *Music in a New Found Land: Themes and Developments in the History of American Music*. Abingdon, UK: Routledge, 1964.

Menand, Louis. *The Metaphysical Club: A Story of Ideas in America*. New York: Farrar, Straus and Giroux, 2001.

Merrill, Linda. *The Peacock Room: A Cultural Biography*. Washington, DC: Smithsonian Institution, 1998.

———. *A Pot of Paint: Aesthetics on Trial in Whistler v. Ruskin*. Washington, DC and London: Smithsonian Institution, 1992.

Metzer, David. "The Ascendancy of Musical Modernism in New York City, 1915–1929." PhD diss., Yale University, 1993.

Meyer, Leonard. *Style and Music: Theory, History, and Ideology*. Philadelphia: University of Pennsylvania Press, 1989.

Mirbeau, Octave. *Torture Garden (Le Jardin des Supplices)*. Translated by Alvah C. Bessie. New York: Citadel, 1948.

Mirka, Danuta. "Introduction." In *Oxford Handbook of Topic Theory*, edited by Danuta Mirka, 1–57. Oxford, UK: Oxford University Press, 2014.

Monelle, Raymond. *Linguistics and Semiotics in Music*. Chur, Switzerland: Harwood Academic Publishers, 1992.

———. *The Musical Topic: Hunt, Military, and Pastoral*. Bloomington: Indiana University Press, 2006.

———. *The Sense of Music: Semiotic Essays*. Princeton, NJ: Princeton University Press, 2000.

Monoghan, Patricia, ed. *Encyclopedia of Celtic Mythology and Folklore*. New York: Facts on File, 2004.

Monson, D. A. "Andreas Capellanus and the Problem of Irony." *Speculum* 63, no. 3 (1988): 539–72.

Monzingo, Elizabeth, and Daniel Shanahan. "The Expression of Self and Grief in the Nineteenth Century: An Analysis through Distant Readings." *Nineteenth Century Music Review* 18, no. 1 (April 2021): 83–107.

Morgan, Luke. *The Monster in the Garden: The Grotesque and Gigantic in Renaissance Landscape Design*. Philadelphia: University of Pennsylvania Press, 2016.

Muecke, Donald C. The Compass of Irony. London: Methuen, 1969.

———. *Irony*. London: Methuen, 1970.

Müller-Muth, Anja. "White Symphonies with Red Spots: Color and the Representation of Women in Four Songs by Oscar Wilde." *Women's Studies* 32, no. 7 (2003): 785–814. https://doi.org/10.1080/00497870390221954.

Murray, Isobel. "Introduction." In *Oscar Wilde, Complete Poetry*, edited by Isobel Murray, ix–xvi. Oxford, UK: Oxford University Press, 1997.

Nattiez, Jean-Jacques. *Music and Discourse: Toward a Semiology of Music*. Translated by Carolyn Abbate. Princeton, NJ: Princeton University Press, 1990.

Needham, Rodney. *Belief, Language, and Experience*. Chicago: University of Chicago Press, 1972.

———. "Polythetic Classification: Convergence and Consequences." *Man*, New Series 10, no. 3 (September 1975): 349–69.

Newman, William S. "The Climax of Music." *The Music Review* 13 (1952): 283–93.

Nicholls, David. "Transethnicism and the American Experimental Tradition." *The Musical Quarterly* 80 (1996): 569–94.

Nietzsche, Friedrich W. *Basic Writings of Nietzsche*. Edited and translated by Walter Kaufmann. New York, NY: Modern Library, 1968.

Noonan, Brenna. "Sibelius as Lament Singer." Master's thesis, Mills College, 2015.

Oja, Carol J. *Making Music Modern: New York in the 1920s*. Oxford, UK: Oxford University Press, 2000.

Orr, Lynn Federle and Stephen Calloway, ed. *The Cult of Beauty: The Victorian Avant-Garde, 1860–1900*. London: V&A, 2011.

Parnas, Josef. "Differential Diagnosis and Current Polythetic Classification." *World Psychiatry* 14, no. 3 (2015): 284–87.

Passler, Jann. "Race, Orientalism, and Distinction in the Wake of the 'Yellow Peril.'" In *Western Music and Its Others: Difference, Representation, and Appropriation in Music,* edited by Georgina Born and David Hedsmondhalgh, 86–118. Berkeley: University of California Press, 2000.

Pater, Walter. *Studies in the History of the Renaissance*. London: Macmillan, 1873.

———. *The Renaissance: Studies in Art and Poetry*. Edited by D. L. Hill. Berkeley: University of California Press, 1980.

Patterson, Annabel. *Pastoral and Ideology: Virgil to Valéry*. Berkeley: University of California Press, 1987.

Pedrycz, Witold, and Fernando Gomide. *An Introduction to Fuzzy Sets Analysis and Design*. Cambridge, MA: MIT Press, 1998.

Peirce, Charles Sanders. *Collected Papers of Charles Sanders Peirce*. Edited by Charles Hartshorne, Paul Weiss, and Arthur W. Burks, 8 volumes. Cambridge, MA: Belknap, 1931–66.

———. "Prolegomena to an Apology for Pragmaticism," *The Monist* 16 (1906): 492–546.

Piotrowska, Anna G. *Gypsy Music in European Culture: From the Late Eighteenth to the Early Twentieth Centuries*. Translated by Guy R. Torr. Boston: Northeastern University Press, 2012.

Poggioli, Renato. *The Oaten Flute: Essays on Pastoral Poetry and the Pastoral Ideal*. Cambridge, MA: Harvard University Press, 1975.

Pollack, Howard. "Edward Maisel and the Historiography of Charles Griffes's Homosexuality." *Newsletter for the LGBTQ Study Group of the American Musicological Society* 16, no. 1 (Spring 2006): 3–11.

Praz, Mario. *Romantic Agony*. New York: Meridian, 1956.

Prettejohn, Elizabeth, ed. *After the Pre-Raphaelites: Art and Architecture in Victorian England*. New Brunswick, NJ: Rutgers University Press, 1999.

———. *Art for Art's Sake: Aestheticism in Victorian England*. New Haven, CT: Yale University Press, 2007.

Puri, Michael. *Ravel the Decadent: Memory, Sublimation, and Desire*. Oxford, UK: Oxford University Press, 2011.

Ransome, Arthur. *Oscar Wilde: A Critical Study*. New York: Mitchell Kinnerley, 1913.

Ratner, Leonard G. *Classic Music: Expression, Form, and Style*. New York: Schirmer Books, 1980.

———. *Music: The Listener's Art*. New York: McGraw-Hill, 1957.

———. *Romantic Music: Sound and Syntax*. New York: Schirmer Music, 1992.

———. "Topical Content in Mozart's Keyboard Sonatas." *Early Music* 9, no. 4 (1991): 615–19.

Reeves, David M. "Selected Songs of Charles T. Griffes: An Examination of the Relationship Between Words and Music." PhD diss., New York University, 1989.

Rhys, Ernest. *Everyman Remembers*. London: J. M. Dent and Sons, 1931.

Ritari, Katja, and Alexandra Bergholm, ed. *Understanding Celtic Religion: Revisiting the Pagan Past*. Cardiff: University of Wales Press, 2015.

Rosand, Ellen. "The Descending Tetrachord: An Emblem of Lament." *Musical Quarterly* 65, no. 3 (1987): 346–59.

Rosch, Eleanor, Carolyn B. Mervis, Wayne D. Gray, David M. Johnson, and Penny Boyes-Braem. "Basic Objects in Natural Categories." *Cognitive Psychology* 8 (1976): 382–439.

———. "Principles of Categorization." In *Cognition and Categorization*, edited by Eleanor Rosch and Barbara B. Lloyd, 27–48. Hillsdale, NJ: Erlbaum Associates, 1978.

Rosen, Charles. *The Romantic Generation*. Cambridge, MA: Harvard University Press, 1998.

Ross, Alex. *The Rest Is Noise: Listening to the Twentieth Century*. New York: Picador, 2008.

Rumph, Stephen. *Mozart and Enlightenment Semiotics*. Berkeley: University of California Press, 2012.

Saguaro, Shelley. *Garden Plots: The Politics and Poetics of Gardens*. Burlington, VT: Ashgate, 2006.

Said, Edward. *Culture and Imperialism*. New York: Knopf, 1993.

———. *Orientalism*. New York: Random House, 1978.

Satyendra, Ramon. "Liszt's Open Structures and the Romantic Fragment." *Music Theory Spectrum* 29, no. 2 (Fall 1997): 184–205.

Saussure, Ferdinand de. *Cours de linguistique générale*. Compiled by Charles Bally and Albert Sechehaye. Paris: Payot, 1962.

Savan, David. *An Introduction to C. S. Peirce's Full System of Semeiotic*. Toronto: Toronto Semiotic Circle, 1988.

Saylor, Eric. *English Pastoral Music: Arcadia to Utopia, 1900–1950*. Champaign: University of Illinois Press, 2017.

———. "It's Not Lambkins Frisking at All: English Pastoral Music and the Great War." *Musical Quarterly* 91 (2008): 39–59.

Schlegel, Friedrich. "On Incomprehensibility." In *Friedrich Schlegel's Lucinde and the Fragments*, 257–72. Translated by Peter Firchow. Minneapolis: University of Minnesota Press, 1971.

Scott, Derek B. *From the Erotic to the Demonic: On Critical Musicology*. Oxford, UK: Oxford University Press, 2003.

———. "Orientalism and Musical Style." *Musical Quarterly* 82, no. 2 (1998): 309–35.

Seising, Rudolph. "Lotfi Zadeh: Fuzzy Sets and Systems." *Computer Aided Systems Theory—EUROCAST 2019*, 101–8.

Seskir, Sezi. "Musical Topoi in Brahms's 7 Fantasien, Op. 116." *Journal of Musicological Research* 39, no. 2–3 (2020): 99–121.

Sharp, Elizabeth A. *William Sharp (Fiona Macleod): A Memoir*. New York: Duffield, 1910.

Sharp, William. *Poems*, selected and arranged by Mrs. William Sharp. New York: Duffield, 1912.

———. *Sospiri de Roma*. Roma: La Societá Laziale, 1891.

Shea, Nicholas. "Descending Bass Schemata and Negative Emotion in Western Song." *Empirical Musicology Review* 14, no. 3–4 (2019): 167–81.

Sheinberg, Esti. *Irony, Satire, Parody, and the Grotesque in the Music of Dmitri Shostakovich: A Theory of Musical Incongruities*. Burlington, VT: Ashgate, 2000.

Silk, J. A. "What, If Anything, Is Mahayana Buddhism? Problems of Definitions and Classifications." *Numen-International Review for the History of Religions* 49, no. 5 (2002): 355–405.

Singal, Daniel Joseph. "Toward a Definition of American Modernism." *American Quarterly* 39, no. 1 (1987): 7–26.

Sonneck, Oscar. "The American Composer and the American Music Publisher." *Musical Quarterly* 9 (1923): 122–44.

Spiller, Henry. "Tunes That Bind: Paul J. Seelig, Eva Gauthier, Charles T. Griffes, and the Javanese Other." *Journal of the Society for American Music* 3, no. 2 (2009): 129–54.

Stell, Jason T. "Rachmaninov's Expressive Strategies in Selected Piano Preludes: Highpoints, Dramatic Models, and Dynamic Curves." Master's thesis, Pennsylvania State University, 1999.

Straus, Joseph N. *Introduction to Post-Tonal Theory*. 4th edition. New York: W. W. Norton, 2016.

Stuwe, Holger M. "Musical Topics and Ambiguity in Nineteenth-Century Music: Towards a Reappraisal." *Musicology Review* 6 (2010): 57–84.

Sutcliffe, W. Dean. "Topics in Chamber Music." In *The Oxford Handbook of Topic Theory*, edited by Danuta Mirka, 118–40. Oxford: Oxford University Press, 2014.

Tarasti, Eero. *Myth and Music: A Semiotic Approach to the Aesthetics of Myth in Music, Especially That of Wagner, Sibelius and Stravinsky*. The Hague: Mouton, 1979.

Tawa, Nicholas E. *Mainstream Music of Early Twentieth-Century America: The Composers, Their Times, and Their Works*. Westport, CT: Greenwood, 1992.

Thacker, Christopher. *The History of Gardens*. Berkeley: University of California Press, 1979.

Toliver, Harold E. *Pastoral Forms and Attitudes*. Berkeley: University of California Press, 1971.

Upton, William Treat. "The Songs of Charles T. Griffes." *Musical Quarterly* 9 (1923): 314–28.

Van, Gilles de. "Fin de siècle Exoticism and the Meaning of the Far Away." *Opera Quarterly* 11, no. 3 (1995): 77–94.

Varty, Anne. "Introduction." In *Collected Poems of Oscar Wilde*, edited by Anne Varty, v–xxvii. Hertfordshire, UK: Wordsworth Editions, 1994.

Vico, Giambattista. *The New Science*. Translated by Thomas G. Bergin and Max H. Fisch. Ithaca, NY: Cornell University Press, 1984.

Von Glahn, Denise. *The Sounds of Place: Music and the American Cultural Landscape*. Urbana: University of Illinois Press, 2003.

Wands, Harold Ernest. "Appraisal of the Charles Tomlinson Griffes Library." No publisher, undated.

Walton, Peggy Marie. "The Music of Charles Tomlinson Griffes: Harbinger of American Art Music's Transition into the Modern Age." Master's thesis, Rice University, 1988.

Watt, Paul, Sarah Collins, and Michael Allis. *The Oxford Handbook of Music and Intellectual Culture in the Nineteenth Century*. New York: Oxford University Press, 2020.

Weitz, Morris. "The Role of Theory in Aesthetics." *Journal of Aesthetics and Art Criticism* 15, no. 1 (September 1956): 27–35.

Wellek, Rene. *A History of Modern Criticism: The Later Nineteenth Century* 4. New Haven. CT: Yale University Press, 1977.

Wenk, Arthur. *Claude Debussy and Twentieth-Century Music*. Boston, MA: G. K. Hall, 1983.

Wetzel, Linda. *Types and Tokens: On Abstract Objects*. Cambridge, MA: MIT Press, 2009.

White, Robin Anita. "19th- and 20th-Century Exoticism: Pierre Loti, Michel Leiris, and Simone Schwarz-Bart." PhD diss., Louisiana State University, 2004.

Whitman, Walt. *Leaves of Grass, First and Death Bed Editions.* Edited by Karen Karbiener. New York: Barnes and Noble, 2004.

Wilde, Oscar. *Works of Oscar Wilde.* Edited by G. F. Maine. London: Collins, 1948.

Williams, Heathcote. *Falling for a Dolphin.* London: Jonathan Cape, 1988.

Williams, Peter. *The Chromatic Fourth During Four Centuries of Music.* Oxford, UK: Clarendon Press, 1997.

Wittgenstein, Ludwig. *Philosophical Investigations.* 3rd edition. Translated by G. E. M. Anscombe. Oxford, UK: Blackwell, 2001.

Youens, Susan. *Heinrich Heine and the Lied.* Cambridge, UK: Cambridge University Press, 2007.

Zadeh, Lotfi A. "Fuzzy Sets," *Information and Control* 8 (1965): 338–53.

Zank, Stephen. *Irony and Sound: The Music of Maurice Ravel.* Rochester, NY: University of Rochester Press, 2009.

Zbikowski, Lawrence M. *Conceptualizing Music: Cognitive Structure, Theory, and Analysis.* Oxford, UK: Oxford University Press, 2002.

———. "Dance Topoi, Sonic Analogues, and Musical Grammar." In *Communication in Eighteenth-Century Music,* edited by Kofi Agawu and Danuta Mirka, 283–309. Cambridge, UK: Cambridge University Press, 2008.

———. "Music and Dance in the *Ancien Régime.*" In *The Oxford Handbook of Topic Theory,* edited by Danuta Mirka, 143–63. Oxford, UK: Oxford University Press, 2014.

———. "Music, Dance and Meaning in the Early Nineteenth Century." *Journal of Musicological Research* 31, no. 2–3 (2012): 147–65. https://doi.org/10.1080/01411896.2012.680880.

———. "Music, Emotion, Analysis." *Music Analysis* 29 (2011): 37–59.

INDEX

TAYLOR A. GREER is Associate Professor of Music Theory at Pennsylvania State University. He is author of *A Question of Balance: Charles Seeger's Philosophy of Music.*